*SPORT MANAGEMENT
IN NEW ZEALAND*

WANGANUI
COLLEGIATE SCHOOL
LIBRARY
796.06 SPO

*sport management in new zealand
an introduction*

Edited by

**Linda D. Trenberth
Chris W. Collins**

The Dunmore Press

©1994 Linda D. Trenberth and Chris W. Collins
©1994 The Dunmore Press Limited

First Published in 1994
by
The Dunmore Press Limited
P.O.Box 5115
Palmerston North
New Zealand

Australian Supplier:
Nyroca Press
P.O. Box 90, Hawksburn
Victoria 3142
Phone & Fax (03) 888-8307

ISBN 0-86469-195-5

Text: Times Roman 10/12
Page Layout: Mark Shingleton
Printer: The Dunmore Printing Company Limited,
Palmerston North

Copyright. No part of this book may be reproduced without written permission except in the case of brief quotations embodied in critical articles and reviews.

contents

Foreword *Wilson Whineray*	13
Preface	15
Chapter 1. An Introduction to Sport Management	17
Linda Trenberth and Chris Collins	
Introduction	17
Development of Sport Management	18
Definition of Sport	19
The Sport Industry	20
Management Versus Administration	20
Unique Aspects of Sport Management	21
Sport Management	22
Understanding Sport in Society	22
Review Questions	24
References	24
Part I: The Environmental Context of Sport	25
Chapter 2. Historical and Social Perspectives on Sport in New Zealand	27
Anne Hindson, Grant Cushman and Bob Gidlow	
Introduction	28
Origins and Development of Sport in New Zealand	28
Modern Society	34
Conclusions	38
Review Questions	39
References	39
Suggested Reading	42
Chapter 3. Politics and Sport in New Zealand	43
Chris Collins and Mary Stuart	
Introduction	44
The Politics and Sport Connection	44
Government and Sport	47

The Changing Nature of the Role of the State as a Provider in Sport	52
Politics in Sport Organisations	53
Conclusion	56
Review Questions	56
References	57
Suggested Reading	58

Chapter 4. The Economics of Sport — 59
Bob Stephens

Introduction	59
Economic Description of Sport	60
Work Leisure Choices	61
The Market and Sport	62
Valuing Benefits from Sport	67
Conclusion	68
Review Questions	68
References	68
Suggested Reading	69

Chapter 5. Sport and the Economy — 71
Benedikte Jensen

Introduction	71
Definition of Sport	72
Definition of Economic Terms	72
The Commercial Sport Sector	73
The Public Sport Sector	77
Employment in the Sport Industry	80
Sport-related Tourism	82
The Total Sport Industry	83
Summary	83
Review Questions	84
References	84
Suggested Reading	84

Chapter 6. Sport and Education: Give the Kids a Sporting Chance — 85
Bevan Grant and Bob Stothart

Introduction	85
The Connection Between Sport and Physical Education	86
Early Developments	87
1950-1990: A Reflection	88
Seeking Change	90
Sport Education	91
Bursary Physical Education: Sport Education	94
Hillary Commission Initiatives	94
Tertiary Education	96
New Zealand Qualifications Authority	96

Conclusion	96
Review Questions	97
References	97
Suggested Reading	98

Chapter 7. The Structure and Organisation of Sport in New Zealand   99
Lorraine Vincent and Linda Trenberth

Introduction	99
Grass-roots (Bottom-up) Stages of Development	100
Canopy (Top-down) Development	101
The Hillary Commission, Local Bodies and Regional Sports Trusts	101
Role of Local Authorities and Regional Sports Trusts	104
Organisational Interactions	105
National Sports Associations	107
National and International Funding	107
Funding Strategies	108
Review	109
Review Questions	110
References	110

Part II: The Practice of Managing Sport   111

Chapter 8. A Competency-based Approach to Sport Management   113
Linda Trenberth

Introduction	113
Competency Defined	114
Competencies for Sport Managers	115
Industry Changes	120
Conclusion	122
Review Questions	122
References	122
Suggested Reading	123

Chapter 9. The Well Managed National Sport Organisation   124
Deborah Battell

Introduction	124
The Importance of Good Management	125
What is a Successful Organisation?	125
What is Good Management?	126
The Game Plan	126
Structure	130
Managing the Money	131
Managing the People	132
Conclusion	135
Review Questions	135
References	135

Chapter 10. Strategic Planning — 136
David Cullwick
- Introduction — 137
- Key Themes and Concepts — 138
- Application of Principles — 141
- Planning — 142
- From Strategic Plan to Management — 149
- Review Questions — 150
- References — 150
- Suggested Reading — 150

Chapter 11. Budgeting and Financial Control — 151
Graeme Hall
- Introduction — 152
- Scope of Chapter — 152
- Essential Concepts and Definitions — 152
- Definition of Financial Management — 153
- Why Financial Budgeting and Control? — 155
- Internal Requirements of Financial Management — 158
- Financial Management Processes — 160
- Financial Management Structure — 162
- Further Financial Concepts — 162
- Some Key Issues — 164
- Conclusion — 165
- Review Questions — 166
- Suggested Reading — 166

Chapter 12. Human Resource Management – The People Decisions — 167
Katie Sadleir
- Introduction — 167
- Who are the Human Resource Managers? — 168
- Assessing the Organisation's Needs for Unpaid and Paid Staff — 170
- Job Descriptions — 171
- Recruitment — 173
- Induction — 174
- Performance Reviews/Appraisals — 175
- Training — 177
- Acknowledgement/Rewards — 178
- Conclusion — 178
- Review Questions — 178
- References — 178
- Suggested Reading — 179

Chapter 13. Leadership Issues in Sport — 180
Steve Tew
- Introduction — 180
- Who leads? — 183

Volunteer Leadership	185
The Leader's Role	185
Organisation Effectiveness Quadrant	186
What Attributes Must a Leader Possess?	187
Who Should Provide Leadership in the Future?	188
Review Questions	189
References	189
Suggested Reading	190

Chapter 14. Sport Marketing — 191
Peter McDermott and Ron Garland

Marketing Processes	192
Branding	194
Objectives	194
Market Research	195
Market Plan	196
Performance Measure	198
Stakeholders, Consultants and Advisory Organisations	199
Sponsors	199
Advertising Agencies, Marketing Consultants	200
Media, Television	200
Sales Promotions	201
Price	201
Value, Product, Promotion and Venue	202
Conclusion	203
Review Questions	204
References	204
Suggested Reading	204

Chapter 15. Public Relations and Sport — 206
Geoff Henley

How is Sport Seen?	206
Why is Public Support so Important?	207
Brand Loyalty	207
Who are the Audiences of Sport?	208
Stakeholders of Sport	208
What is public relations and what can it do for sport?	209
Who are the stakeholders of your sport and what are they looking for?	209
Is your Product Right?	210
Creating a Vision	210
Building a Positive Image for a Sport	211
Building a Communications Plan	211
Techniques for Building Visibility and Profile	213
What are the Easy Answers?	214
Review Questions	215
Suggested Reading	215

Chapter 16. Sponsorship and Sport   **216**
Paul Carrad
   Introduction   216
   Definitions   217
   Guide to Obtaining Sponsorship   218
   Sponsorship Effectiveness   226
   Conclusion   227
   Review Questions   227
   References   228
   Suggested Reading   228

Chapter 17. Event Management   **229**
Arthur Klap
   Event Management in New Zealand   230
   Organisational Structures   230
   Financial Considerations   235
   Event Planning   237
   Marketing   238
   Public Relations   240
   Administration   241
   Event Implementation   242
   Debriefing   242
   Summary   242
   Review Questions   242
   Suggested Reading   242

Chapter 18. Media Sport   **243**
Judy McGregor
   Introduction   243
   The Sport Mediascape in New Zealand   244
   Does Media Sport Serve the Public Interest?   251
   How to Manage the Sport Media?   251
   Conclusion   254
   Review Questions   254
   References   254

Chapter 19. Sport and the Law   **256**
David Howman
   The Sporting Body and its Legal Entity   257
   Contractual Matters   258
   Disciplinary Matters   259
   Accidents, Injury and Safety   260
   Sponsorship   261
   Facilities   262
   Drugs in Sport   262
   Privacy Issues   262
   Financial Issues   263

Conclusion	263
Review Questions	263
References	263
Suggested Reading	263

Chapter 20. Ethics and Sport Management — 264
Jon Doig

Introduction	264
Definitions	266
Sport's Ethical Base	267
Business Ethics	268
Ethics and Sport Management	268
Writing and Implementing Codes of Ethics	269
Limitations of Codes of Ethics	270
Compliance with Ethical Codes	270
Enforcement of Codes of Ethics	271
Should Ethics be Taught?	271
Common Ethical Issues Raised in Sport	272
Conclusion	273
Review Questions	273
References	273
Suggested Reading	274

Conclusion. Looking Ahead: Sport Management Towards 2000 — 276
Chris Collins and Linda Trenberth

Introduction	277
Continuity and Change	277
Growing Commercialism	278
Future Trends	279
Managing for a Responsible Future	285
Conclusion	287
Review and Discussion Questions	288
References	288
Suggested Reading	289

About the Contributors — 291

Editors	291
Contributing Authors	291

Index — 297

foreword

The sport and leisure sector is a large and vital part of New Zealand society. Directly and indirectly the sector supports more than 22,000 jobs, and total economic activity exceeds $1.6 billion each year. In addition, hundreds of thousands of volunteers contribute their time and energy to assist in the development of sport and leisure activities. At a highly conservative estimate, the economic value of this contribution exceeds $200 million each year.

Another key characteristic of the sport and leisure sector is its capacity to grow. The Hillary Commission exists to both increase the number of people participating in sport and leisure activities and to improve performance and achievement at all levels. These goals cannot be met without increasing the numbers of skilled professional and volunteer leaders.

Sport Management in New Zealand will play a major role in professionalising the management of sport and leisure in New Zealand. The contributions of expert practitioners involved with this book will provide readers with sound theories which have been tempered with practical realism. This text will be essential reading for students, and also those with many years of experience in this exciting and dynamic sector.

Wilson Whineray
Chairman
Hillary Commission for Sport, Fitness and Leisure

preface

We believe that *Sport Management in New Zealand,* will make an important contribution to the sport management literature and to the sport industry. This publication is the result of the challenge to provide a text and resource to support the many courses of study in Sport Management emerging from tertiary institutions in New Zealand. This growth in tertiary programmes is the result of the trend towards increasing professionalism within sport and recreation organisations, the growing commercialisation of many forms of sport, and career structures within the industry becoming more established. Along with this trend has been a call for increased accountability, and government, at national, regional and local levels, has sought over recent years to target management skills as a means of achieving greater effectiveness. This has led to a growing demand for better trained sport and recreational managers.

It is our hope that this text will go some way to supporting what is now recognised as a legitimate field of study in tertiary institutions in New Zealand and throughout the world.

Audience

In increasing numbers, students with a wide variety of backgrounds are choosing a course of study in sport management. The need for a text of this nature has become increasingly clear to us in our role as university lecturers in a sport management programme. This publication therefore is primarily written for undergraduate students, although postgraduate students will also find it useful. We hope this book will also appeal to practitioners in the industry.

Content

This text is both multi and interdisciplinary, reflecting the need for professional conceptual development as well as the acquisition of technical and human skills. It incorporates both theoretical and applied aspects of sport management and is organised into two parts. *Part I* of the text introduces the historical, socio-economic, political and educational context in which sport is delivered in New Zealand. As Editors we consider it important that students studying sport management, and practitioners alike, have some understanding of this context. There are many areas which we would have liked to have included in this section, such as some of the current issues confronting sport in New Zealand – gender and inter-group relations – to name but two, but the size of the text, the related cost of production, and the tight publication deadlines have restricted us to the existing seven chapters.

Part II of the text, *The Practice of Managing Sport,* is more applied in nature and it makes a deliberate attempt to involve practitioners within the field of sport management as contributors to this section. The main objective is to bring together some of the leading authorities in their respective areas to report on their work on various aspects of sport management. These people are involved in the day-to-day operation of managing various aspects of sport in New Zealand, and their contributions ensure the relevance of the subject matter to sport management in the 1990s. General areas of competency specific to the occupation of a sport manager and the much neglected area of human resource management are addressed. Each chapter includes key terms, case studies, review questions and recommended readings to give students further insight into how to apply the theoretical principles. It must be emphasised at this point that the views and opinions expressed by the individual authors are their own and in no way represent the views of the organisations they work for, nor those of the Hillary Commission.

Acknowledgements

We would like to express our gratitude to all who contributed to *Sport Management in New Zealand.* Managing Editor Murray Gatenby and Editor Sharmian Firth made an invaluable contribution to this book.

Much time was taken to consider the many key people in respective fields who could contribute to this text, and we acknowledge the invaluable input of Steve Tew, Katie Sadleir, Jon Doig and Mary Stuart in this process. The result is the most comprehensive compilation of subject matter published to date for the sport management profession in New Zealand. All our authors made a commitment to excellence and made extraordinary efforts to meet extremely demanding deadlines.

Our thanks go to the Hillary Commission for Sport, Fitness and Leisure and to Peter Dale, Executive Director of the Commission, for his support throughout the project.

We extend special thanks to Janet Toogood, Professor Tony Taylor and Naomi Collins for their editorial assistance; to Trish Bradbury, Department of Management Systems, Albany Campus for her review and comments; to Bob Goddard for his help with the illustrations; and to Stephanie Pearson for her help in the preparation of the work. We thank also our colleagues in the Department of Management Systems and the Recreation and Sports Centre who have coped with our stressed presence at various stages in the process of compiling this text.

We are especially grateful to Professor Tony Vitalis, Head of the Department of Management Systems, Business Studies Faculty, Massey University, without whose support and coercion, this book would not have happened!

A final thanks to our families who have supported us throughout this very demanding but rewarding project.

Linda Trenberth and Chris Collins
Editors
Massey University
Palmerston North
New Zealand

An Introduction to Sport Management

Linda Trenberth and Chris Collins

In this chapter you will become familiar with the following terms:

The development of sport management

The sport industry

Management versus administration

Conflict theory

The definition of sport

The uniqueness of the sport industry

Functionalist theory

Critical theory

Introduction

Sport is pervasive in modern society and is not only requiring higher levels of performance from competing athletes but is also demanding increasing professionalism from today's sport managers. This text has developed in response to this demand for professionally trained people in sport management to meet the manifest needs of the market place. They include meeting the employer's, consumer's and voluntary worker's needs for a technical knowledge of sport, management skills, and continuing education. Through examination of environmental factors which have influenced both sport and the way it is organised and the introduction of foundation and application areas of sport management, this text endeavours to provide a valuable contribution to the body of knowledge and skills relating to the sport industry in New Zealand. It is targeted at students and new managers alike.

A glimpse of overseas trends indicates that sport is a rapidly growing multi-billion dollar industry. In the United States, for example, Parkhouse (1991) notes that if all the elements of the sport industry were combined, sport would be bigger than other industrial giants such as the automobile, petroleum, lumber, and air transportation sectors of the US economy. She suggests that by the year 2000, the Gross National Sports Product (GNSP) for the next century could increase by 141 per cent.

The first major study attempting to measure the size of the sport industry in New Zealand (Jensen, Sullivan, Wilson, Berkeley and Russell, 1993) demonstrates similar trends in New Zealand. The study indicated that the commercial, public and non-profit sectors of the sport industry contributed at least $301m, $461m, and $70m respectively to the GDP in 1991. This equates to approximately 1.0 per cent ($831m) of GDP, and furthermore, the industry was responsible for some 14,000 jobs, or 1.1 per cent of total employment for that year. Chapter 5, which addresses the size of the industry in detail, notes that the actual contribution of the sport industry to the economy is almost certainly larger than these figures indicate, particularly when one considers the contribution of sport-related tourism and also the imprecise data that the study was forced to use at times. Nevertheless, the sport industry in New Zealand is comparable to the entire clothing and footwear industry and the electrical machinery industry in terms of its contribution to GDP. Furthermore, the prospects for growth in the commercial and non-profit sectors of this industry are strong.

It is clear then, that New Zealand's sport managers are involved in a multi-million dollar industry which represents a significant component of the New Zealand economy and which is beginning to make unique demands on its personnel and increasingly requires them to have specialised training. As managers they face increasing legal technicalities, complexities of computerisation, financial responsibilities, sponsor requirements, media demands, public and private sector negotiations and an increasingly discerning and demanding membership. To meet the complex demands a new breed of specialist is emerging – the sport management specialist. Already the field of sport management has become recognised as a legitimate field of university study, but lacking is an adequate range of text-books and related resources on the topic. This book begins to fill this gap and, to date, represents the most comprehensive compilation of subject matter related to the New Zealand context.

Development of Sport Management

Thus far sport in New Zealand has been well served by part-time voluntary administrators, who, likely as not, met around the kitchen table. However, for reasons already given, the management of sport is in a state of veritable transition, with the dedicated volunteers and informally trained individuals beginning to be replaced by more business orientated managers. The change is a direct result of an increasingly volatile economic, political, social and legal environment coupled with increasing levels of commercial investment and government expenditure. Considerable pressure has been applied to sport organisations, particularly in the voluntary sector, for them to transform themselves from loosely structured bodies, administered on a casual basis by interested volunteers, to highly purposeful and productive corporate entities managed by professional managers. Yet it has to be said that sport management has not developed professionally as rapidly as management in other industries. For most sport there is a need to make up ground in matters of financial control, decision making and policy formulation. Other areas that require attention concern the formal structure of sport organisations, sponsorship, marketing and public relations, strategic planning and legal issues (Trenberth and Love, in press) and these are addressed in this text.

During the last decade an evolution has occurred in the power-base of professional preparation for sport management. Initially there were traditional programmes in physical education and coaching, and then the emphasis switched to recreation and leisure studies. Now a liaison is emerging between physical education and sport science on the one hand, with business management on the other. The indications are that the sport industry favours the hard-core focus upon business and management skills provided by the business schools. Shuttleworth (1990), from research undertaken by the Hillary Commission with Executive Directors of sport organisations, obtained a rank order of preferred competencies. They were general management, business planning, accounting and financial management, human resource management, marketing, economics, sport science and leisure and recreation theory. Although this text is primarily a management text, it must be emphasised here that sound business and management skills are not to be acquired at the expense of equally sound social concerns or the dictates of sport science and leisure theory.

Definition of Sport

Sport has been defined in many different ways, but a common contemporary view would define sport as an institutionalised physical activity with recreational and competitive components. According to the authors of the *Sport on the Move* report (1985), an activity is classified as sport if each of the following factors are present to some degree:

- It involves all levels of performance regardless of age, sex, ability and disability;
- It has an objective of improving performance through practice, training and coaching;
- It has some form of administrative structure, generally nationally based;
- It has some form of disciplinary or regulatory code;
- It includes a competitive element;
- It includes a degree of physical effort and skill.

Recreation and Government in New Zealand (1985), the companion report to *Sport on the Move*, identifies two further criteria:

- external motivation and rewards;
- public performance.

In determining whether a sporting organisation is eligible to receive funding, the Hillary Commission adopts similar criteria to those used in the *Sport on the Move* report. For such public agencies as the Hillary Commission, which are involved in the distribution and allocation of funds, the task of defining what is and what is not a sport moves from the realm of academic debate to functional necessity.

Loy (1968), Snyder and Sprietzer (1989), and Coakley (1990) also support the multi-component definition. Coakley, for example, defines sport in the following way:

> Sport is an institutionalised competitive activity that involves vigorous physical exertion or the use of relatively complex physical skill by individuals whose participation is motivated by a combination of intrinsic and extrinsic factors (1990, 15).

Essentially such a definition refers to what is popularly referred to as 'organised sport' and this definition is adopted in this text. It serves as a tool to clarify what we mean by sport and is useful in the creation of workable concepts with which to understand the rapidly changing sport industry.

The Sport Industry

The term sport industry itself is a term used to describe all organisations and groups involved in the private, public and voluntary provision of sport services, goods and programmes. The industry embraces a considerable number of products and services, consumer market segments, service delivery system sectors and occupations. Its influence has widened considerably because of its interrelationships with several cognate industries, public and commercial health and fitness agencies, sport science and technology and medicine, sports goods, entertainment, tourism and recreation – many of which have come into prominence only in recent years.

Essentially the sport industry revolves around sports clubs and associations, with the community, public and commercial sectors. The community-based or non-profit sector includes the organisation of local clubs, sport interest groups, private clubs, local and national associations. The commercial sector includes the provision of facilities, services, materials and equipment in the form of sport and leisure centres, sports clubs, sponsorships, tourism in the form of sport packages and the formation of events such as triathlons. The public sector includes government servicing through formulating policy, developing strategic coordination of industry sectors and the provision of independent advice, guidance, and responsibility for the allocation of funds. Each of these sectors will be examined in some detail later in the text.

Management Versus Administration

Although the terms sport management and sport administration are often used interchangeably, a distinction should be made because the first describes this field from a universal or global perspective and the second, from a parochial or narrow perspective. Kerr Inkson (1990) defines management as a set of ideas and also as a set of people who are concerned with administering organisations in order to achieve stated objectives. This book favours the global perspective and does not therefore concern itself with procedural or routine matters which have come to be known as administration. It is about the philosophy, the vision and the practice of management that produces results in organisations. Administrative procedure, although important, is in the end a servant to the philosophy. The thesis is that the principles and practices which have been proven in business management are transferable to sporting organisations whether they be professional or voluntary. The belief is that by acquiring such skills, officials in any capacity can significantly increase the contribution they make to the development and indeed perhaps the survival of their sporting codes.

In the realm of semantics, there has been some academic debate on the use of the word *sport* as opposed to *sports*, although more often than not the terms are used interchangeably.

Parks and Zanger (1990) argue that sports is 'singular in nature', whereas the term sport is more 'all-encompassing', and there is a move within North America (North American Society for Sport Management) to encourage the use of the collective noun 'sport' (Parkhouse, 1991). For the sake of standardisation, we have elected to follow suit.

Unique Aspects of Sport Management

It has to be said, however, that there are some unique aspects of sport management which render it different from the management of other business enterprises and, hence, justify it as a separate, distinct area of professional expertise. These include issues such as sport marketing, the structure and financing of sport organisations and the career paths within the industry (Parks and Zanger, 1990).

The marketing of sport is unique, because sport and fitness services are unlike other products purchased by consumers. For example, those providing the sports experience cannot predict the outcome because of the spontaneous nature of the activity, the inconsistency of various events, and the uncertainty surrounding the results. Marketers of sport face special challenges dictated by the nature of the enterprise.

The financing and budgeting for sport organisations also differs from that of a typical business in a number of ways. Although their income might be more definite in that subscription levels are set and their membership levels and grants may be known in advance, their cash flow is likely to be more erratic. Their objectives will also be more varied and difficult to quantify, with the likelihood of greater problems of accountability existing due to the spreading of responsibility among members. This structural issue is particularly pertinent. The sporting landscape is littered with examples of sporting codes which respond too slowly, if at all, to the changing environments within which they operate, because of their cumbersome organisational structures.

With regard to revenue, sport enterprises nowadays also earn a significant income, not from the sale of service (e.g. a game or a 10 km run), but from sources extraneous to the sale of the service (e.g. sponsorship and television rights). Sport managers also compete for the discretionary dollar of consumers through the sale of items that may or may not be related to what might be thought the primary focus of the enterprise. Another difference is that sport attracts customers (spectators) who spend more money outside the sporting arena than on the sport itself. As a result of such a unique financial base, sport managers require a different practice within their setting from that which obtains in business, although obviously similar basic accounting and budgeting principles will still apply.

It could be argued that the economics of sport are unique. Undoubtedly the goal for those in the business of baked bean production is not only to be the best baked bean producers but to be the only producers. The goal is to eliminate competition. Sport, however, requires competition for its economic survival. Managers of sport find themselves striving for a state of affairs where participants are able to remain competitive in relation to other participants. Owners/managers of teams wish to be the best, but only just the best, not to be so much better than others that there is a loss of spectacle. The Americans, for whom professional sport is business, are masters at manipulating the variables to ensure even competition, thus spectator appeal and economic success. Rule changes and draft systems are obvious examples of such management. As sport becomes more commercialised in New Zealand we can expect to see similar concerns facing sport managers.

In passing, it should be said that career paths associated with sport management are not as well defined as in other vocational areas. Traditionally many sport managers were hired from such highly visible groups as successful athletes or coaches. In some cases the absence of managerial expertise would raise the question that their employment might have depended less on what they knew and perhaps more on whom they knew and the nature of their relationships. Fortunately there is growing evidence to show that contemporary practice deviates from this tradition and that managerial appointments depend more and more on knowledge of finance, marketing and management than success in the sporting arena.

Sport Management

As a combined term, sport management can be misleading. In the strictest sense management is limited to subject matter that focuses on the processes of planning, organising, directing and controlling. But primary areas of study that relate to sport and are included in this text include accounting, marketing, economics, organisational behaviour and legal studies. Sport management, then, is composed of two basic elements – sport and management. The job of management is to get things done with and through other people via planning, organising, leading (directing) and evaluating (controlling). Hence we could define sport management as including the functions of planning, organising, leading and evaluating within the context of an organisation, with the primary objective of providing sport or fitness-related activities, products and/or services (Mullin, cited in Parkhouse, 1990: 5). This definition provides a framework for the present text. Overall, this book addresses the substantive aspects of the profession by presenting theoretical principles and the subsequent application of these principles in each topic area. It will raise questions and issues through case studies, and give readers insight into areas of management from sport settings in New Zealand. The current level of economic investment and competition within the sport industry mandates the consideration of sound business and management training and expertise in employment practice.

Understanding Sport in Society

The book begins by examining a number of contextual issues which impact on the sport manager, such as the economic, social, political, educational and structural environments within which sport operates. Of course how we understand the relationship of sport to such issues depends on the theoretical framework we use. Differing theoretical frameworks can lead to quite different explanations. Debate on the validity of each approach is often intense amongst sport sociologists, whose primary concern is to understand the relationship between sport and society. Coakley (1990) provides a simple but useful overview of the different theoretical frameworks, suggesting that the major theoretical positions can be described as either functionalism, conflict theory or critical theory.

The *structural functionalist* is more likely to focus on the positive functions of sport in society, perceiving that sport contributes to the efficient operation of society. This position draws on the organic analogy, viewing sport as one interdependent part of the social system, functioning to meet the needs of both the individual and the social system as a whole. Hargreaves (1986) notes that in such an approach sport is seen as providing meaningful activity for an individual, which enhances the acquisition of stable personal identities, integrates the individual into society and stabilises the social order by reinforcing common norms and values.

Using rugby as an example, the functionalist is likely to view the game as socially valuable with positive consequences for participants, the community and New Zealand society as a whole.

It could be perceived as a vehicle for socialising young males into an appropriate male role with its emphases on strength, endurance, toughness and manliness. Furthermore, it could be regarded as teaching participants that success is achieved through hard work, commitment to the team and working in cooperation with others. It could be seen as providing a healthy outlet for pent-up frustrations which, if not released, could spill over into other spheres of life in less legitimate ways, and for the lower socio-economic groups in society, it provides an avenue for social and economic advancement. In summary, as Leonard (1993) states, functionalists 'while not denying negative features of the social system, tend to view the social world in more positive images'.

Such an understanding of sport and its relationship to society closely resembles the popular and 'commonsense' views of sport. It is an approach which is frequently adopted by sport advocates and sport managers when lobbying for public funds, and is usually the position of politicians who support the notion of government as a provider in sport. The latter is evidenced by the Minister of Sport, Fitness and Leisure, Hon. John Banks, who in a speech to sports bodies in 1990, advocated the 'clear connection between being *into* sport and being *out of* court'.

By contrast, the *conflict theorist's* attention is drawn to the negative aspects of sport, seeing it as an opiate which dulls people's awareness of societal problems and oppression. The concern of the conflict theorist is to change current structures, which manipulate and oppress for the profit and personal gain of the powerful in society. The goal is to de-institutionalise sport, to render it more 'play-like' and put power in the hands of the 'players', hence making it a source of freedom and liberation. Hence the conflict theorist's view of rugby is likely to contrast sharply with that of the functionalist. The level of preoccupation with the game that exists in New Zealand, is likely to be viewed as manipulative, diverting time and energy away from social injustices, and camouflaging pressing societal problems. Likewise for young participants, particularly those from lower socio-economic groups, it could be seen as creating a false hope, raising a 'false consciousness', which diverts participants' energies from taking more realistic steps towards improving their situation, whether through education or political activism. The commercialism and links with the business world could be viewed as increasing the alienation of participants so that they become mere objects, instruments, a technical means to a commercial end, a reified factor of output and productivity which will ultimately only serve to continue to promote the interests of those who hold the power (Brohm, 1978).

The *critical theorist* is drawn to the way in which sport is an expression of people's 'interests, resources and relationships'. Sport is seen both as a product of historical and social conditions and as a potential mechanism for bringing about change. The goal is that sport should facilitate a variety of opportunities for all members of society, enhance personal development and enable participants to become involved in shaping both their own participation and other aspects of their lives.

Hence the critical theorist might view rugby in a way which identifies how it has developed out of on-going struggles between groups in society who have differential access to resources and power. It is not simply a source of inspiration for society, helping it to function more effectively, nor is it simply shaped in some deterministic way by economic interests which inevitably leads to alienation. It would more likely be regarded as being shaped and defined by being involved in 'never-ending processes of negotiation, compromise and coercion between various groups in society' (Coakley, 1990: 31).

Coakley's overview could be criticised for oversimplifying complex areas of theorising, but it nevertheless provides a useful starting point for understanding three of the major theoretical frameworks. Such frameworks are merely tools for understanding society; they are not sacred, nor ends unto themselves, and each has various strengths and weaknesses. The purpose here is not to advocate one over the other, but to alert the reader to the existence of differing theoretical positions which may lead to different explanations. Each approach sheds light on attempts to understand more about the sport-environment relationship. Contributors to this book have not been asked to adopt any particular framework but have been free to develop their analysis of contextual issues as they deem appropriate.

Review Questions

1. What are some of the reasons for the development of the sport industry?
2. How would you define sport?
3. What are some of the aspects of sport management which make it unique?
4. In what ways could it be argued that management differs from administration?
5. What are some of the different theoretical frameworks which can be used to understand sport in society?

References

Brohm, J. (1978), *Sport: A Prison of Measured Time,* London: Ink Links Ltd.
Coakley, J. (1990), *Sport in Society, Issues and Controversies*, St Louis: Times Mirror/ Mosby College Publishing.
Community Services Institute (1985), *Recreation and Government in New Zealand, Report to the Minister of Recreation and Sport*, Wellington: Government Print.
Hargreaves, J. (1986), 'Where's the Virtue? Where's the Grace? A Discussion of the Social Production of Gender Relations in and through Sport', *Theory, Culture and Society*, vol. 3, no.1, pp. 109-21.
Inkson, K. (1990), *Managing Clubs and Societies*, Auckland: Bateman.
Jensen, B., Sullivan, C., Wilson, N., Berkeley, M. and Russell, D. (1993), *The Business of Sport and Leisure: The Economic Importance of Sport and Leisure in New Zealand*, Wellington: Hillary Commission.
Leonard, W. M. (1993), *A Sociological Perspective of Sport*, New York: Macmillan Publishing.
Snyder, E. and Sprietzer, E. (1989), *Social Aspects of Sport,* Englewood Cliffs, N.J.: Prentice Hall.
Loy, J. (1968), 'The Nature of Sport: A Definitional Effort', Quest 10, 1-15.
Parkhouse, B. (1991), *The Management of Sport: Its Foundations and Applications*, St Louis, MO.: Mosby-Year Book,
Parks, J. and Zanger, B. (1990), *Sport and Fitness Management: Career Strategies and Professional Content*, Champaign, IL.: Human Kinetics.
Shuttleworth, J. (1990), *Sport Management: Professional Preparation in New Zealand: Position Report*, Wellington: Hillary Commission.
Sports Development Inquiry Committee (1985), *'Sport on the Move'*, *Report to the Minister of Recreation and Sport*, Wellington: Government Print.
Trenberth, L. and Love, M. (in press), 'Business and Sport', in Deeks, J. and Enderwick. P. (eds), *Business and New Zealand Society*, New Zealand: Longman Paul.

part one

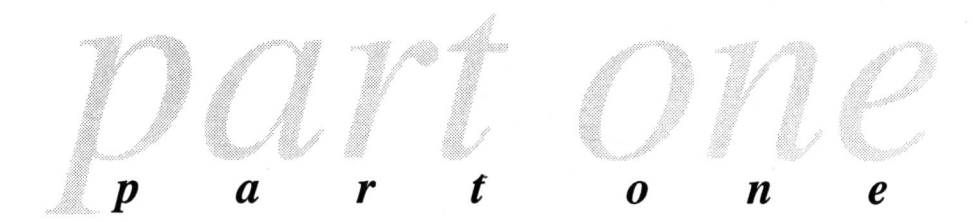

The Environmental Context of Sport

Historical and Social Perspectives on Sport in New Zealand

Anne Hindson, Grant Cushman and Bob Gidlow

In this chapter you will become familiar with the following terms:

'periodisation' of the history	*cultural continuity*
cultures of origin	*colonial and imperial aspirations*
the frontier society	*Victorian-derived values*
manliness	*mateship*
inequality	*gender division of leisure pursuits*
the settled society	*industrial capitalism*
capitalist values	*national identity*
egalitarianism	*urban-based youth culture*
the modern society	*commercialisation*
commodification	*professionalism*
sports-media complex	*televisual sport*
Physical Welfare and Recreation Act, 1937	*Recreation and Sport Act, 1973*
Recreation and Sport Act, 1987	*market ethos*
voluntary, commercial and public sector provisions	

Introduction

While the cultural and economic importance of sport in our society has been recognised (Fougere, 1989; Jensen, Sullivan, Wilson, Berkeley and Russell, 1993), it is somewhat surprising that historians have paid little critical attention to the role of sport in society. Historical writings about New Zealand have tended to focus on settlement patterns, on economic and political developments and, more recently, on bicultural issues and women's experiences (herstory). Apart from the writings of particular individuals with an interest in sport, play and games (e.g. Thompson, 1969, 1975, 1980; Crawford, 1977, 1978a, 1978b; Cleveland, 1967; Pearson, 1978; Sutton-Smith, 1979, 1982), there is no continuity of study and certainly no sub-discipline in the history of sport or leisure. Indeed, a recent important contribution by James Watson (1993) noted that much work on the history of leisure in New Zealand has been written by people trained in other disciplines, particularly sociology and geography. Few historians have focused on the specialist study of sport and leisure, although some have made reference to sport and recreation when examining the more 'mainstream' concerns of their discipline. This 'mix' of writings, together with material from general sports history books (mainly from overseas), informs the following history of sport in New Zealand.

The chapter will consider several historical periods and themes. The discussion will draw attention to the way sport reflects the wider structural processes of the society in which it is located, including historical, economic, technological, political, social and cultural. Separate coverage of Pakeha and Maori involvement in sport and its delivery is not provided, for both cultures have made important contributions. Europeans brought the concept of modern sport with them to New Zealand, but some sports reflect a distinctly Maori contribution in the way they have evolved. This is most clearly the case with respect to team games such as rugby.

Origins and Development of Sport in New Zealand

Pearson (1978) suggests that the nature of New Zealand sport today is a mixture of what was imported by Pakeha settlers, changes made on arrival and changes introduced at a later date. A 'periodisation' of the history of leisure, recreation and tourism in European New Zealand, such as that of Watson (1993), emphasises themes of continuity and change. This brief history of sport in New Zealand emphasises the same themes and locates sport in the context of the wider processes identified in our Introduction.

Colonial Development and Sport

Cultural Continuity

Many modern sports in New Zealand are derived from the games and sports of the first major colonial settlers, the British. The first large-scale influxes of British migrants began to arrive in New Zealand after 1840. The majority of early migrants were agricultural labourers, town craftsmen and domestic servants (Sutch, 1966). Initially, the population was predominantly male and from English country districts, mainly in the South of England. Large populations of Scottish migrants also settled and congregated in the south of the South Island, making Dunedin their 'capital'. Many settlers were hoping to escape the pervasive class structure of their homelands. In their sea-chests and cases these migrants brought the paraphernalia of the sporting traditions of

Victorian England, and they carried with them knowledge of the pastimes and games which were part of their cultural heritage, whether it be Cornish wrestling or Scottish curling. These activities helped to lighten the bleak and harsh conditions in this strange land and reinforced their cultures of origin as well as providing a basis for social interaction and group identity.

Sport, particularly organised sport, was an important vehicle for Britain's early colonial and imperial aspirations (Cushman, 1989). When sport spread to the British colonies, including New Zealand, value patterns, not simply codes of practice, were disseminated. In England the development of organised sport occurred in the prestigious 'public' schools and universities responsible for educating England's upper classes. Sport itself was permeated by the values of these institutions. Mallea (1972) identifies three values which have been associated with sport organisation and participation and which were clearly present in Great Britain at that time. The first is humanism: balanced moral, intellectual and physical development, or a sound mind in a sound body. The second is the gentlemanly tradition of physical prowess, fair dealings, modesty in victory and cheerfulness in defeat. The third is the tradition of manliness, of courage, endurance, loyalty, cooperation and patriotism. Fair play, gentlemanly behaviour, honest competition, manly courage and cooperation in sport were values associated with the imperial élite, the development and maintenance of the British Empire and colonial manhood. Later these values were abbreviated still further and *good sportsmanship* and *playing the game* became phrases which epitomised the desirable approach to New Zealand sport. Even today these Victorian-derived values still retain meaning, as evidenced by the Hillary Commission's recent publicity campaign to maintain or bring back 'fair play' in sport.

Early Colonial Period: Frontier Society

Frontier New Zealand was dominated by extractive industries such as whaling, flax-cutting, gold-mining, timber-milling, and later, gum-digging. Such industries, often set in remote locations, involved heavy manual labour and unpleasant and dangerous working conditions. Frontier settlements were populated by young, transient males (Watson, 1993). The harsh conditions faced by early settlers, the nature of their work, their reliance on each other for survival and the gender imbalance of the frontier, all influenced the choice of sports and the way they were played.

Rugby was quickly transposed from the sport of the élite in Britain to a game for the (male) masses in New Zealand, for it was suited to the social needs of the frontier and the uneven terrain which was typically the field of play (de Jong, 1991). The important contributions which hunting, boxing, wrestling and foot races made to the pursuit of manhood have also been documented (Phillips, 1987; May, 1962; Crawford, 1978a). These activities were often accompanied by the heavy consumption of alcohol (May, 1962; Watson, 1993), which was used to ... *blot out the pain of social isolation* (Fairburn, 1989). Gambling and prostitution were part of frontier life for many, but more respectable forms of recreation, such as shearing, tug-o-war and log-splitting, developed as an extension of work activities. Even frontier children were involved in physically demanding pastimes such as brawling and shinty (an undisciplined form of hockey)(Watson, 1993). In the North Island the games which children played showed a strong Maori influence (Sutton-Smith, 1982).

Horse-related recreational activities were important from earliest colonial times. Whereas in England horses were associated with the gentry, most New Zealand settlers used them not only for work and travel, but also for sport and recreation. An exception to this *democratisation* of horse-based recreation occurred in the Anglican settlement of Canterbury, where attempts were made to use it to preserve class distinctions. Eldred-Grigg (1980, 1982) describes how wealthy landowners rode to hounds and hosted hunts on their properties. The early appearance of horse racing, rowing, tennis, cricket, croquet and polo in European New Zealand had much to do with the British élite (Watson, 1993), who comprised some of the wealthiest landowners in the new colony. These aristocratic sporting traditions however, made little headway. As with rugby, horse-racing symbolised the triumph of the 'ordinary New Zealand bloke' over the élitist values of the 'Old Country'.

Given that the roots of the new society were located in a frontier economy, rural traditions and rural values proved to be the most important determinants of popular New Zealand games, sports and pastimes, and the values which infused them. The need for hard, co-operative work to conquer a harsh environment supported 'mateship', a value system which embodied courage, masculinity and equality. This value system was clearly at odds with the élitism and class structure of British society, which influenced the development of organised sport in that country. Nevertheless, 'mateship' institutionalised its own form of inequality in frontier societies such as New Zealand, Australia and Canada: that between men and women. The significance of the gender division of leisure pursuits became more apparent later in the century, when the population imbalance between men and women corrected itself.

As the frontier receded, and settled communities developed in their wake, recreational opportunities were still sought locally, for transport was difficult and hazardous, particularly in the North Island where open conflict between Maori and Pakeha continued until the 1870s. The church was often the focus of recreational activities. Status was determined by commitment to work, the church and acceptance of group attitudes (Stothart, 1993). In the developing urban towns the influence of the church was more muted (Collins and Lineham, 1993). Extended holidays were unknown in either rural or urban areas, except for the privileged few. For rural people and for the 'respectable' urban working class (Eldred-Grigg, 1982), opportunities for spare time were typically limited to Sunday afternoons and to the occasional day set aside to observe important religious, royal and communal events, such as Queen's Birthday and Anniversary Days.

Anniversary Days were typically used by settler communities to celebrate their survival in an alien land and to reaffirm, by the choice of games and activities, their cultural traditions and the value they accorded physical prowess. Despite the spread of urban values later in the century, the Anniversary Days of different provinces continued to retain some aspects of the founding cultures.

To summarise, in the early colonial period many forms of physical recreation were spontaneous and often rugged, infused with frontier values and having few uniform rules and standards. Except for the sports and pastimes directly imported from Britain and preserved for their élite values, the level of development and organisation of physical activities was insufficient to allow a clear delineation between activities, games and sport. Strong regional differences were apparent in preferred activities, reflecting the cultures of origin of different settler communities.

Late Colonial Period : the Settled Society

By the 1890s the white settler population was numerically, politically and economically dominant, the sex ratio of the population had become more balanced, a settled family life was the norm, and a network of community institutions had been established. Watson (1993) refers to this as the 'settled' period.

An early manifestation of such settlement was the increasing communal organisation and formalisation of sport, especially the establishment of sports and recreation clubs. Yachting, croquet, cycling, curling, prize fighting, fishing, archery, hockey, quoits, skiing, greyhound racing, canoeing, water polo, draughts, and badminton were all established prior to 1900 (Stothart, *circa* 1980), and many of these activities developed on a club basis.

Team sports commonly drew membership from local areas, workplaces or schools (Watson, 1993). As a proportion of the total European population, attendances at sports matches and race days were massive, perhaps reflecting the long working hours, lack of facilities for individual recreation, lack of private transport and inability of most people to afford sports equipment (Stothart, *circa* 1980).

The development of sports clubs was mainly confined to urban centres. In the rural communities the organisation of most team games continued to be a more spontaneous affair. The Church imposed restrictions on the use of the Sabbath (Collins and Lineham, 1993; Stothart, 1993). While small towns remained the repositories of traditional values, urban centres increasingly adopted different, secular, values. Exceptions were working-class Catholic suburbs, such as Addington in Christchurch, where the Church continued to exert a strong control on all aspects of life until well into the 20th Century.

New Zealand was settled by European peoples already familiar with the technology which accompanied the Industrial Revolution. Railways were quickly introduced and while progress on improving communications was slow in some parts (the 'main trunk line' was not completed until 1908), by the 1890s a nationwide series of rail-links was established, joining major centres, facilitating the development of a national economy and the spread of urban values, and creating greater opportunities for inter-provincial and national sporting events. Long before the arrival of motorised transport, provincial teams were able to challenge each other. By the late-1890s at least twelve national sporting associations had been established, beginning with the N.Z. Rifle Association in 1860. By 1894 major codes such as tennis, rowing, athletics, golf, rugby, horse racing and cricket were covered (Sutherland, 1961; Todd, 1966; both cited in Stothart, *circa* 1980). Stothart (1993) suggests that 'our national preoccupation with forming committees was given birth in these early days'.

The technology and values associated with industrial capitalism, together with New Zealand's economic ties to Great Britain, quickly ensured our pre-eminence as a producer of food for the British table. Although there were and continue to be some value differences between rural and urban sectors of New Zealand, reflecting the society's agricultural base, both were permeated by capitalist values which supported hard work, thrift, division of labour, discipline, and cost efficiency, as was the case in other Western, industrialised societies. These values were carried over into sport. Time periods for games were established, equipment for measuring and timing sports became more sophisticated, and sporting, coaching and managing roles became differentiated. Constitutions were drawn up to formalise the rules and to regulate events and competitions. Winning, rather than simply participating, began to be as important in sport as it was in business. Whereas the rough paddock was still the home of many contests in rural New Zealand, more prescribed spaces for sport were made available in urban indoor and outdoor venues.

Alongside team sports, a number of outdoor individual pursuits became popular. Participation was usually club-based rather than informal. These clubs, including a number of tramping, skiing, hunting and fishing clubs, developed after the First World War. The number of participants remained small in comparison with team sports and they were predominantly drawn from more affluent social groups.

Despite the growing popularity of sports and the increasing complexity and organisation of sport in the late colonial period, the involvement of Government continued to be minimal. The major involvement of central and local government was in the provision of land for playing fields. In Christchurch, for example, land was made available for cricket in Hagley Park in 1867, and a polo ground followed (Barnett, Gilpin and Metcalf, 1963).

While gender differences continued in this period, and women were conspicuously discouraged from participating in active forms of recreation and sport, Coney (1986) notes that independent-minded and usually well-educated women were prepared to defy convention. Women's physical activities and sports predominated where groups of women congregated. The history of the YWCA in Auckland indicates that basketball, gymnastics, hockey, fencing, tennis, swimming, cricket, marching, athletics, cycling, and baseball/softball were popular among this group of women early in the twentieth century.

The variety which marked sport, leisure and recreational opportunities by the late nineteenth century is conveyed by Edward Gibbon Wakefield's verbal sketch of 1889:

> The great mass of the people give themselves up wholly to amusement. Horse races, which are exceedingly common in New Zealand, are fixed for these seasons, as are also athletic sports, cricket and football matches, volunteer reviews or camps, agricultural or pastoral shows which are popular and attended by great crowds, regattas, boat races, excursions by sea and land and all sorts of dramatic and musical entertainments in the evenings (cited in Stothart, 1993:4).

Sport and Nationhood

The earliest national sporting associations predated the establishment of a unified political system in New Zealand in 1876. Sporting contacts were important avenues for developing a sense of loyalty and identity and for establishing wider affiliations in the period before political integration (Fougere, 1989). Rugby Union was particularly important in the development of regional, then national, identity, because its popularity was all-pervasive, drawing support from both town and country. The domination of rugby over other sports was established early in the history of European settlement. A form of rugby was played by pupils of Christ's College in 1853, and eight years later inter-provincial matches began. By 1890 there were 700 clubs and 16 major unions, and a national controlling body was established in 1892 (Stothart, *circa* 1980). In England rugby retained an association with élite education, but in New Zealand it became a symbol of egalitarianism. The sport cut across social class and ethnic boundaries, and Maori were represented in early national teams, apart from those touring South Africa (Pearson, 1978). The physical and disciplined nature of rugby was used to promote the values essential for work, family and military service (Phillips, 1983, 1987; Watson, 1993). Culturally, rugby also contributed to the sense of nationhood once national teams proved themselves capable of defeating the 'Mother Country' with a 'classless' team (see Chapter 3). The enthusiastic reception given to the 1905 All Blacks on their return from defeating the British was a harbinger of things to come (Chester and McMillan, 1984).

The 'functional' contribution which rugby made to British upper-class society, as well as to Rugby School itself, has been documented by Dunning and Sheard (1979). A similar analysis can be provided for New Zealand. Rugby represents a classic fusion of two, apparently contradictory, sets of values. One set emphasises equality and 'mateship', while the other emphasises authority.

The former helped to ensure physical survival on the frontier, while the latter encouraged qualities needed by capitalist labour relations and by Imperialism. Not surprisingly, many prestigious New Zealand boys' schools provided no alternative winter sport to rugby until the early 1950s or even later.

Attempts to instil discipline and national pride through sport and physical activity were also evident in the philosophies of the developing voluntary sector. This sector provided young people with structured programmes based on healthy physical activity and moral guidance (Collins and Lineham, 1993). Between 1880 and 1914, Boy Scouts, Girl Guides, Boy's and Girl's Brigades and the YMCA and YWCA were all introduced into New Zealand. By 1914, sport was also firmly established as a compulsory part of the school curriculum, valued for its character-building qualities and for promoting values of teamwork, cooperation, and discipline. As a result, ' ... formal sports, especially rugby, cricket and netball came to occupy much school leisure time, with or without adult supervision' (Watson, 1993: 22).

Government Involvement in Sport

Until the 1930s the voluntary and commercial sectors met most of the organised sporting and recreational needs of New Zealanders with little assistance from the public sector (Perkins, Devlin, Simmons and Batty, 1993). Government involvement in the provision of sport was a consequence of the movements for physical fitness, community health and social reform. These began in the late nineteenth century in a number of Western industrialised societies, and reflected concern that urban-industrial conditions were deleterious to healthy lifestyles, particularly of the urban working class. They gained considerable public strength during the late 1930s. Prior to the Second World War, central government, and to a lesser extent local government, was slow to become involved in sports provision. Sport was regarded as an individual responsibility and government limited its role to providing selected physical facilities such as national and local parks, sports facilities, playgrounds and community halls. Rather than promoting sport, central government's major preoccupation was controlling and regulating undesirable 'recreational' activities such as prostitution, gambling and the abuse of alcohol. As sports became more regular and organised, and youth organisations more active in physical recreation programmes, local governments took a greater role in the provision of playing fields and sporting facilities such as swimming pools, parks, tennis courts and gymnasia. There was much less concern, however, with providing for the sporting needs of Maori and non-European immigrant groups, such as the Chinese, than with meeting the needs of the majority group of British settlers (Perkins and Gidlow, 1991).

In 1937 the Labour Government passed the Physical Welfare and Recreation Act, a bold attempt to coordinate the development of recreation and sport in New Zealand through the Department of Internal Affairs. The Act was driven by concern about the physical condition and fitness of young New Zealanders and the implications of their lack of fitness for the defence of the nation and the Empire (Perkins *et al.*, 1993). The Act contained both educational and practical components. It provided infrastructures for physical training, exercise, sport and recreation and gave financial resources and power to local governments and voluntary organisations to act as community facilitators of leadership courses, programmes and the training of fitness instructors (Sikking, 1992).

While many of the weaker national sports organisations welcomed the physical welfare programme, other better established organisations resented what they saw as government intervention in autonomous organisations. Full implementation of the programme was impeded by New Zealand's entry into the Second World War. Implementation of the Act after the War was dogged by poor administration. The programme withered when the National Party, philosophically opposed to extending Government's welfare role in society, came into office in 1949 (see Chapter 3). At the same time, however, a National Council for Sport was established by a group of enthusiastic sports administrators, whose aim was to coordinate efforts to secure government funding of sport. Unfortunately, the Council's life was short. Powerful and well-resourced sports, such as rugby, tennis and bowls, failed to lend their support, and it was not until the 1970s that any further attempts were made to centrally coordinate sporting and recreational activities.

Modern Society

By the early 1950s seventy-two per cent of the population lived in urban areas (Perkins *et al.* 1993), and New Zealand was beginning to enjoy the benefits of the 'long boom', which lasted until the late-1960s. This was a period of economic prosperity based mainly on high prices for the country's agricultural products and was marked by changes in leisure and recreational behaviour facilitated by the expansion of motor-car ownership. The 'stratified diffusion' of car ownership in the post-war period (Young and Willmott, 1975) had a powerful influence on sport in that it provided the means for people to break away from mass activities and structured team and club sports. Some of the sports to benefit from this were running and squash, which suited the new urban environments where space and time were limited (Watson, 1993).

The period was also marked by shifts in social attitudes and by the first manifestations of a distinct, urban-based youth culture. The teenagers of the 1950s were more physically and socially mobile than their predecessors, possessed greater discretionary income, and questioned what they saw as the suffocating orthodoxies of the 'steady-as-we-go' Holyoake years. Many of them sought freedom to experiment in new, informal leisure activities with their peers rather than commit themselves to 'organised' sport structures dominated by people of their parents' generation. In the 1960s particularly, their experimentation extended into sex, drugs and other activities unacceptable to older people. In response to growing concerns about youth morality and delinquency, governments supported a range of programmes in the 1950s administered through traditional, often uniformed, youth organisations. Generous financial support was provided to organisations for leadership training and administration. These organisations, however, held little attraction for those young people who were seen to be most at risk, and their programmes were largely ineffectual in imposing conformity.

The relationship between public, voluntary and commercial sector involvement in sporting provision changed dramatically from the late 1950s. The voluntary sector, so powerful in the early part of this century, suffered most from the emergence of individualistic values and the rebellion against formal, frequently value-laden, provision. The growth of individual sporting pursuits, involving increasingly sophisticated technology, created new opportunities for the commercial sector. In some cases, however, the voluntary sector was also able to take advantage of new leisure and sporting trends, by becoming more commercial in its outlook. Profitable programmes, such as fitness, were used to support uneconomic services, such as introductory sports skills programmes for children.

Public sector involvement in sport was limited to trying to rectify the negative effects of urbanisation mentioned above, by encouraging youth leadership programmes and the provision of community facilities. The aim was to reinstate traditional social values and controls. The ethos involved, that of using sport and recreation to solve urban social problems, was hardly different to that which fuelled the 1937 Act. A change in ethos began to emerge in the early 1970s however. Encouraging participation in sporting and physical recreation activities for its own sake, and ensuring opportunity of access to such activities, became more important than promoting the moral fibre of the nation and its youth.

Labour's Recreation and Sport Act 1973 was instrumental in resourcing and developing sport and recreational activities in New Zealand (see Chapter 3). At the time, sport leaders such as Arthur Lydiard spearheaded demands for more resources to be provided at a central level, and more organisation to achieve greater international sporting success and policies to bring more young people into competitive sport. Two bodies were created, the Ministry of Recreation and Sport (under the Department of Internal Affairs) and the Council for Recreation and Sport. The Ministry's main role was to encourage local government involvement in recreation planning, provide funding for community recreation initiatives and partially fund recreation personnel in local authorities. Whereas earlier public sector initiatives were concerned with constructing facilities, efforts were now directed to encouraging community-and individual-initiated programmes through community development processes. Local government, in particular, took a major role, employing recreation staff in programming and community development. The Council for Recreation and Sport, which was an autonomous body, had an advisory role at Ministerial level and promoted national programmes. In campaigns such as 'Have-A-Go' and 'Come Alive', emphasis was placed on experimenting with, and participating in, new activities.

Commercialised and Industrialised Sport

For Watson (1993: 24) modern society is marked by:

> ... greater diversity, particularly in the ranges of choices for the individual consumer; further mechanisation and commercialisation; greater urbanisation; a relaxation of official attempts to police behaviour; an emphasis on youth; greater opportunities for women; and a fading of ideologies based on race, empire, and, to some extent, the nation.

As the British Empire dissolved, the gradual fading of the ideology of nationhood and of economic ties to Britain also saw a changed attitude to rugby, the *national* game. Stothart (1993) and others have suggested that the prolonged single-minded relationship with South Africa and its rejection of Maori players, the upsurge of female resistance to the game and the growth of a range of other sports, also contributed to a weakening of the near-exclusive hold of rugby over male leisure. The 1981 Springbok Tour broke the rugby allegiance of many urban New Zealanders, and the New Zealand Rugby Football Union spent much of the 1980s repairing the damage it caused. Its support of women's rugby has been one recent, positive outcome of attempts to reinstate the popularity of the game.

While rugby administrators of the 1970s and early 1980s ignored major social and cultural changes, other sports and alternative approaches to sports participation and presentation flourished. The growth of the commercial and industrialised sport sector in particular, was rapid, and has had significant effects on New Zealand culture.

Beamish (1982: 178) argues that:

> Sport is no longer a mere process of utility that is enjoyed by the player for his (or her) health, welfare, amusement, distraction, or whatever. Nor is it solely a concrete use-value to be matched by bystanders. Sport is a commodity ....

This commodification of sport has had a number of ramifications.

First, sport and general fitness became arenas for commercial sponsorship and investment and also for major property development, gambling (both legal and illegal) and highly competitive selling of specialised clothing, equipment, facilities, books and magazines.

Second, older cultural or sporting forms were sometimes replaced or were simply swept aside by the cult of the new, the novel and the fashionable, in the pursuit of 'market share'. The decline in popularity of horse-race gambling (especially on-course betting) and the increasing popularity of other forms of individualised (and increasingly mechanised) gambling, such as Lotto and poker machines, are examples of this trend (Syme, 1992). Of course, some changes to sport came from external sources. For example, pressures to deregulate the economy led to the introduction of Saturday and Sunday trading. The traditional Kiwi notion of the 'working week' has faded and with it the tradition of Saturday as a sports day. Many New Zealanders now find that opportunities to participate in regular sporting competition have been removed. Such wider economic trends increase the popularity of individualist sporting and recreational pursuits, and further erode the popularity of team sports and the willingness of people to commit themselves to voluntary organisations and activities.

Third, the values which today sustain team sports such as rugby and cricket, are no longer based solely on the values which nurtured and sustained them during the colonial period. Values of equality and team-work or 'mateship' are threatened by commercial opportunities such as product endorsements, which tempt individual 'star' players to stand out from the team. Moreover, teams are expected to uphold a different set of public standards than hitherto. The application of professionalism to sports, including amateur sports, means for example that rugby teams which were once proud to publicise how beer drinking contributed to their match preparation, must now demonstrate their preoccupation with fitness, health and body image.

Fourth, leisure ceased to remain a separate sphere of life, free of the pressures which mark other life spheres.

> As we get richer, more and more areas of our lives become monetised. This means that the freedoms we gain from toil are increasingly the object of attention of the markets ... (Seabrook, 1988).

As sport has become increasingly central to the New Zealand economy (Jensen *et al.* 1993), entire manufacturing industries now rely on the constant stimulation of consumer demand in *free* time (Rowe and Lawrence, 1990). There are more pressures to purchase 'good times' rather than to create them.

Fifth, performance criteria became as stringent in sport as in *work*, and the division between them has grown increasingly blurred. The expectations of performance and the emergence of a 'win at all costs' mentality have forced athletes to push their bodies to new levels of exertion and accomplishment, either naturally or with performance-enhancing aids including drugs. Not surprisingly, amateur athletes experience more pressure to turn professional or to accept many of the material benefits which amateurism makes possible.

Sixth, an institutionalised dislocation between suppliers and consumers of sport emerged. The provision of sport, even of amateur sport, is increasingly dominated by market considerations. Specialists with expertise in marketing and promotion are employed to 'shape' the game. The centralised development and promotion of sport removes it from local communities, from community neighbourhoods and workplaces where it arose. One consequence of this dislocation is a lack of connection between those interested in the community development and welfare aspects of sport (e.g. sport for the unemployed) and those motivated by purely commercial possibilities. Another consequence is that while there has been an increase in the sporting participation of individuals, players and spectators have less control over the game or sport.

> ... sport was at one time an activity engaged in in the streets, on the village greens and so on. Now it takes place in the local sports centre which is expensively provided by the local authority and managed by professional managers. Children used once to play in relatively safe, stimulating environments, near their homes, watched by grandparents and neighbours: now playschemes and playcentres with trained staff and expensive equipment are required. Sport and play have become commodities (Veal, 1987: 157).

Seventh, a distinction emerged in sports funding. Élite sportsmen and sportswomen are increasingly able to attract financial support from commercial sponsors and, if they compete in codes represented at the Olympic and Commonwealth Games, they may also receive assistance from government-funded sources, such as the New Zealand Olympic and Commonwealth Games Association. Non-élite competitors, on the other hand, struggle to finance themselves and are heavily dependent on government funding and support. Sport has thus become a tool of commerce at the high performance level and the responsibility of government at the mass participation level.

Eighth, commercial considerations began to strongly influence the structure of sports events. For example, the five-day test match, with its discipline and tightly structured code of conduct, has been joined by the one-day game, a commercialised spectacle (Harriss, 1990). According to cricketing purists, the one-day game has done nothing to improve the technical aspects of batting and bowling. To take a second example, netball is now divided into four quarters rather than two halves, creating more opportunities for advertising breaks and thus making the game more presentable to television networks.

The Sports-media Complex

A profound influence on modern sport, and one that has facilitated its rapid commercialisation, is the mass media, particularly television (see Chapter 18). Jhally (1989) has adopted the term sports-media complex to describe the relationship between commercial interests, media and sport. Jhally argues that this complex of institutions has a profound effect on people's perceptions, tastes and preferences with regard to sport. Sports are increasingly dependent upon commercial sponsorship, via the media, for their survival. This is particularly, but not exclusively, true of professional sports. Commercial television networks find that coverage of many sports is a relatively cheap way to fill programme schedules, and they 'sell' their viewers to sponsors via coverage of 'televisual' (Barnett, 1990) sports such as rugby league and sporting events such as the America's Cup, the Olympic Games and the Rugby World Cup. Most people, according to Jhally, do the vast majority of their sports spectating via the media, which means that their cultural experience of sport is highly mediated. There is some evidence that in New Zealand, as elsewhere, 'couch potato' viewers are replacing ardent sideline spectators (Cushman and Laidler et al., 1991).

The importance of the sports-media complex in New Zealand is apparent from the fact that Television New Zealand provides free coverage only to selected codes – rugby union, rugby league, cricket and netball. Other codes must pay for coverage. Some of these are able to attract commercial sponsors, but others, particularly minority-interest and less televisual codes, are effectively locked out. The growth in the power of the media is highlighted by the treatment of Erin Baker, one of the best female triathletes in the world, who was denied lucrative sponsorship deals because the New Zealand media considered her too outspoken and too *unfeminine* in appearance. The power and money of major corporate sponsors is clearly evident in major sporting codes. Rugby League initially held little television appeal for New Zealand viewers, but massive promotion, fuelled by corporate sponsorship, generated the present healthy level of interest in the sport (Hyde, 1993).

The Public Sector and the Market Ethos

Traditionally, the public sector has tried to balance or supplement the growth of commercial sporting enterprise, although on unequal terms and without much coordinated planning (see Chapter 3). Prior to 1984, sporting and recreational opportunities were seen to constitute a public good which the state should provide. Central and local government funding was traditionally used to provide sports infrastructures and to support a wide range of recreations and sports, particularly minority-interest sports. Public sector facilities, such as the public hospital system and the Accident Compensation Corporation, were routinely used to meet the social and personal service needs of sports-related activities.

Assumptions about the economic wisdom of the state's involvement in service provision were examined critically, and in most cases rejected, following the election of the fourth Labour Government in 1984. Central government became no longer concerned with the provision of services and the strict regulation and control of private-sector services, but with the privatisation of its own services wherever possible, and with the development of partnerships with commercial organisations. Following the passing of the Recreation and Sport Act 1987, the Ministry of Recreation and Sport and the Council for Recreation and Sport were replaced by a quango, the Hillary Commission for Recreation and Sport (now Sport, Fitness and Leisure), which removed recreation and sport from direct government control. Local government moved away from a near-exclusive concern with direct service provision and accepted private sector involvement in facility ownership and management. Some services and facilities, such as swimming pool complexes, have been contracted out to the commercial sector. That local government has come to recognise the value of commercial initiatives is also apparent from its adoption of more corporatist approaches to the management of parks, recreational and sporting services since the mid-1980s (Perkins, 1992).

Conclusions

In Chapter 1, Trenberth and Collins outlined Coakley's (1990) distinction between three theoretical frameworks or perspectives which provide different insights into sport-society relationships. These are the functionalist, conflict and critical perspectives. It is not the intention to revisit these theoretical frameworks here, except to indicate that whether sport is seen as reaffirming, recreating or challenging societal structures, depends heavily on which framework is adopted. The tension between the perspectives reflects the associated conflict between two conceptually distinct processes – the capitalist exploitation of sport, and its popular celebration as pleasure (Rowe and Lawrence, 1990). Notwithstanding contemporary insights provided by postmodernism, explanations of the evolution of sport must be grounded in an appreciation of the economic conditions faced by groups of people, the economic system they follow, the power relations they create and the effectiveness of challenges to those relationships (Coakley, 1990; Rowe and Lawrence, 1990; Cameron, 1993). In a capitalist society such as New Zealand, where power is unequally shared, a struggle ensues as individuals and groups compete for the right to determine sport outcomes, including the way sport is to be defined, played and organised. An instructive example is provided by the struggles to have women's sport recognised and resourced in New Zealand (Cameron, 1993). Such struggles involve not just players and officials, but also patrons-sponsors, spectators and commentators (Baker, 1982).

In conclusion, the purpose of this chapter was to provide an overview of the social, economic and political conditions which have influenced sport over the one hundred and fifty years of European settlement of New Zealand. Changes in sport, including the growing diversity of codes, the emergence of individualist sports, changing sport values, the role of the media and the increasing professionalisation and commercialisation of sport, reflect and reinforce other, broader, change processes. These impacts are likely to continue into the twenty-first century, and are likely to result in an expanding range of sporting services, products, facilities and management practices. Historical precedents in New Zealand suggest that sport administrators and managers will ignore the historical, social and cultural contexts of sport at their peril.

Review Questions

1. Explain and give examples of the way sport has reflected and reinforced wider social, economic and political developments in New Zealand.
2. Describe the British influences on the development of sport in New Zealand in the early Colonial period, giving examples.
3. Contrast the later Colonial period with 'Modern' New Zealand, with regard to the characteristics of sport participation.
4. Describe and contrast the conditions which led to the introduction of the:
    (a)   Physical Welfare and Recreation Act 1937;
    (b)   Recreation and Sport Act 1973;
    (c)   Recreation and Sport Act 1987.
5. What is the commercialisation of sport? How has it arisen? How has it been manifest in the participation, delivery and resourcing of sport in New Zealand?

References

Baker, W. (1982), *Sports in the Western World*, New Jersey: Rowman and Allanheld.
Barnett, M. Gilpin, H. and Metcalf, L. (1963), *A Garden Century*, Christchurch: Pegasus Press.
Barnett, S. (1992), *Games and Sets: The Changing Face of Sport on Television*, London: British Film Institute.
Beamish, R. (1982), 'Sport and the Logic of Capitalism', in H. Cantelon and R. Gruneau (eds), *Sport, Culture and the Modern State*, Toronto: University of Toronto Press.

Cameron, J. (1993), 'The Sociology of Sport', in H. C. Perkins and G. Cushman (eds), *Leisure, Recreation and Tourism*, Auckland: Longman Paul.
Cashmore, E. (1990), *Making Sense of Sport*, New York, Routledge: Chapman and Hall.
Chester, R. and McMillan, N. (1984), *Centenary: 100 Years of All Black Rugby*, Auckland: Moa Publications.
Cleveland, L. (1967), 'Pop Art, Politics and Sport in New Zealand', *Politics*, vol. 2, no. 2.
Coakley, J. (1990), *Sport in Society: Issues and Controversies*, 4th Edition, St. Louis: Times Mirror/Mosby College Publishing.
Collins, C. and Lineham, P. (1993), 'Religion and Leisure', in H. C. Perkins and G. Cushman (eds), *Leisure, Recreation and Tourism*, Auckland: Longman Paul.
Coney, S. (1986), *Every Girl. A Social History of Women and the YWCA in Auckland, 1885-1985*, Auckland: YWCA.
Crawford, S. (1977), 'Recreation Activity in the Otago Goldfields', *New Zealand Journal of Health, Physical Education and Recreation*, vol. 10, no.1.
Crawford, S. (1978a), 'A Social History of 19th Century Sport in Otago', in J.J. Hinchcliff (ed.), *The Nature and Meaning of Sport in New Zealand*, Auckland: Centre for Continuing Education, University of Auckland.
Crawford, S. (1978b), 'A National Cult: A Study of Rugby in New Zealand', *Momentum*, June.
Crawford, S. (1987), 'One's Nerves and Courage are in Very Different Order Out in New Zealand: Recreational and Sporting Opportunities for Women in a Remote Colonial Setting', in J.A. Mangen and R. J. Park (eds), *From Fair Sex to Feminism: Sport and the Socialisation of Women in the Industrial and Post-Industrial Eras*, London: Frank Cass.
Cushman, G. (1989), 'Trends in Sport in New Zealand', in T. Kamphorst and K. Roberts (eds), *Trends in Sport: A Multinational Perspective*, The Netherlands: Giordano Bruno Culemborg.
Cushman, G., Laidler A. Russell, D., Wilson, N., Herbison, P. (1991), *Life in New Zealand Commission Report*, Volume IV, Dunedin: University of Otago.
de Jong, P. (1991), *Saturday's Warriors*, Palmerston North, Massey University: Sociology Department.
Dunning, E. (1970), *The Sociology of Sport,* London: Frank Cass.
Dunning, E. and Sheard, K. (1979), *Barbarians, Gentlemen and Players*, Oxford: Martin Robertson.
Eldred-Grigg, S. (1980), *A Southern Gentry: New Zealanders Who Inherit the Earth*, Wellington: A.H. and A.W. Reed.
Eldred-Grigg, S. (1982), *A New History of Canterbury*, Dunedin: McIndoe.
Fairburn, M. (1989), *The Ideal Society and Its Enemies: The Foundations of Modern New Zealand Society, 1850-1900*, Auckland: Auckland University Press.
Fougere, G. (1989), 'Sport, Culture and Identity: The Case of Rugby Football', in D. Novitz and B. Willmott (eds), *Culture and Identity in New Zealand*, Wellington: GP Books.
Gidlow, R., Perkins, H., Cushman, G. and Simpson, C. (1990), 'Leisure', in P. Spoonley, D. Pearson and I. Shirley (eds), *New Zealand Society*, Palmerston North: Dunmore Press.
Hargreaves, J. (1986), *Sport, Power and Culture*, Cambridge: Polity Press.
Harriss, I. (1990), 'Packer, Cricket and Postmodernism', in D. Rowe and G. Lawrence (eds), *Sport and Leisure: Trends in Australian Popular Culture*, Sydney: Harcourt Brace Jovanovich.
Hinchcliff, J. (1978), 'Some Philosophical, Moral and Theological Assumptions About

Sport', in J. Hinchcliff (ed.), *The Nature and Meaning of Sport in New Zealand*, Auckland: Centre for Continuing Education, University of Auckland.

Hyde, T. (1993), 'Taking the Lion's Share', *Metro*, No. 145, July.

Jensen, B. Sullivan, C. Wilson, N. Berkeley, M. and Russell, D. (1993), *The Business of Sport and Leisure: The Economic Importance of Sport and Leisure in New Zealand*, Wellington: Hillary Commission.

Jhally, S. (1989), 'Cultural Studies and the Sports-Media Complex', in L. Wenner (ed.), *Media, Sport and Society*, California: Sage.

Kelly, J. (1990), 'Leisure and Common Life in New Zealand', Paper presented to the Life in New Zealand Survey, Data Release Conference: Wellington.

Mallea, J. (1972), 'Class and Sport: The Victorian Legacy', Paper presented to the American Sociological Association Annual General Meeting.

May, P. (1962), *The West Coast Gold Rushes*, Christchurch: Pegasus Press.

Pearson, K. (1978), 'Meanings and Motivation in Sport', in J. Hinchcliff (ed.), *The Nature and Meaning of Sport in New Zealand*, Auckland: Centre for Continuing Education, University of Auckland.

Perkins, H. C. and Gidlow, R. (1991), 'Leisure Research in New Zealand: Patterns, Problems and Prospects', *Leisure Studies*, vol.10, no.2, pp.93-104.

Perkins, H.C. (1992), 'Local Government Reform, Case Study 9.3: Recreational Service Provision in Christchurch', in S. Britton, R. Le Heron and E. Pawson (eds), *Changing Places in New Zealand: A Geography of Restructuring*, Christchurch: New Zealand Geographical Society.

Perkins, H. Devlin, P. Simmons, D. and Batty, R. (1993), 'Recreation and Tourism' in A. Memon and H. C. Perkins (eds), *Environmental Planning in New Zealand*, Palmerston North: Dunmore Press.

Phillips, J. (1987), *A Man's Country? The Image of the Pakeha Male – A History*, Auckland: Penguin.

Rowe, D. and Lawrence, G. (eds) (1990), *Sport and Leisure: Trends in Australian Popular Culture*, Sydney: Harcourt Brace Jovanovich.

Sansome, D. (1988), *Greek Athletes and the Genesis of Sport*, Berkeley: University of California Press.

Seabrook, J. (1988), *The Leisure Society*, Oxford: Blackwell.

Sikking, M. (1992), 'Subcultures and Outdoor Pursuits: An Interpretive Study of Therapeutic Outdoor Recreation Programmes for Youth-at-Risk', Master of Applied Science thesis, Lincoln University.

Sinclair, K. (1959), *A History of New Zealand*, Harmondsworth: Penguin.

Stothart, R. (circa 1980), 'Sport in New Zealand – A Critical View', Unpublished Paper.

Stothart, R. (1993), 'History is About Chaps', Paper presented to the *Women in Action '93* Conference: Wellington.

Sutch, W. B. (1966), *The Quest for Security in New Zealand*, Wellington: Oxford University Press.

Sutton-Smith, B. (1979), 'The Development of Folklore and Games in the Pacific', *History of Sport and Physical Education*, Dunedin: University of Otago.

Sutton-Smith, B. (1982), *A History of Children's Play: New Zealand, 1840-1950*, Wellington: New Zealand Council for Educational Research.

Syme, D. (1992), 'A History of Horse-Race Gambling in New Zealand', PhD. thesis,

Victoria University of Wellington.
Thompson, R. (1969), 'Sport and Politics', in J. Forster (ed.), *Social Processes in New Zealand*, Wellington: Longman Paul.
Thompson, R. (1975), *Retreat from Apartheid: New Zealand's Sporting Contacts with South Africa*, London: Oxford University Press.
Thompson, R. (1980), 'Sport and Politics', in J. Shallcrass, B. Larkin., B. Stothart (eds), *Recreation Reconsidered Into the Eighties*, Auckland: Auckland Regional Authority and New Zealand Council for Recreation and Sport.
Veal, A. J. (1987), *Leisure and the Future*, London: Allen and Unwin.
Watson, J. (1993), 'The History of Leisure, Recreation and Tourism in New Zealand', in H. C. Perkins and G. Cushman (eds), *Leisure, Recreation and Tourism*, Auckland: Longman Paul.
Young, M. and Willmott, P. (1975), *The Symmetrical Family*, Harmondsworth: Penguin.

Suggested Reading

Cushman, G. (1989), 'Trends in Sport in New Zealand', in T. Kamphorst and K. Roberts (eds), *Trends in Sport: A Multinational Perspective,* The Netherlands: Giordano Bruno Culemborg.
Fougere, G. (1989), 'Sport, Culture and Identity: The Case of Rugby Football', in D. Novitz and B. Willmott (eds), *Culture and Identity in New Zealand*, Wellington: GP Books.
Gidlow, R. Perkins, H. Cushman, G. and Simpson, C. (1990), 'Leisure', in P. Spoonley, D. Pearson and I. Shirley (eds), *New Zealand Society,* Palmerston North: Dunmore Press.
Perkins, H. C. and Cushman G. (eds) (1993), *Leisure, Recreation and Tourism*, Auckland: Longman Paul.
Phillips, J. (1987), *A Man's Country? The Image of the Pakeha Male – A History*, Auckland: Penguin.
Rowe D. and Lawrence G. (eds) (1990), *Sport and Leisure: Trends in Australian Popular Culture*, Sydney: Harcourt Brace Jovanovich.

Politics and Sport in New Zealand

Chris Collins and Mary Stuart

In this chapter you will become familiar with the following terms:

hegemony	nationalistic values
dominant groups	old-boy-network
institutional nature of sportpolitics in sport	politics of gender
Physical Welfare and Recreation Act 1937	government involvement
Ministry of Recreation and Sport	Recreation and Sport Act 1973
Sport Fitness and Leisure Act 1992	Recreation and Sport Act 1987
the managerialist critique	traditional pluralism
resources for influence	welfare reformism
Hillary Commission for Recreation and Sport	The New Right
Hillary Commission for Sport, Fitness and Leisure	hierarchy of authority
	New Zealand Council for Recreation and Sport

Introduction

That sport and politics should not mix is a proposition that has provoked much debate in New Zealand. For example, while government involvement in sport at the funding or advisory level seems now to be readily accepted and even expected, it has not always been the case. Such issues in New Zealand in the 1970s divided political parties and became platforms for election campaigns. At the time, the suggestion of setting up a centralised government-linked sport organisation and bureaucracy, with its own significant funding base, would have been anathema to many. At the prospect of the establishment of a Ministry of Recreation and Sport, for example, Mr Highet, a National Party Member of the Opposition, commented that from a first glance the proposal confirmed his worst fears, namely government interference in the administration of sport, and that he thought this was a 'lot of humbug and ballyhoo' (NZPD, 1973: 800). Ironically, Mr Highet was eventually to become the Minister responsible for the Ministry of Recreation and Sport when the National Party was returned to power. Sport has unquestionably been a political football in New Zealand in a number of different ways.

The aim of this chapter is to explore links between politics and sport from a New Zealand perspective. The chapter also examines motivations for government involvement in sport, highlights examples and the changing nature of New Zealand government involvement, and then considers the issue of politics within sport organisations.

The Politics and Sport Connection

Commentators such as Baker (1982) argue that sport and politics are closely intertwined and that it is, in fact, extremely difficult to identify a period in history in which sport has not been integrally related to the dominant political structures of the day. Coakley (1990) similarly maintains that throughout history the emergence, nature and organisation of sport has been influenced by the relationships between various groups of people in society and the distribution of power and resources between these groups.

This is not to suggest that sport has necessarily been used by the powerful as a political tool to *force* values and ideology upon the general populace. Rather, many social scientists advocate the use of the Gramscian notion of 'hegemony' to understand the influence of sport in society (for a more detailed discussion refer to Hargreaves, 1985; McKay, 1991; Cameron, 1993). Hegemony refers to the dominance and subordination of particular groups within society by the dominant groups, not through coercion or sanction but through compliance and consent. It is a dynamic all-encompassing process involving subtle persuasion rather than ideological imposition. The result is a general assumption of the values of the dominant group among all members of society. The benefits however, typically accrue to the dominant group. Utilising the notion of hegemony as it relates to sport, Cameron (1992: 172) argues that,

> ... subordinate groups are not forced into sport. They are won over, given apparent status and perhaps financial reward; they are given some of the trappings of power. But they are not given power itself. Power remains with the dominant group – the promoters, sponsors, national associations and governments.

There are several characteristics inherent in sport which serve to guarantee a strong relationship between sport and politics (Eitzen and Sage, 1993). The hegemonic potential of sport will become evident as some of these characteristics and government motivation for involvement in sport are explored.

Sport – Representing Others

One important factor, note Eitzen and Sage (1993), is that as sports participants typically represent and have allegiance to some social organisation, through sporting representation, others inevitably become bound up in the performance of the sports person. Hence, when the Silver Ferns walk onto the court, their victory becomes 'our' victory, their defeat 'our' defeat. Furthermore, victory is frequently taken to be an indication of group superiority and the outcomes of contests, most particularly at international level, are often interpreted politically. Phillips (1987) highlights an example of this when examining the significance of the 1905 All Black tour to Great Britain. It was a tour which, apart from establishing the game at the core of the male identity for New Zealanders, indicated a great deal about underlying social pressures, anxieties and overtly political concerns. The All Blacks, notes Phillips (1990: 131-132), provided reassurance for those worried about the decline of the Anglo-Saxon race, demonstrating that in the colonies 'were men toughened on the frontier who could ... uphold the honour of the race in future military conflict'. The virtues of the pioneering life were still evident and certain nationalistic values were read into the All Blacks' success, namely mateship, the outdoor life, modesty, honesty and mental quickness. In the context of imperial rivalries, the tour was so important, notes Phillips, that then Prime Minister Seddon rewarded the team with a 'free tour' of the United States on the way home, no doubt providing a chance to demonstrate their 'superior manhood' to their American kin.

Sport and International Politics

The representative nature of sport often means that sporting events and political situations have reciprocal effects, as was demonstrated by the NZRFU 1970s' rugby tours to South Africa. As a result of the 1976 tour, New Zealand found itself at the centre of the international stage when the African nations boycotted the 1976 Montreal Olympics in protest at New Zealand's sporting contact with South Africa and New Zealand's presence at the Olympic games. Returning from a visit to the United Nations, the purpose of which was to attempt to quell the troubled international waters, Prime Minister Sir Keith Holyoake stated that 'we have to face the fact that in international affairs sport is already deeply involved in politics and it is no longer possible to keep the two completely separate' (cited by Thompson, 1980: 51). On numerous occasions, sport has clearly been used as a tool of foreign policy by both small and large nations, with more recent examples being the USA-led boycott of the 1980 Moscow Games and Soviet-led boycott of the 1984 Los Angeles Games.

The Politics Inherent in Organisation

Politics is also inherent in the process of organisation. As a young colony it was not long before a variety of national sport associations were formed; at least 14 were created between 1886 and the turn of the century (Stothart, *circa* 1980). Sports people form associations and organisations to further their chosen sport, and these associations acquire power, which almost invariably is distributed unequally (Eitzen and Sage, 1993). Sport has its own internal government and politics, rendering meaningless the suggestion that sport and politics should not mix.

In one sense politics is about the exercise of power, which can be evidenced in the influence, regulation and control of decision-making processes that occur within organisations. There are many ways of influencing such processes; Brager and Holloway (1987), for example, identify the following 'resources for influence':

- the control of resources, in particular money, or financial power;
- information as a basis for decision-making, including specialisation and length of service;
- networks or alliances with powerful others, sub-unit membership, inner/outer circles of influence; and,
- status or position in the decision-making hierarchy, access to decision makers, prestige and reputation.

The decision-making processes usually take place within a 'hierarchy of authority', and while such authority relations are intrinsic to bureaucratic structures, they also often bring conflict in their wake. This is evidenced in the internal conflicts and plays for power that occur within New Zealand sport organisations. Political nous is clearly required in order to be successful and to survive in the governance of sport.

Very often significant power and influence is also held in the hands of a few influential leaders in the management of New Zealand sport (notable in the last two decades were Ces Blazey, Sir Lance Cross and Sir Ron Scott). As Thompson (1980) points out, it does not matter how democratically structured an organisation is, eventually the real power in decision-making rests in the hands of a few. The 'old-boy-network' in sport management is alive and well; it has also, particularly in the past, been literally for 'boys'. On the basis of her recent study, Cameron, (1992) argues that even in the 1990s, sport management in New Zealand is still an overwhelmingly male enterprise, with very few women senior sports administrators, coaches or officials. In her study of 70 sports organisations, for example, she notes that only 21 per cent of paid executive officers, 20 per cent of volunteer administrators, and 11 per cent of elected national directors were women.

The Institutional Nature of Sport

Eitzen and Sage (1993) argue that a further source of the strong relationship between sport and politics is the institutional nature of sport, which, as with other institutions, tends towards conservatism. More often than not sport 'serves as a preserver and a legitimator of the existing order' (ibid.: 218) and its politicisation usually tends to lag behind that of other areas of culture (Hargreaves, 1990). Thompson (1980) argues that there is strong evidence to demonstrate that New Zealand sports people have appeared to be supportive of what they perceived as established beliefs, and have tended to be opposed to what they regarded as new, permissive or radical. Citing examples, he concludes that there are significant grounds for assuming that New Zealand's sporting administration is both political and conservative.

Thompson suggests that in practice New Zealanders have not objected to politics interfering in sport, provided it was the right kind of politics. In the 1960s, for example, the exclusion of Maori players from All Black teams touring South Africa was not considered to be a case of political interference, but to protest against their exclusion was. Sport leaders appeared to adopt an attitude that limited the definition of politics in sport to any attempt to change the status quo.

This tendency towards conservatism is also evidenced in the politics of gender in New

Zealand sport. As noted, sport is still overwhelmingly male and 'often appears as intrinsically and naturally male' (Clarke and Clarke, 1982). Up to 1991 for example, New Zealand women were still being nominated for the 'Sportsman of the Year' award. Commentators such as Cameron (1992) argue that women are marginalised in New Zealand sport, both in regard to participation and management, and by the 'prevalence of masculine ritualistic, symbolic and practical barriers'.

Changes are beginning to happen, particularly through the education and training efforts of organisations such as the Hillary Commission. Unquestionably, however, there is evidence to suggest that sport is some way from being at the forefront of change in New Zealand society. Cameron (1992: 181) argues, for example, that in sport,

> ... the inequalities and patterns of domination which underlie society are maintained, not questioned. Because of this tendency to conservatism, sport can be seen to fulfil a hegemonic role. It presents as 'natural' and unchallenged ideas and values which are in the interests of the dominant groups of society: those who are male, white, upper class (professionals, managers, owners of production) and are able-bodied.

Summary

Sport events can also arguably be seen as political occasions; certainly much wider social significance can be read into them than merely the 'spectacle' of athletic excellence. Furthermore, the fact that sport is popularly thought of as being essentially value-free and non-ideological in character, gives it considerable hegemonic power. Sport is a vital and pervasive force in most modern societies. As an institution it tends towards conservatism. In New Zealand and internationally sport has at times become a central political issue in this century's conflicts. Sport and politics are clearly intertwined and the issues involved are becoming ever more complex.

Government and Sport

Motivations for Involvement

As stated at the outset, it is not long since the prospect of government involvement was perceived by many as inappropriate interference by the state in the lives of New Zealanders. Coakley (1990: 303) notes however, that as societies have become more complex and the relationships within societies more interdependent, government involvement in sport as in all spheres of life has increased, and he suggests several motivations for this. He notes for example, that as governments have responsibilities for control and regulation, the need for the safeguarding of public order frequently motivates government involvement in sport. As discussed in Chapter 2, prior to the 1930s this was a main preoccupation of New Zealand governments with regard to recreation and sport, with its role orientated towards controlling those leisure activities which were considered undesirable and undisciplined (e.g. controlling liquor, gambling and prostitution) (Watson, 1993).

More typically, government, be it local or central, involves itself in the establishment of legislation and by-laws to ensure appropriate planning, allocation and use of resources, guarantee of access, and the protection of public assets and the rights of members of the community, whether users or non-users. Most New Zealanders are satisfied with this justification for government involvement, although the application of the principle frequently involves controversy.

Governments also become involved in sport in order to maintain and develop the physical abilities and fitness of citizens. This often stated motivation is clear from the content of parliamentary debates in New Zealand when recreation and sport related issues are on the agenda. In 1987 the Hillary Commission published a report entitled *The Cost of Doing Nothing* to demonstrate that the cost to the community of people being inactive and sedentary was significant. Against this the benefits of a healthy population are generally perceived as being numerous, from a reduction in expenditure on health care costs and increased productivity or output of citizens, to reductions in neurosis and anxiety and so forth. Interestingly, Wagner (1987) maintains there are flaws in political justifications of reductions in health care expenditure through sport participation, arguing that the two are often either unrelated or that increased participation in some sport may in fact lead to an increase in health-care costs.

Two further motivations for government intervention in sport are the quest for prestige for a community or for the nation itself, and the promotion of a sense of identity, belonging and unity among citizens (Coakley, 1990). These are evidenced in the political significance of the early All Black tours to the United Kingdom as has been noted, and also in events such as Auckland's 1950 Empire Games. According to Phillips (1990), the Auckland Games was a vehicle to express national identity. The Games demonstrated our ability to organise and be up-to-date, our friendly, neighbourly qualities (a quality emphasised again at the 1974 Christchurch Commonwealth Games) and portrayed New Zealand as a rural paradise, a beautiful country in which people enjoyed healthy, open-air living. The Games also provided an opportunity to tout our 'positive' race relations, further evidence of our 'God's own country' status with 'God's own people'. New Zealand was portrayed as a country with 'friendly natives', a united people and the best race relations in the world. Phillips (*ibid.*: 139) reports how the Prime Minister of the day, in a speech to competitors visiting the famous Marae of the Waikato Tribes at Ngaruawahia, spoke of the unity between Maori and Pakeha. The *Evening Post* reports him stating that,

> ... the Empire Games visitors would feel that the demonstration of unity between the two peoples of New Zealand was something that completed the spirit of unity seen at the games. At this time in world history it was fitting the visitors should be given a demonstration that two peoples could live together without any impediment of language or colour. (*Evening Post*, 13 February 1950. Cited by Phillips, 1990: 140).

Among the listeners were South African athletes, and Phillips notes the irony of this pride in the absence of impediments of colour, given the fact that it was only the previous year that Maori rugby players had been excluded from the All Black team selected to tour South Africa.

More recently, clear recognition of the value of sport in promoting the prestige of the nation, was reflected in the appointment by the Minister of Recreation and Sport in the fourth Labour Government, of a number of prominent sporting celebrities as sporting ambassadors. Another example is the government allocation of grants to the New Zealand Sports Foundation and the New Zealand Olympic and Commonwealth Games Association and their desire to produce winners. While not directly offering financial rewards to winners of Olympic or Commonwealth Games' medals, as governments of some other countries have done, the Government-supported Sports Foundation announced the Challenge Award Scheme in July 1991. Under this scheme, winners of designated World Championship events, or the equivalent, receive monetary rewards ranging from $25,000 for individuals, to $150,000 for certain team events. In the Award's information material the Foundation clearly links sporting success with the enhancement of national pride, unity, morale, and confidence in New Zealand, both economically and socially.

Coakley (1990) suggests that yet another motivation for government involvement in sport lies in the opportunity it provides to emphasise or align citizens' values with its own ideology. In this sense the power of sport to transmit dominant ideologies has already been highlighted, as was alluded to with respect to race relations. Phillips (1990) also notes that the 1950 Empire Games, for example, was an important vehicle for expressing New Zealand's Imperial connection. The Games reinforced New Zealand's bonds to the 'British' Empire.

Nevertheless, over the years the bonds and connections with the Empire and the 'old country' have weakened and New Zealand has had to come to terms with being a very small country in a large and competitive world. Arguably, sport in New Zealand has been accorded the virtues previously associated with the pioneering frontier life (Phillips, 1987), and it is through sport in particular that New Zealanders have come to understand that they can compete in the 'big wide world'. New Zealanders seem to take pride in the David versus Goliath type contests where success is against all odds, particularly when their athletes defeat athletes from large nations with budgets to match. New Zealanders are quick to make the medals-per-head-of-population calculations for reassurance. Links between success and hard work, and between building character and achieving excellence through competition, are frequently made in connection with participation in sport. Such attitudes are consistent with the capitalist values required in today's market driven society. Government promotes sport in the belief that participation will also positively affect productivity in other areas. Government also promotes participation in the belief that it will create better citizens and a better community. The government youth programmes in the 1960s (see Chapter 2), which aimed at reinstating traditional social values and controls, are clear examples of government involvement motivated by a desire to promote certain values and ideology. Sport will quickly lose governmental support if government ever perceives sport participation as being detrimental to the promotion of values consistent with good citizenship.

Sport is also used to increase the legitimacy of government (Coakley, 1990). This occurs even in political systems which profess to separate sport and government (Johnson, 1982, cited by Coakley, ibid.). Certainly government, be it local or central, likes to be associated with winners, and opportunities are readily taken to be seen at high-profile sports events. In a sports hungry society such as New Zealand, politicians can ill afford to appear disdainful of sport. As Johnson (1982) comments, if those in power were to lose the support of sport, their opposition would attempt to capture it for themselves. This was seen clearly with the third Labour Government who lost considerable electoral support when they forced the cancellation of the proposed tour by the South African Springboks. Adopting this as an election issue, the National Party included in its 1975 Manifesto a pledge that it would be supportive if the NZRFU were to invite the Springboks to tour. Subsequently National swept into power in a landslide victory, and most commentators recognised that their pledge was a key non-economic factor in the victory.

Interestingly, however, while politicians and governments are quick to use sport for their own ends when it suits them, sport has not always been able to capitalise on this link. Despite active representation, sport leaders are often unable to convince governments to alter legislation which will adversely effect sport, such as the changes to the accident compensation legislation, and the removal of sport's earthquake insurance exemptions.

Direct Government Influence

As highlighted, sport in New Zealand has been a proverbial political football. In line with their respective political philosophies, successive Labour Governments have sought to establish and implement direct influence via programmes and agencies and, up until the 1990 National Government, succeeding National Governments have sought to curtail or reduce commitment to those initiatives.

As discussed in Chapter 2, in the 1930s concerns for health, fitness and social integration, particularly for youth, overcame the traditional resistance towards state intervention in sport and recreation and the Labour Government passed the 1937 Physical Welfare and Recreation Act creating a Physical Welfare Branch in the Department of Internal Affairs. The change of government in 1949 caused the initiative to be wound down, and during the 1950s and 1960s public sector involvement in sport remained limited (see Chapter 2 for discussion of this period).

More direct government involvement in sport became one of the issues in the 1972 election when the Labour Party advocated the establishment of a Ministry of Recreation and Sport. The National Party argued that this represented government interference in sport and announced support for the newly formed non-government Confederation of Sport (Stothart, 1980). As discussed in Chapter 2, after winning the election the Labour Government introduced the 1973 Recreation and Sport Act, which established a Ministry of Recreation and Sport and a statutory body called the New Zealand Council for Recreation and Sport. Several high-profile programmes and initiatives resulted and three funding schemes were launched: one for national sport and recreation organisations; one for sport and recreation organisations at the local level; and a third for regional facilities.

Stothart (1980) notes that when the government changed in 1975, many associated with these new programmes were uncertain as to whether the new National Government would retain the initiatives, given its pre-election stance of non-government interference in sport. The Ministry and the Council were in fact retained, albeit with reduced funding, although the regional funding scheme was abandoned and for example, the high-profile initiative, the 'Come Alive' programme, was discontinued as it was perceived by many National Party politicians as a Labour Party promotion (Stothart, 1980). By the 1978 election, however, recreation and sport policies were included in the manifestos of both main political parties and it was significant that 'community development' was the rationale adopted for government involvement (Garrett, 1980). Funding, however, continued to decline (in real terms) under three successive National Governments and it was not until Labour was returned to power in 1984 that funding ever approached the levels first established in 1973. Interestingly, leaders in the Arts world, who were perhaps more accustomed to receiving government patronage, were more effective than sports leaders in countering prospects of reduced funding (Stothart, 1980: 49).

While the 1973 Ministry and Council initiatives were considerably more successful than those in 1937, it became clear that some confusion between the roles of the Ministry and the Council, and the resulting duplication of activities, was beginning to cause concern. Furthermore, the relationship between recreation programming and sport programming was a perennial difficulty. Many sports people were critical of the more nebulous recreation activities which they believed were receiving too much attention, to the detriment of sport, while recreationists, who were in influential positions at this time, were wary of an undue focus on élite top level sport. (Concern about this and funding issues led to the establishment of the New Zealand Sports Assembly in 1985 in order to provide a united voice for sport and to lobby for increased funding.)

With a change in government in 1984 and in the context of these various concerns, the Labour government instigated a major review of recreation sport (see Community Services Institute, 1985; Sports Development Inquiry, 1985).What resulted, as discussed in Chapter 2, was the 1987 Recreation and Sport Act which replaced the Ministry and the Council with a single body, the Hillary Commission for Recreation and Sport. Funding was increased, and, perhaps most significantly, adopting the recommendation of the *Sport on the Move* report (1985), Lotto was introduced with the intent of funding recreation and sport, together with other activities and programmes. The Hillary Commission has expanded considerably since its establishment, developing a number of new initiatives such as KiwiSport as well as programmes for women, Maori, older adults, and people with disabilities. The Commission's level of expenditure on administration, however, and the public availability of funding was criticised by some who saw its growth as representing little more than an expanding bureaucracy.

In 1990 the National Party was returned to government and there was some uncertainty as to how it would respond to Labour's initiatives, with rumours abounding of programmes being dropped. The new Minister of Recreation and Sport, Mr John Banks, expressed concern about expanding bureaucracies, and appeared to reflect sport's institutional conservative character, stating that he was not interested in sexism or apartheid or selective morality, but treated New Zealanders as New Zealanders, regardless of their ethnic or cultural background (Romanos, 1991).

The most significant result from the change in government, however, was the passing into law of the 1992 Sport Fitness and Leisure Act. This altered the priorities of the Hillary Commission, and renamed it the Hillary Commission for Sport, Fitness and Leisure. Sport was accorded a high priority and was no longer to be a 'bed fellow' of the vast array of cultural and non-physical recreational groups. This change was criticised, particularly by recreationists, who argued that it reflected a return to the more narrow definitions of the 1937 Act.

Sport as an activity has the potential to have greater political capital than activities more broadly conceived as recreation, and government intervention will always benefit some interest groups more than others. Those who benefit most from policy are more likely to be those most able to influence the policy makers. Coakley (1990) suggests that while government policy does not always reflect the interests of the powerful and wealthy, it does reflect the political power struggles between different groups in society. Historically when Governments do intervene, they are generally more interested in fitness over fun, discipline and physical skills over expression and self-development, élite sport over mass participation, and records and victories rather than participation and relationships (Coakley, ibid.). At times, the same tendencies have been evident in New Zealand and the 2000 Sydney Olympic Games are undoubtedly likely to increase the pressure for the targeting of greater resources towards the development of élite level sport.

The 1992 Act also allowed the National Government to make changes in the composition of the Hillary Commission and facilitated the appointment of an entirely new set of commissioners, effectively individuals whose political and sporting philosophies were compatible with those of the government. However, unlike previous National Governments, which had reduced funding, the Minister of Sport, Fitness and Leisure was responsible for ensuring an increase in funds to the Hillary Commission and a guaranteed future funding policy of 20 per cent of the Lottery Commission's profits. Funding for the Hillary Commission has steadily increased from $7.3 million in 1987, to some $25.9 million in 1992. The primary source of funding has changed however, with government reducing its own financial commitment (from 79 per cent of total funds in 1987 to only 4 per cent in 1992) and the New Zealand Lotteries Board increasingly providing the bulk of the Commission's funding (see Figure 3.1).

Figure 3.1: Hillary Commission Funding, 1987-1993

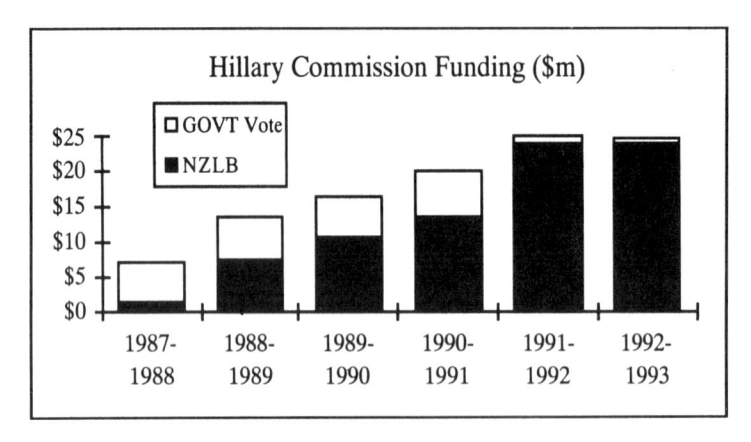

(Source: Hillary Commission)

Indirect Government Influence

Government legislation in other areas can also have a significant and sometimes direct impact on sport. A case in point was the series of developments arising out of government legislation on broadcasting in the late 1980s and early 1990s. These developments threatened the estimated $17 million sponsorship of sport by liquor industries, as sponsorship of sporting and other cultural or artistic events became a less viable and attractive means of product marketing and promotion. In response to these concerns, the New Zealand Sports Assembly facilitated an agreement between interested parties to protect this source of sponsorship income. The proposed ban on tobacco advertising by the fourth Labour Government similarly had significant implications for several sports codes and resulted in considerable lobbying by high-profile sportsmen and women.

The Changing Nature of the Role of the State as a Provider in Sport

Henry's (1990) analysis of the state's involvement in sport in post-war Britain indicates that the same debate between conservative and more socialist-leaning politicians has occurred on both sides of the world, with at times a remarkable coincidence in timing. Henry cites various stages to summarise the changing nature of the role of the state as provider in sport, namely traditional pluralism, welfare reformism, the managerialist critique, and the New Right. This analysis has some relevance to the New Zealand setting.

Until the immediate post-war years the state's role was typified by a 'traditional pluralism' in which the market and voluntary sectors were seen as the primary providers of sporting opportunity. The state involved itself only to the extent of supplementing the provision of those sectors when externalities were deemed to accrue or where other types of market failure resulted in inefficient distribution (see Chapter 4). Thus, sport was regarded by the state as the individual's responsibility, with government provision largely restricted to aspects such as national and local parks, playgrounds, selected sport facilities, and community halls (see Chapter 2).

The second stage in the development of state involvement in sport can be characterised by 'welfare reformism' with its emphasis on the proactive role of the public sector in meeting the needs of groups who were disadvantaged in the commercial and voluntary sectors. Government subsidy and funding were provided not merely because of some externalities or market failure, but because recreation and sporting opportunities were deemed worthy of support in their own right. While this welfare-reformist thinking viewed sport and recreation as representing a right of citizenship, it did not, however, 'necessarily supersede the traditional-pluralist rationale with its emphasis on externalities'; rather it augmented it (Henry, 1990: 44).

Hence recreation and sport provision were supported as a 'need' and a 'right', as well as a vehicle for other social benefits. This stage involved a developing shift from viewing recreation and sport as an antidote to social problems, to viewing them as a social good in their own right, worthy of efforts to remove constraints to provision and ensuring access by all groups. In other words, it involved a shift from viewing 'recreation and sport as welfare' to 'recreational and sporting welfare' (Coalter, 1987). The developments of the 1970s discussed earlier, characterise this stage.

Arguably, economic recession, concerns about state welfare spending, questions about the value of directing funds to mass participation programmes with their egalitarian goals, and doubts about the confusing bureaucracy of the Ministry and the Council for Recreation and Sport led during the mid to late 1980s to the third phase of the 'managerialist critique'. With a market-orientated ethos driving the fourth Labour Government, a new corporatised approach resulted in the establishment of the Hillary Commission for Recreation and Sport – a quango removed from direct government control – which was headed by a senior executive from industry as the CEO, rather than a recreation professional as had been the case in the past. The incoming National Government in 1990, with an even more purist market-orientated ethos, continued the development set in train by the previous Labour administration. The goal of the New Right was to reduce state spending and state machinery and this was regarded as being morally desirable rather than merely a regrettable, temporary expedient (see Figure 3.1). Countering this ethos with respect to state involvement in sport, however, was the perceived virtue of national success in the sporting arena, providing as it did national prestige and international profile with supposedly all sorts of potential commercial spin-offs. Furthermore, any tendency for government to withdraw from involvement in sport was countered by the perceived value of sport in addressing social ills. This perception is clearly reflected in the Minister of Sport's (1990-1993) view that a 'kid in sport is a kid out of court'.

Nevertheless a more commercial orientation now exists and policy is more than ever directed towards corporatist styles of sport management. Whereas facilitation might have been the buzz word of the late 1970s and early 1980s, business values, such as strategic planning, profitability and accountability, dominate the 1990s. This trend is well established and is discussed in greater depth in Chapter 2.

Politics in Sport Organisations

As noted earlier, politics is inherent in the process of organisation. Sport organisations provide frequent media copy as various interest-groups within a sport or between sports codes vie for power or influence over decision making. As discussed, the use of various key resources for influence (Brager and Holloway, 1987) are critical in this process.

Sport politics is concerned with the use of elements of power inside hierarchical structures, as the majority of sports organisations have established hierarchies of authority with a National Executive or Management Committee as the apex of the pyramid (see Figure 3.2).

Figure 3.2: A hierarchy of authority typical to sport organisations

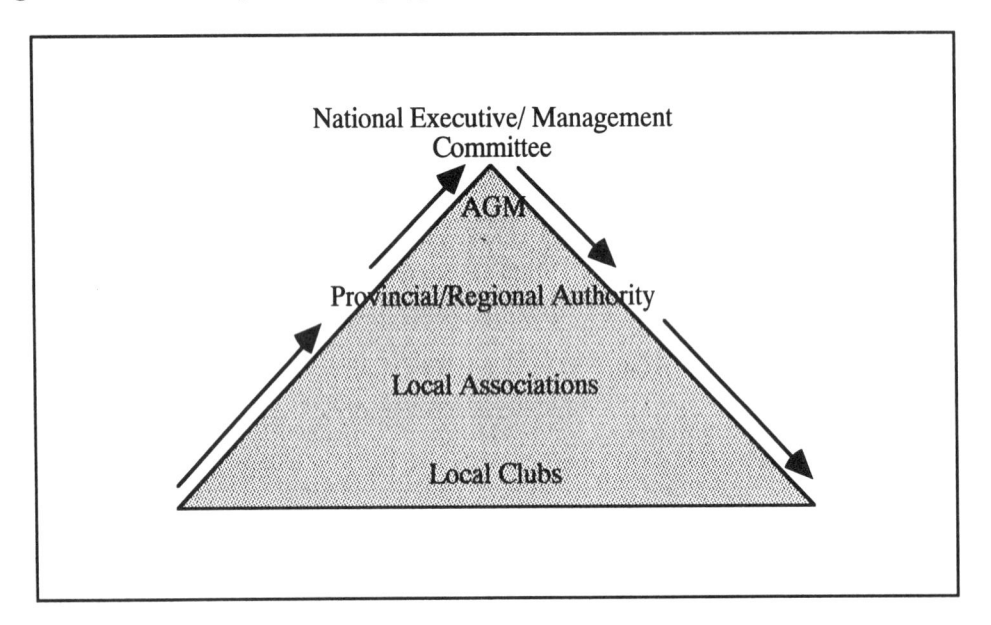

Most sports, however, begin at the bottom of the pyramid when a group of enthusiasts at the local level join to share in an enjoyable activity. As groups develop from the grassroots, informal structure, decision making moves up the hierarchy. The national body which inevitably develops, adopts specific goals/objectives, roles, responsibilities, functions and powers which are usually detailed within constitutions and rules and are usually consistent with those at the regional and club level. Paradoxically, however, the organisation of structures simultaneously constrains and enables individuals to reach certain objectives (Pitter, 1990).

Pitter (ibid.) notes that hierarchy is associated with a 'differential distribution of organisational power' and he regards control as the capacity some people have to be able to influence circumstances or actions of others. He suggests that while one may possess power without having control, one cannot have control without possessing power (ibid.: 310-311). Pitter defines and describes several key resources for power and control, namely, information, access to funds, status in hierarchy, networks, time and commitment. It is the informed use and deliberate interplay of these resources for influence by elected volunteer members of a national executive or management committee and by the paid sport manager which will control and decide the decision-making processes.

Funding issues, for example, often engender change, as is evident where sponsorship requirements have impacted on rules and playing conditions of some sport (e.g. one-day cricket), sometimes causing internal conflict amongst administrators and supporters. Also with the emphasis on finance for survival, individuals with perceived financial status and prestige are frequently recruited to decision-making levels within sport structures. This is evidenced in the membership of the Board of Governors of the New Zealand Sports Foundation, which comprises individuals with strong links to major corporations. Status also often influences the political process, as witnessed by the appointment in 1993, in highly controversial circumstances, of a triple gold Olympic medallist national coach to a coaching position.

The control of information and the building of networks by committee members are less obvious to identify and record than financial influence or status. The existing corps of volunteer administrators who served on executive or management committees, became adept at both using the knowledge of structures and rules, and building networks of support amongst affiliates to ensure a viable working organisation. The modern, paid executive staff, with more managerial responsibilities than before, must also attend to the control of information and the building of networks, although care has to be taken to link only into those which are appropriate. When various factions within organisations compete for leadership, a delicate situation exists for sports managers; their loyalty and support lies with the elected committees, as they are the paid servants of the policy makers.

The Influence of the Hillary Commission

As stated earlier, one of the key fundamental forces in sport in New Zealand is the Hillary Commission. In the same manner that the 1992 Act gave government a means of influence in sport in New Zealand, it also ensured that the Hillary Commission itself was an agency with a significant and powerful political presence through its funding, research and advisory status.

For example, the Commission has mandated control of direct and indirect government provided funds, the size of which has increased in a climate in which the funding from other sources has been considerably reduced. Therefore decisions about the allocation of funds and the mechanisms to ensure proper use and accountability provided a powerful means for influencing and regulating the activities of sports organisations. As Brager and Holloway (1987) note, the control of funding is one of the key resources for influence. Sporting organisations can ill afford to alienate themselves from the Commission, and funding control enables the Commission to set new directions, such as the creation of new bodies (for example the New Zealand Sport Sciences Technology Board).

The Commission has also exerted influence through information initiatives via funded research projects such as the *Life in New Zealand Survey* (1990) and the *Business of Sport and Leisure Report* (Jensen, Sullivan, Wilson, Berkeley and Russell, 1993). Furthermore, information provided by sports organisations who apply for funding assistance comprises the basis for future funding allocation decisions and also, in turn, provides the Commission with a basis for seeking additional funding and support for sport, fitness and leisure from government, local bodies, sponsors and the public.

Commissioners and staff also build powerful formal and informal networks on a continuing basis with Ministers of the Crown, government officials, leading sport administrators, national sport organisations, regional sport structures and others. This networking expands the influence of the Commission and enables it to take an informed and influential position in many sport related issues. In turn, the above factors increase the status and prestige of the Commission and ensure that it has a clear position at the top of the hierarchy of authority in

New Zealand sport. As such, government has created a centralised, powerful and influential organisation servicing New Zealand sport, the prospect of which would have generated considerable debate only two or three decades ago. The fact that it is now a generally accepted and expected presence on the New Zealand sporting landscape, demonstrates the changing expectations of New Zealand sport organisations with regard to government's role within sport, and perhaps a changing ideology regarding the mix between politics and sport.

Conclusion

The basic premises of this chapter are that there are several characteristics inherent in sport which serve to guarantee a strong relationship between sport and politics, that as an institution sport tends towards conservatism, and that it frequently can be seen to fulfil a hegemonic role in society. Sport is pervasive in modern society and is part of the life experience of many New Zealanders, whether as participants, organisers, officials, or spectators. Thus sport is connected to the processes that exist in everyday life. An analysis of international and national sport clearly confirms Coakley's (1990) contention that sport and politics are two parts of our social lives that cannot easily be separated.

Historically, despite the rhetoric, government involvement in sport has been shown to be significant and has been motivated by different reasons. As our society becomes increasingly complex and the relationships within society more interdependent, governmental influence is likely to continue to increase. The influence and power of the Hillary Commission has been noted, and as 'outside' funding for sports organisations becomes increasingly difficult to obtain, the public funds controlled by the Commission ensure it will remain at the top of the hierarchy of authority in New Zealand sport.

How one attempts to understand the relationship between politics and sport in society is dependent on the theoretical framework one adopts, as alluded to in Chapter 1. Given the constraints of space, it has not been the intention here to revisit this debate. The purpose of this chapter has been to introduce readers to the interaction between sport and politics. The approach has been to recognise that sport is a product of historical, social and economic forces. Individuals and groups within society use power and resources to define and culturally construct sport into something that fits their interests and concerns. As a result, as Coakley (1990) states, sport is inevitably involved in ever-continuing processes of conflict, negotiation, compromise, coercion and subtle persuasion between various groups in society.

Review Questions

1. What are some of the characteristics inherent in sport which serve to guarantee a strong relationship between sport and politics?
2. List, providing New Zealand examples, some of the motivations government has for involvement in sport.
3. What are specific examples of the New Zealand government passing legislation directly related to sport?
4. How would you describe the changing nature of the role of the state as a provider in sport over the last three decades?
5. What are the key 'resources for influence' that can be identified as being used to control or manage the decision-making process?

6. What is meant by the phrase 'hierarchy of authority', and how does that apply to New Zealand sport?
7. What are some of the reasons which make the Hillary Commission such an important influence in New Zealand sport?

References

Baker W.J. (1982), *Sport in the Western World,* Totowa, N.J.: Rowman and Littlefield Co.
Brager, G. and Holloway, S. (1987), *Changing Human Service Organisations – Politics and Practice*, New York: The Free Press, Collier Macmillan Publishers.
Cameron, J. (1992), 'Gender in New Zealand Sport, A Survey of Sport and its National Administration', Unpublished Paper.
Cameron, J. (1993), 'The Sociology of Sport', in Perkins, H. and Cushman, G. (eds), *Leisure, Recreation and Tourism*, New Zealand: Longman Paul.
Clarke A. and Clarke J. (1982), 'Highlights and Action Replays – Ideology, Sport and the Media', in Hargreaves, J. (ed.) *Sport, Culture and Ideology*, Boston and London: Routledge and Kegan Paul
Coakley, J. (1990), *Sport in Society: Issues and Controversies*, St Louis: Times Mirror/ Mosby.
Coalter, F. (1987), *Rational for Public Sector Investment in Leisure*, London: The Sports Council and Economic and Social Research Council.
Community Services Institute (1985), *Recreation and Government in New Zealand, Report to the Minister of Recreation and Sport*, Wellington: Government Print.
Eitzen, D. and Sage, G. (1993), *Sociology of North American Sport*, USA: Wm. C. Brown Communications Inc.
Garrett, T. (1980), 'Government – Its Role in Recreation', in Shallcrass, J., Larkin, B. and Stothart, B. (eds), *Recreation Reconsidered Into the Eighties* (pp.41-45), Auckland Regional Authority and New Zealand Council for Recreation and Sport.
Hargreaves, J. (ed.) (1985), *Sport, Culture and Ideology*, London: Routledge and Kegan Paul.
Hargreaves, J. (1990), 'Gender of the Sports Agenda', *International Review for the Sociology of Sport,* vol. 25, no. 4, pp. 287-305.
Henry, I. (1990), 'Sport and the State: The Development of Sports Policy in Post-war Britain', in Kew, F. (ed.), *Social Scientific Perspectives on Sport* (pp. 42-49). British Association of Sport Sciences, National Coaching Foundation.
Hillary Commission (1987), *The Cost of Doing Nothing*, Wellington: Hillary Commission.
Jensen, B., Sullivan, C., Wilson, N., Berkeley, M. and Russell, D. (1993), *The Business of Sport and Leisure: The Economic Importance of Sport and Leisure in New Zealand*, Wellington: Hillary Commission.
Johnson, A. (1982), 'Government, Opposition and Sport: the Role of Domestic Sports Policy in Generating Political Support', *Journal of Sport and Social Issues*, vol. 6, no.2, pp. 22-34.
Life in New Zealand Survey (1990), Wellington: Hillary Commission.
McKay, J. (1991), *No Pain, No Gain? Sport in Australian Culture*, Australia: Prentice Hall.
New Zealand Parliamentary Debates, (1973), vol. 382, 14 March.
Phillips, J. (1987), *A Man's Country? The Image of the Pakeha Male: A History*, Auckland: Penguin.

Phillips, J. (1990), 'Sons and Daughters of the Empire – The meaning of the 1950 Empire Games', in *Conference Proceedings, Sport, Commonwealth and International Conference on Physical Education, Sport, Health, Dance, Recreation and Leisure*, vol. 2, NZAHPER.

Pitter, R. (1990), 'Power and Control in an Amateur Sport Organisation', *International Review for the Sociology of Sport*, vol. 25, no. 4, pp. 309-320.

Romanos, J. (1991), Sport's Funding Mess', *Listener and TV Times*, April 15, pp.43-45.

Sports Development Inquiry (1985), *Sport on the Move, Report to the Minister of Recreation and Sport*, Wellington: Government Print.

Stothart, R. (*circa* 1980), 'Sport in New Zealand: A Critical View', Unpublished Paper.

Stothart, R. (1980), 'The New Deal in Recreation and Sport', in Shallcrass, J., Larkin, B. and Stothart, B. (eds), *Recreation Reconsidered Into the Eighties* (pp.47-50), Auckland Regional Authority and New Zealand Council for Recreation and Sport.

Thompson, R. (1980), 'Sport and Politics', in Shallcrass, J., Larkin, R. and Stothart, R. (eds), *Recreation Reconsidered into the Eighties* (p.51-54), Auckland Regional Authority and New Zealand Council for Recreation and Sport.

Wagner, G.G. (1987), 'Sport as a Means for Reducing the Cost of Illness – Some Theoretical, Statistical and Empirical Remarks', *International Review for the Sociology of Sport*, vol.22, no. 3, pp. 217-227.

Watson, J. (1993), 'The History of Leisure , Recreation and Tourism in New Zealand', in Perkins, C. and Cushman, G. (eds), *Leisure, Recreation and Tourism*, Auckland, New Zealand: Longman Paul.

Suggested Reading

Brager, G. and Holloway, S. (1987), *Changing Human Service Organisations – Politics and Practice*, New York: The Free Press, Collier Macmillan Publishers.

Cameron, J. (1993), 'The Sociology of Sport', in Perkins, H. and Cushman, G. (eds), *Leisure, Recreation and Tourism*, New Zealand: Longman Paul.

Coakley, J. (1990), *Sport in Society: Issues and Controversies*, St Louis: Times Mirror/ Mosby.

The Economics of Sport

Bob Stephens

In this chapter you will become familiar with the following terms:

allocation of scarce resources

demand, supply and market places

efficiency

market failure

non-market valuation techniques

work-leisure choices

clubs

economic impact

elasticity of demand

income

opportunity costs

market failure, public goods, externalities and merit goods

Introduction

Using a broader definition of sport than that outlined in the introductory chapter, the next chapter demonstrates that sport and sport-related industries make a small but significant contribution to the overall size of the New Zealand economy. To many people this would represent the contribution that economics can make to sport management. But economics is not restricted to an analysis of the aggregate number of jobs created through the sporting sector, nor is it simply the analysis of total expenditure on sports equipment and facilities, as these are summed from the individual's demand for sport to give the economic impact.

Economists are also interested in the individual and household decision on how much time to devote to sport as opposed to work or other leisure activities, and how much limited income received from work effort will be allocated to sport rather than spent on consumer durables or food and clothing. Decisions by local authorities and firms to build sports facilities are made on economic and financial criteria, with the use of those resources for sport precluding alternative uses. The choice of sport, or the way in which leisure time is used, is largely determined by the social context, physical characteristics and psychological development of the individual. The essence of microeconomics is the analysis of these choice decisions and the variables which influence them, irrespective of whether a dollar label is attached to them.

In this chapter sport is taken to be a sub-set of recreation, which can be considered to represent a purposeful use of leisure time to provide a leisure experience. Any definition of sport runs into boundary problems with recreation, but in this chapter sport is restricted to active participation in organised games. A casual game of squash would be included, whilst a hike would be classified as recreation. Jogging, recreational skiing and aerobics are harder to categorise, but the microeconomic analysis is similar irrespective of the label. Professional sport is more difficult because its commercial nature makes it more akin to productive activity than leisure.

The chapter commences with an economist's description of sport and a justification for a separate economic analysis of sport. It then proceeds to provide an analysis of the separate concepts, starting with discussion on work-leisure choices, the role of markets and the factors influencing supply and demand for sport, the role of governments and non-profit organisations such as clubs. The chapter finishes with an outline of specific techniques used to determine the benefits which accrue from participation in sport.

Economic Description of Sport

The essence of sport is competition between individuals and/or teams. This seems similar to the market game, but in the market the objective is to dominate and monopolise the industry, whereas in sport maintaining the opposition is essential. El-Hodiri and Quirk (1971) state that 'as the probability of either team winning approaches one, gate receipts fall substantially, consequently, every team has an economic motive for not becoming too superior in playing talent compared to other teams in the league'. In organised sport, individuals and teams will normally be members of a club, and the various clubs will be administered by an umbrella organisation, with a monopoly over its jurisdiction, such as the Wellington Rugby Union or the New Zealand Amateur Athletic Association. Individuals will normally pay a membership fee to the club (including registration with the national association), plus a smaller charge each time they participate. In most clubs the organisation and administration will be undertaken on a voluntary basis, with fees and charges being based on estimates of costs.

All sport requires a venue, whether it be a custom-built facility such as Mt Smart Stadium or Titirangi Golf Course, or one adaptable for a variety of sport and recreational uses such as an indoor gymnasium which can be used for netball, basketball, badminton, indoor soccer and table tennis as well as gymnastics and aerobics. Alternatively, it might be a field which can be used for picnics and kite flying as well as cricket, athletics or soccer. Sport can be provided at a variety of levels and may be amateur or professional, although as the rewards for success in the modern Olympics or All Blacks indicate, this distinction is rather blurred. There is financial pressure to attract spectators through the gate, especially at the upper grades and professional levels, as well as funding from TV and radio broadcasts, and sponsorship. At all levels there is keen competition between clubs for members and victories, and between sports for both sponsorship and members, coupled with competition between sport and other recreational uses of leisure time.

Sport can also be analysed in terms of individual and household decision making as to the use of leisure time (between informal recreation and organised sport, between different types of sport, and between clubs within a sport), the provision of facilities (gyms and sport stadiums), and the purchase of equipment (for example rugby boots and golf clubs). This decision-making analysis requires an allocation of a limited time budget, while the provision of facilities requires a capital expenditure analysis, and the purchase of equipment requires a derived-demand analysis based on the allocation of income.

Work Leisure Choices

For most participants sport represents a purposeful use of discretionary leisure time (i.e. the amount of non-work time not required for household chores and activities). Participation in sport, also requires some expenditure, which comes from discretionary income, that is the income available after necessary household items such as food, clothing and utilities have been purchased.

Economists have long recognised that there is a trade-off between work, undertaken primarily because it provides income and thus enables consumption, and leisure, which requires both time and money for full utilisation (Becker, 1965). Higher after-tax wage rates and economic growth have offsetting effects on the amount of leisure time. They increase the effective price of leisure, since more income is foregone by increasing leisure time (substitution effect in technical jargon). For example, a person earning $25/hour who takes time off for a sports tournament, loses greater potential income than the person earning only $10/hour. However, the increase in wage rate also allows for more leisure without foregoing income (the income effect). In other words the $25/hour earner is more able to afford to take the time off and forego income than the $10/hour earner. Only empirical studies can determine which effect is stronger. The unemployment benefit, by contrast, reduces the price of leisure and provides an income independent of work effort. The extent to which this reduces work effort depends on the level of benefit compared to after-tax earnings (the replacement ratio).

The time commitment required for professional sport makes it difficult for athletes to earn adequate income from non-sport related employment, thus requiring compensation from the sport itself. Because professional sport life is short and normally precludes education and development of skills within another occupation, rewards have to be structured to compensate for this loss. Those receiving the highest rewards (e.g. Carl Lewis, Steffi Graf) are those in greatest demand.

Long-term trends indicate reductions in the average hours of work per week and increases in length of annual holidays, although this does not necessarily indicate a new leisure-age with an increase in time available for sport. Offsetting this trend has been an increase in the female labour force participation rate (best regarded as a shift from household and child-minding duties to paid employment), increased commuting time, weekend shopping, and higher work loads for those still in employment. The increasing number of unemployed, especially youth, have time for sport but have little income and few opportunities.

The distribution of leisure time has a significant impact on the structure of demand for different forms of sport and their inter-relationships with other recreational interests. An extra hour of leisure time after work, for example, may be useful for sports training or for providing an alternative time for organised games, thereby relieving congestion on the use of facilities. In the absence of organised activity, however, the extra hour will probably only result in passive recreation at home. Similarly, an extra week's holiday is more likely to be utilised for extra recreation and travel rather than sport. Increased time spent in education by the young has the potential for increasing sports participation. At the other end of life, earlier retirement will have a smaller impact, except possibly for activities such as bowls and recreational golf.

The Market and Sport

Economics is concerned with the efficient use of resources, with efficiency defined as the allocation of resources which maximises social benefits over social costs. Economists argue that a perfectly functioning market will automatically achieve this, although market failure is also recognised, providing a rationale for the involvement of government to improve upon the market outcome.

Market prices are set by the interaction of supply and demand, with price rationing consumption of each product to those with the highest valued demands, with only the most cost-efficient firms finding it profitable to supply. Changes in the factors influencing supply and demand lead to a new price and quantity of the product bought and sold (Horsman and St John, 1990). For example, a sudden increase in the demand for squash (following Susan Devoy's successes) would permit squash court managers to raise the price to eliminate excess demand, with the increase in profitability of squash leading to extra investment in squash facilities, returning the price to its original level. Changes also occur in the demand for squash equipment (known as derived demand). Product supply should be in private hands to permit the profit incentive, with this profit motive allowing rapid adjustment to changes in economic circumstances.

Demand

Traditional economic analysis is useful for choice decisions concerning whether to buy a squash racquet or running shoes, or to invest in a gymnasium or hotel chain. Even then, as the factors influencing demand demonstrate, the analysis requires adaptation to deal with the complexity within the sports industry. Individual demand has to be totalled to give market demand, where the size of the population and its age and income distribution are important influences.

Relative Prices

Economists argue that when the price of a good rises relative to other prices, less of that good will be purchased. The extent to which demand is reduced when price rises is given the technical name of elasticity of demand. For a sport manager, the issue is whether a rise in entrance fee to a sports arena increases total revenue (inelastic demand – a relatively small reduction in quantity resulting from the price rise) or reduces total revenue (elastic demand – a relatively large quantity change from the price change). There are several potential dilemmas here for sport managers; whilst raising the price for watching the Silver Ferns could increase revenue, it could also lead to the odium of empty seats. A price rise may alienate some customers, resulting in a switch in sport, whilst others may no longer be able to afford it. Non-price rationing, such as first-come-first-served or waiting lists, may be the preferred strategy.

Gratton and Taylor (1985) argue that price affects quantity of sport demanded in two ways. First, there is the participation decision. This is based on the average price or cost of participation, and takes into account all aspects of costs, such as equipment, entrance charges, membership fees, travel and time costs. Second, there is the frequency of participation, which is more related to the additional, or marginal, cost of each participation (entrance costs and travel/time costs). Higher average prices will reduce demand for a particular sport, especially if there is an acceptable substitute. Once the average price has been paid, variations in the marginal price will have little impact upon current demand, certainly where there is a given schedule of fixtures. Equally, changes in the price of items such as of squash racquets, derived from demand for squash, for example, are likely to have little impact on immediate participation, once a person is committed to a sport, but it may influence replacement, and hence future participation decisions.

Income

For most products, increases in income lead to greater demand. As sport participation is influenced by discretionary income, allowance should be made for family size and stage of the life cycle. Teenagers, for example, may have low pre-tax income, but substantial discretionary income, whilst those with young families may have little discretionary income (and time availability). With sports such as yachting and skiing, expenditure and participation probably grow faster than income (income elasticity of demand greater than one), but with many sports, especially popular sports such as rugby and netball, changes in income will have little effect on participation. There is some evidence from surveys of beneficiaries, however, that the 1991 benefit cuts substantially reduced participation by children of beneficiaries in many sports (Cody and Robinson, 1992).

Consumer Preferences

Although preferences are a major determinant of both participation in sport and between sports, economic theory has little to say about preference formation except to assume that individuals are rational in their choice decisions. It is recognised that advertising and media exposure can influence participation decisions, but participation is more a function of physical attributes, socio-economic background, cultural heritage, intra-family decision making, age and sex, than any economic variable. Thus active participation in sport tends to be male dominated, declining with age (see Chapter 2), with emphasis on sports such as rugby in New Zealand and soccer in Europe.

As well as work/leisure choices, Becker's (1965) household production model suggests that sport can be seen as an investment in health status – 'to feel better' and 'to reduce stress' – with the increase in health capital resulting in greater productivity. Professional sport provides a financial return on time invested in training, whereas amateur levels give only a psychic and stimulatory effect (Scitovsky, 1976), in addition to enhanced health status. Scitovsky argues that sport is skilled consumption, and that to obtain the benefits from sport, one needs considerable training in order to develop a 'taste' for sport. Gratton and Taylor (1985) use this to argue that the government has a role in educating people in sport, as this positive activity will reduce the socially unacceptable substitutes of vandalism and delinquency (see Chapter 3 for further discussion on this and other government motivation for involvement in sport).

Supply

The supply of sport and sports facilities comes from three sets of providers: the commercial or profit sector; the public sector, especially local and regional councils; and the voluntary or non-profit sector based upon sports clubs. Each sector has different objectives, and with different cost structures there is scope for specialisation, although there is significant inter-dependence between the sectors (see Chapter 5 for a discussion of the size of these three sectors).

The Commercial Sector

- Provision of sport facilities (and manufacture of sports equipment), where the return on investment is paramount. There is often direct competition in the provision of facilities with the public and voluntary sectors. Location decisions are important; the least-cost sports complex may be a large multi-purpose facility on the city outskirts, but the increase in travel costs will reduce demand. Smaller and specific facilities may raise construction costs, but lower travel costs. Competitive pricing is essential, with decisions required on a number of fronts, such as peak-pricing to spread demand, price discrimination to encourage some users and to switch demand between facilities, and the mix between membership fee and usage charge.

- Sponsorship of sport (events, teams, individuals) to promote products, such as Smoke-free Netball or the Chelsea Development Athletic Squad. Sponsorship is best seen as a form of marketing of a product by an indirect means, and thus has similarities with the economics of advertising (Hay and Morris, 1991). Sponsorship is also becoming an increasingly important form of revenue for many sports, allowing lower membership fees or entrance fees. Sponsorship is a function of the media coverage a sport is able to achieve and the level of club/sport support (Gratton and Taylor, 1985).

- Provision of sport facilities for employees as a fringe benefit. There is relatively little provision of such facilities in New Zealand, although both the USA and Japan have recognised their importance in developing company identification, morale and productivity.

The Public Sector

Local authorities are a major supplier of sport facilities such as tennis courts and soccer grounds. Local authority objectives vary, but incorporate the minimisation of rate demands against the need for provision of general recreational and sports space. The facilities are usually multi-purpose, providing general recreation as well as sport, with clubs paying for the hire of these grounds to obtain exclusive use of the facilities. A hire charge is justified on the grounds that it precludes other potential users, and to cover the costs of preparing the ground for that sport. A variety of pricing mechanisms are feasible, and, as Crompton (1984) indicates, the first issue is to determine what proportion of the costs incurred in delivering a service should be recovered from direct pricing (marginal cost, average cost or full cost recovery). The second issue relates to determining the acceptability of the charge, and the third involves varying the price for specific user groups for equity reasons.

Central government involvement relates to the encouragement of sport and recreation, through subsidisation, and to the benefits of prestige accruing from success of sports teams (see Chapter 3). Caves (1981) argued that a successful exporting policy requires the importing country to have an understanding of the culture of the exporter, and one may argue that visits by, or success of, national sports teams helps achieve this. The clean/green image is also assisted by outdoor sport success. Guidelines and regulations are essential to ensure that parks are set aside in urban areas to permit recreation and sport, although these are under the control of local authorities. Forecasting future demand is also necessary to ensure an adequate supply of land and facilities for sport for years to come (Walsh, 1986).

Economic theory provides sound reasons for government involvement in these areas (Gwartney and Stroup, 1980; Stephens, 1985). The theory of public goods indicates that direct charging is not always feasible (requiring financing from general tax or rate revenue) as it is not possible to exclude people from the activity (or costs of exclusion exceed any gain from revenue). Furthermore, where the activity is not congested, there are no additional costs incurred in an extra person participating or watching, implying that the efficient price at point of use is zero. Public goods relate to both the provision of parks and the general feeling of euphoria derived from the success of a national or regional team in sports competitions.

External benefits are also derived from participation in sport, in terms of improved health and fitness, which lower health costs and increase productivity in the workplace. Furthermore, because sport provides a positive use of leisure time; there is a reduction in crime, vandalism and general delinquency (Department of Environment, 1977). External benefits arise because individuals do not take into consideration the benefit that the rest of society obtains from the fitter, healthier, more relaxed and productive society. A government subsidy is required, structured so as to increase the proportion of the population participating, rather than the frequency of participation of those already involved. Calculation of the size of the externality is very difficult, and to maintain government involvement, sport administrators need to enumerate and quantify these external benefits.

External costs, such as injuries, are associated with sport, although this could be addressed through the direct charging of Accident Compensation Commission (ACC) levies, with the charge being related to incidence and severity of accidents in each sport. A different external cost relates to control of sports crowds (soccer crowds in Europe demanding huge resources, for example) although again direct charging of the sports club for the policing of crowd control largely internalises the externality.

Sport is often regarded as a 'merit good', 'indicating a good that is socially desirable independently of the valuation placed on it by beneficiaries' (Mishan, 1982). The argument is that people do not recognise the benefits of sport, due to ignorance or a lack of information. Solutions relate to the provision of information about active recreation, which successive governments have done through campaigns to encourage participation, and active programmes of sport at school (to provide the 'taste' for sport) (see Chapter 6). Stephens (1985) argues that recreation, but not necessarily sport, comes under the 'domain of rights', as there is a social need for recreation, and the provision of recreational facilities is a prerequisite for a just and caring society.

Economics also cautions against taking a benign view of government. The development of public choice theory (Gwartney and Stroup, 1980) infers that much government involvement within the economy is not to correct for market failure, but instead to satisfy the objectives of politicians seeking re-election and bureaucrats seeking to increase their budget or have a quiet life (see Chapter 3). Governments may under-provide in areas where the benefits are diffuse and in the future, such as children's sport or recreational facilities, while over-providing products where the benefits are clear for a particular group, such as élite sport or sports already commercially viable with a large following and substantial sponsorship. The issue is not necessarily to remove government altogether from involvement in sport, but to ensure that it is clearly accountable for its actions, with the domain of rights argument over recreational and sport facilities devolved to the local level.

Non-Profit Sector

Most sports activities are organised through clubs which aim to maximise benefits to members, with non-members excluded. With most sports involving teams, clubs reduce the transaction costs of having to organise and arrange a team and provide the stability required for organised fixtures. Clubs normally operate on a non-profit basis, aiming to cover costs from a combination of joining fees, subscriptions, donations, fund-raising, sponsorship, government subsidies, events, entrance fees, and over-the-counter sales. The precise mix will vary according to the objectives of the club, the type and level of sport, and the drive and enthusiasm of the members. For example, an exclusive golf club will have a high joining and membership fee (and even a waiting list), paid staff and subsidised food and bar facilities. An athletic club will have open membership and a low annual subscription, with fees kept low through a combination of voluntary office-bearers, profits on bar sales, fund-raising and payments for assisting in event management.

Individuals join a particular club for such reasons as the camaraderie of fellow members, its reputation and organisation, the ability of the individual relative to the club, location of the club, and finally, relative costs of membership. In other words, economic decisions may not be paramount in the choice between clubs, although they may be important in the decision to participate. Individuals may also voluntarily offer their services to manage clubs, partly to reduce costs, but generally through a sense of community spirit. The economists argument – that individuals volunteer because they derive a personal benefit – does not capture this sense of community obligation and responsibility.

Professional sports teams (such as the Auckland entry in the Winfield Rugby League Cup) are a combination of club and commercial enterprise. In the USA, profit maximisation is the motive of the owners, whereas in the United Kingdom, playing success while remaining solvent seems more applicable (Gratton and Taylor, 1985). But success leads to larger gates, and thus increasing ability to purchase better players, a virtuous circle. A major function of an umbrella league is to prevent any club from achieving too much power by restricting competition through the provision of property rights in players being given to clubs, and cross-subsidisation of poorer clubs by richer ones.

All three supply sectors are interrelated. The more extensive the provision of sport facilities by government, the less viable it is for commercial operators, but the greater the likelihood that clubs will try to hire public facilities for exclusive use. Where sports attract high income consumers (or substantial sponsorship), there may be some 'skimming' of the market by the commercial sector, but equally this provides the opportunity for exclusivity of a club. In general, the more collective the goods or facilities are, the more difficult it is for the market to provide, because free-rider problems make it difficult for the market to levy a fee. However, the more diverse the demand for collective goods and facilities, the more difficult it is for government to supply, providing an opening for the voluntary and club sector (Gratton and Taylor, 1985).

Valuing Benefits from Sport

For most commercial recreation and sport, market prices represent a reasonable estimate of the underlying costs and benefits. Where governments are involved in the provision of facilities for sport, or the provision of a subsidy to sports groups and individuals, they need to be able to justify this, because the land will have alternative commercial uses, and their subsidy will either increase taxation or reduce other government expenditure options.

Economists have developed several techniques which estimate the benefits from intangible and non-traded sport and recreational experiences, in comparison with commercial use (Stephens and Wallace, 1993). One technique is to use questionnaires to determine the value that people place on a particular activity (Kerr and Sharp, 1987). An Australian study used a tax/expenditure trade-off questionnaire to determine the value that Australians obtained from government subsidising the arts. The study found that the preferred level of subsidy was four times that provided by the government, with the size of the preferred subsidy only increasing slightly with income and education level (Thompson *et al.*, 1983). Other studies have similarly valued the preservation of wildlife or scenery which was under threat from development. Most questionnaires on sport have been designed to measure the frequency and type of participation, but these could be widened to include estimates of the value of sport.

A second technique is to use 'hedonic pricing', where a surrogate market for the non-traded good is developed. Thus, the value of a nearby sport facility can be calculated by comparing the value of similar dwellings in suburbs near to the facility compared to those further away. The argument is that people are prepared to pay a premium on houses with ready access to the facility.

Also the Clawson-Knetsch travel cost technique can be used in outdoor recreation to construct a demand curve for a recreational site. Where there are time and travel costs to get to a site, it is assumed that the benefits of visiting the site at least equal the costs of getting there. Costs will be higher for those further from the site, but they are likely to have a lower per capita visitation rate than those closer to the site who will have lower costs. A downward sloping demand curve can then be calculated, and the area under the demand curve (consumers' surplus) represents the total benefits from the recreational experience, to be compared with the opportunity costs of providing the site. Although Vickerman (1974) has outlined the well-known weaknesses of the approach, it can be used for specific sports events (cricket tests, golf tournaments), for both participants and spectators, but is inapplicable to most local games.

Another approach is to calculate the impact of an event on the local economy. Kennedy (1990) looked at the impact of the Wellington motor-race by considering the changes to tourist flows from the event, their additional spending in Wellington less displacement spending (bringing forward trips or people leaving because of the noise), plus construction costs, and compared this with the City Council's financial commitment.

None of these approaches measure the external benefits from participation in sport, nor the option value of keeping facilities available even though the consumer may not want to use them at present. The estimates are probably lower-bound estimates, not incorporating the actual pleasure of the training and competition itself. But the approaches value sport in the same terms as the financial and opportunity costs of the provision of the facilities.

Conclusion

Whilst most people play or watch sport in order to escape from, or relax after, productive activity, economics enters into virtually every stage of decision making in sport. Resources have to be allocated to the construction and provision of facilities, and these have an opportunity cost in terms of the alternative use of these resources. To participate in sport, individuals have to allocate both time and money. As a result, changes in incomes, price of participating and time availability all influence both the participating decision and its frequency. Nevertheless, social, cultural, weather, age, and stage of family life cycle considerations, are probably the dominant determinants of participation.

Although there is little detailed literature on the economics of sport, it requires separate analysis due to its distinctive features: the interdependence between public sector activity (especially local government), the commercial sector and club provision of facilities; the role of sponsorship; the voluntary nature of much organisational activity; the nature of competition between clubs in both organised games and for members; the distinction between amateur and professional sport; and the requirement of being a team-player.

The market is supplying increasing sport opportunities. In other areas, pricing is often required to ration the available supply to the demand, though price may often deter the young and poor, who are in fact most likely to benefit from sport participation. Where prices are not used, other rationing devices have to be employed. User charges for facilities are appropriate if they provide exclusive access to a sport, with the charge based on the direct and additional costs of providing that facility. But most benefits from sport are not captured by the market system, and here economics can provide an array of techniques which attempt to measure these benefits, thereby ensuring that non-market values are incorporated into decision-making, along with market values.

Review Questions

1. If your real take-home pay increased, what factors would influence your decision whether to work longer or take more time in leisure activities? What is the opportunity cost of increasing your time spent on sporting activities?
2. What factors influence your willingness to participate in sport, and the frequency of that participation? How many of these could be classed as economic variables?
3. Is there a role for subsidies to sport through central government? What kind of sport facilities should local governments provide, and how should they charge for them?
4. Why do some sportspeople become millionaires through sport, while most have to pay to participate in sport?
5. Why do private companies sponsor individuals or sports teams? What factors influence the sponsors decisions, and what do you think the impact of sponsorship is on entrance and membership fees, participation in the sponsored sport, and in other sports?

References

Becker, G. (1964), *Human Capital*, New York: Columbia University Press.
Becker, G. (1965), A Theory of the Allocation of Time', *Economic Journal*, Vol.75, No.3, pp.493-519.

Brown, C. and Jackson, P. (1990), *Public Sector Economics*, 4th ed, Oxford: Basil Blackwell.
Butson, P. (1983), *The Financing of Sport in the UK*, Sports Council Information Series, No.8, London.
Caves, R. (1981), 'Intra Industry Trade and Market Structure in the Industrial Countries', *Oxford Economic Papers*, No. 33, March, pp.203-223.
Cody, J. and Robinson, D. (1992), 'Minimum Adequate Income Estimates for Households in Porirua', *Signpost*, Dec, pp.4-5.
Crompton, J. (1984), 'How to Establish a Price for Park and Recreation Services', *Trends*, Vol.21, No.4, pp.12-21.
Department of Environment (UK) (1977), *Policies for Inner Cities*, Cmnd 6845, London: HMSO.
El-Hodiri, M. and Quirk, J. (1971), 'An Economic Model of a Professional Sports League', *Journal of Political Economy*, Vol. 79, pp.302-319.
Fletcher Challenge (1989), 'Impact of the 25th Fletcher Challenge Marathon on Rotorua', *Race Report*, Rotorua, Fletcher Challenge.
Gratton, C. and Taylor, P. (1985), *Sport and Recreation: An Economic Analysis*, London: E. and F. Spoon.
Gwartney, J. and Stroup, R. (1980), *Economics: Public and Private Choices*, New York: Academic Press.
Hay, D. and Morris, D. (1991), *Industrial Economics and Organization*, 2nd ed, Oxford: Oxford University Press.
Horsman, J. and St. John, S. (1990), *Economics: a New Approach*, Auckland: Longman Paul.
Kennedy, M. (1989), 'Wellington City Motor Race – A Partial Impact Study', MBA thesis, Victoria University of Wellington.
Kerr, G. and Sharpe, B. (eds) (1987), *Valuing the Environment: Economic Theory and Applications*, Christchurch: Centre for Resource Management.
Maani, S. (1993), 'Post-Unemployment Wages, the Probability of Re-employment, and the Unemployment Benefit', *New Zealand Economic Papers*, Vol. 27, No.1, pp.35-55.
Mishan, E. (1982), *Introduction to Political Economy*, London: Hutchinson.
Scitovsky, T. (1976), *The Joyless Economy*, New York: Oxford University Press.
Stephens, R. (1985), 'The Economic Analysis of Recreation', in Community Services Institute (ed.), *Recreation and Government in New Zealand: Change in Relationships*, Wellington: Ministry of Recreation and Sport.
Stephens, R. and Wallace, C. (1993), 'Recreation, Tourism and Leisure Through the Lens of Economics', in Perkins, H and G. Cushman (eds), *Leisure, Recreation and Tourism*, New Zealand: Longman Paul.
Thompson, B. Throsby, C. and Withers, G. (1983), 'Measuring Community Benefits from the Arts', Research Paper No. 261, Macquarie University.
Vickerman, R. (1974), 'The Evaluation of Benefits from Recreational Projects', *Urban Studies*, Vol.11, pp.277-288.
Walsh, R. (1986), *Recreation Economic Decisions: Comparing Benefits and Costs*, State College: Venture Publishing.

Suggested Reading

Gratton, C. and Taylor, P (1985), *Sport and Recreation: An Economic Analysis*, London: E. and F. Spoon.

Houlihan, S. and DeBrock, S. (1991), 'Economics in Sport', in Parkhouse, B. (ed.) *Sport Management,* St Louis, MO: Mosby Year Book, pp. 198-209.

Jensen, B., Sullivan, C., Wilson, N., Berkeley, M. and Russell, D. (1993), *The Business of Sport and Leisure: The Economic Importance of Sport and Leisure in New Zealand,* Wellington: Hillary Commission.

Stephens, R. (1985), 'The Economic Analysis of Recreation', in Community Services Institute ed. *Recreation and Government in New Zealand: Change in Relationships,* Wellington: Ministry of Recreation and Sport.

Stephens, R. and Wallace, C. (1993), 'Recreation, Tourism and Leisure Through the Lens of Economics', in Perkins, H. and G. Cushman (eds), *Leisure, Recreation and Tourism,* New Zealand: Longman Paul.

Sport and the Economy

Benedikte Jensen

In this chapter you will become familiar with the following terms:	
Gross Domestic Product (GDP)	*value added*
non-profit sector	*public sector*
commercial sector	*local government*
central government	*gross output*
employment profile	*sport-related tourism*

Introduction

The purpose of this chapter is to place sport in the context of the New Zealand economy in order to gain an appreciation of its economic significance. Effective sport management conditions the enjoyment of sport spectators and participants, but its ramifications go much further. The economic influence of sport managers is conditioned by the level of economic activity, which is dependent on sport participation. A primary objective of this chapter is therefore to describe the boundaries of the sport industry and to measure its size.

When studying the economic importance of sport to the New Zealand economy, the primary interest is in the contribution of sport-related industries to the number of jobs and the standard of living enjoyed by New Zealanders. This entails the need to estimate the value of goods and services produced within New Zealand, but not the value of imported goods and services. Imported sports goods are relevant to the number of workers employed in the countries from which these imports are sourced but have no influence (other than possibly a negative one) on the number of people employed in New Zealand. Hence the focus is on the value of goods and services produced by New Zealand companies regardless of whether they are purchased by New Zealanders or exported overseas. In both cases the sale of goods is associated with employment in New Zealand-based companies, and the wages earned from this employment, together with the profits earned by the owners of these companies, contributes to the standard of living in this country.

The analysis of the economic significance of sport should not be restricted to measuring the size of commercial businesses producing goods and services for the sport community. Government and non-profit or community-orientated activity supporting the sport sector, are equally valid components of the sport industry. The various activities making up the sport industry therefore fall under three main sectors: the commercial or profit-orientated sector; the non-profit sector; and the public sector (refer also to Chapter 4). The economic impact of sport-related tourism is a fourth aspect which must also be measured to gain an impression of the size of the sport industry. The significance of each of these areas within the overall sport industry is described in the relevant sections below.

This chapter is based on a study commissioned by the New Zealand Hillary Commission (Jensen, Sullivan, Wilson, Berkeley and Russell, 1993), which was the first study to attempt to measure the size of the sport industry in New Zealand. This chapter largely represents a summary of the chapters in that study which refer to the economic importance of sport and leisure in New Zealand. Readers who are interested in more specific information concerning the methodology underlying the findings summarised here, are referred to the original study.

Definition of Sport

The original study, Jensen *et al.* (1993) defined sport and leisure according to the activities within the brief of the Hillary Commission. This entailed the consideration of all leisure activities requiring physical exertion and coordination but excluded physical pastimes which could be categorised as belonging to the Performing Arts, such as dancing. This means that sport in the context of this chapter is somewhat broader than that of organised sports (refer to the definitions discussed in Chapter 1). It includes individual outdoor pursuits such as tramping, fishing and flying, although the differences in definition tend to be at the margin, with much of the activity falling within the organised sport definition. In the case of economic statistical analysis, the limitations of the data tended to further restrict the analysis to more conventional sport activity. The precise coverage of the economic analysis as it relates to each sector of the sport industry is described in more detail below.

Definition of Economic Terms

There are three key economic terms used in this chapter which may be unfamiliar to some readers, thus, explanations are provided as follows:

- Value added: If you subtract the cost of intermediate products used to produce a good or service from the sale price of the end product, you derive the product's value added. For example, of the $100 retail price for a sports shirt (excluding GST), $45 could be staff salary costs and the profit margin. This means that only $45 of the total price of $100 represents the value added contributed by the sports shop in supplying the service of retailing the shirt to consumers. The rest of the price relates to inputs supplied by other industries, such as the wholesale distribution industry which supplied the shirt to the retail shop, or the electricity industry which supplies the shop's energy requirements.
- Gross domestic product: The sum of all value added produced by firms in the economy is the gross domestic product (GDP). GDP is therefore a measure of total output of the economy and is derived by summing value added to ensure that the output of one firm used as an input to the output of another firm is not counted twice. Since the incomes of workers and producers are directly related to the value of domestic production, GDP is also used as a proxy for the standard of living.
- Gross output: This refers to the total sales or turnover of the firm. Gross output therefore includes the value of intermediate goods used in production.

The Commercial Sport Sector

This section describes the significance of commercial economic activity associated with sport. The firms included in the commercial sport sector are highly varied, ranging from sport shoe manufacturers to professional sport persons. These firms are grouped together into industry groupings called component industries to make clear that they are merely component parts of one sector of the overall sport industry.

The coverage of commercial activity associated with sport is as comprehensive as was possible given the available data at the time of writing (see Table 5.1). A lack of data in some potentially important areas means, however, that the list is not exhaustive and that the final estimate of the size of this sector may underestimate the actual size. The commercial component industries covered in this study are as follows:
- Services to sport consist of professional sports persons, sporting and recreation clubs, ski fields and ski-hire, health and fitness centres, swimming pools, indoor cricket centres and ten-pin bowling, amusement parks, roller and ice skating centres, and an assortment of outdoor recreational services, such as jet boats and river rafting, sports grounds and stadium operation, horse show operation and grand prix motor racing. The sporting and recreational clubs included in the value of output of this component industry exclude central, local government and non-profit organisations, as the public and non-profit services are estimated separately in later discussion.
- Manufacture of sporting and athletic goods consists of the manufacture of sporting and athletic goods in New Zealand and includes, in addition to the more typical sports and athletic goods, the manufacture of billiard balls and cues, fishing tackle and flies, playground equipment, rod and gun cases, golf clubs and caddy bags, and surf-boards.
- Distribution of sport and camping goods consists of the services provided by sports and camping goods shops in distributing sports and camping goods to consumers. It also includes the services provided by wholesale retail chains which act as the link between sport goods manufacturers and retail shops. This component industry only includes the wholesale and retail distribution of sports clothing where it is sold through sports shops.

- Manufacture of sports clothing consists of all New Zealand-based producers of sports clothing.
- Manufacture of sports footwear consists of all New Zealand-based producers of sports footwear.
- Racing (excluding gambling) covers the operation of racing and trotting clubs, racehorse ownership, training and racing, excluding the activity of the Totalisator Agency Board.
- Manufacture of yachts and other pleasure craft consists of all New Zealand-based producers of yachts, dinghies and other pleasure craft.

The Value of Production in 1987

Time lags in the production of economic statistics means that the most accurate data on the commercial sport sector relate to the year ended March 1987. The commercial sector of sport contributed $251m to Gross Domestic Product in 1987. The largest contribution to the value added of the sector was made by the self-employed sports persons and recreational services industry. This industry represented 34.4 per cent of the total sport commercial sector. The distribution of sport and camping goods was the second largest component, producing 22.2 per cent of the industry total. The third largest component was the non-gambling portion of the racing and associated services industry, contributing 17.8 per cent of the total sectoral output.

Table 5.1: Value added in industry as percentage of total value added in the sport sector 1987.

Description	Value Added $m	Gross Output $m	%
Manufacture of sports clothing	23.68	64.71	9.4 %
Manufacture of sports footwear	11.02	28.72	4.4 %
Manufacture of yachts and other pleasure craft	18.98	44.10	7.6 %
Manufacture of sports and athletic goods	10.36	36.74	4.1 %
Distribution of sports and camping goods	55.69	61.61	22.2 %
Racing (excludes gambling)	44.58	81.53	17.8 %
Services to sport	86.32	180.56	34.4 %
Total	250.62	497.96	100.0 %

(Jensen *et al.*, 1993). Figures may not add due to rounding.

Comparison with Other Sectors

The study compared the sport commercial sector with other (more well defined) sectors of the economy in the year to March 1987, the results of which are presented in Table 5.2. In 1987 the sport sector was almost as large as the iron and steel products sector in terms of gross revenue or sales, while contributing more in terms of value added. The sector was comparable in size to the sanitary and cleaning services industry and the rail transport industry in terms of gross revenue, while contributing considerably more than rail transport to GDP. It was larger than the road passenger transport, water works and supply, and agricultural services industries.

Sport and the Economy

Table 5.2: Output of the commercial sector compared with other sectors in 1987.

Description	Value Added	Gross Output
Sport	251	498
Agricultural services	223	405
Iron and steel products	113	574
Water works and supply	102	225
Rail transport	95	386
Road passenger transport	266	423
Sanitary and cleaning services	238	457
All Sectors (including those not shown)	51,240	118,740
Sport sectors as % of all sectors	0.49 %	0.96 %

(Jensen *et al.*, 1993).

Growth of the Commercial Sector

The estimates of output for the 1991 March year are based on data relating to changes in employment, some specific production data (footwear), labour productivity trends for some component industries (clothing and footwear), household expenditure, export and import data for the constituent industries, and changes in the prices of producer inputs and outputs for the constituent industries (Table 5.3).

Table 5.3: Growth in the commercial sport industries 1987-1991.

Description	Value Added March Years 1987 $m	Value Added March Years 1991 $m	% Change in Value Added 1987-1991 Nominal	% Change in Value Added 1987-1991 Real
Manufacture of sports clothing	23.7	32.3	36.5 %	21.7 %
Manufacture of sports footwear	11.0	13.5	22.5 %	9.2 %
Manufacture of yachts and other pleasure craft	18.9	24.8	30.8 %	12.7 %
Manufacture of sports and athletic goods	10.4	6.2	-39.7 %	-44.0 %
Distribution of sports and camping goods	55.7	70.6	26.7 %	6.0 %
Racing (excludes gambling)	44.6	44.9	0.7 %	-25.1 %
Services to sport	<u>86.3</u>	<u>108.9</u>	<u>26.3 %</u>	<u>-11.8 %</u>
Total	250.6	301.2	20.2 %	-5.6 %

(Jensen *et al.*, 1993)

The estimates for 1991 show the largest increase in output in the sport clothing and footwear industries, and in the manufacture of yachts and other pleasure craft industry. These are estimated to have grown by 22 per cent, 9 per cent and 13 per cent respectively. The largest decline is estimated for the sporting and athletic goods manufacturing industry, where output is estimated to have declined by 44 per cent based on the change in employment recorded for that industry between 1987 and 1991. This industry represents a small proportion of the total commercial sport sector however, and this large decline therefore has a smaller impact on total sectoral output. Estimated declines in the self-employed sports-persons and amusement and recreational services industry of 12 per cent, and in the racing and associated services industry of 25 per cent, have a larger impact on the total since these are large components of the total sector. This decline is partially off-set, however, by an increase of 6.3 per cent in the second largest component industry, namely, the distribution of sporting and camping goods.

Overall, these estimates suggest a slight decline in the size of the commercial sport sector, from 0.45 per cent of GDP in 1987 to 0.41 per cent in 1991. Readers should note the disproportionate influence of the racing component industry on this outcome as the racing industry has been declining in significance for some time and the introduction of Lotto during this period hastened its demise. This decline is therefore not representative of sport industries in general. The decline in the sporting and athletic goods manufacturing component industry, reflects the removal of tariffs and import controls which contributed to the erosion of New Zealand's overall manufacturing base during this period. The experience of the sports clothing and footwear component industries is all the more remarkable due to the fact that they have prospered at a time when manufacturing generally has been in decline. Declining household incomes causing a slackening in demand for non-essentials services, is likely to explain the reduction in output from the services to sport component industry.

Prospects for the Commercial Sport Sector

The preceding analysis has shown that the commercial sport sector in New Zealand represents a significant industrial sector in its own right. Given the significance of sport to the New Zealand lifestyle, some readers may be surprised that sport does not represent an even greater proportion of commercial economic activity. One reason for the apparent discrepancy between the size of the commercial sector shown here and the level of involvement in sport in New Zealand, relates to the import content of goods and services purchased by sports people. In 1991 New Zealand imported approximately $96m worth of sport goods, so that imports exceeded exports of sport goods by a factor of four to one. The commercial sport industry shown here relates only to the domestic production of sports goods and services.

Whatever the relative size of the commercial sport sector in New Zealand in 1991, there is reason to be optimistic about its future prospects. On the basis of empirical and theoretical economic research concerning the spending behaviour of individuals with respect to leisure or luxury goods, it is possible to predict that the demand for sport goods and services will grow faster relative to the overall demand for goods and services in coming years. Spending on non-essential goods and services, to which sport goods generally belong, is highly responsive to changes in real income. Economists call demand for these goods income elastic (refer to Chapter 4). In a recessionary period such as New Zealand experienced between 1986-1991, households cut back on non-essential expenditure in order to maintain spending on necessities such as basic foodstuffs and power. When real incomes begin to rise once again, as some economists expect them to do over the next few years, spending on non-essential goods will rise at a faster rate than spending on essentials. The appetite of consumers for luxury goods in growth periods is relatively unlimited, as long as producers continue to bring new products out and to market these products successfully. There are limits, however, to the demand for basic household goods. This means that as incomes rise, households will spend a greater proportion of their income on non-essential goods, such as sport goods and services. Economic growth will therefore disproportionately benefit the commercial sport sector. As long as New Zealand producers are able to compete against foreign firms to capture the rising demand for sport goods, then the sport sector is set to expand in the near future. Producers of non-tradeable sport services, such as organisers of sport events and fitness centre owners, are in a more enviable position, since they are less likely to have to contend with foreign competition for the local sports dollar.

The Public Sport Sector

Society as a whole views government production of goods and services as a contribution to its welfare, and this is reflected in the conventional treatment of government production (as distinct from government transfer payments) as a component of GDP. To estimate the value of sport-related goods and services produced in the public sector, it is assumed that the value of production is equal to the cost of production. This in turn is equal to government expenditure on sport-related goods and services and the following discussion examines the expenditure by central and local government on the production of sport goods and services.

Central Government Expenditure

The expenditure data summarised here relates to the following: current expenditure on the acquisition, development and administration of recreational facilities; the administration of and expenditure on grants to sports bodies; and expenditure on sport promotional programmes, sport education and research. This emphasis on current expenditure means that this examination does not include estimates of the value of existing government assets used for sports purposes, such as swimming pools and sports stadiums. It does include expenditure on the construction of sport facilities, however, provided it occurred in the year for which data was collected (1991)(Table 5.4).

Information on central government expenditure on sport was extracted from the Budget Estimates, annual plans of government departments and from direct discussions with departmental officials. This is summarised as follows:

- The Department of Conservation (DoC)
  The expenditure by the Department of Conservation covered in the Jensen *et al.* (1993) study, falls under three areas of the Department's activities. The first relates to the provision of recreational facilities and services (such as huts, camp grounds) and the management of sports fishing; the second to the management of recreational leases, licences and concessions; and the third, to the Department's educational role with respect to recreational activities. In combination these three areas accounted for $34.9m of a total $134.4m in appropriations in 1990/91.

- The Department of Internal Affairs
  Sport expenditure by the Head Office of the Department of Internal Affairs was related to funding for the Mountain Safety Council, the New Zealand Water Safety Council and the

Royal Life Saving Commonwealth Council. This amounted to $435,000 in 1991. The Department also spent $392,000 on providing policy advice to, and administering grants on behalf of, the Minister of Recreation and Sport. The grants it administered for the Minister of Recreation and Sport were funding to the Hillary Commission ($6.1m), a payment for the Commonwealth Games deficit ($2.4m) and $48,000 in miscellaneous grants.

- The New Zealand Tourism Board (NZTB)
  The New Zealand Tourism Board has funding for promoting 'event tourism' in New Zealand which largely consists of sport events. In 1991 this amounted to $75,000.

- The New Zealand Lottery Grants Board
  The New Zealand Lottery Grants Board spent $21.8m on sport-related activities in 1991. It contributed $13.6m to the Hillary Commission's budget. The remaining $8.2m was used for funding of sport activities recommended by the Board's various targeted committees (youth, older adults, welfare, and so forth). Approximately $2m of these latter funds went to sport facility development.

- The Hillary Commission
  The Hillary Commission spent $20.3m in 1991. The New Zealand Lottery Grants Board contributed $13.6m, the Department of Internal Affairs $6.1m, with the remainder coming from interest on savings, commercial sponsorship and miscellaneous sources.

- The Ministry of Education
  Expenditure on sport-related education and research at the primary, secondary and tertiary levels was estimated at approximately $125m for 1991.

- The Accident Compensation Corporation
  In 1990/91 the ACC spent $222,000 on sport-related research. The ACC funded eight research projects investigating methods of injury prevention in sport activities.

Table 5.4 summarises expenditure in each of the categories of central government sport expenditure described above.

Table 5.4: Central government expenditure on sport by agency in 1991 financial year.

Central Government	Expenditure $m
Department of Conservation	34.8
Department of Internal Affairs	9.3
New Zealand Tourism Board	0.1
Hillary Commission	20.3
New Zealand Lottery Grants Board	21.8
Ministry of Education (estimated)	125.1
Accident Compensation Corporation	0.2
Total	211.6

[Note: The sum of each agency's expenditure does not equal the total expenditure shown because the expenditure of some agencies is financed by income sourced from the expenditure of agencies included here.] (Jensen, et.al., 1993)

Local Government Expenditure

The type of local government expenditure on sport summarised here relates mainly to the acquisition of land and the development/extension of sport, fitness and leisure assets and facilities. This includes local government expenditure on parks and reserves. Table 5.5 shows estimated local government expenditure for 1990/91.

Table 5.5: Estimated local government expenditure on sport in 1991 financial year.

Local government	Expenditure $m
Territorial local authorities	281
Regional councils	21
Total local government	302

(Jensen et al., 1993).

The Contribution to GDP Made by the Public Sport Sector

To calculate the final contribution of government production of sport goods and services to GDP it is necessary to subtract the value of expenditure which is simply a transfer payment from Government to other sectors of the economy or households. Transfer payments are small in relation to total expenditure, estimated to amount to $28.5m or 5.8 per cent of total expenditure, and relate to grants made by the Hillary Commission and the New Zealand Lottery Grants Board. The public sector consequently contributes $460.5m to GDP in the form of sport goods and services, such as parks and other recreational facilities and sport-related education.

The contribution by the public sector to GDP is therefore estimated to be greater than the contribution of the commercial sport sector in New Zealand, ($460.5m as compared to $301m). The contribution of local government to the sport sector is one and a half times greater than the contribution of central government. This is largely explained by the greater responsibility borne by local government for the provision and maintenance of recreational facilities (Table 5.6).

Table 5.6: Summary of government expenditure on sport in 1991 financial year.

	Expenditure $m
Central Government (net of grant to Local Government)*	187.0
Local Government	302.0
Total Government Expenditure	489.0
Contribution to GDP/Value added	460.5

* Includes estimated expenditure on sport education.   (Jensen et al., 1993)

The Non-profit Sport Sector

An important part of the provision of sport services in New Zealand is provided by non-profit making or non-commercial bodies. This sector largely comprises the vast array of national, regional and local sporting and recreational bodies. In addition, the Olympic and Commonwealth Games Association (OCGA) and the Sports Foundation, form part of the non-profit sector. However, these two bodies provide a very specialised input into the sporting sector.

Size of the Non-profit Sport Sector in 1991

In 1991 the total income of the sport non-profit sector was approximately $135.4m (see Table 5.7). The national sport bodies accounted for 36.2 per cent of these funds, the sub-national bodies for 59.7 per cent, while the Sports Foundation and the OCGA accounted for 2.9 per cent and 2.1 per cent, respectively. These funds are mostly sourced from membership fees, sponsorship and fundraising. In addition, there is some funding from the Hillary Commission and the New Zealand Lottery Grants Board.

Table 5.7: Total funding of the non-profit sport sector in 1991.

Non-profit sectors	Funding $m	Funding %
National sport bodies	49.0	36.2
Sub-national sport bodies	80.9	59.7
Sports Foundation	3.9	2.9
OCGA	1.5	2.1
Total funding	135.3	100.0

(Jensen *et al.*, 1993)

The total funding of this sector has been used as the estimate of the sector's gross output. This is consistent with standard methods of estimating non-market services where gross output is assumed to be equivalent to the cost of providing those services. Assuming that the ratio of value added to gross output for the total non-profit organisations within the economy is the same in non-profit sport organisations, gives an estimate of the value added of $70.3m.

Comparison with the Total Non-profit Sector

It is appropriate to compare the gross output of the non-profit sport sector estimated here, to the gross output of the total non-profit sector. The non-profit sector as a whole comprises all bodies servicing households that operate in a non-commercial manner. It therefore includes religious bodies, private schools, private hospitals, cultural bodies, as well as the sport non-profit bodies described above. In 1991 the total income of the non-profit sector was around $1,070m. Its contribution to the overall level of economic activity was $556m, around 0.8 per cent of GDP. Sport non-profit organisations represent at least 12.6 per cent of the non-profit sector.

Employment in the Sport Industry

Employment Coverage

While the preceding sections have described the contribution of the commercial, public and

Sport and the Economy 81

non-profit sectors of the sport industry to GDP, this section focuses on the number of jobs directly dependent on the sport industry. The analysis uses employment data from the 1991 New Zealand Census of Population and Dwellings, although the Census data refers only to employment in private profit-making organisations, non-profit organisations, and central and local government activities providing sport goods and services. Government administrative positions, which may relate to the administration of sport services are excluded, as the Census categorises them together with all other central and local government administrative workers. A significant number of sport local government administrative workers may also be excluded from the Census sport services category. In the absence of robust data on local and central government sport administrators, however, there is no choice but to restrict this analysis to the Census employment coverage.

Sport Employment Profile

In 1991 the sport industry provided approximately 14,530 full-time equivalent jobs (full-time equivalent means that every part-time worker is counted as half a full-time worker). People employed in the sport industry represented 1.1 per cent of the New Zealand workforce, with employment directly associated with the industry falling into the following three broad sectors:

- the manufacture of sport goods;
- the distribution and retail of sport goods; and
- the provision of sport services to people and households.

Figure 5.1: Composition of employment in the sport industry in 1991.

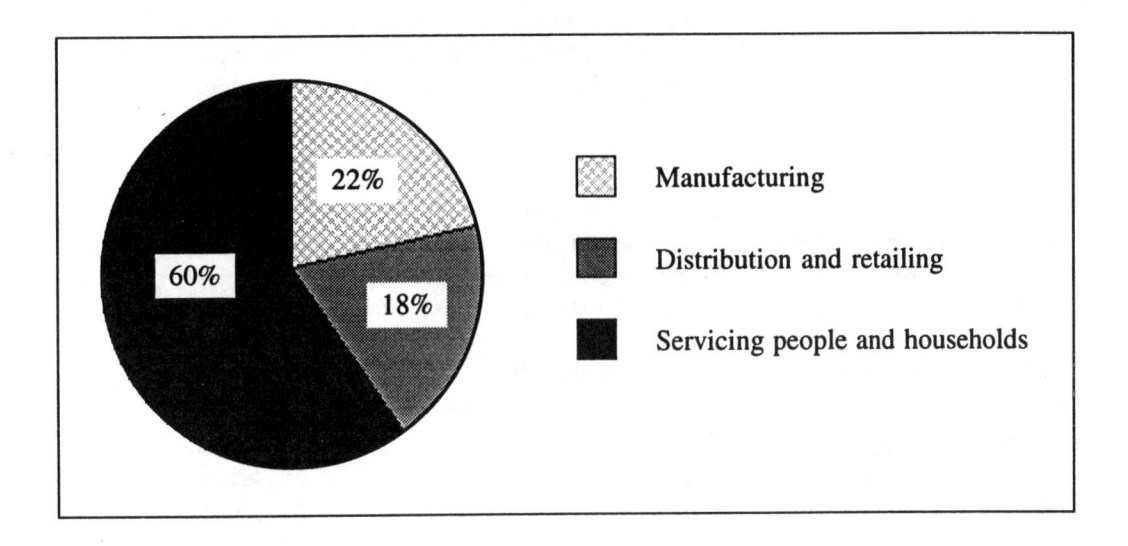

- Manufacturing: 22%
- Distribution and retailing: 18%
- Servicing people and households: 60%

(Jensen *et al.*, 1993).

As evident in Figure 5.1, most people are employed in the firms and organisations that service people and households in their pursuit of sporting and recreational pastimes. In 1991 service firms and organisations accounted for 60 per cent of all those employed in the overall sport industry, with the next largest in terms of employment being the manufacturing sector, which accounted for 22 per cent of those employed in the sport industry. The distribution and retail activities of sport goods is the smallest in terms of employment, accounting for only 17.9 per cent of the labour force directly associated with the sport sector.

Sport-related Tourism

This chapter has been concerned with the level of GDP and employment in New Zealand which is dependent on sport activity, and in this context it is necessary to consider whether tourism related to sport activities and sport events is a significant source of income and employment in New Zealand. The treatment of sport-related tourism as a component of the sport industry is slightly different to that of the sport industry sectors described above. When analysing the economic significance of the commercial, non-profit and public sport sectors, attention is focused on the value of goods and services produced by firms or agencies within those sectors. In the case of sport-related tourism, the emphasis is on the value of expenditure by foreign and domestic tourists whose primary reason for their trip is a sport attraction, even though only a certain proportion of this expenditure will be on sport goods and services. Consider, for example, the foreign tourist who comes to New Zealand primarily to go skiing. This tourist will purchase ski-passes, and hire or purchase ski equipment and clothing. A significant proportion of the tourists expenditure will, however, be on non-sport goods and services such as restaurant meals, accommodation and transport to and from the ski-fields. Since the ski-attraction is the primary reason for the tourist visiting New Zealand, it can be assumed that in the absence of ski facilities the whole of the tourists expenditure will be lost. This means that it is appropriate to include the total of this expenditure for the purpose of estimating the contribution of sport-related tourism to GDP.

Contribution to GDP and Employment

To estimate the contribution of sport-related tourism to GDP, expenditure by tourists is adjusted to remove the import content of the value of goods and services purchased. The resulting estimated contribution to GDP may then be used to derive the number of jobs which are dependent on sport-related tourism. Table 5.8 summarises this information.

Table 5.8: Summary of sport-related tourism 1991.

Total expenditure ($m)	$382m
Value added/contribution to GDP ($m)	$210m
Employment	4,013

(Jensen *et al.*, 1993)

While the output of the commercial, non-profit and government sectors may be added together to form the output of the total sport industry, it is not appropriate to simply add on the output attributable to sport-related tourism. To do so would be to engage in some double counting. Some of the goods and services consumed by tourists are produced by the sport industry and so will have been counted already in the sum of output from the commercial, non-profit and public sport sectors. In order to determine how much of the tourism attributable output can be added to the sport industry, information is required on the proportion of sport-related tourism expenditure which relates to each industry type. Unfortunately, the required level of detail of information on sport-related tourist expenditure patterns is not available.

The Total Sport Industry

By adding together the commercial, public and non-profit sectors it is possible to obtain an estimate of the size of the total sport industry. Table 5.9 shows the results.

Table 5.9: Value added/contribution to GDP in the total sport industry 1991 ($m)

	$m
Commercial sector	301
Public sector	461
Non-profit sector	70
The total sport industry	832

(Jensen et al., 1993)

The sport industry as a whole represented approximately 1.0 per cent of GDP in 1991. It is comparable to the entire clothing and footwear industry and to the electrical machinery industry in terms of its contribution to GDP. The sport industry was responsible for approximately 14,000 jobs in 1991 or 1.1 per cent of total employment.

Arguably, the actual significance of the sport industry is much greater than these estimates suggest. Sport-related tourism contributed approximately $210m in GDP in 1991 and was responsible for over 4,000 jobs, although, as was explained earlier, some of the contribution of sport-related tourism is already counted in the output of the sport industries. One would intuitively expect that most of the contribution of sport-related tourism could, however, be added directly to the estimated contribution of the individual production sectors. In the absence of additional statistical information, no attempt has been made to estimate the magnitude, but readers should be alert to the potential implications of omitting this aspect of the sport industry from the final estimate.

Summary

This chapter has shown that it is possible to make reference to a sport industry in the same way that one refers to the dairy or the banking industries. New Zealand leads the world in the manufacture of some specific sports goods, such as tramping equipment and high quality sports clothing. In addition to these high-profile goods, the total range of sports goods and services produced in New Zealand represents a sizeable proportion of total economic activity. The level of economic activity directly related to sport means that successful sport managers can make an important contribution to the performance of the

New Zealand economy. While the sport industry is already a significant component of the New Zealand economy, the prospects for growth in the commercial and non-profit sectors of this industry are encouraging. These facts underline the importance of sport management to the economic fabric of New Zealand society.

Review Questions

1. Why did the commercial sport sector remain virtually the same proportion of GDP in 1991 as it had been 1987?
2. What factors are likely to determine the growth of the sport industry over the next decade?
3. How does sport-related tourism contribute to the New Zealand economy?
4. How can effective sport management influence the course of economic development?

References

Jensen, B., Sullivan, C., Wilson, N., Berkeley, M. and Russell, D. (1993), *The Business of Sport and Leisure: The Economic Importance of Sport and Leisure in New Zealand*, Wellington: Hillary Commission.

Suggested Reading

Gratton, C. and Taylor, P. (1985), *Sport and Recreation, an Economic Analysis*, London: E. and F. Spon.
Henley Centre (1992), *The Economic Impact of Sport in the United Kingdom in 1990*, United Kingdom: Henley Centre.
Jensen, B., Sullivan, C., Wilson, N., Berkeley, M. and Russell, D. (1993), *The Business of Sport and Leisure: The Economic Importance of Sport and Leisure in New Zealand*, Wellington: Hillary Commission.
Stephens, R. (1985), 'The Economic Analysis of Recreation', in Community Services Institute' (ed.), *Recreation and Government in New Zealand: Change in Relationships*, Wellington: Ministry of Recreation and Sport.

Sport and Education:

Give the Kids a Sporting Chance

Bevan C. Grant and Bob Stothart

In this chapter you will become familiar with the following terms:

New Zealand Qualifications Authority (NZQA)　　*physical education*

youth sport　　*sportfit*

Hillary Commission initiatives　　*sport education*

Sport, Fitness, Recreation Industry Training Organisation (SFRITO)

Introduction

Many people who read this book will have had positive experiences from their involvement with school and community sports programmes. For them, the sport culture has been a dynamic, evolving enterprise providing significant personal meaning, reward and identity. For others, however, sport has become exclusive or élitist with little, if any, positive outcome. The structures used to promote sport in schools reduce the opportunity for participation at an appropriate level, and the chance to develop confidence and competence gradually escapes the once playful nature of many individuals. While much has been written about the role of education in contributing to the supposed Kiwi ethos of *sport for all*, the success of what has occurred through education and physical education in contributing to this, can be questioned. All young people will be subject to a variety of physical experiences during their school years but many grow to dislike participating in sport and to reject other forms of physical activity. The real challenge is to learn from what we know and to identify ways which prevent such attitudes being formed.

The first section of this chapter provides a brief historical overview of the links between education, physical education and sport and puts some of the current concerns into context. It becomes clear that there is need for change. The second part of the chapter discusses several developments which make participation in physical activity, and in particular sport, more attractive to greater numbers of young people.

The Connection Between Sport and Physical Education

Any discussion on the management of sport in schools raises questions about physical education in schools, and it is important to differentiate between the two. Physical education (physical training) became part of the primary curriculum in 1877, but it was not a required subject in secondary schools until after the Thomas Report of 1942. Nevertheless, the majority of secondary schools saw the value of physical activity and employed drill instructors, gamesmasters (or gamesmistresses). Girls schools in particular, appointed women with training gained in Britain, and some very good physical education programmes were developed in the 1920s and 1930s. But sport and physical education have not always been amiable colleagues. For many teachers of physical education, sport exemplifies attitudes and values incompatible with the aims and objectives of physical education. On the other hand, many sports people see physical education as irrelevant or pointless. While it is important to consider the differences between sport and physical education, differences in the main are in attitudes and values.

Sport in schools is about school teams, and sometimes about individuals, competing in regular, organised inter-school and community events which usually take place out of school time. The events may be organised and managed by teachers, sports officials or volunteer parents. Good physical education programmes taken regularly by qualified teachers can enhance the learning of sport specific skills, contribute to fitness preparation, and make the experience personally meaningful and rewarding. Inevitably sport is about winning and losing, about being in the team and sharing in these experiences with friends. Unless the school has a comprehensive and well managed and appealing sports programme, many students may feel excluded and disadvantaged.

Physical education is about skill learning, fitness, health, outdoor education, dance, aquatics and the development of attitudes which encourage life-long physical activity. It is less concerned with high levels of achievement in specific sports than it is in developing in students a range of fundamental movement skills which enable them to make intelligent choices about recreation and sport. Physical education is provided for every student, whereas sport may become the goal of the proficient and skilled.

This difference in approach between sport and physical education was clearly defined for the first time in the 1987 revision of the physical education syllabus published by the Department of Education. The revised syllabus, which covered Junior classes to the Seventh Form, stated:

> Physical education and sport are closely linked. Sport is a significant part of New Zealand's culture. It is formalised physical activity involving challenge or competition against oneself, others, or the environment. It begins in play, develops through games, and culminates as a structured competitive activity (Department of Education, 1987: 12).

The syllabus also suggests that the role of the school is to provide opportunities, regardless of the abilities of the students, to experience the special benefits of sport, and where possible to promote links with community sports groups. This can be achieved, the syllabus contends, if students play, officiate, coach, respect opponents, appreciate skill in others and know the rules of games. Sport begins with spontaneous play in junior classes, develops through a wide range of modified and low-structured games and culminates in organised competitive games. It is well documented (e.g. Roberts and Treasure, 1993) that many students find competition stressful because of fear of failure, conflict, being separated from friends, or pressure from adults. In spite of this evidence, present-day structures still promote negative outcomes and make sport an unpleasant experience for many young people.

It is therefore not surprising that the debate on sport in schools is problematic and threaded with varying attitudes towards mass participation and leisure choice on one hand, and competition, élitism and hierarchy on the other. It is bound to be ongoing and contentious with entrenched attitudes and practices difficult to change.

Early Developments

The early secondary schools of New Zealand were replicas of the 'public' schools of England, where sport was an integral component of school culture and sportsmanship and attitudes of fair play were inculcated at an early age (see Chapter 2). Along with Latin grammar and the prefects system, sport was transplanted into New Zealand secondary schools (particularly rugby and cricket) and it has not only become a feature of life in the schools, but has been woven into the cultural fabric of life in New Zealand. As a society we have gradually attached greater status and value to sporting success and endeavour. Taggart (1988) asserts that sport is now a significant component of Western culture.

From the earliest times sports in New Zealand boys' secondary schools flourished and rugby was quickly established as the pre-eminent game for boys. In girls' schools, however, it was not as straight-forward. Girls schools had to combat entrenched attitudes about what was 'proper' for young women. According to Coney (1986) there was widespread concern that the reproductive organs of the girls would be damaged by vigorous sporting activity, thus threatening the very survival of the nation. In addition, opponents to vigorous sport maintained that girls should pursue elegant, graceful, feminine activities, not games that were aggressive, boisterous or unladylike. While boys played rugby, hockey and soccer in winter, and cricket and a little tennis in summer, girls were limited at first to tennis, croquet, some dancing, swimming and perhaps a little postural correction to avoid sway-back. Lacrosse, popular in England, did not catch on, while hockey did. The girls who played it, however, were deemed to be tomboys. Annie Whitelaw, first principal of Auckland Girls' Grammar went so far as to comment in reference to hockey that she 'wouldn't dream of allowing her girls to play so unladylike a game' (Coney, 1986: 174). Elsewhere, Dr Maud Ferey of Christchurch was asserting 'soccer is the finest sport for girls that exists' (cited in Coney, 1986: 162).

For most girls schooling terminated at primary level, and in that environment girls were often included in cricket, rounders and hockey, especially in rural schools. Most town schools, however, maintained separate playgrounds for boys and girls. By 1928 about half of the primary school leavers were going on to secondary school. Tennant (1986) noted there were powerful opponents to the education of girls, many of whom believed that educating girls was a waste of time and money, and that anyway, they should only learn the wifely arts of domesticity. One example of this was Sir Truby King, founder of the Plunket Society, who was strongly opposed to equal educational opportunities for boys and girls and proclaimed it one of the most preposterous farces ever perpetuated. Views such as these (promoted in the main by men), regarding what was proper for young females, were a powerful negative influence on female participation in physical activity. These attitudes still influence public attitudes towards female sport.

Fry (1985) highlights the discrepancy between the provision of land (see Table 6.1) in boys' and girls' state secondary schools. Clearly, girls were not expected to be as active in games and sports as boys.

Table 6.1: Acres of land available at selected boys' and girls' secondary schools.

Boys School	Area	Girls School	Area
Auckland Grammar	17	Auckland Girls Grammar	3
New Plymouth Boys	40	New Plymouth Girls	6.5
Wellington College	60	Wellington Girls	3
Christchurch Boys	28	Christchurch Girls	7.5
Waitaki Boys	25	Waitaki Girls	3.5

In spite of the many constraints (e.g. space, expectations for boys and girls), in management terms the locus of control and the organisation of sport remained the prerogative of teachers. Inter-school games were established, coaching was organised and loyal and enthusiastic teachers dedicated time and skill to their students. In girls' schools in particular, games mistresses were employed to improve the sports performance of girls in their schools. Teachers of physical education were often expected to teach physical education to every class and in addition to manage, coach and organise a whole range of sports teams. It was frequently an intolerable expectation.

1950 – 1990: A Reflection

Until the 1950s, sport in secondary schools had been limited to a handful of traditional games. However, the increasing affluence of the post-war period saw a proliferation of games and sports in New Zealand society, in particular the growth of individual sports (see Chapter 2). Whereas schools could insist that every boy in the school had to play rugby, and teachers were prepared to coach and turn out on Saturdays, the rapid diversity of post-war sports began to place real pressures on schools. Squash, gymnastics, badminton, archery, softball, basketball, volleyball, golf, skiing, rowing, and many more sports were demanding equal time and resources within the structure of school sport. Many schools were not able to respond to all of these demands, and the social changes of the post-war period were beginning to put increasing pressure on schools. Teachers gradually began to reject the task of coaching sports teams in their own time while the parents of the students went about their own recreation.

Some occasional relief was provided for beleaguered teachers in the 1960s by the Rothmans Foundation, which employed a variety of national sports coaches who travelled extensively, visiting educational institutions as well as assisting the sports organisations with their particular sport. Highly skilled people were employed and very good coaching was delivered. However, for some educators the association of sport with tobacco was an anathema. Nevertheless, standards of excellence in sports coaching were demonstrated in many schools and tertiary institutions. The Rothmans coaching scheme was eventually overtaken by the funding schemes of the New Zealand Council for Recreation and Sport in the 1970s.

The Post-Primary Teachers Association eventually took a strong stand, and the involvement of teachers in Saturday sport gradually diminished. The tradition of the enthusiastic teacher giving up time for the greater glory of the school was changed forever. The situation was clearly unsatisfactory. Some schools were well organised, while others struggled with poor equipment, limited finances, inadequate playing fields and no indoor space suitable for sport. Although teachers bore the brunt of parental criticism for a gradual decline in the numbers of sports teams, they were powerless on their own to transform the situation. Sport was not the responsibility of schools alone. Nationally, secondary school sport was controlled by sports associations (for specific sports) comprised of teachers. At the local level committed teachers and local sports associations tried valiantly to keep sport going. It was not an ideal situation and by the mid-1970s the pressures on teachers to manage school sport, in effect in their own time, were becoming onerous and burdensome. McKenzie (1974), typically for the time, reported that delegates at the Secondary School Hockey Association had resolved to write to the Ministers of Education and Sport to urge them to provide as much assistance as possible with finance, facilities and time allocation to teachers to improve the position of sport in schools.

The Minister of Recreation and Sport, the Hon. Mike Moore, commissioned a Sports Development Inquiry Committee. This was chaired by Sir Ron Scott, and its task was to examine the nature, structure and meaning of sport in New Zealand (see Chapter 3). The inquiry resulted in the publication of a report titled *Sport on the Move* (1985). The Minister wanted a report that provoked reaction and discussion in every sports community. In this context therefore, it was not surprising that some comments were highly critical of physical education and condemnatory of the role of the Department of Education in failing to properly recognise the importance of sport in schools. For example, the report asserted that 'sport has been buried within the current school physical education syllabus' and that 'the declining standard and status of physical education has also affected the quality of school sports education' (ibid.: 68). Most damning was the Committee's comment that it saw 'sport as seriously disadvantaged at the present time within the physical education curriculum' (ibid.: 69).

These criticisms are understandable given that the Sports Inquiry Task Force comprised prominent sportsmen and sportswomen and that sport in education had been addressed primarily from a technical and competitive perspective, at the expense of a social framework. There was also a confusion in the report between the responsibilities of the Department of Education and the freedom of schools to conduct physical education and sports programmes as they saw fit. After all, sport is not an official subject within the school curriculum. Of more significance in terms of concern were remarks made to the Sports Inquiry Committee by an Inspector of Secondary Schools with specific responsibilities for school sport, who contended that, 'Sport in secondary schools has many symptoms of chronic illness... . Unless remedial measures are applied, sport as we know it could slowly disappear' (ibid.: 75). However, as noted earlier, at the time of the Sports Inquiry the physical education syllabus (Department of Education, 1987) was being completely revised. Members of the Syllabus Review Committee included several prominent sports people appointed by the Minister of Education. The role that physical educators could have in preventing this so-called demise of sport from occurring, if indeed it should be prevented, is more difficult to identify.

By 1990 the structure of educational administration had been dramatically changed by the Picot reforms and Tomorrow's Schools. In the new environment, schools with their controlling Boards of Trustees are legally free to plan sports (and other programmes) to suit their own needs. While the consequences (for sport) of such reforms may not be known for a few years, the message is clear: many of the known structures and programmes of the past will require significant attention if they are to survive in the new climate of more rigid forms of accountability and control. Gilroy (1993) noted that sport now has to compete for participants with a plethora of other entertainment. As schools have become self-managing, much power resides with the Boards of Trustees, and schools and communities are free to determine their own priorities.

Traditionally, school management exercised proprietary rights over the students in the school but that attitude has changed and the interface between physical education, school sport and the community sports club, often the source of conflict, is also changing. McKay (1991: 177) suggests that sport has 'become subjugated to the instrumental rationality and profit-making imperatives of the entertainment industry and consumerism'. If this is so, current practices must be challenged. Many aspects of the adult model for sport are not appropriate for use in schools and alternative structures need to be developed. The way sport for young people is organised, who organises it, and who benefits from it is now being addressed in several different ways.

Seeking Change

Many ways have been suggested to increase the number of young people participating in regular physical activity and organised sport. While there is debate about how this can be achieved, it is apparent that if more young people are to be 'turned on' to sport, then many of the current attitudes and practices in both school and community must be changed. Grant (1992) suggests present concerns will only be amplified if we continue to pay lip-service to such issues as the goals of sport, fair play, sport for all, equal opportunity, cost structures, meaningful competition, the successful acquisition of motor and manipulative skills, the enjoyment factor and the role of the school and teacher in the process. This notion challenges the reality of the Kiwi *sport-for-all* philosophy and suggests it is time for resolve rather than rhetoric. Irrespective of the difficulties, if sport is to be preserved as a component of our culture, it must be made more accessible to young people. Sparkes (1990) suggests in Figure 6.1 (opposite) that without a significant shift in how we personally approach the issues and concerns, the matter at hand will continue to be characterised by superficial rather than real change.

Figure 6.1 also helps to explain why some practices and innovations from the past have not fulfilled their assumed potential in promoting sport as a worthwhile leisure activity. Although the opportunity exists, many students do not belong to school or community sports clubs or participate in formal or informal competition. Csikszentmihalyi (1990) noted that it was difficult for teenagers to be actively involved in sport because of the time, money, and effort necessary compared to other activities. Furthermore, the market-driven society and the difficulty of attracting appropriate volunteer coaches has made some aspects of organised sport unattractive for many students. The question arises as to who or what structure is best equipped to provide and manage sport for young people to make it more attractive and a viable leisure activity in the future.

Figure 6.1: Levels of Change (Sparkes, 1990).

```
┌─────────────────────────────────────────────────────────────────────────┐
│                    Surface Change (relatively easy)                      │
└─────────────────────────────────────────────────────────────────────────┘
                                    ↓
┌─────────────────────────────────────────────────────────────────────────┐
│                                Level 1:                                  │
│   The use of new and revised materials and activities, e.g. curriculum   │
│                    resources, instructional packs                        │
└─────────────────────────────────────────────────────────────────────────┘
                                    ↓
┌─────────────────────────────────────────────────────────────────────────┐
│                                Level 2:                                  │
│   The use of new skills, teaching approaches and styles, i.e. change in  │
│                  teaching practice and teaching role.                    │
└─────────────────────────────────────────────────────────────────────────┘
                                    ↓
┌─────────────────────────────────────────────────────────────────────────┐
│                                Level 3:                                  │
│ Changes in belief, values, ideologies and understanding with regard to   │
│ pedagogical assumptions and themes. This may require a major orientation │
│                            in self-image.                                │
└─────────────────────────────────────────────────────────────────────────┘
                                    ↓
┌─────────────────────────────────────────────────────────────────────────┐
│                      Real Change (very difficult)                        │
└─────────────────────────────────────────────────────────────────────────┘
```

Several school-based innovations have been introduced during the last few years. Each is an attempt to make quality physical activity, and sporting experiences in particular, more accessible to young people. In doing so they have the opportunity to learn about the many positive values to be gained from participating. A description of several separate developments is provided:

- A sport education curriculum as part of the secondary school physical education programme.
- Sport education as part of Bursary Physical Education.
- Initiatives from the Hillary Commission for Sport, Fitness and Leisure.
- KiwiSport Leadership Award, Sportfit/School Partnership, Sportfit/Regional Partnership, and the New Zealand Secondary Schools Sports Council.

Sport Education

There is no evidence to support or refute the inclusion of sport education as opposed to teaching sport skills in time scheduled for physical education. A sports education curriculum model (Siedentop, Mand and Taggart, 1986) is a student-managed, school-based programme within physical education time that has recently been introduced into many New Zealand secondary schools. The model has six main characteristics:

- Sports education uses seasons (e.g. 18-20 lessons) instead of short units (e.g. 4-6 lessons) of instruction, and typically involves a modified sport.
- Students become members of teams and stay in these groups throughout the season.
- The season is organised to include practise sessions, pre-season games, and a formal competition.
- The season ends with a culminating event involving all participants.

- Records (emphasising team performance) are kept and publicised during the season.
- Students learn the roles necessary for sport to take place, such as manager, selector, captain, sports committee, referee, duty team, and the teacher assumes a less intrusive role as students are gradually given more responsibility.

Siedentop (1982) claims sport education can be implemented in a manner that is both sane and exciting, both humane and competitive, and can contribute to the culture's growth and survival. The primary objective of sports education is to help students become skilled sports participants and good sports persons through both rhetoric and behaviour. Students learn to be:

- Competent   -   acquire skills, execute strategies, become knowledgeable games players;
- Literate   -   learn to understand and value the roles, rituals and traditions in sport and to discriminate between good and bad sports practices;
- Enthusiastic   -   learn to want to participate in sport;
                 -   develop tendencies and behaviours that preserve, protect and enhance the sport culture.

The sports education model requires the full involvement of all class members, with the interests of the student placed ahead of the sport. This varies from the typical club-based system, where management tends to be more parochial in terms of attracting young people towards their particular sport (Evans 1990). Within the club-based system, students are relatively powerless agents as most decisions are made for them, their advice is rarely sought and what occurs is typically dominated by the adults and more capable performers. Many students are socialised into roles of passive conformists and their particular social and physical needs are frequently ignored.

Sport education is student centred. What tends to happen is that the teacher becomes less visible as the dominant figure in the class, even though guidance and leadership is still provided. Students become directly involved by being required to accept such roles as member of the sports committee, a selector, a coach, a manager, a first aid person, a publicity officer, a referee or umpire, a scorer, on duty, or a captain, and all are participants in the games. Each role has a specific task with identifiable responsibilities and known consequences and together they influence the efficiency of the sports education programme. By fulfilling these roles all students share in the ownership and overall control of the sporting experience (Grant, Sharp and Siedentop, 1992). The manner in which the student is involved and perceives the worth of their effort, influences their interest level, their enthusiasm for participating, their enjoyment and their desire to achieve. Unity and fairness within and between teams is also a factor.

Teachers who have incorporated sport education into the physical education programme, identified several significant differences between what they believe traditionally occurs in physical education and in community sport (Grant, 1992). Teachers reported that sport education:

- Makes sport accessible to all students for no cost and does not compete against other leisuretime activities;
- Involves all students in decision making and ensures they share responsibility for what occurs throughout the programme;

- Enables all students to establish realistic goals for self, team and the programme;
- Provides better opportunities, particularly for the less skilled and not so enthusiastic students;
- Ensures all students in the class participate in all aspects of the sporting experience;
- Puts all students, irrespective of their skill level or enthusiasm, into situations where their contribution is more easily recognised and valued by peers;
- Ensures the level of intensity during training and competition is controlled by students rather than adults, thus contributing to the enjoyment factor;
- Uses more developmentally appropriate sport through modifications allowing both boys and girls, and the highly skilled and less skilled, to participate together in a way that engenders success for all;
- Uses organised competition, but winning and losing is put into a different context by students than what typically happens in community sport.

Although there were many positive outcomes from the programme, it should be noted that where the sports education model was not applied in full, the experience was not particularly successful. The results from this project were very clear: those who have a particular interest in promoting participation in sport for young people, must first challenge their own understandings, beliefs and values about what to expect from sport, and then change some of their current practices and beliefs used to promote sport. It is probable that adult values intertwined with student desires may conflict and be one reason why many students drop-out from playing community-based sport. Perhaps adults unknowingly pervade the boundaries of play and dismantle the elements of fun and spontaneity.

The most controversial aspect of including sport education in physical education is the use of structured competition. There are many arguments which oppose and support the notion of competitive sport with young people in education. However, competition involves more than a team or individual playing against another. For students, competition is about having the opportunity to participate and experience personal success as defined by the individual. Mastery of skill performance at an appropriate level is valued more than winning. Arnold (1988: 62) reminded us of this when suggesting 'trying to win may be considered a necessary feature of competing but this should not be confused with a person's reason or motive for playing'. Therefore factors such as team selection, game rules, scoring systems, and the role of the teacher/coach, must all be considered when designing a programme.

Appropriate competition provides an ideal environment for teaching the values associated with self and sport. Thorpe (1990) suggests that when competition is organised and structured effectively, students find appropriate ways to make it work. If students can see what it means to act honestly, fairly, resolutely, and generously while competing in sport, they are more likely to be impressed by such acts than by a discussion of them. Fair competition will promote team affiliation, enhance relationships among team members (who in many cases were not previously close friends), create interest when watching other teams play, and elevate enthusiasm among many students who previously appeared to dislike sport. Young people have a desire for and enjoy competition appropriately structured, but at the completion of the event they typically move on to the next exciting part of their life.

Sport education has the potential to help students understand and value what is required to make sport personally rewarding. It can also change the way they think about themselves and each other while improving their capacity to be competent and confident sport performers, without detracting from the elements of enjoyment and fun.

However, in the school setting, Ross (1970: 23) alluded to what was and still is a real challenge for teachers when stating, 'There is no easy way to implement a physical education programme which aims to educate as well as activate its students'. While the pedagogical process encouraged by sport education may help motivate students in the short term, it will require more than a curriculum model to change the dominant discourses currently used to promote sport as a viable leisure activity for young people.

Bursary Physical Education: Sport Education

In 1990 Physical Education became a Bursary subject in the 7th Form. The course was developed in a way that kept the needs of the student to the fore, rather than merely replicating a tertiary programme. The role of physical activity has been accorded centre stage in Bursary Physical Education. In addition to increasing the status of physical education as a part of the senior school curriculum, Bursary Physical Education provides students with an opportunity to study the subject at a high level. Over 230 schools now offer Bursary Physical Education and student demand for the course is increasing every year (for example, 1990 – 650; 1993 – 2,600). A survey of students registered in the course in its first year indicated that the main reason for choosing physical education as one of their Bursary subjects was a love of sport, outdoor education or physical activity. It was noted (Grant, 1991: 10) that 'many students claimed they were not top performers in their respective activities but valued the opportunity to study a subject at this level which has high personal interest'.

The course is organised on a modular basis and requires students to complete three modules. There is a compulsory module (i.e. Lifestyles Concepts) and seven optional modules, the most popular of which is sports education. This has a completely different conceptual basis to the sport education curriculum model previously explained. In the sports education module the students are required to analyse, practise and assess their own performance in a chosen sport. The module emphasises personal development through a considerable variety of physical and cognitive tasks. Being student centred, there is an opportunity for ensuring a high level of personal success, which is one important factor that contributes to the desire for continued participation in any physical activity.

Hillary Commission Initiatives

The Hillary Commission for Sport, Fitness and Leisure has invested considerable amounts of money and time into trying to keep in touch with young people's interests in physical activity and sport in particular. Their own inquiries through surveys and contact with schools, consistently show students want greater opportunities to participate in sport. Based on this premise, a new concept called the *Sportfit* programme was developed and introduced in 1992. Sportfit aims to increase the numbers of young people participating in physical activity and sport, improve the quality of sports programmes, provide better trained sports people and administrators and to make the transition from sport in school to the community easier (Hillary Commission for Sport, Fitness and Leisure, 1993). Sportfit also provides a coordinating and communications role and helps reduce the costs of administering some aspects of school and community sport.

Four components of the Sportfit programme are described in brief:

KiwiSport Leadership Award aims to develop leadership and teaching skills through involvement in KiwiSport and endeavours to increase the pool of qualified volunteer coaches. This award is typically incorporated into the 6th Form Certificate Physical Education programme and is administered by the physical education teacher. However, it can be offered through clubs and other agencies. The practicalities of the Leadership Award require students to participate in a twelve-hour course which includes demonstrating their ability in skills teaching, communication, planning and management with a primary or intermediate school-age group. Students self-assess and the teacher also rates them from 1 (low) to 5 (high) on each aspect. All students who complete the requirements of the course are eligible for the award.

Sportfit/School Partnership was introduced in 1991 with the intention of increasing participation in sport and improving the quality of school sports programmes. Schools are offered a 50 per cent subsidy for an initial two-year period, in order to expand their sports programme. This generally involves the appointment of a qualified person to coordinate predetermined aspects of the sports programme. Examples of how schools use the funding include: employing a full-time sports coordinator, paying for teacher release to allow the teacher in charge of sport time to organise the programme, employing a part-time coordinator to manage the sports programme, and employing a part-time recreation officer to improve the sport and leisure opportunities for the students in the school and community. In 1993 there were 112 schools involved in the partnership, resulting in approximately 8,000 more students participating in a variety of school or community sports programmes.

Sportfit/Regional Partnership was initiated in 1992, with 17 Regional Secondary School Sports Directors being appointed. The directors' (who have been teachers) salaries are shared by the regional schools that utilise their services. The task for each director is to improve the quality of inter-school sport, provide opportunities for more students to participate in sport, promote fair play, expand coaching programmes, assist local sports bodies to align themselves to school sport more easily and to coordinate sports tournaments and festivals. There is also an expectation the directors will significantly improve the management of secondary school sport within their region and help make the sporting experience more accessible and attractive to increasing numbers of young people. But the employment of *experts* and the adoption of an alternative management structure is insufficient on its own to produce change. There must be an accompanying change in adult attitudes and expectations towards sport for young people.

New Zealand Secondary Schools Sports Council was established in 1993 to assist organisations that host either South Island, North Island or National Secondary School sporting events (e.g. regional cross-country, South Island netball tournament, national U16 soccer tournament). The administration of each event is coordinated through the Regional Sports Directors. It is proposed that this system will improve the efficiency of the sporting experience and ensure the best use is made of both physical and personal resources. Furthermore, this proposed management structure should release teachers from the onerous task of accepting total responsibility for planning and implementing these large-scale events on a voluntary basis.

Tertiary Education

Thus far the discussion has predominantly been about secondary school sport, but some knowledge of developments in the post-school sector is also important. There is now a complex mix of courses available for a variety of awards and qualifications. Until recently university studies relating to sport, leisure and recreation were only available through the School of Physical Education at the University of Otago, the Parks and Recreation degree at Lincoln University and the Masters of Arts (Applied) in Recreation at Victoria University. While these course have seen some revision to cope with new demands (e.g. sport and fitness management courses), the 1990s has seen the emergence of two new undergraduate degrees – a Bachelor of Leisure Studies at the University of Waikato, and a major in Sports and Recreation Management through the Bachelor of Business Studies at Massey University. Most of these university courses are available at bachelors, masters and doctorate level.

New Zealand Qualifications Authority

When education was restructured in 1989, the New Zealand Qualifications Authority (NZQA) was established. One component of their work is to coordinate the myriad of qualifications – be they certificates, diplomas degrees – into a cohesive, meaningful and interrelated framework. An eight-level national framework has been devised to embrace all education and training courses above Form 5 (Level 1 = Form 5, to Level 8 = post-graduate studies). The framework will gradually be applied to the many courses, certificates and diplomas in recreation, sport, fitness and leisure offered through the universities, polytechnics and other training agencies. The coordination of all courses will ensure the needs of the industry (in other words sport, fitness, recreation and leisure) are being provided by the various agencies and institutions.

Sport, Fitness, Recreation Industry Training Organisation

In an effort to maintain (in some cases improve) the quality of current courses and minimise the mass production of technocrats with limited vision and knowledge about the issues and needs within sport, fitness, recreation and leisure, SFRITO (Sport, Fitness, Recreation Industry Training Organisation) a controlling board for the industry has been established. The members on the board represent the Sports Assembly, Fitness New Zealand, Community Recreation and the Outdoor Recreation sector, including Maori interests. Through a wide consultative process and needs analysis, SFRITO determined what training programmes are required. This resulted in a series of units of learning being written for each industry at the different levels. These courses will eventually become a part of the framework and may be offered by accredited individuals or institutions. In time the framework should produce a well coordinated and structured national training programme for those interested in sport, fitness, recreation, and leisure, that meets the various needs of the industry.

Conclusion

In these times of unpredictable and continual change, the structure and management of sport requires careful monitoring if it is to flourish. What happens to sport in schools cannot be considered in isolation from society. Many of the images young people have about sport and what it represents are provided by the media. Whilst this may create unrealistic ideals, young people do aspire to the efficiencies and excitement portrayed in this form and expect some similarity in their own sporting experience, albeit on a smaller scale.

If sport is to become a more attractive leisure option in the future for an increasing number of young people, there is a need to find alternative structures to those of the past. The foundations can be provided through alternative forms of physical education and sports programmes in schools. However, any modification in schools needs to be matched with sensitive and informed adults providing well managed and stimulating programmes in the community. The developments described in this chapter may be the first steps to giving more kids a sporting chance!

Review Questions

1. If you had the power and the resources, what would you do to improve sport in secondary school?
2. Draw up a list of adjectives for sport and one for physical education then comment on the significant differences and similarities?
3. 'Sport in many secondary schools has the symptoms of chronic illness.' Discuss this statement with reference to present-day circumstances.
4. Describe the ideal training programme for prospective leaders of youth sport.

References

Administering for Excellence (1988), *Report of the Task Force to Review Education Administration*, (The Picot Report) Wellington: Government Print.
Arnold, P. J. (1988), *Education, Movement and the Curriculum,* London: Falmer Press.
Csikszentmihalyi, M. (1990), 'What Good are Sports? Reflections on the Psychological Outcomes of Physical Performance', *New Zealand Journal of Health, Physical Education and Recreation*, vol. 23, no. 2, pp.3-11.
Coney, S. (1986), *Every Girl*, Auckland: YWCA .
Department of Education (1987), *Physical Education Syllabus for Junior Classes to Form 7,* Wellington, New Zealand: Government Printer.
Evans, J. (1990), *Sport in Schools,* Geelong, Victoria: Deakin University Press.
Fry, R. (1985), *It's Different for Daughters*, Wellington: New Zealand Council for Educational Research.
Gilroy, S. (1993), 'Whose Sport is it Anyway? Adults, and Children's Sport', in M. Lee (ed.), *Coaching Children in Sport: Principles and Practice*, Great Britain: E. and F. Spon, pp.17-26.
Grant, B. (1991), 'A New Era in Physical Education', *The New Zealand Journal of Health, Physical Education and Recreation*, vol. 24, no. 3, pp.7-12.
Grant, B. (1992), 'Integrating Sport into the Physical Education Curriculum in New Zealand Secondary Schools', *Quest*, vol. 44, no. 3, pp.304-316.
Grant, B., Sharp, P. and Siedentop, D. (1992), *Sports Education in Physical Education: A Teacher's Guide*, Wellington: Hillary Commission for Sport, Fitness and Leisure.
Hillary Commission for Sport, Fitness and Leisure, (1993), *Sportfit: A Hillary Commission Programme*, Wellington: Hillary Commission for Sport, Fitness and Leisure.
McKay, J. (1991), *No Pain, No Gain: Sport and Australian Culture*, Sydney, Australia:

Prentice Hall.
McKenzie, P. (1974), 'The Trauma of ...The Decline of Sports in Schools', *New Zealand Journal of Health Physical Education and Recreation*, vol. 6, no. 4, pp.38-41.
Roberts, G. and Treasure, T. (1993), 'The Importance of the Study of Children in Sport: an Overview', in M. Lee (ed.), *Coaching Children in Sport: Principles and Practice*, Great Britain: E. and F. Spon, pp.3-13.
Ross, B. (1970), 'Individual Fitness: The Aim of Physical Education'. *New Zealand Journal of Health, Physical Education and Recreation*, vol. 3, no. 2, pp.21-26.
Siedentop, D. (1982), 'Movement and Sport Education: Current Reflections and Future Directions', in M. Howell and J. Saunders (eds), Proceedings of the VII Commonwealth Conference on Sport, Physical Education, Recreation and Dance: Movement and Sport Education, Brisbane: University of Queensland Press, pp.3-13.
Siedentop, D., Mand, C. and Taggart, A. (1986), *Physical Education: Teaching and Curriculum Strategies for Grades 5-12*, Palo Alto, CA: Mayfield.
Sparkes, A.C. (1990), *Curriculum Change and Physical Education: Towards a Micropolitical Understanding*, Geelong, Victoria: Deakin University Press.
Sports Development Inquiry (1985), *Sport on the Move*, Report to the Minister of Recreation and Sport, Wellington: Government Print.
Taggart, A. (1988), 'The Endangered Species Revisited', AAURER National Journal, No. 121, pp.34-35.
Tennant, M. (1986), 'Natural Directions', in B. Brooks, C. Macdonald and M. Tennant (eds), *Women in History: Essays on European Women in New Zealand*, Wellington: Allen and Unwin.
Thomas, W. (1944), *Report of the Consultative Committee on the Post Primary School Curriculum*, Wellington: Department of Education.
Thorpe, R. (1990), 'New Directions in Games Teaching', in N. Armstrong (ed.), *New Directions in Physical Education*, Champaign, Ill.: Human Kinetics, pp.79-100.
Tomorrows Schools (1988), The Reform of Education Administration, Wellington.

Suggested Reading

Coney, S. (1986), *Every Girl*, Auckland: YWCA.
Fry, R. (1985), *It's Different for Daughters*, Wellington: New Zealand Council for Educational Research.
Grant, B., Sharp, P. and Siedentop, D. (1992), *Sports Education in Physical Education: A Teacher's Guide*, Wellington: Hillary Commission for Sport, Fitness and Leisure.
McKay, J. (1991), *No Pain, No Gain? Sport and Australian Culture*, Sydney, Australia: Prentice Hall.
Sports Development Inquiry (1985), *Sport on the Move*, Report to the Minister of Recreation and Sport, Wellington: Government Print.

The Structure and Organisation of Sport in New Zealand

Lorraine Vincent and Linda Trenberth

In this chapter you will become familiar with the following terms:

National Sports Organisations (NSOs)   *Regional Sports Trusts (RSTs)*

Local Funding Scheme (LFS)   *Volunteer Involvement Programme (VIP)*

Hillary Commission's Five Year Strategic Plan 1993-1997

Introduction

Sport is an organisation or industry in which close attention should be paid to the bureaucratic structures that exist to ensure its viability. The efficiency of any organisation is always reflected not only in the quality of its goals, strategies, facilities, staff, funding, products and market satisfaction, but also in the quality of the bureaucratic structure that has evolved or developed to ensure these various qualitative elements are kept in some balanced relation. The structures that evolved will have begun by serving certain limited purposes and, over time, will have expanded and gained strength and at some point will have been forced to change and adapt to prevailing conditions, demands and opportunities. By contrast, those that have been specifically developed will perhaps have begun more pragmatically, with a systematic appraisal of the organisational structure required to meet a certain pattern of detectable needs.

But whether it came about through evolution or developmental design, the effectiveness of the structure of any organisation is vital to its survival. If, therefore, an organisation is beginning to falter, its structure, as much as any other organisational component, has to come under critical review. This observation applies to every organisation, whether it be commercial or non-commercial; large, medium or small; local, regional, national or international; staffed by voluntary or paid workers or a mixture of both.

The intention of this chapter is to describe and comment on structures that exist currrently in New Zealand sport. At the outset a distinction can be made between structures which can be classified as emanating from grass-roots (bottom-up) and those which developed from a canopy construction. The grass-roots structures are typified by part-time and voluntary activities of enthusiastic players and administrators of particular sports. The structures emanating from canopy (top-down) construction tend to be dominated by full-time, paid professional administrators – perhaps including paid professional players as well – who apply techniques of business analysis and management to sporting activities.

Occasionally there might be organisations found with an effective blend of both grass-roots and canopy structures. If they function satisfactorily it will be because their particular organisational resources and needs are best served by the voluntary and professional structural combinations that have developed. Otherwise they will be organisations in a state of change which should be assessing their strengths, weaknesses, opportunities, and threats, before adopting a managerial structure and methods with which to become more efficient and effective.

The design/structure of a sports organisation is also a result of its nature, that is, volunteer driven, non-profit or involving competition. Almost without exception a sports organisation has been established by volunteers/participants whose desire is to achieve a competition structure which allows each individual to achieve her or his maximum potential. Despite the rising number of paid executive staff and paid participants in some sporting codes, it is highly unlikely that the nature of sports organisations will ever be entirely professional and profit-driven to the exclusion of volunteer effort in some crucial form or other.

Grass-roots (Bottom-up) Stages of Development

Koopman-Boyden (1991) presented a five-stage model of the growth of organisational structures that has some applicability to New Zealand sport. In this model, organisations are identified as developing through foundation, orientation, stabilisation, differentiation, and institutionalisation stages. At the *foundation* stage, the seeds of an idea are sown among likely supporters by enthusiasts who are prepared to devote time, energy, and money in its promotion. Then follows the *orientation* stage, in which aims, objectives and policies are framed in constitutional form. Numerous discussions take place, and consensus is reached in an atmosphere of optimism and progress, with assurances that modifications could be introduced democratically as events unfold. This leads on to the stage of *stabilisation,* in which administrative routines are established to implement policies, to deal with internal and external issues, to recruit members, and to monitor finance. Subsequently the stage of differentiation occurs in which functional groups are set up to focus on specific tasks, such as coaching, fund-raising and young-player recruitment from schools. Finally there is the stage of *institutionalisation,* in which formal hierarchies of responsibility are established, bureaucratic procedures are confirmed and publicised, a national network of regional and local adherents fostered, and a central agency created both to coordinate the membership and to liaise with international equivalents. The central agencies also liaise with their national equivalents of other sports for political, economic, and fraternal purposes.

This model reflects the character of each organisation as it proceeds at its own pace through the different stages according to the energy, enthusiasm, opportunities and urgency of the personnel involved. None is guaranteed survival to the next stage, and survival in perpetuity is not assured at the final stage. Each stage also involves a shift from individual to group responsibility, from spare-time to full-time commitment, from voluntary to paid organisational staff, from ad hoc to managerial decision making, and from ambiguous and casual procedures to those involving clear lines of responsibility and practice.

Canopy (Top-down) Development

The alternative organisational structure – the transfer of prefabricated systems from successful business ventures – is more instant than organic in its formation. It is designed on the principles of rationality, efficiency, and cost-effectiveness. It gives little weight to commitment, convention, past performance, and voluntary work. Instead the focus is on viability and adaptability in an ever-changing climate. It emphasises the function rather than the functionaries, and so prevents the entrenchment of individuals in key areas of responsibility, no matter how much they and their small group of supporters might have found such practices useful in the past.

The canopy or top-down formation can be as a result of an international initiative. For example, in order to establish a New Zealand branch, Taekwando placed an instructor in New Zealand with a mandate to set up a local organisation with affiliated clubs (Mary Stuart, 1992, personal communication). At a special General Meeting of interested people, a National Council was elected before a regional level with affiliated clubs was in existence.

For the top-down structure to be successful, it requires a supporting robust statement of intent which declares the objectives, core values, strategies, time-frame, and performance indicators for the organisation as a whole, and for its component working parts. This statement should be prepared from intensive working group sessions in which commercial principles and practices, stakeholders and responsibilities are clearly identified. The statement is then able to be promulgated throughout the organisation and to relevant supra-organisational bodies, such as the Hillary Commission for Sport, Fitness, and Leisure, which has statutory obligations with regard to funding. Top-down organisational statements need to be prescriptive but flexible, as organisations are subject to change if they wish to match changing circumstances and capitalise on opportunities for growth and development.

The Hillary Commission, Local Bodies and Regional Sports Trusts

The Hillary Commission is probably the most significant agency in New Zealand sport, and it provides a good example of a top-down construction of an organisation. As discussed in Chapters 2 and 3, the Hillary Commission was set up by Parliament in 1987, and was specifically 'dedicated to helping all New Zealanders participate and achieve' via the targeting of grant-aid to national sport and recreation organisations and the delivery of direct control programmes. Its full title, the Hillary Commission for Recreation and Sport, disclosed its responsibility for fostering recreation and sport. The government, in line with those of Australia and Britain, assumed the task of creating a central framework, with substantial Lottery Board Grant Funding (see Chapter 3 for funding breakdown), for the purpose of bolstering, coordinating and creating more effective sports organisations in the community.

Much of the impetus for this development came from the review *Sport on the Move* (1985). This review also argued that local authorities should be encouraged to do more than merely provide public facilities by way of open space, sports fields, swimming pools and libraries. However, because of a concurrent restructuring and amalgamation of Local Authorities that forced 238 Local Authorities to amalgamate into 74, it was evident that in some cases Local Authority recreation and sport provision was actually under threat. This was confirmed by the Review of the Hillary Commission's Support for Recreation and Sport at the Local Level (1991), which stated that amalgamation had had a significant negative impact on the provision of recreation and sport services in some local governments. The report listed the following five reasons for this negative impact:

i. There was ineffective lobbying to protect leisure services during amalgamation and, as a consequence, those services were often marginalised.
ii. One of the prime motivations for enforced amalgamation was to effect economies of scale. Most senior staff are on performance contracts that make a specific reference to 'cost containment' as the bottom-line measure. This has resulted in enforced economies to reach anticipated bottom lines, and these economies often bear no relationship to need or to service quality.
iii. In line with the above, there has been a rush to contract out some services. The result is contracts based on net cost bottom lines rather than constituent needs or quality of service.
iv. Many elected representatives and officers see the provision of leisure services as a burden not appropriate to the local government function. They have taken the current period of fiscal restraint as the means by which to divest themselves of such services and return to the basics of roads, rats and rubbish.
v. Those services which have remained have often been told to do more with less. This inevitably leads to a deterioration in standards, as there is no 'fat' in the system.

The range of leisure services varies within councils, but traditionally councils have restricted themselves to basic 'public good-type' provision such as open space, sports fields, swimming pools and libraries. More recently they have provided courts, recreation centres, programmes, marinas, community centres and grants to recreation and sport organisations and individuals.

By way of response, in 1992 the Hillary Commission reinforced the funding scheme it had established through local authorities, and it created a special Local Government and Technical Services Unit to strengthen the partnership, by giving advice to local authorities on policy and its implementation. Simultaneously the Hillary Commission sought directly to promote effective administration and management in the infrastructure of sport, fitness and leisure organisations. It also changed its own name to the Hillary Commission for Sport, Fitness and Leisure, to indicate its changing pattern of priorities. Although a professional body itself, it recognised the contribution made by volunteers and accepted the estimate of $200 million contributed from such sources (Jensen, Sullivan, Wilson, Berkeley and Russell, 1993). The Commission's aim now is to ensure that by 1997, 75 per cent of local authority and national sporting organisation managers will have attended at least two Commission-sponsored training sessions per year. Simultaneously it also intends to expand and extend its highly successful volunteer involvement programme (VIP) through which business methods, such as accountability, critical evaluation, market research, and sponsorship, are disseminated as skills for augmenting the specifics of coaching and performance with which most volunteers will be familiar.

The Hillary Commission also set up a country-wide contractual pattern of funding through Regional Sports Trusts (RSTs), with annual performance reviews and random audits. The first RST was established in Otago in 1983, with the second in Waikato in 1986, and shortly after their activities were reviewed, a recommendation was made that their organisational model be used for establishing similar sports trusts throughout the country. In its report to the Commission, the review team recommended that the following set of objectives be incorporated into the statement of interest of all sports trusts:

- To increase participation in all aspects of sporting involvement. This should include all people no matter what their age, race, sex, location or economic circumstances.
- To prepare a plan of development with short- and long-term goals, for sport in the region. The plan should take account of local recreation planning and be subject to regular review and evaluation.
- To establish liaison with existing regional organisations, sports associations and local authorities.
- To promote sport in the region through close association with all media.
- To develop coaching programmes for players and officials at all levels.
- To prepare, collate and disseminate information about sport through publications and research.
- To improve the administration of sport through initiatives such as provision of secretarial services, courses for administrators and other support services.
- To coordinate existing resources such as coaching, tertiary facilities, accommodation, documentation, administration, secretarial services and sports science.
- To work with education authorities to initiate and support programmes in schools.
- To raise finance from sponsorships, charitable trusts, central and local government and other sources.
- To foster attitudes towards sport which embody respect for opponents and officials, through codes of fair play. Where appropriate, the review team stated that RSTs might wish to include the following objectives:
  - To develop assessment of performance programmes with sports medicine authorities and experts in physiological and psychological testing. Such programmes should lead to talent identification.
  - To initiate sports scholarships for tertiary students to enable them to reach their full potential.

The team also recommended that RSTs should have complementary relationships with such organisations as:

- national and local sports associations;
- Local Authorities – for access to facilities, grounds, personnel and general services;
- Coaching New Zealand (CANZ) – for support, assistance and specific skills;

- local recreational workers – for professional support and assistance with specific programmes, planning and resources;
- local universities or tertiary institutions – for access to research libraries, personnel and students who can act as coaches for certain Regional Sports Trust programmes.

The Hillary Commission's response to the review team's report recognised the function of Regional Sports Trusts as representing the regional voice of sport and as constituting an autonomous regional delivery system for sport services. It also saw the two main functions of sports trusts being the coordination, development and servicing of existing sport delivery systems, and the planning, provision, promotion and management of new programmes and services. Consequently it established the following funding principles by which RSTs should operate:

i. The Hillary Commission funding policy of grant-subsidising sports associations' executive and organisational development will be applied to each individual RST. Funding will thus consist of subsidising operational and establishment costs but exclude the subsidisation of maintenance, programmes and services, and capital budgeting costs.
ii. The Hillary Commission subsidisation of operational and establishment costs will decrease over a prescribed period, with RSTs becoming increasingly self-supporting. (This has been further identified in the Commission's five-year strategic plan which states that by 1995 RSTs should be providing 50 per cent of their own administration costs.)
iii. The RSTs portfolio of programmes and services will be funded in the main from commercial sponsorship, although certain programmes such as KiwiSport may be funded in part by the other sport delivery agencies.
iv. Hillary Commission funding will be contingent upon the strict adherence by sports trusts to accountability procedures.

Currently there are 17 Commission-recognised RSTs which give a comprehensive coverage across New Zealand. Some trusts are still embryonic while others are well-established. While these all differ in nature and direction, there can be no disputing that collectively they are an important part of the country's sport, fitness, and leisure structure. Already they have had a major impact on the local and regional scene and should continue to do so for some time to come.

As their name suggests, Regional Sports Trusts help the Commission achieve its goals on a regional basis, and the security of Commission funding and long-term commitment to RST development will assist trusts to plan ahead in the same way as national organisations. The funding will continue to be contingent on the achievement of agreed performance targets and will include a commitment to management development, both at trustee and employee level.

Role of Local Authorities and Regional Sports Trusts

The relationship between RSTs and national sports organisations, and also between RSTs and Local Authorities requires further development to meet the sport, fitness and leisure needs of communities. There was, and in some instances still remains, tension between the Trusts and Local Authorities or personnel within these authorities because of the diverse nature of Trusts. Some have clear direction and relationships with Local Authorities, while others (particularly the more politically active Trusts), are antagonistic. A competitive element exists between the different groups which is not unhealthy as long as there is no great conflict nor duplication of effort. It is a huge waste of personnel and resources to resolve conflict and also to reinvent the wheel when discussion and shared planning could prevent overlap. Regional Sports Trusts and Local Authorities need to integrate recognisable structures to avoid inefficiency. Sports Trusts must complement existing provision and be careful not to formulate aspirations that are too grandiose and serve only to alienate other key providers. They should also concede, as numerous reviews suggest, that local government is the major provider of leisure facilities and the major provider of funds to support public leisure. For their part, Local Authorities need to pay attention to the new voices of their RSTs, rather than persisting only with previous information sources.

Clarification of roles is important if tensions are to be avoided, though it is difficult to set down specific tasks for either Sports Trusts or Local Authorities because of variation in resources and goals. The overall goal of RSTs has emerged, however, from the desire to strengthen the local and regional delivery structure of sport, fitness and leisure. Their mission statements were to articulate and serve the needs and wants of the sports market in a designated region, and the objectives were to coordinate, develop and service the existing sports delivery systems, and to plan, provide and manage new programmes and services. In order to support the work of Sport Trusts, the Regional Network Sports Trust has been established, which has identified the following goals:

- To advance the interests of regional sports foundations and trusts in New Zealand through a central body or a network of regional sports foundations and trusts by the communication of ideas and the utilisation of coordinated activities and resources.
- To assist and promote regional sports foundations and trusts through coordinated fundraising, promotion and advertising.
- To arrange regular meetings of regional sports foundations and trusts with the aim of sharing ideas and resources.
- To promote recreation and sport and sport education in all its aspects including (but not limited to) health, fitness, training, sportsmanship, seminars, coaching and 'KiwiSport' in schools.

Organisational Interactions

The Hillary Commission was also required to contribute to the work of Key Sports Organisations and Sport Service Organisations (see Figure 7.1 over page).

Key Sports Organisations included the New Zealand Olympic and Commonwealth Games Association (NZOCGA), the New Zealand Sports Foundation (NZSF), and the New Zealand Sports Assembly (NZSA). Sport Service Organisations included the Coaching Association of New Zealand (CANZ), the New Zealand Sport Science and Technology Board (NZSSTB), and the New Zealand Federation of Sports Medicine (NZFSM).

Again, the roles and responsibilities of each organisation were presented in organisational statements. For example, those of NZOCGA were primarily:

- To establish and maintain New Zealand as one of the best sporting nations in international competition involving current and potential Olympic and Commonwealth Games sports.

Figure 7:1

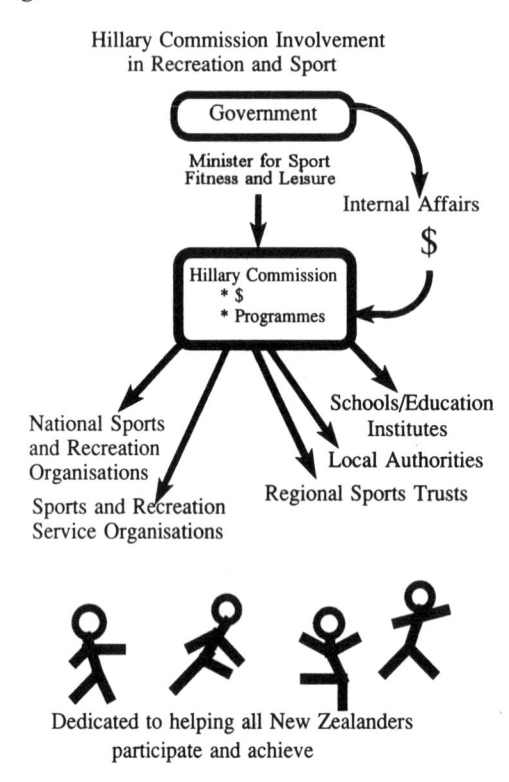

Hillary Commission Involvement
in Recreation and Sport

[Diagram: Government → Minister for Sport Fitness and Leisure → Hillary Commission (* $ * Programmes); Internal Affairs → $ → Hillary Commission. Hillary Commission distributes to: National Sports and Recreation Organisations, Sports and Recreation Service Organisations, Schools/Education Institutes, Local Authorities, Regional Sports Trusts.]

Dedicated to helping all New Zealanders
participate and achieve

- To increase the number of participants of National Sports Associations at Olympic and Commonwealth Games.
- To control, select and appoint participants in New Zealand Olympic or Commonwealth Games teams.
- To promote the principles of 'Olympism'.

The goals of the NZSF were primarily:

- To provide financial assistance to high performance New Zealand sportspeople giving them the opportunity to achieve their full potential in international sport.
- To ensure that such assistance was targeted solely at the élite performance sport area to maximise the star medal/podium winning team and/or individual potential.

The goals of the NZAS were primarily:

- To be a focal point for all sport within New Zealand and to provide one representative view on behalf of all sport within New Zealand as the principal representative organisation for New Zealand sport.
- To support and correlate the administration and efforts of sports governing bodies in New

Zealand and to advance the development of the administration of sport.
- To liaise with government and international agencies and to bring before government and international agencies such recommendations as are approved by the Assembly.

Similarly, the expressed aim of CANZ was to develop a comprehensive education programme to meet the needs of sport, to initiate an accreditation scheme and specialist seminars, and to provide an accessible library resource centre. The NZSSTB was established to promote and develop the use of sport science to improve the performance of New Zealand sportspeople. Finally, NZFSM was established to encourage and promote the dissemination of current knowledge and research into the causes and prevention of any illness or accident which might be associated with sporting activity.

National Sports Associations

Beyond the organisational systems described already, and usually preceding them in date of origin, are those representing national sports such as netball and tennis. By way of example, the object of Netball New Zealand is:

- To foster, develop and promote the game by providing enjoyment and recreation for all parties.
- To stage, control and conduct netball matches in New Zealand including national tournaments and international fixtures and matches in accordance with the Rules of the International Federation of Netball Associations.
- To publish and uphold the rules of netball.
- To make and enforce rules and regulations for the control of the game of netball in New Zealand.

The comparable purpose of the New Zealand Tennis organisation is:

- To foster, control and develop (i.e. promote the organised growth of) the sport of tennis in New Zealand.
- To provide opportunities and access for all New Zealanders to participate in tennis at all levels of competition and recreation.
- To provide opportunities for élite performers to fulfil their potential in tennis.
- To maintain a significant presence on the international tennis scene.
- To participate, with distinction, in international tennis competitions, particularly the Davis Cup and Federation Cup.

National and International Funding

Both national and international funding is directed through a client base of more than 133 organisations which have a total of 1.7 million members. It includes the National Sports Organisations (NSOs), the New Zealand Olympic and Commonwealth Games Association, and the New Zealand Sports Foundation. Categories of funding at this level incorporate participators, volunteers, and service and management development.

The New Zealand Sports Foundation, whose Board comprises prominent business leaders, was established in 1979 to raise money for the country's high performance athletes.

The New Zealand Olympic and Commonwealth Games Association comprises representatives of sports that conventionally participate in such events, and it raises funds to select and send teams to the venues. More recently it has come to provide funds for the preparation and training of participants, and for some of these purposes it receives funding from the International Olympic Committee (IOC).

The New Zealand Sports Assembly was established immediately prior to the formation of the Hillary Commission in 1987. There has been occasional friction between the two bodies as each sought to establish roles in the national sporting structure, but clearly both have parts to play in New Zealand sport. The NZSA has been active in combating or modifying policies which it believed would have a negative impact on New Zealand sport. For example, it has brought an amendment to the Accident Compensation and Rehabilitation Insurance Bill to avert the imposition of a levy on national sports organisations. It lobbied for an expansion of the definition of an 'accident' to include sprains and strains, and it influenced liquor legislation concerning liquor sponsorship, liquor brand advertising codes, and legislation on gaming machines, taxation issues, and human rights.

To ensure the continuation of Commission funding, the Assembly recently clarified its role and contribution to the national sporting scene. The process, performed in conjunction with Commission personnel, confirmed the Assembly's commitment to advocacy and representation as its core activity. For its part the Hillary Commission publicly stated that its goal will be to provide funds at national level, in bulk form for a three-year period, to be expended on the basis of management plans agreed with the Commission. It believes that through such funding true partnerships will evolve, and through partnerships on a national scale of operation, there will be significant developments made in the field of sports.

Funding Strategies

The funding functions of the Hillary Commission are crucial to its goals. Its Strategic Plan identifies the following three funding strategies:

i. To support the total development of sport and leisure through bulk funding for national organisations based on the projected growth management plans as follows:

- 1993 – 10 organisations
- 1994 – 50 organisations
- 1995 – 75 organisations
- 1997 – 100 organisations.

ii. To provide long-term security of financial support to clients in the form of a three-year growth commitment to national organisations as follows:

- 1993 – 10 organisations
- 1994 – 50 organisations
- 1995 – 75 organisations
- 1997 – 100 organisations.

iii. To provide fully integrated funding support on a one-stop-shop annual basis as follows:

- 1993 – 10 organisations
- 1994 – 30 organisations
- 1995 – 50 organisations.

The Commission also provides funds to national organisations on the basis of planned development and clear objectives. Much of the dollar contribution supports management, administration, training, coaching and marketing operations.

Sadly, however, there can be little dispute that the impact of national funding is negligible at local level. Monetary 'trickle down' to club level – and ultimately the participants – is ad hoc, and in many cases non-existent. In fact, while progress in the professionalism of sport and leisure management has been made, there is a noticeable chasm between national organisations and regional clubs and associations. It is in this area that regional sports trusts could effectively act as intermediary bodies, advising and guiding grass root sport and leisure groups on general criteria. This might include human resource management, volunteer training, public relations and strategic planning. Sports trusts are like charitable trusts which adhere to the Hillary Commission philosophy of improving quality of life through sport and leisure. As such they have huge potential but have been under-utilised.

Review

The Hillary Commission evidently has no intention of limiting itself to the coordination, development, funding and liaison tasks of sport organisations. Rather with the recent publication of a draft strategic plan (Hillary Commission, 1993) it sets out a bold eight-point plan with 42 specific target objectives which it intends to implement in the next five years. Its intention is to provide the nation with well-organised structures for sport, fitness and leisure. The structure will offer a continuum of progression for participants, from initiation to the level of their choice and ability. More particularly, and expressed in fulsome terms, the Commission has identified the following visions for the future:

- Vision One – Education. A nation with high levels of sport and leisure literacy, i.e. the lifelong interests, skills and attitudes that lead to active lifestyles.
- Vision Two – Active Lifestyles. A nation of participants choosing active lifestyles through sport and leisure.
- Vision Three – Achievement and Excellence. A nation of people achieving to the level of their ability in the sport or leisure of their choice.
- Vision Four – International Success. A successful sporting nation taking pride in its achievements.
- Vision Five – Great Outdoors. A nation of people enriched by experiences in natural surroundings.
- Vision Six – Successful Organisations. A nation with well-organised structures for sport, fitness and leisure that offer a continuum of progression for participants from foundation levels to the level of their choice and ability.
- Vision Seven – Active Communities. Communities with access to active living opportunities.

- Vision Eight – Volunteer Involvement. Communities volunteering their help for sport and leisure in ways that are rewarding for all concerned.

It should be noted that a special strength of New Zealand's sport, fitness and leisure structure has been the access to the country's education system (see Chapter 6). This relationship is a point of envy for many overseas counterparts, and hopefully it will be further enhanced during the next decade.

Overall, a nation with well organised structures for sport fitness and leisure is a tangible goal (Hillary Commission, 1993). Such aspirations can only lift the ability, commitment, and endeavours of all people at all levels of any multifaceted organisation, and enhance the performance and satisfactions of participants, funders, sponsors, spectators, and administrators. However, it has to be remembered that ultimately any such benefits will accrue only to organisations whose structures and processes are expressed in modern managerial terms. The hope is that people in all spheres of sport, and in all states and phases of its operation will feel impelled to learn and to apply the lessons of successful business management. Towards that end this chapter is dedicated.

Review Questions

1. Identify an organisational structure that can be classified either as emanating from top-down or bottom-up. Perhaps it is a mixture of both. Does the organisation function satisfactorily or could it be more efficient and effective?
2. In accordance with the Koopman-Boyden (1991) five-stage model of the growth of organisational structures, describe those of a sports organisation with which you are familiar, and analyse its areas of responsibility, staff composition, managerial decision making and procedure.
3. Examine the eight visions outlined in the Hillary Commission's five-year strategic plan. Now formulate your own strategies to achieve each vision through specific targets. Upon completion of your plan, compare to the original documentation and explain variances and the reasons for them.

References

Hillary Commission (1991), *Review of Hillary Commission's Support for Recreation and Sport at the Local Level*, Hillary Commission: Wellington.

Hillary Commission (1993), *Moving a Nation, Draft Strategic Plan for 1993-1997*, Hillary Commission: Wellington.

Jensen, B., Sullivan, C., Wilson, N., Berkeley, M. and Russell, D. (1993), *The Business of Sport and Leisure: The Economic Importance of Sport and Leisure in New Zealand*, Wellington: Hillary Commission.

Koopman-Boyden, P. (1991), 'Volunteering in the 1990s', *Social Work Review*, Vol 4, pp.14-18.

Smith, K.S. (1992), *Observation of Sports Administration and Activities – United Kingdom, Norway, Sweden, Switzerland, Canada*, Hillary Commission: Wellington

Sports Development Inquiry (1985), *Sport on the Move*, Report to the Minister of Recreation and Sport, Wellington: Government Print.

part two

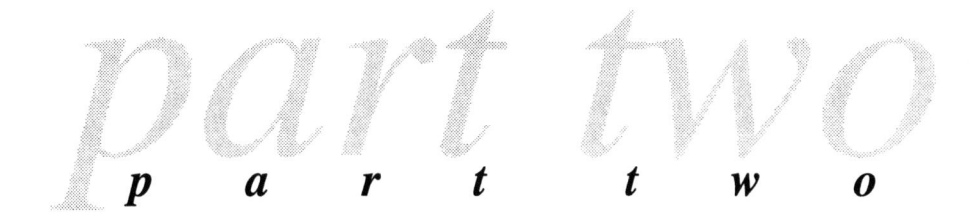

The Practice of Managing Sport

A Competency-based Approach to Sport Management

Linda Trenberth

In this chapter you will become familiar with the following terms:

competency

competency-based approach

commercialisation

management functions

Introduction

New Zealand has always been regarded as a sporting nation, and the enormous demand for sport in this country has developed a strong tradition of involvement in and support for sport at all levels. Historically, the management of sport has been essentially based on a voluntary structure, and were this not the case, sport would not have survived, (see Chapter 12). However, with the proliferation of sport opportunities and the commercialisation of many forms of sport during the 1970s and '80s, notions of how to effectively and efficiently manage a sport organisation have undergone marked and profound changes. Today sporting organisations must justify their operations to consumers and sponsors (public and private) and therefore must respond in a more professional, business-like manner. The economic pressures and commercialisation of sport have put an emphasis on reducing deficits and improving the management of facilities, clubs and associations, and programmes, whereas in earlier times much effort was put forth by volunteers towards increasing participation numbers and improving the skills of athletes, coaches, officials, sport administrators and managers. Political (see Chapter 3), legal (see Chapter 19), and social (see

Chapter 2) factors have also influenced the changing roles of sport managers (Cuneen, 1992; Hogg, 1989). Sport has been rapidly transformed into a major business activity worldwide. According to Karlin (1988), in Britain, and no doubt the world over, sport businesses are looking for quality sport management graduates instead of the retired athlete.

This chapter will address the changing nature of the sport industry in relation to the competencies now required of sport personnel to enable them to deal with the variety of circumstances that they might encounter in the management and administration of a sporting business. Competency will be defined, research studies relating to competencies of sport managers overseas and in New Zealand summarised, and the new set of skills required of personnel in the sport industry will be outlined.

Competency Defined

Competency is the knowledge, skill and attitude needed to carry out an activity successfully in professional life (Butler, 1978). In management those competencies are the characteristics, traits or skills that a person possesses and uses in their job. Smale, Luyks-Ledgerwood (1989) and Cyrs, Dobbert and Grussing (cited in Anschel and Webb, 1990) go further to include the intellectual, attitudinal and performance capabilities derived from a specified role and setting. Shuttleworth (1990), for his part, defines competence as the standards an employee undertakes at work and the skills and knowledge required to fulfil them effectively. McClearly (cited in Zeigler, Bowie and Paris, 1988) defines competency as the 'presence of characteristics (or the absence of disabilities) which render a person fit, or qualified, to perform a specified task or to assume a defined role. To be competent is to possess sufficient knowledge and ability to meet specified requirements in the sense of being able, adequate, suitable and capable'.

A competency-based approach not only focuses on the acquisition of knowledge, but also on the ability of an individual to demonstrate competence in the tasks which comprise a professional role (Bradley, cited in Zeigler, Bowie and Paris, 1988).

Whilst not identical, these definitions do identify the components of traits, skills, knowledge and attitudes as attributes of the term competency. Although competence standards, that is the standards to which tasks have to be performed, are not identified here, areas of competence specific to the occupation of sport management will be discussed. In particular, an attempt will be made to understand the functions, roles and skills required to effectively conduct the business of sport organisations.

Competencies are manifested through the activities which make up the four most widely recognised functions of effective management: *planning* (see Chapter 10), *organising* (see Chapters 7, and 12), *directing* (see Chapter 13) and *controlling* (see Chapters 11 and 19).

Planning requires competencies in such diverse managerial activities as budgeting, marketing, policy making, and research. Organising – the way in which plans are put into action – involves competencies tied to the selection and management of personnel and other resources to meet declared objectives, and it includes job analysis, organisation structure, scheduling, recruiting and performance appraisal. Dimensions of management competency can be seen in Table 8.1. Directing requires the ability to guide and motivate the organisation towards the achievement of goals and objectives, and it involves competencies such as communication, leadership, motivational skills and working with groups. Controlling ensures that things happen as they were intended, and consequently, it requires the ability to measure current performance against expected outcomes.

Table 8.1: Dimensions of management competency.

Dimension	Description
Planner	Competencies which involve the identification, formulation, and the defining of goals, plans, and objectives pertaining to an organisation.
Evaluator	Competencies which involve various aspects of the evaluation processes pertaining to an organisation.
Educator	Competencies which involve various educational aspects pertaining to the needs of the personnel within the organisation.
Fiscal Officer	Competencies which involve various aspects of the monetary processes pertaining to an organisation.
Leader	Competencies which pertain to the directing and coordinating of tasks within an organisation.
Communicator	Competencies which involve the preparation and delivery of information, both within and outside an organisation.

(Zeigler, Bowie and Paris, 1988)

In turn this involves competency in evaluating, financial record-keeping, information processing, legal knowledge, and coordination.

Here it has to be said that although much has been written about the competencies linked to these principal management functions, in general little attention, and even less research has been devoted to the competencies required of sport management in particular.

Competencies for Sport Managers

Shuttleworth (1990), in a survey undertaken for the Hillary Commission, examined the general areas of competency specific to sport management, with students and managers respectively.

First, the responses of the physical education and recreation administration students were obtained with regard to the competencies not adequately catered for in their programmes. The results, expressed in rank order, showed the need for their training programmes to include human resource management (communication skills), public relations, media skills, marketing and sponsorship, and financial management (Table 8.2). They underscore the point that New Zealand programmes have been remiss in their exclusion of essential business and management skills.

Table 8.2: Shows the responses of students to perceived inadequacies in their courses.

Competencies under-provided	%
- Human resource management (communication skills)	60
- Public relations, publicity, media skills	50
- Marketing and sponsorship	50
- Financial management	50
- Planning	30
- General management	30
- Administration	30
- Practica/Internship	20

(Shuttleworth, 1990)

The comparative opinions were then obtained from professional executive directors, selected chairpersons of National Sport Organisations and commercial agencies. The results showed that marketing, business planning, accounting and financial management, and general management were ranked the highest (Table 8.3) requirements for executive directors.

Table 8.3: Shows the responses of Executive Directors to competencies their job requires.

Competencies	Rank
- Marketing	1
- Business planning	2
- Accounting and financial management	3
- General management	4
- Economics	5
- Sport science	6
- Human resource management	7
- Leisure and recreation theory	8

(Shuttleworth, 1990)

In more detail:

- *Marketing* – was identified as the area requiring greatest emphasis in any training programme (over 60 per cent). This reflects the current emphasis at the time resulting from media attention, sponsorship requirements, and falling participation rates. It also indicates the input of the commercial sector to the sport industry.

- *Business planning* – was marginally second (55 per cent), reflecting the requirements of public and private sponsors for rigorously prepared management plans prior to grant-aiding or sponsorship.

- *Accounting and financial management* – (45 per cent) reflected the increased accountability for spending and control in all National Sport Organisations.

- *General management* – did not achieve as high a rating (35 per cent) as was expected and generally thought to be required. The result suggested that the respondents perceived technical skills to be more important than conceptual or human skills.

- *Economics* – the 30 per cent was higher than might be expected, in view of the theoretical nature of the topic in contrast to its direct applicability to the immediate requirements of management.

- *Human resource management* – the relatively low 15 per cent showed an obvious lack of appreciation by managers at the time of the needs of staff and volunteers on whom sport in the private and public sectors depend.

- *Sport science and leisure theory* – the mention of these factors by 15 per cent and 20 per cent respectively, reflected a failure of managers to appreciate the need for basic conceptual skills in disciplines which underpin their sport organisations.

Finally, comparable opinions were obtained from chairpersons and student managers on Executive Director requirements (Table 8.4). Here the results largely reinforce those of the Executive Directors, with one marked inconsistency, that of marketing.

Table 8.4: The perceptions of chairpersons and student sport managers to competencies required for Executive Directors.

a. Executive Director Functions	Chairpersons	Students
- Policy Implementation	1	3=
- Administration	2=	2
- Policy Advice	2=	0
- Programme Development and Implementation	4	3=
- Policy Formulation	5	5
- Marketing, Promotion, Sponsorship	0	1
b. Competencies		
- Business Planning	1=	4=
- Human Resource Management	1=	1
- Accounting and Financial Management	3=	3
- Marketing	3=	2
- Sports Science	5	6
- Economics	6	8
- Leisure and Recreation Theory	7	7

(Shuttleworth, 1990)

Except for business planning, the results of these groups correspond closely. For example, both rated competency in human resources management high, and both rated sport science, economics, leisure and recreation theory low. It could be that such a spread reflected the growing importance attached to the introduction of business methods into the sport industry at the time, at the expense of the traditional Arts and Science subjects which were the mainstay of early sport-orientated programmes.

Similar trends were noticed by studies overseas. For example, Parks and Quain (1986) surveyed sport practitioners in the six careers of physical fitness, sport promotions, sport marketing, sport administration and management, sport directing, and aquatics management in the United States. But instead of asking the subjects to nominate the competencies they thought were required by sport managers, they provided them with a list of eight and were asked to indicate which of them were relevant for their careers. Although groups were of uneven size and the researchers did not weight the responses accordingly, their results (Table 8.5) showed that human relations, personnel management and time management were the competencies the groups rated most essential, and finance management, knowledge of sports, and personal fitness the least essential of the eight options provided.

Table 8.5: The competencies and ranking per career category of 365 sports practitioners in six career groups in the United States.

Competency	N=	PFI 55	SP 49	SMKTG 39	SAM 82	SD 81	AQM 59	Total 365
Writing		5	1	1	4	6	7	4
Personnel management		3	6	2.5	2	3	1.7	2
Public speaking		6	2	2	6	7	6	5
Time management		4	4	3.5	5	5	3	3
Finance management		7	2	6	3	4	4	6
Human relations		2	3	5	1	1	1.5	1
Personal fitness		1	8	8	8	8	5	8
Knowledge of sports		8	5	7	7	2	8	7

PFI = Physical fitness industry; SP = Sport promotion; SMKTG = Sport marketing; SAM = Sport administration and management; SD = Sport directing; AQM = Aquatics management

(Parkhouse, 1991)

Lambrecht (1987) identified 33 competencies required to manage sport and athletic clubs, and tried to determine whether sub-groups of different sizes of the International Racquet Sports Association had different requirements among them. The sub-groups in effect were local clubs classified according to membership size. Group I had 500-999 members, Group II 1,000-2,000 members, and Group III had more than 2,000 members. The top 10 competencies rated by the total sample and the three club group classifications show a remarkable uniformity (Table 8.6). The results this time ranked the competency needs in human relations above those required for skills in business and evidently far ahead of the unreported competencies that were at the tail-end of the list of 33 provided.

Table 8.6: Showing the competencies and rankings for three groups of different sizes.

Competency	Total sample	I	II	III
Communication with clientele	1	1	1	1
Employee motivation	2	3.5	3	2
Handling complaints of customers	3	3.5	2	4
Staff communications	4	2	4	3
Decision-making process	5	5	5	5
Supervision of staff and personnel	6.5	7.5	7	6
Evaluation of club as a business	6.5	7.5	6	7
Time management	8	6	8	9
Strategic planning	9	10	9	10
Budget preparation	10	11	11	8

(Mean rankings across columns I, II, III)

(Parkhouse, 1991)

Then Farmer (cited in Parkhouse, 1991) utilised the same competency instrument designed by Lambrecht to survey members of the Australian Society of Sport Administrators (ASSA). This time the top 10 of the list of 33 competencies placed the emphasis squarely upon competencies in the managerial functions of communication, decision making and budget preparation, closely followed by those of writing, programme preparation and development and strategic planning (Table 8.7).

Table 8.7: Shows the rank order of competencies of sports administrators of ASSA.

Competency	Rank
Communication	1
Decision making	2
Budget preparation	3
Writing skills	4
Program preparation and development	5
Strategic planning	6
Time management	7
Programme goals and objectives	8
Marketing	9
Legal liability	10

(Parkhouse, 1991)

Finally, a study was carried out by Tait, Richins and Hanlon (1993) to identify and compare management training knowledge and skill priorities of sport, recreation and tourism managers. In lists of the highest and lowest knowledge and skill priorities for each of the three fields of tourism, recreation and sport, only one – communications ability – was rated as a maximum priority by all three fields. Table 8.8 (over page) shows a breakdown of responses on the prioritisation of management skills for sport managers. The study identified a greater number of similarities as compared to differences amongst sport, tourism and recreation managers' knowledge and skill priorities and begs the suggestion that it would be worthwhile considering the feasibility of introducing a common core management programme in tertiary institutions, with specialist strands in sport, tourism and recreation.

In considering the different studies, the variations of outcome, whether major or minor, are of less importance than the fact that they reflect the needs of particular populations of embryo and mature sport managers at a given time. They show that the need for business competencies is well recognised, and it follows that university training courses in the field of sport, recreation, and leisure were wise to meet the need – notwithstanding the evidence that in contemporary academia there are diverse views on what is essential, peripheral and unnecessary knowledge and skill in sport, tourism and recreation management (Tait, Richins and Hanlon, 1993). All three fields are widely acknowledged as having considerable economic, political and social impact (Jensen, Sullivan, Wilson, Berkeley and Russell, 1993), and all three are expected to operate in a fiscally secure manner in an increasingly demanding environment.

Table 8.8: Perceived sport training needs. Highest and lowest knowledge and skill priorities for sport managers. Percentage of respondents indicating importance.

High level importance	Percentage of respondents	Low level importance	Percentage of respondents
Organising	100.0	Survey analysis	40.0
Leadership	100.0	Research methods	40.0
Public relations	100.0	Merchandising	40.0
Communication ability	100.0	Financing of Aust. tourism industry	40.0
Group dynamics	100.0	Structure of Aust. tourism industry	40.0
Conflict resolution	100.0	Work with people/participants in tourism	40.0
Planning	93.5	Psychological concepts	36.0
Understanding financial statements	93.0	Compensation law	33.5
Practical experience in sport	92.3	Supply/demand analysis	33.5
Methods of evaluation	87.0	Workplace influences	33.5
Employee responsibility	87.0	Survey design	33.0
Value and function of networking	87.0	Structure of Aust. recreation industry	33.0
Customer service	87.0	Equipment purchase	30.0
Problem solving	86.5	Trust and trustees	28.5
Marketing	86.0	Statistical methods	27.0
Current issues and trends	85.5	Group/individual dynamics in tourism	25.0
Decision making	82.5	Retailing	20.0
Practical experience in recreation	82.0	Teaching activities in tourism	17.0
Working with people in recreation	80.0	Practical experience in tourism	17.0
Event organising	80.0	Qualifications/certificate in tourism	12.5
Liability	80.0		
Self evaluation	80.0		
Self confidence	80.0		
Effective writing skills	80.0		
Dealing with customers/participants	80.0		

Industry Changes

There is general agreement that commercialisation has made sport become more or less closely linked to market forces (Maguire, 1990), and to meet the demands of this dominant movement, dedicated volunteers are being replaced by business oriented managers who are influenced by management theory, administrative strategies and concern for the balance sheet (Shuttleworth, 1990). In New Zealand, the governing boards of sport organisations are known to have few trained executives at present, but they do have large and unwieldy boards, extensive regional and provincial administration networks and thousands of volunteers (officials, coaches and administrators), members and affiliates. Generally they are under-resourced, and subjected to an increasing demand for effective and efficient management in a commercially-driven, government grant-aided environment. Shuttleworth (1990) found that the competencies and qualifications of the executive directors were limited to a technical knowledge of the operations of particular sports, to service delivery (coaching and teaching) and to a long record of local service to an organisation, particularly at the national level.

The traditional competencies required by sport coaches and physical educators were in the main based upon experiential knowledge, which it was assumed could be transferred successfully to sport management. But since the recent advent of the liaison of sport science and business, and the leadership of business schools via the professional preparation of sport managers, such experience alone is insufficient. Instead the emphasis has shifted to the specific competencies of human communication, conceptual and technical skills and to the categories of procedural, fiscal, health and safety, and facility management. Human skills are those skills used in the understanding of human perceptions, attitudes and behaviours, and adjusting one's own behaviours accordingly (Katz cited in Parkhouse, 1991). Katz describes conceptual skills as those that go towards understanding the organisation as a whole, how its own parts fit together, how the total organisation meshes with the economies, social and political realities. Technical skills are those skills involving methods, procedures, or techniques associated with the tasks of the organisation. Such skills are commonly found in business management, but they are new to the sport industry and they are effecting changes.

One such change is the emphasis now being placed on business management and accountability for funds. For example, the Hillary Commission provides funds to National Sport Organisations on the basis of planned development and clear objectives (*Draft Strategic Plan*, 1993, p.14) and as a provider it regards the business focus as critical to economic self sufficiency. Yet such a focus was foreign previously to many well-intentioned volunteers and it has required them to retrain for competency in management and administration.

For this reason the Hillary Commission *Draft Strategic Plan* for 1993-1997 adopted the strategy of investing in professional development throughout its sector for national level volunteer administrators, coaches and officials. It regards effective administration and management as a key requirement for the development of successful sport organisations.

Consequently the advent of the business orientation heralds major changes in the sport industry that require personnel to develop a new set of skills and a new business line and entrepreneurial attitude to:

- the promotion and running of sport events, with associated media coverage, and sponsorships;
- the import and export of personnel, goods, and services;
- the accountability within clubs and associations, with particular regard to obtaining and utilising government funds and encouraging private investment;
- sporting and leisure facilities being managed on a far more competitive and commercial level under the pressure of increasing economic constraints;
- the need to report to executive committees or boards of management with a clear picture of operations in order to obtain endorsement/approval for areas of need.

With the increasing emphasis on commercialisation, efficiency, accountability and structured work practices, the employment of professional, trained staff rather than volunteers is an emerging trend. It is often difficult to hold volunteers accountable for particular tasks (see Chapter 12). Therefore, increasingly it is seen advisable for sport organisations to employ paid staff. This creates the need for organisations to have staff with special management skills to obtain the desired result without putting pressure or heavy expectations on volunteers, and thus risking losing them. In addition, personnel need to be sensitive to the reasons and the personal satisfactions that volunteers derive from their voluntary participation in sport.

Conclusion

The key skills required to perform the role of sport manager effectively and efficiently are the conceptual, technical and human skills of business management that have been identified in this chapter. The leisure field in general is growing quickly, and the public, private and voluntary sectors need to upgrade their management skills to match those of the commercial sector. Sport needs well-trained and motivated managers at all levels in response to clients demand for a higher standard of service than previously they were prepared to accept from volunteers. As sport management is a field that has not yet received total acceptance among scholarly disciplines, it is of utmost importance that a competency-based approach to management training in sport be encouraged.

Review Questions

1. What does the term competency mean and how does the use of the concept help in understanding the field of sport management?
2. Are competencies specific to particular settings of sport management or can they be generalised across settings?
3. What does an analysis of competencies over time tell us about the development and evolution of sport management?

References

Anschel, M. and Webb, P. (1990), 'Model for Determining and Evaluating Competencies in Sport', in *Management and Sport Conference Proceedings*, Vol 1, pp.49-60, Canberra: Centre for Sports Studies.

Butler, F. (1978), 'The Concept of Competence: An Operational Definition', *Educational Technology*, Vol 18, pp.307-321.

Cuneen, J. (1992), 'Graduate-Level Professional Preparation for Athletic Directors', *Journal of Sport Management*, Vol 6, No 1, pp.17-20.

Curriculum Research and Development Unit (1989), *Sport and Recreation Industry Training Needs Analysis*, Victoria: Frankston College TAFE.

Hillary Commission for Sport, Fitness and Leisure (1993), *Moving a Nation – Draft Strategic Plan 1993-1997*, Wellington: Hillary Commission for Sport, Fitness and Leisure.

Hogg, D. (1989), 'Professional Development Needs of Sports Administrators', Canberra University, Management and Sport Biennial Conference, Vol 1.

Jensen, B., Sullivan, C., Wilson, N., Berkeley, M. and Russell, D. (1993), *The Business of Sport and Leisure Report*, Wellington: Hillary Commission for Sport, Fitness and Leisure.

Karlin, L. (April 1988), 'A Class Compendium', *Sports Incorporated*, pp.42.

Lambrecht, K. (1987), 'An Analysis of the Competencies of Sport and Athletic Club Managers', *Journal of Sport Management*, Vol 1, No 2, pp.116-128.

Maguire, J. (1990), 'The Commercialisation of Sport and Athletes Rights', in Kew, R. (ed.), *Social Science Perspectives on Sport*, Britain: British Association of Sports Sciences.

Parkhouse, B. (1991), *The Management of Sport: Its Foundation and Application*, St Louis, M.O.: Mosby Year Book.

Parks, J. and Quain, R. (1986), 'Curriculum Perspectives', *Journal of Physical Education, Recreation and Dance*, Vol 57, No 4, pp.22-26.

Shuttleworth, J. (1990), *Sport Management Professional Preparation in New Zealand*, Wellington: Hillary Commission.

Smale, B. and Luyks-Ledgerwood, D. (1989), 'A Case Study of the Management Competencies of Municipal Recreationists', *Recreation Research Review*, Vol 14, No 3, pp.51-58.

Tait, R. (1989), 'Study and Employment in Sport and Fitness'. Paper presented at the conference in Management and Sport, Canberra.

Tait, R., Richins, H. and Hanlon, C. (1993), 'Perceived Training Needs in Sport, Tourism and Recreation Management', *Australian Journal of Leisure and Recreation*, Vol 3, No 1, pp.12-26.

Zeigler, E.F., Bowie, G.W., Paris, R.H. (1988), *Competency Development in Sport and Physical Education Management: A Primer*, Champaign, Illinois: Stipes Publishing Company.

Suggested Reading

Chelladurai, P. (1985), *Sport Management: Macro Perspectives*, London, Ontario: Sports Dynamics.

Farmer, P.J. (1989), 'A Model Curriculum for Sport Administration at Tertiary Institutions in Australia', *Arena Review*, Vol 4, No 3, pp.1-10.

Jamieson, L. (1987), 'Contemporary-based Approaches to Sport Management', *Journal of Sport Management*, Vol 1, No 1, pp.48-56.

Mullin, B.J. (1980), 'Sport Management: The Nature and Utility of the Concept', *Arena Review*, Vol 4, No 3, pp.1-10.

Slack, J. (1991), 'Sport Management: Some Thoughts for Future Directions', *Journal of Sports Management*, Vol 5, pp.95-99.

Tait, R., Richins, H. and Hanlon, C. (1993), 'Perceived Training Needs in Sport, Tourism and Recreation Management', *Australian Journal of Leisure and Recreation*, Vol 3, No 1, pp.12-26.

Zeigler, E. (1987), 'Sport Management: Past, Present, Future', *Journal of Sport Management*, Vol 1, No 1, pp.4-25.

The Well-managed National Sport Organisation

Deborah Battell

In this chapter you will become familiar with the following terms:

National Sporting Organisations

well-managed organisations

culture

outputs-based accounting

stakeholders

structure

strategic management

Introduction

In considering National Sporting Organisations (NSOs), none stands out as being the model of a well-managed organisation. A number of NSOs, however, have managed aspects of their operations well, and these will be illustrated in this chapter.

To be really well-managed, NSOs need to be strategically managed to ensure that they have appropriate strategies, structures, systems, management styles, people and values, and that they meet the needs of all stakeholders, i.e. the players, spectators, sponsors, supporters, administrators.

In this chapter it will be argued that an organisation is more likely to achieve its desired results if it is well managed, and that while there is no magic formula for good management, there are basic management principles and practices to be followed which will enhance an organisation's prospects for success.

The principles and practices derive from the author's experience of reviewing the performance and management of twelve organisations in the sport and recreation sectors, as well as from reviewing a considerable number of organisations in the public, private, and voluntary sectors.

The objective of this chapter is to help all those involved in managing sport, and NSOs in particular, to identify opportunities to improve their management skills so that their chances of success are improved.

The Importance of Good Management

As one recent television series was entitled, sport is now 'more than just a game'. It is more than achievement for the players on the field. It has become a business, and therefore it has to be well managed simply to survive. The survival of NSOs, and indeed sports, has been jeopardised by a range of factors, including competition from the myriad of new sports which have emerged, for example touch, and parapenting, and from a wide range of other recreation, entertainment and leisure pursuits.

Sport has also been affected by the downturn in the economy which has prevailed since the mid-1980s. Increasing unemployment and falling incomes have made for difficulties at all levels in recruiting and retaining volunteer organisers, and in encouraging players. The effects have been felt throughout sport, from bar-takings to subscriptions and gate-takings, and sponsors being more discriminating and less generous except for major events.

Such factors as these challenge the management skills of all those involved in sport, and they call for professional management skills to ensure that a sport not only survives, but thrives.

What is a Successful Organisation?

NSOs are more likely to be successful if they are well-managed, set appropriate goals and objectives, and have gone about achieving them systematically within a predetermined timetable. Figure 9.1 below depicts the central thesis of this chapter.

Figure 9.1 Influence of Management

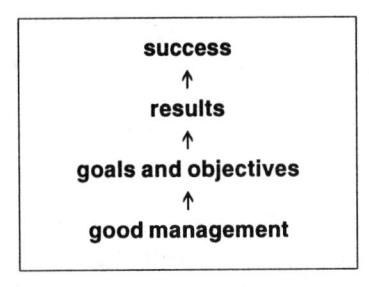

```
        success
           ↑
        results
           ↑
   goals and objectives
           ↑
      good management
```

In other words, a well-managed organisation will define good goals and objectives, which will in turn lead to results and finally to success (Thompson and Strickland, 1992). Good management may not be the only determinant of success – other factors, such as luck, the weather, and politics can play a part (as New Zealand Cricket can testify only too well after the terrorist incident during the 1993 tour to Sri Lanka) – but it is a major determinant over which there can be some degree of control.

The above statement is significant in that it does not necessarily refer to winning national and international championships, or surviving financially, or increasing the number of active participants and spectators. It simply declares that for the organisation to be successful it must achieve its goals and objectives. This assumes that goals and objectives have been set, that they are appropriate, and that the means and strategies by which they can be achieved are in place.

What is Good Management?

So what constitutes good management, and what does a well-managed organisation do? If there were just one recipe for good management, someone or perhaps everyone would be very successful at it. Unfortunately, there are as many ways of managing well as making a good stew! Based on experience and observation of successful organisations, however, a number of good management principles and practices can be distilled and they will be described in the following sections. Again it has to be said that there is no perfect model, but examples will be taken from a number of organisations where parts have been seen to work well. It also has to be said that management does not refer solely to the role of paid staff. Volunteers also have a valuable role to play and NSOs could not operate without them (see Chapter 12). They are also under tremendous pressures from their other obligations, and part of the managerial task therefore is to ensure that all stakeholders – i.e. interested parties such as staff, volunteers, affiliated association members, sponsors, funders, players, coaches, etc. – are not only able to contribute, but are able to do so in a way which enables the organisation to achieve its goals and objectives, and spreads a sense of achievement and satisfaction to all concerned.

The Game Plan

Managing well means managing strategically, and managing strategically means:

- taking a longer-term (more than three-year) view;
- identifying where the organisation in question has an advantage over competitors (including other sporting and leisure pursuits) (Porter, 1985);
- overcoming weaknesses and threats;
- taking advantage of, and building upon strengths and opportunities;
- addressing the factors which are critical for success, e.g. media coverage, star performers, successful teams, depth of talent; and
- ensuring that the organisation's systems, structure, values, management style, staff and skills support the strategy.

The well-managed NSO will have a vision which is encompassed in a strategic plan (see Chapter 10). In the case of cricket, for example, the vision is to have every New Zealander participating in some way. A vision such as this enables administrators to consider how all the groups in our society could be involved, e.g. as spectators, as television viewers/radio listeners, as family groups playing on the beach, as Pacific Islanders playing kilikiti, as school children playing kiwicricket, as élite players, administrators, and sponsors. It commits the organisation to actions, and although the efforts and plans have their detractors, there are also a number of success stories. The most well-publicised story is that of the New Zealand Golf Association that began in 1986 with an internal review which resulted in a paper entitled *In Search of Success* (Clements, 1986).

The paper identified five prime areas upon which the Association needed to concentrate. These were to:

- give opportunities for as many New Zealanders as possible to play the game of golf;
- make golfing clubs efficient and financially viable;
- improve playing surfaces of golf courses;
- improve the profile of the game in the media;
- succeed at national and international competitions.

Projects were attached to each of these goals as well as targets. The Association set itself a target of winning the 1992 Eisenhower Trophy and went about this by identifying and coaching 14-15 year olds. The rest is history – the Eisenhower was won, and this has had a tremendous flow-on effect enabling the Association to better achieve its other four goals. From this it can be seen that strategic plans are very useful for a number of reasons. For example, they:

- provide a means of communicating to members, players, volunteers and staff what the national body will be doing, and what it expects to achieve;
- form a 'contract' with funding bodies – i.e. for funders and sponsors to see what they are purchasing, and that their money is going to an organisation which is managed in a professional way;
- enable the organisation to demonstrate achievement of results. This in turn helps organisations more easily to justify continued or increased levels of funding;
- help focus the effort of all those involved in the sport, and motivate them towards achieving results;
- provide a means of holding key staff and volunteers accountable.

One exercise which really gets a planning session going is to ask participants why they are working for their particular sport – why, for example, cricket and not swimming? And why are they spending so much time on it? What are they really trying to do? Is it, for example, to keep the game of cricket and the values it represents alive? The responses often disclose a surprising amount of passion from people who are normally reserved!

Managing well also means ensuring that the organisation is clear about what it is doing. This involves being quite clear about its role, i.e. how it adds value to its current and future stakeholders. It also involves, to use the current jargon, identifying the organisation's outputs, i.e. the goods and services it produces. Typical examples of outputs for NSOs include:

- coaching and development;
- administration of competitions;
- administration of grants to affiliated clubs/members;
- management of national teams; and
- promotion of the game.

Achievement of results implies that targets have been determined. These targets are known by a number of labels – mission statements, outcomes, goals, and objectives are the most common, and will be explained in Chapter 10 on strategic planning. In brief, there are four main types of targets:

- long term;
- short term;
- outward looking (external); and
- inward looking (internal)

(Thompson and Strickland, 1992).

Mission and 'outcome' statements tend to be long term and more outward looking. A mission statement is the ultimate outcome or goal for an organisation, and states its purpose. The word outcome is used here as in the financial management reforms which have been taking place in the public sector, i.e. the desired impact on society (Treasury, 1989). For example, the mission statement from the Water Safety Council is 'To prevent/reduce drowning within New Zealand'. As such, it makes absolutely clear why the Water Safety Council exists and how it aims to benefit society. It is the kind of mission which is much more likely to motivate staff than some of the more staid and nebulous statements of purpose which have been produced in the past.

There are differences between goals and objectives. For example:

Goals are fairly long term (say 3-5 years or longer), and can be both externally and internally orientated. An example of goals from the Surf Life Saving Association's plan is shown below:

- to reduce and prevent drownings and accidents at beaches and water-related events;
- to increase community awareness of beach safety; and
- to encourage care for the beach and coastal environment.

Objectives tend to be shorter term (say 1-2 years), and are the milestones along the way towards achieving goals. Good objectives are defined as being SMART – i.e. specific, measurable, achievable, realistic and timebound. They should also address those factors which are critical to the success of the organisation and they should be challenging. They should not merely state what the organisation does. For example, five of New Zealand Cricket's objectives are:

- to double the number of women players by 1995/96;
- to increase accumulated funds by 15 per cent by 1995/96;
- to increase financial assistance to affiliated associations by 25 per cent by 1995/96;
- to win the next men's and women's World Cup; and
- to increase attendance at matches by 25 per cent by 1995/96.

Note that in the case of New Zealand Cricket, performance measures have been embedded in objectives. However, Surf Life Saving have separated their objectives and performance measures – for example:

Objective

- To ensure all clubs are strong, viable and efficient.

Performance Measures

- All clubs are using beach management plans by 1995.
- All clubs are carrying out contracted patrols by 1994.

Publishing a plan is a sensible way of focusing the attention of those who will be judged by it. Once these people realise that they are responsible for achieving the stated objectives and performance measures, they have a tendency to respond in two ways – they try to remove specific activities or objectives, or they begin to move out the dates! Both these responses might be perfectly valid, but they might also be adopted by those who wish to avoid being held accountable. In particular those who simply repeat the responsibilities contained in their job descriptions rather than list their specific projects or improvements, could be stagnating.

A good planning system for NSOs will most likely include:

- Participation and commitment of staff and a range of affiliates and volunteers. This is essential if a plan is to be successfully implemented. Involve those who are critical because they can help to bring about more improvements than those who either agree with everything or do not contribute.
- External input. NSOs would find it useful to have an external facilitator at their planning workshops who can both challenge thinking and run an enjoyable session.
- Linked budgets. Budgets should be based upon intentions, and reflect strategic priorities. Too often, budgets are prepared in isolation from the plan, and even in advance of its preparation.
- Opportunities to review and alter a plan. A plan is simply a way of measuring whether a new strategic option or course of action is better than the previous method of operating.
- Specific performance measures. These performance measures will be both qualitative and quantitative, and they will assist in evaluating the efficiency, economy and effectiveness of the plan.
- Operational plans. These are sometimes called business plans, or annual plans, and they differ from strategic plans in that they have a shorter-term horizon. They are the means by which individuals or groups within the organisation state how they are going to contribute to the achievement of the strategic plan. This requires them to produce operational plans which state their objectives, the actions they will take to achieve them, who is responsible, who approves them, when they will be complete, and how much they are expected to cost. In New Zealand Tennis, for example, operational plans were prepared for the following areas: coaching, representation of New Zealand, management, ground authorities, umpires, marketing, associations, and development of the game in New Zealand.
- Linked marketing and/or revenue-raising plans. Organisations often fail to state how they are going to meet their financial targets but marketing plans should identify the organisations intended to be targeted for sponsorship, methods for raising the profile, promotion and pricing strategies for public attendance at games and merchandise, how sponsors/funders will be serviced, how the sport will be positioned relative to other sports or competing recreational pursuits, and how the sport will be developed.
- Linked human resource and information systems plans. Note that it is not necessary to have large amounts of information technology but it is important that decision makers are presented with high-quality, timely, and accurate information with which to make decisions.

Strategic plans must be useful for an organisation, and used by it, instead of being simply produced to meet the requirements of funders. One NSO was even adamant in stating that planning had no place in its organisation. It was no surprise that this NSO was experiencing difficulty with recruitment and retention of members.

Plans are often also used as a tool for evaluating effectiveness and efficiency. Effectiveness is the extent to which the organisation has achieved its objectives (either stated or unstated), and the extent to which it has benefited the New Zealand public. By efficiency is meant what the organisation achieves with its funding – i.e. the outputs it produces for the inputs it receives. Funders and sponsors like to know that the money they have given to NSOs is being used effectively and efficiently. They are particularly interested in ensuring that the funding meets their own goals and objectives, as well as those of the NSO. Typically they will require organisations to submit strategic plans along with their applications for funding. The plans then form the basis of a contract between the funder and the provider – i.e. they tell the funder what it will get for its money. Funders will then want to be assured at the end of the financial year that the money has been spent as per the plan or contract. This can take the form of a simple report provided by the NSO, or an independent compliance audit/performance evaluation.

The strategic plan is a very important document, because the subsequent funding of an organisation might depend on the results of reports and audits. An NSO must be able to demonstrate that its activities are producing results, are benefiting society, are contributing to the desired outcomes of its funders, and are worthy of its funding. This requires skills in evaluation, particularly in evaluating the effectiveness of the programmes it has devised. Such evaluation requires NSOs to define appropriate objectives and performance measures. The results of the evaluations should be publicised, success stories published and 'opportunities for improvement' identified.

Structure

A variety of structures have been adopted by NSOs, and none is ideal. The golden rule is that 'structure follows strategy', i.e. that the structure should support the organisation's strategy and not determine it. Common nowadays is a company structure in which a management committee is elected from the wider board, and each member is given a portfolio, or area of responsibility. Moreover, the Board and its committees may have a number of non-elected members. These people are generally co-opted for their specific expertise, often business experience. A typical structure appears in Figure 9.2 (see also Chapter 10).

The role of the full Board is to set and approve policy, to set delegations, to approve strategic plans and annual budgets, and to appoint the Executive Director.

The role of the Management Committee is to provide more regular oversight of the operations of the organisation. This involves monitoring of budgets, approval of operational and capital expenditure, monitoring and appraising the performance of the Executive Director, monitoring of progress towards achieving objectives and, in some cases, initiating and recommending policy.

Little can be said about staffing structures because NSOs vary greatly in the number of staff employed. The general principle to observe when designing structures, however, is to ensure that there is adequate accountability and control. This function usually involves having a position such as an Executive Director whose area of responsibility would cover the following range of activities, (although many of these may be picked up by volunteers in smaller organisations):

Figure 9.2: Company Structure

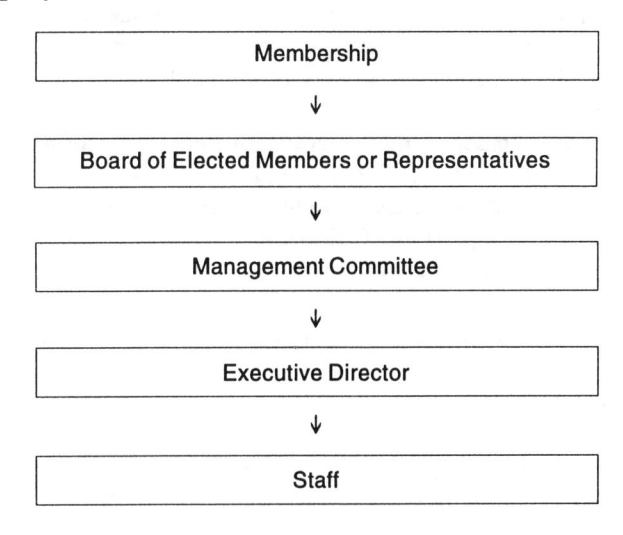

```
                    Membership
                        ↓
     Board of Elected Members or Representatives
                        ↓
                Management Committee
                        ↓
                  Executive Director
                        ↓
                        Staff
```

- Staff management, including recruitment and retention.
- Planning – initiating strategic planning and ensuring operational plans are produced.
- Budgeting, and budget monitoring.
- Public Relations – promoting the organisation.
- Fundraising.
- Setting sporting standards.
- Monitoring objectives and achievements.
- Supporting the Subcommittees.
- Ensuring that the sport itself is developed.
- Implementing Board policy.
- Reporting to the Board.
- Servicing the affiliated associations/members and other external stakeholders – e.g. public, sponsors.
- Liaising with professional bodies, government, etc.

Staff will be accountable to the Executive Director, but may well have responsibility to a particular sub-committee, for example a technical director such as the Director of Coaching may report to a Coaching Committee. Having staff accountable to committees as well as the Executive Director can cause problems unless all parties communicate well, and the directions and policies are clear.

Managing the Money

The principles of financial management will be covered in Chapter 11. Here it will suffice to cover the main challenge for NSOs in the 1990s which has been to adapt to the requirements of their funders. Funders generally want to know what they have purchased for their money as they have their own accountability requirements to meet – either to their boards or to government, or both. This has resulted in a move to an outputs-based way of accounting, from the more traditional one that is inputs-based, (State Services Commission, 1990).

An outputs-based accounting system requires NSOs to define their outputs (see previous section), and then to cost them. As NSOs are providing services (e.g. coaching, education) as well as products (e.g. merchandise), staff may have to keep timesheets so that they know how much time is being spent on each output.

The change to an outputs-based method of accounting can cause difficulty for those who are used to budgeting and reporting by such input categories as travel, accommodation, and rent. It can also be difficult to understand. Inputs are still important, but they must be related to the goods and services produced. For example, Field Officers may be required to budget and report on how much time they have spent on the following categories:

- Providing assistance to members (e.g. planning, fundraising, administration, etc.).
- Coaching.
- Public Education.

They will also be required to state how much they spent on travel and accommodation for each output. This information enables NSOs to know how much each of their services is costing, which in turn assists them to make decisions about where to place their resources most effectively. To illustrate further, consider an anonymous NSO which has the following outputs, and expenditure:

- Coaching $12,000
- National Team Management $ 6,000
- Promotion of the Sport $40,000
- Fundraising for Members $10,000

At the time this particular NSO's budget was set, its primary objective was to increase participation. After a planning session, however, it decided that it had a sufficient number of new players, and that it now needed to provide its member clubs with more support to cope with the influx. Having the financial information enabled it to decide to reduce its promotion budget, increase its coaching budget, and add a new output called 'Assistance to Clubs' which consisted of helping affiliated clubs produce three-year plans.

Defining outputs also enables NSOs to decide which ones will be provided by the organisation itself and which ones will be contracted out. Some NSOs have contracted out some or all of their fundraising and promotional activities.

Other key financial management practices are the need to report regularly against budgets, and to update budget forecasts. Some organisations make the mistake of changing their budgets each time the forecasts are reviewed. This does not allow those charged with oversight of the finances to keep a good grip on what is happening. For this reason, unless it is the annual budgeting process, only the forecasts should be revised.

Managing the People

A well-managed NSO need not have overly bureaucratic human resource systems, but it does need to ensure that its people are motivated, effective and accountable. This includes both staff and volunteers. When reviewing organisations, the following are used as indicators of effective and efficient people management.

Human Resource Systems

All staff should have signed employment contracts, and current job descriptions. Job descriptions should be reviewed at least annually, or when strategic changes take place. They should be linked to the organisation's plan so that it is quite clear how the individual contributes to its objectives, and they should spell out what the person is expected to achieve for the coming year – i.e. individual performance measures. In addition, they should state the general responsibilities and duties of the position, and the core competencies (skills and abilities) which the individual is expected to have (see Chapter 12).

Job descriptions should also be prepared for volunteers, including members of the Board. While this may be anathema to those NSOs that have difficulty attracting volunteers, job descriptions have actually proved to be a successful strategy for increasing the quality and numbers of volunteers. This is partly because the job descriptions signalled that the NSO was well organised, and that volunteers could expect professional service from the staff. Staff and volunteer performance should be appraised at least annually. Staff performance appraisals should be conducted by the Executive Director; the Executive Director's performance should be appraised by a Board member, or sub-committee of the Management Committee; and volunteer performance should be appraised by the Chairperson of the Board. Performance appraisals should take into account the extent to which individuals have attained their objectives as per their job descriptions, how they have performed against the expected competencies, and how well they have performed their ongoing or day-to-day tasks. Appraisals should also be forward-looking, and identify the training and development needs of staff, and link them to both the strategic plan and to personal objectives.

Increases in pay no longer appear to be awarded just for service, or even because employees meet their objectives. Employees are expected to perform well, and should generally be rewarded for exceeding expectations, for making outstanding contributions or significant improvements in their performance.

Staff

Long gone are the days when NSOs would employ those whose only merit was that they had played the game. This is not to decry the value of having staff who understand sport, but this should not be their only attribute. Also long gone are the days when the Executive Director was simply regarded as a secretary to the volunteer management, with the one major task being to take and write the minutes, and to keep everyone informed.

Today every employee must add value. Staff must be innovative, be able to implement initiatives, have other professional qualifications or experience, and management ability as well as knowledge of the sport. NSOs need staff who can raise money, have marketing skills, be good at public relations, manage the finances, and motivate to superior performance. NSOs need leaders not followers, and they need staff who are initiators.

In order to obtain the best staff possible, vacancies should be advertised openly. When recruiting staff there is a need to be very clear about selection criteria. A variety of selection tools gives a more rounded picture of each applicant, and while this can be time consuming, choosing the right person might be the most important investment an NSO makes. Selection methods include appraisal of résumés, holding personal interviews, making reference checks, using appropriate psychological and other tests, and obtaining work sample exercises.

Communication

Good communication between all external and internal interests is important. Staff need to know what is happening and what is planned. Communication between staff and volunteers should be regular and constructive; staff members and external parties, such as sponsors, should be kept informed and involved.

There are a number of mechanisms for ensuring that good communication takes place. One is the strategic plan because it is a statement to everyone of where the organisation is heading and what it expects to achieve. Another would be regular meetings between the Executive Director and staff on an individual and collective basis, regular board and committee meetings, appropriate written communication (not too expensive, not too often!), and plenty of communication with the media and sponsors/funders.

Some NSOs have been remarkably successful with obtaining and retaining sponsors. They take every opportunity to show their sponsors how much they are appreciated, acknowledge them publicly, provide them with opportunities to meet players, and to be promoted, thereby increasing their target market's awareness of their organisation or product. They also clearly identify for sponsors the benefits of being associated with their sport, and demonstrate how these can be translated into bottom-line profits. To paraphrase John F. Kennedy, the adage is: 'Ask not what my sponsor can do for me, rather what can I do for my sponsor' (see also Chapter 16).

Culture

By culture is meant the values, attitudes and beliefs which pervade the organisation. The culture of each organisation is unique, and there is no 'right' one, but those organisations which demonstrate the following attributes are more likely to succeed:

- Focus – everyone knows where they are going, what they are doing, and can explain this clearly. Decisions are made quickly and easily because people know whether opportunities are consistent with the strategic direction of the organisation. Staff demonstrate an understanding of what makes their sport tick, and what they have to concentrate on if they are to be successful.

- Energy – staff and volunteers are enthusiastic and give extra effort. They are also full of ideas, are committed to the success of their sport, and are passionate about it.

- Cooperation – all parties work together to attain the common goals. There is no unnecessary or destructive internal competition and politicking.

- Customer orientation – the primary customers are known, and there is a commitment to servicing their needs. Internal customers (colleagues) are treated in the same manner as external ones.

- Results orientation – staff are motivated by a desire to achieve results, and can demonstrate their achievements.

Conclusion

In this chapter, a number of practical suggestions have been made to show NSOs how they can lift their game, manage more professionally, and achieve the results that they need to be successful. In summary, the key points for managers are:

- to know where they are going and what they want to achieve;
- to have a published plan so that everyone else knows the direction, goals, and objectives;
- to know how much the products and services cost;
- to ensure the structure supports the strategic direction;
- to employ the right people with the right skills;
- to have good human resource systems and practices so that staff and volunteers are both motivated and accountable;
- to remember that they are working for stakeholders and listening to their needs; and
- to enjoy and publicise successes!

Review Questions

1. Identify the stakeholders in a National Sport Organisation. Suggest what goals each set of stakeholders is likely to hold for a National Sport Organisation.
2. Explain what is meant by the term 'structure follows strategy'.
3. Outline an outputs-based method of accounting.
4. Identify the key components of a well-managed sport organisation.

References

Bungay, S. and Goold, M. (1991), 'Creating a Strategic Control System', *Long Range Planning*, Vol 24, No 3, pp.32-39.

Carpenter, M.A. (1986), 'Planning vs Strategy – Which Will Win?' *Long Range Planning*, Vol 19, No 6, pp.50-53.

Clements, G. (1986), 'In Search of Success', New Zealand Golf Association, Wellington.

Goold, M. and Campbell, A. (1987), *Strategies and Styles: The Role of Centre in Managing Diversified Corporations*, Oxford: Blackwell.

Porter, M.E. (1985), *Competitive Advantage*, New York, Free Press.

State Services Commission: A Guide to Corporate Planning and Annual Reporting, SSC, Wellington (1990).

The Treasury (1989), 'Putting it Simply: An Explanatory Guide to Financial Management Reform', Wellington: Treasury.

Thompson, A.A. and Strickland, A.J. (1992), *Strategic Management*, 6th edition, Homwood Ill.: Irwin.

Vancil, R.F. (1992), *Implementing Strategy: The Role of Top Management*, Harvard Business School Press.

Waterman, R.H. (1979), 'Structure is Not Organisation', McKinsey Staff Papers, June.

Strategic Planning

David Cullwick

In this chapter you will become familiar with the following terms:

strategic planning process	strategic plan
vision	mission
critical success factors	key capabilities
goal	objective
strategy	ownership of plan
implementation	monitoring of performance

There are three types of organisations:

- *Those who make things happen*
- *Those who watch things happen*
- *Those who wonder what happened*

(Anon)

Strategic Planning

▷ Introduction

Each organisation has the power to choose where it belongs and how to achieve that position. If your preference is for watching or wondering, then you should perhaps read no further, but if you are curious perhaps you should read on.

This chapter demonstrates how to 'make things happen'. A strategic planning approach is used which fundamentally focuses on the factors which will make an organisation successful in achieving its longer-term goals. It outlines and demonstrates how the *strategic planning process* can be undertaken to position a sport organisation as a healthy growing organisation.

Figure 10.1

```
              WHY?
            (Reason)
                              WHAT?
                           (Definition)
  WHEN?      STRATEGIC
 (Timing)    PLANNING
                              HOW?
   WHO?                     (Process)
  (People)
```

These strategic plan elements are developed as principles and then later in the chapter they are examined in a sport management situation.

An integral part of the planning process is for members of every organisation to have a clear picture of how they see their organisation developing over the next few years. Organisations will have their own sets of pictures. Sometimes the picture has become tired, in others the picture is out of focus, and for some the picture is broken.

The key challenge in planning is to assist organisations to ensure they have a clear and vibrant picture of where they want to be in a given time and how they will seek to get there. The pictures may range from:

- staying the same or merging with other clubs;
- achieving a national title or avoiding relegation from the premier grade;
- building a new multi-purpose stadium complex or buying new equipment.

The picture held collectively is termed the *vision* and this chapter explores how to work toward the vision, either for the organisation as a whole, or for a particular area. Any sporting organisation, from the local pub pool playing team to a national sporting organisation, must undertake planning to develop the necessary 'building blocks' for the future. Without them organisations often float along haphazardly.

Examples of the benefits of strategic planning include New Zealand Golf's vision to win the Eisenhower Trophy in 1992 (for international amateur national teams) and the systematic development plan which resulted in its achievement (Clements, 1992). New Zealand Soccer developed and rode a wave of success to a big high after the World Cup in 1984 – but why has it lost momentum since?

Other examples include the growth of sports academies and national development squads in various sports codes. Have these been developed with clear visions supported by appropriate objectives, strategies and resources? How will their performance compare with the longer-established Australian Institute of Sport? There are also the new sports categories of rollerblading, parapenting, mountain biking, corfball, and triathlons. How well will these 'minor' sports fare? Have they got the necessary vision and strategic positioning to be a longer-term winner?

Always remember *strategic planning* is to assist an organisation to grow or remain strong so that it can provide an enjoyable and developing environment for both recreational and competitive participants.

Planning is not about becoming an end in itself to benefit sports administrators – that is a disease all sports administrators need to be vigorously alert to stamp out!

Key Themes and Concepts

Why Plan? (The Reasons)

'Why bother with (strategic) planning? It just involves endless meetings.'

The environment in which organisations operate is undergoing continual change, and with far less predictability than previously. These changes include individuals or groups changing their preference as to which sports they wish to pursue, e.g. the swing of schoolboy interest from rugby to soccer and then later switching back, plus the rapid increase in cricket-playing after New Zealand's success in the 1992 one-day series.

Key benefits from strategic planning include:

- creating a forward looking organisation;
- providing direction for organisations and their members;
- providing a common management framework for improving overall decision making;
- improving communication and coordination and encouraging leadership, teamwork and motivation;
- benefiting the sport.

Despite these benefits, the organisation should be alert to the following factors which are often associated with *failed* planning initiatives – 'We've spent time planning but nothing happens'.

Planning will fail:

- when a Chairperson or Executive Director does not believe in it;
- where an Executive Director makes decisions alone;
- where all activities of the organisation have not been considered;

- where the organisation is in survival mode;
- in smaller organisations which have insufficient time and resources.

What? (Definitions)

A *strategic plan* defines the vision and mission of the organisation, the key capabilities the organisation requires to achieve them, and the key objectives and strategies which must be pursued to achieve the organisation's goals, and performance measures.

A *vision* is the picture of how key people in an organisation see it developing over time. A good vision has a 'stretch' or 'challenge' within this picture, and it provides the focal point and integrating glue to hold together all the parts of the organisation.

A *mission* is the statement which outlines the key customers or participants of an organisation, the main activities the organisation will provide, and the main ways by which the organisation will provide benefits to them and which in turn will ensure a financially viable organisation.

The *key capabilities* of an organisation are those success factors which the organisation views as critical in achieving its vision. Typically in a sport organisation, critical success factors must include the following:

- Membership
- Facilities
- Coaching
- Development programmes
- Competitive excellence
- Volunteer support
- Profile or publicity
- Fundraising
- Refereeing.

The key capabilities are the elements from this type of grouping which are critical. For example in golf, most clubs need a sustained, sizeable and active membership level to remain financially viable. Key capabilities to achieve this are both excellence of facilities (makes a club attractive to members) and international success or high-profile national competition (this accentuates member or potential member participation). Equally for water polo clubs, success at club national level is important, but a strong capability in coaching and development programmes is essential to keep building a club's talent base for tomorrow.

The theme of critical success factors and the subset of key capabilities ensures that a strategic plan is focused on the elements for an organisation's longer-term success. Clearly the elements are interactive, and the relative importance will vary within a sports club over time and across sports at any given time.

An *objective* is a specific and measurable activity which will be achieved by a specific time. Objectives will be set in terms of agreed directions outlined in the vision and when achieved on an implementation basis will result in the achievement of the *goal* (or direction statement).

Note that the language of planning varies, and goals/objectives terminology are often reversed. In this chapter the specifics are as follows:

Goal: Direction statement, generally developed from critical success factors or key capabilities. (note: synonymous with outcome).

Objective: A specific measurable activity to be achieved at a certain date at a specified quality level (note: synonymous with output).

A *strategy* is the means by which a specified objective(s) is to be achieved and refers to the 'how' elements of a plan from which specific actions are developed.

A Sport Organisation's Goals

- To seek and gain members and ensure their needs are satisfied.
- To promote participation in the skills and strategies of the sport.
- To provide coaching programmes and specific instruction.
- To develop an appropriate balance between recreational and competitive activities in the sport.
- To effectively administer the financial and planning aspects of the club.

How? (Planning Process)

This phase emphasises the process by which the Strategic Plan will be created. It will combine a series of elements under the headings of analysis, strategy development, strategy implementation, and performance review, as follows:

Analysis
- What is the organisation's current situation?
- What are the key trends, likely future scenarios?
- What are the strengths and weaknesses?
- What are the threats and opportunities?
- What are the competitors' success factors?
- What are the stakeholders' requirements?
- What are the critical success factors?

Strategy Development
- What is the Vision?
- What is the Mission?
- What are our key capabilities for success?
- What strategy choice(s) will be made?
- What are the specific goals?
- What will the specific objectives be?
- What are the key strategies to achieve these?

Strategy Implementation
- What are the specific tasks/action programmes to implement the strategy?
- Who is going to do what by when?
- What are the implementation obstacles?

Performance Review
- What criteria will be used to judge success?
- How will these criteria be measured?

The planning process needs to be quite systematic *but not* bureaucratic and should show individuals a building-block approach to creating the overall plan. Traditionally planners put too much emphasis on *analysis* and insufficient on *strategy development* and *implementation*.

Who? (The participants)

A key element of planning today is that a plan has 'ownership' by key members of an organisation and at a range of levels within the organisation. For example, if the plan emphasises the importance of a professional attitude, then it is essential that the behaviour required from this professional approach is exhibited in all teams and by all officials throughout the club or organisation. Key decision makers in the organisation need to be committed to the principle of participation and consultation. The planning process can have a powerful role in making this approach work.

Key members of an organisation should be involved in its development, as well as key customers, participants and supporters, especially in terms of, for example, volunteers or coaches. This emphasis in particular needs to be carefully managed to prevent the planning process getting bogged down. Planning processes should be succinct, should get the key ideas clearly articulated, as well as provide a challenge and team-building focus for the organisation. The plan should then become a living document which sets the scene and the priorities to be pursued over time.

Timing

There should be an annual update of a strategic plan which itself should have a time horizon of say three years. In sports clubs or organisations where there are often a significant number of key people changes from year to year, it is important to build the new team into the current strategic plan, and then adapt as necessary.

Hence the plan update should be done as soon as the new committee is established, as well as being done in parallel with the budget process. There may be other cycles that a particular organisation wishes to pursue. The key factor is to use a timing relevant to the organisation.

At the end of each season it is necessary to review performance overall as well as individual parts of the plan.

Application of Principles

Recently the Greenfields Rugby Club (hypothetical) decided it needed a focus for club development over the next few years, and it gave one of its committee members the task of finding out the best way to go about it. First the committee member borrowed a book and photocopied the pages entitled 'strategic planning and your organisation' an outline (shown below). He contacted a few like-minded people from Greenfields and they spent an evening going through the steps demonstrated in the outline and put together a list of the type of questions which would need to be answered during the planning process.

Planning

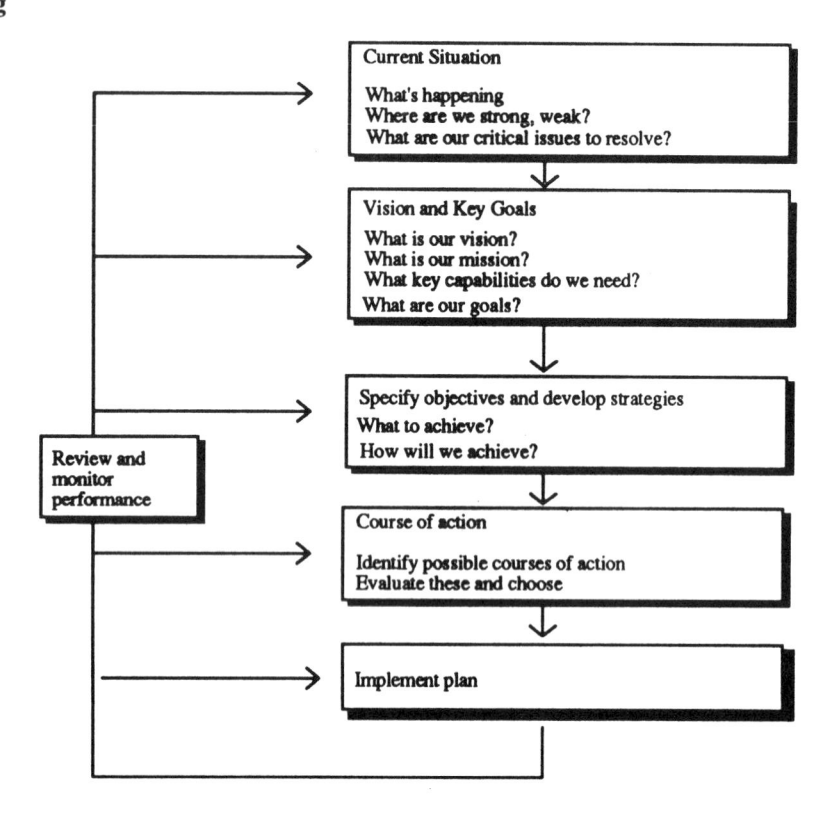

```
              ┌─────────────────────────────────────┐
              │ Current Situation                   │
         ───▶ │ What's happening                    │
         │    │ Where are we strong, weak?          │
         │    │ What are our critical issues to resolve? │
         │    └─────────────────────────────────────┘
         │                     │
         │                     ▼
         │    ┌─────────────────────────────────────┐
         │    │ Vision and Key Goals                │
         │    │ What is our vision?                 │
         ───▶ │ What is our mission?                │
         │    │ What key capabilities do we need?   │
         │    │ What are our goals?                 │
         │    └─────────────────────────────────────┘
         │                     │
         │                     ▼
  ┌──────────┐  ┌─────────────────────────────────────┐
  │ Review and│  │ Specify objectives and develop strategies │
  │ monitor  │──▶│ What to achieve?                    │
  │performance│  │ How will we achieve?                │
  └──────────┘  └─────────────────────────────────────┘
         │                     │
         │                     ▼
         │    ┌─────────────────────────────────────┐
         │    │ Course of action                    │
         ───▶ │ Identify possible courses of action │
         │    │ Evaluate these and choose           │
         │    └─────────────────────────────────────┘
         │                     │
         │                     ▼
         │    ┌─────────────────────────────────────┐
         ───▶ │ Implement plan                      │
              └─────────────────────────────────────┘
```

Current Situation

This is an essential first step in the planning process, which involves a stocktake of the organisation in terms of strengths, weaknesses, opportunities and threats. For Greenfields Rugby Club it would involve a series of questions identifying how well they are doing under the following headings:

Teams:	Competition, recreation
Players:	New members, loyalty/retention
Coaching:	Numbers, standards, programmes
Facilities:	Degree of excellence, average, excellent, usage levels
Finance:	Sources of income, vulnerability? New options? Expense control.
Sponsorship:	Have we tried? What linkage with our sponsor?
Tradition:	What is the tradition? How to keep building, adapting?
Morale:	What is it like? Differences between players and volunteers, or by age group
Club Management:	Competence? Administration or management?
Equipment:	Standard, availability?
Image:	Awareness level, peer attitude.

The output of this phase could be:

Strengths	Weaknesses
• Senior team is in top three of club competition. • Solid core of administrators. • Strong financial support – bar facilities, wide membership.	• Drop-off in junior teams. • Bigger drop out of youth-age players. • Increased competition from other sports (e.g. triathlons).
Threats	**Opportunities**
• Increased social concern about violence in sport, rugby injuries bad for image. • Soccer growth at junior level. • Fewer former players available to coach – alternate sports. • Reduced membership with financial impact. • Increased public support for rugby league.	• Create more recreation teams/competitions. • Merge with another senior team club to create strength. • Create 'sports clubs' with other sports (i.e. summer season). • Seek funding support for top youth-age players.

Vision and Mission

Moving on then to consider Greenfields' vision highlights, the *real challenge* that needs to be presented as the 'vision' was developed and debated. To ensure success the 'vision' must provide *stretch* to the club in the context of its present strengths and weaknesses, as well as *position* in respect to emerging threats and opportunities. Overall the vision represents the 'believable dream' of the future. If the 'vision' is set low and inward looking, then Greenfields will have either a 'myopic' or 'tunnel' vision which could lead to their future downfall, i.e. the Club will not adapt sufficiently or quickly enough to changes which are occurring in the market around them. It may, however, decide it wants to be a 'top three' contender in local club championships, with player representation at provincial and national level. If so it could assess that it must be big enough to field, for example, 10 junior or mid-age teams, that would ensure a feed-through of sufficient top players for the future.

In parallel with this player and team base, would be the need for 'excellence in coaching'. Consideration of vision in these terms could result in Greenfield seeking to merge with another senior grade club to ensure size, coaching strength and financial viability for the future. See next page for possible Vision and Mission for Greenfield.

Key Capabilities and Goals

As outlined earlier, key capabilities are a subset of critical success factors for the organisation to consider for the present and the future (say a three to five-year period). They are a consciously developed set of factors for an organisation which facilitate above average results, by comparison to a competitor, over the longer term (Pumpin, 1990).

Generally the capabilities are based on four key attributes: efficiency of operations, extent of differentiation, excellence in people factors, and timing (being first is important), but the danger

> **Greenfields' Vision**
>
> To be a top three competitor in the local club competition within three years.

> **Greenfields' Mission**
>
> To provide competition and recreational playing opportunities in rugby for the community of Greenfields, with a sound coaching programme at all levels, and a philosophy that to enjoy is better than to win at all costs, and that today's juniors are tomorrow's seniors, so a good balance between these groups is required.

is that general issues are considered, and very general responses obtained, which could be similar for a range of clubs or national sporting organisations.

For example, Greenfields Club should consider what it can learn from other competition clubs by way of areas of excellence? Then, having reviewed them and innovative factors in other sport organisations, the capability factors should be tested against a more general list of success factors such as:

- Image and Publicity
  To have the image and performance to be the number one club preference of the top players and sponsors, i.e. to promote success and events actively.

- Membership and Participation
  To achieve sufficient membership to ensure growth in participation at all levels, i.e. number of teams, managers and coaches. Club strength depends upon overall strength, not just that of the top team.

- Coaching and Development
  To provide an internationally recognised coaching programme at all competition levels, i.e. be prepared if necessary to employ an internationally recognised coach.

- Access and Standard of Facilities
  To have excellent training and competition facilities, i.e. a key capability element was the move by many clubs to have floodlit training areas.

- Fundraising
  To achieve an improved revenue base, which is not dependent on annual subscriptions, i.e. to involve a range of fundraising initiatives, including sponsorship.

- Quality of Management
  To ensure management excellence that supports player excellence, i.e. a club may have been served well by voluntary administrators and coaches but there may be a need to have a near full-time manager or coach to ensure that 'quality' management is in place.

On a national basis, the Hillary Commission has emphasised in its funding priorities the importance of full-time Executive Directors. Equally at a club level there is a need to ensure that this capability is in place and operating at the quality level required in an increasingly competitive situation. Clearly to have either a near full-time person in management or coaching requires a certain scale and funding base. The challenge is to ensure that 'part-time effort does not result in part-time results'.

Finally, goals reflect the direction statement of the key capabilities and should be integrated with the Vision as follows:

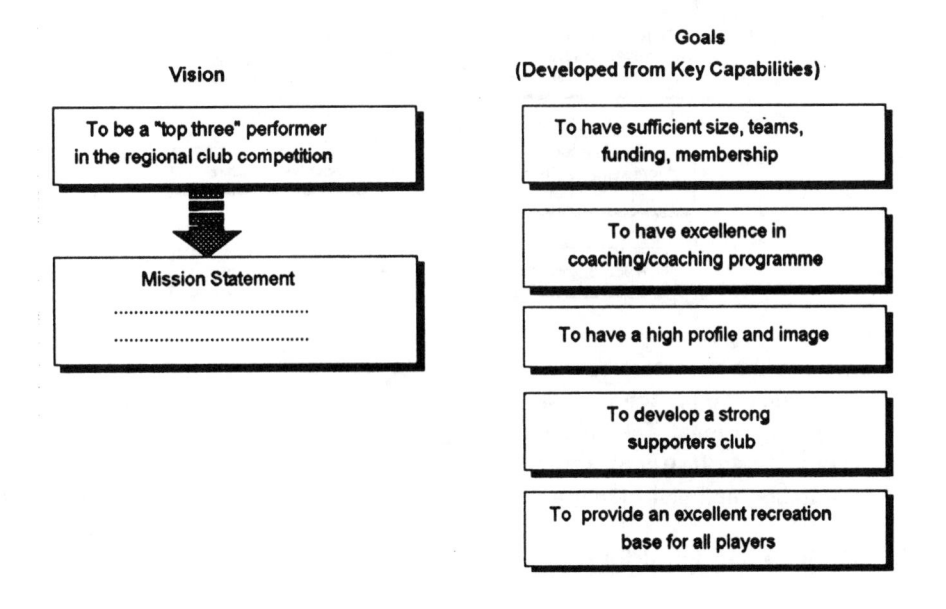

Vision

- To be a "top three" performer in the regional club competition
- Mission Statement

Goals (Developed from Key Capabilities)

- To have sufficient size, teams, funding, membership
- To have excellence in coaching/coaching programme
- To have a high profile and image
- To develop a strong supporters club
- To provide an excellent recreation base for all players

Objectives

This phase of the Plan is in a hierarchy from the Vision → Key Capabilities (Goals) → Objectives (Outputs) → Strategies → Action Tasks → Accountability/Timing → Funding. A case study of a national organisation – *New Zealand Association of Disabled Skiers (NZADS)* (1991) – will be used to highlight the preparation of objectives and strategies (see figure next page).

The Mission of the Association is to foster skiing for the disabled through enhancing individual skills to achieve safe skiing, personal growth and to have fun and fellowship. In 1991 the Association identified the importance of increasing the 'learn to ski' base, and specified objectives in these terms:

- Increase the number of beginner skiers from 50 to 180 by 1994
- Increase the number of intermediate skiers from 50 to 120 by 1994
- Increase the number of advanced recreational skiers (higher technical proficiency) from 20 to 40 by 1994
- Maintain 10 skiers in a racing programme.

Five key strategy areas were identified to achieve the above objectives:
    i   Increase the instructor base for skill enhancement programmes.

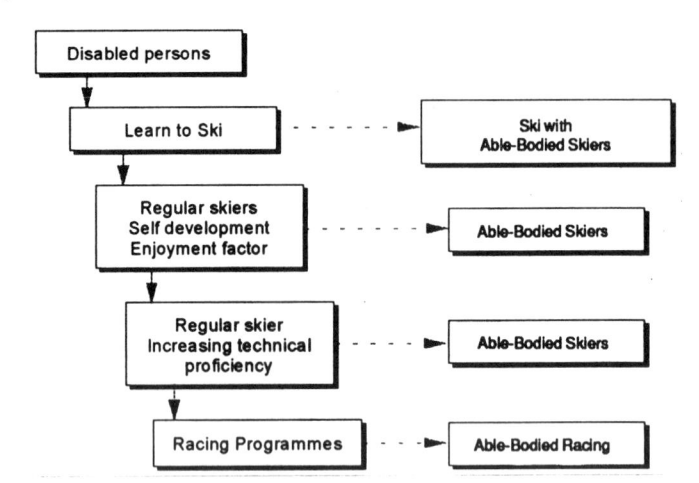

The 'development' focus for NZADS can be visualised as:

```
┌─────────────────┐
│ Disabled persons │
└────────┬────────┘
         ▼
┌─────────────────┐         ┌──────────────────┐
│  Learn to Ski   │ ──────▶ │    Ski with      │
└────────┬────────┘         │ Able-Bodied Skiers│
         ▼                  └──────────────────┘
┌─────────────────┐
│ Regular skiers  │         ┌──────────────────┐
│ Self development│ ──────▶ │ Able-Bodied Skiers│
│ Enjoyment factor│         └──────────────────┘
└────────┬────────┘
         ▼
┌─────────────────┐
│ Regular skier   │         ┌──────────────────┐
│Increasing technical│─────▶ │ Able-Bodied Skiers│
│   proficiency   │         └──────────────────┘
└────────┬────────┘
         ▼
┌─────────────────┐         ┌──────────────────┐
│Racing Programmes│ ──────▶ │ Able-Bodied Racing│
└─────────────────┘         └──────────────────┘
```

ii Improve the volunteer base, including a broader awareness programme.
iii Strengthen the branch network, including support to 'at risk' branches.
iv Create a national development programme, including a coaching network, ski weeks and an instructor programme.
v   Maintain a national racing programme and link with Winter Park Group, USA.

Specific tasks were developed for each strategy as below:

Strategy 1 – Increased Instructor Numbers

1.1 Association appointment in North Island
1.2 Funding support to maintain coaches with Christchurch and Dunedin Branch
1.3 Targeted instructor support to Nelson
1.4 Offer an instructors' training course

Related objectives and strategies were adopted to ensure the needed finance was available. In 1993 the plan was updated, following significant success in reaching the earlier objectives. The original plan and the new one are quite simple documents, but they have the key purpose of providing a common picture of where the organisation wanted to go (Vision), where it had to be strong (Capabilities), and then the translation of these elements into specific objectives and strategies.

Courses of Action

A plan is only of use if it can be implemented and this requires getting down to the detail of tasks which can be allocated to individuals for action, and for which they are accountable. These actions flow from the strategies, and need to be developed and agreed to prior to execution.

Strategic Planning

Courses of action for sub-strategy 1.4 (in preceding section) 'offer an instructors' training course', could lead to something like this:

- Design a training programme
- Identify potential trainers and select
- Identify instructors
- Invite instructors to attend training
- Arrange administrative details (this of course can be broken down into a variety of tasks).

Action: Coaching Director
Deadline: Programme by a specified date.

Implementation

Planning fatigue is a potential problem because often so much energy is expended in creating a plan that little is left for its implementation. To avoid this situation it is best to focus on a smaller number of issues and get them implemented. In general there are three key dimensions to achieving effective implementation. These are (a) achieving ownership of the plan, (b) having specific action tasks, accountabilities and a time schedule, and (c) having the necessary resources.

Ownership of the Plan

In the past, two models of involvement in the planning process have been advocated, either 'top-down' or 'bottom-up'. Features of these are given below, along with the 'mixed' model which combines the best elements of both. For sports organisations a 'mixed' planning process is recommended, which is half-way between 'top-down' and 'bottom-up' planning. Profiles of these three planning processes are as follows:

Ownership of Plan:

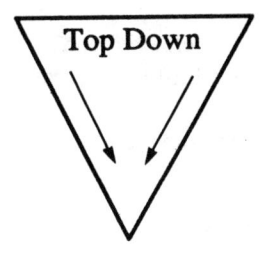

Top Down
- We know
- Trust us
- We lead – you follow
- Traditional
- Successful in some small organisations

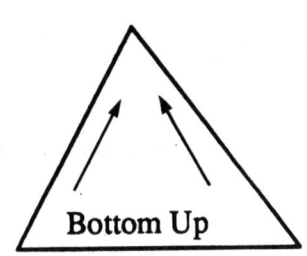

Bottom Up
- Grass roots building blocks
- Consultation
- Often committee dominated
- Can empower individuals

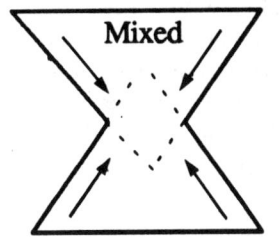

Mixed
- Grass roots
- Consultation
- Focused decision making
- Empower individuals
- Should assist team building

Traditionally most sports organisations have operated on a 'top-down' basis as identified in three planning seminars for executive directors of national sports organisations, (Cullwick, 1992), but a move specifically to the 'mixed mode' approach which involves more people in the process is an important factor, especially with the volunteer based organisations that prevail in sport.

Building people/involvement:

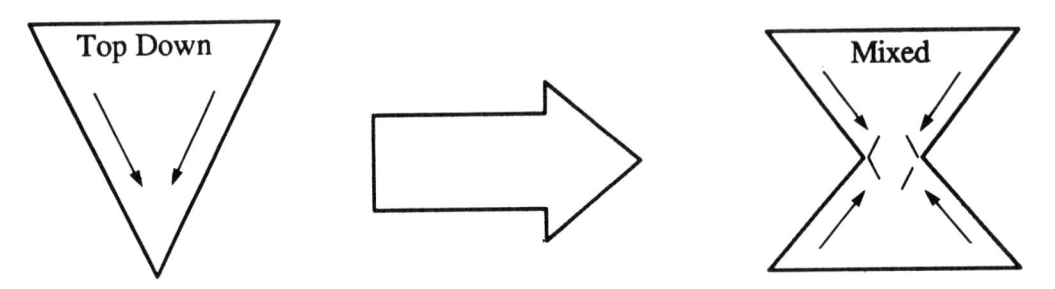

Key steps to achieve ownership include:

- Informal discussion exploring planning problems and opportunities.
- Setting up of a multi-level planning project group – key issues and options for dealing with the issues.
- Draft strategic management plan – based on outcome from informal discussions and the findings of the planning project group.
- A review process by the Committee or Board and key influencers.
- Ongoing communications and discussions between all parties. This helps to share direction and create interest.
- Setting of tasks and accountabilities and monitoring achievement.

Specific Action Tasks and Accountabilities

- The establishment of a written Strategic Plan which is concise and user friendly, and updated annually.
- The Plan should specify responsibility areas, key tasks and timing for achievement.
- The setting up of sub-committees to work on key areas, delegate responsibility, encourage wider involvement.
- The Plan should be the basis for ongoing management and regular meetings, and not be divorced from the day-to-day functioning of the organisation.

Performance Review

Monitoring of Performance

The failure to monitor performance means that plans can take on a life of their own and go way off course, like an owner building a boat, getting some people to sail it, and sending it off (hopefully with clear instructions) but never requiring them to get back in contact to see how the trip is going and how storms have been weathered.

In the sport management area, successful performance monitoring has these features:

- Expectations that have been established that objectives are set to be met.
- Meetings that have a clear agenda and involve focused discussion.
- Progress that is specifically reviewed monthly on action tasks.
- Every three months, progress is reviewed against overall objectives to:
  - Identify resource gaps
  - Modify plan if required.

Internal Measures

- Measures need to be stated and yardsticks put in place. These may include the following:
  - Clubs with volunteer register
  - Membership increase, participation increase
  - Participants with access to excellent facilities
  - Coaches accredited to A grade.

External Measures

- Media coverage (positive, negative)
- Competitive position in school sport
- Relative financial support by funding agencies

From Strategic Plan to Management

Throughout there is a need for recognising that the Strategic Plan is an integral part of the management process. Creating the plan is often a change process and its effective implementation is essential. 'Keeping the sports machine well oiled is the real work of the sport manager' says Ramish Patel, (cited in Watt, 1992) the executive director of the Hockey Federation. 'You have to ensure the quality of the people is right, put them in position and keep them there. That's the hardest thing.'

The same article observes that the medium-sized sports, such as hockey and men's basketball, have the hardest battles in New Zealand. They lack the reputation of the 'big four' – cricket, netball, rugby, and rugby league – and must fight for television coverage and corporate sponsorship, let alone for the success of their own competitors, (see Chapter 18).

Overall it can be seen that sport business involves a number of events at local, national and international level. The publicity from success in any major event can *make* a sport, e.g. world cup soccer, one-day cricket wins or international golf wins. The downside is that failure can mean loss of public interest, sponsorship and support. The reality is that to be successful, a sport needs to have a clear direction plan (Strategic Plan), effective management to make it happen, and strength in marketing to differentiate it from other sports.

Review Questions

1. You are the Executive Director for New Zealand Netball. Identify your vision, key capabilities and goals for the next three years.
2. Identify the relative roles and responsibilities in the National Hockey Association between management and players in developing a strategic plan.
3. Describe how you would judge the success of the many Executive Directors in national sporting organisations in strategic planning and management.

References

Clements, G. (1992), 'New Zealand Golf – the 1992 Eisenhower'. Unpublished presentation to Hillary Commission, December 1992.
Cullwick, D. (1992), 'Strategic Planning for Sports Organisations'. Unpublished presentation to Hillary Commission, December.
New Zealand Association of Disabled Skiers (NZADS) (1991), 'Development Plan 1991-1994', June 1991, Wellington.
Pumpin, C. (1990), *Strategic Management,* London: Gower Press.
Watt, L. (1992), 'Sports Management: The Pros Take Over', *Management*, September, pp.56-59.

Suggested Reading

General

Day, G.S. (1990), *Market Driven Strategy*, New York: Free Press.
Hamel, G. and Prahalad, C.K. (1989), 'Strategic Intent', *Harvard Business Review,* Vol 67 pp.63-76.
Pumpin, C. (1990), *Strategic Management,* London: Gower Press.
Shanklin, W.L. and Ryans, J.K. (1985), *Thinking Strategically*, New York: Random House.
Steiner, G.A. (1979), *Strategic Planning,* New York: Free Press.

Sporting Organisations

Crompton, J.L., (Summer 1990/91), 'Strategies for Improving the Image of Park and Recreation Agencies', *Recreation Australia*, pp.4-12, Perth.
Robb, D. (1992), 'Introducing Strategic Planning into Australian Sporting Organisations', *Sports Industry Conference,* Sydney.
Stewart, B. (1991), 'A Strategic Planning Model for Sport', *Management and Sport Conference Proceedings,* Vol 2, pp.141-163, University of Canberra.
Stewart-Weeks, M. (1991), 'Planning Performance and Power: New Models for the Management of Australian Sports', *Management and Sport Conference Proceedings*, Vol 2, pp.41-60, University of Canberra.

Budgeting and Financial Control

Graeme Hall

In this chapter you will become familiar with the following terms:

budgeting and financial control

delegated powers and responsibilities

entity concept

statement of financial position

budget

monitoring

accountability

stewardship

annual plan of stated objectives

strategic plan

specific performance measures

general ledger

sub-systems

accrual concept

depreciation

control regime

common unit of measure

statement of income and expenditure

statement of cash flows

resource allocation

benchmark

governance

stakeholders

outputs

business plan

variances

chart of accounts

matching concept

accounting period

Goods and Services Tax (GST)

Introduction

Many readers seeing the above title might be tempted to skip this chapter, because budgeting and financial control hardly evoke the same fervour as organising a sports meeting, or an overseas campaign, or perhaps evolving a major new strategy. The challenge is to keep reading, for the subject can be interesting, and it is a critical element of sport management.

Why is financial management in general, and budgeting and financial control specifically, critical to sport management? The proposition here is, that managing an organisation without maintaining control through budgeting and subsequent monitoring and reporting is the equivalent of playing a game without keeping the score.

As a species, humans are predominantly competitive and goal seeking by nature. This applies in a sporting or a recreational activity, e.g. witness the response as 100 comes up on a cricket score-board, but there are strong parallels between keeping the score in sport and maintaining a record of an organisation's financial progress and position. If we accept that keeping the organisational score is necessary, the key issue is either how it is done or how it should be done.

Scope of Chapter

The dimensions covered in this chapter are:

- Why is there a need to budget and control the financial performance?
- Who are the interested parties and what are their accountabilities?
- How is progress to be planned and reported?
- How are positions planned, measured and reported?
- What are the control mechanisms and how are these used?

As this is the only chapter in this book relating to financial management, some background and context will be provided prior to examining the questions above.

Essential Concepts and Definitions

Common Unit of Measure

The first requirement in any planning, reporting, and control system is to identify a common unit of measure. Imagine if in rugby there was no common points system, but progress was described by way of the number of scrums, lineouts, passes, kicks, and yardage. Also imagine there was no formula to convert all these aspects into equivalent points on the board. The outcome would be confusion. No one would understand who had won, being faced with a welter of statistics, all expressed in different measures. To solve this dilemma, different sports and recreations have converted the outcome of a large number of activities into standard units, to express relative success or progress.

Financial planning, reporting and controlling has been formulated on the same basis. Whilst there is more to an organisation than the financial aspect, especially in sport management with its large volunteer contingent, there is a need to report progress and position using a common unit of measure. For this purpose the 'dollar' or monetary unit is used.

This common unit of measure has often been misinterpreted as a ploy by accountants or financially orientated personnel to capture the organisation, the view being that financial people are a little myopic and see operations in financial terms only, rather than in terms of effort, perseverance, morale, ethics, and values. Whether readers subscribe to this view or not, what all accountants recognise is the impossibility of reporting the progress and position of diverse organisations in anything but common terms. Therefore they find it helpful to convert all effort into financial points.

Entity Concept

Financial management draws on the concept of a separate reporting entity, i.e. when an organisation is established, a separate entity reflecting only that organisation is nominally created, whether or not it has separate legal form at the time. The entity can further support this concept through legal incorporation as a society, or body corporate. However, this is not necessary to achieve the separate financial entity form.

The financial implication of the entity concept is to describe all financial results as they affect the entity. There will be financial reports relating to the entity concerned primarily with:

- What progress has been made?
- What is the present position?
- What has been the flow of funds?

Definition of Financial Management

Management has been defined earlier in this book as getting things done with and through other people, via planning, organising, directing and controlling. The sports perspective has been accommodated by changing the latter two strategies from directing to leading, and from controlling to evaluating. Sport financial management is therefore concerned with all management matters relating to finance and financial reporting. It is pertinent here to define briefly four of the key documents used in financial management: statement of income and expenditure; statement of financial position; statement of cash flows; and finally, the budget.

Statement of Income and Expenditure

('Profit and Loss Account' is the commercial equivalent)

The income and expenditure statement defines the characteristics of the organisation's financial progress (or otherwise) over a specific period (usually a year, but can be a lesser period). It details the revenue gained and the expenditure undertaken in each of the organisational areas, e.g. coaching, training, and competition, and for each expenditure category, e.g. travel, uniforms. In other words, an income and expenditure statement is equivalent to the score at the end of a game, i.e. it describes the quantum and characteristics of the progress made.

Statement of Financial Position

(Balance Sheet)

A balance sheet represents the current organisational position (not progress). It is an absolute position, and is analogous to a stocktake at the end of the game to identify:

- current position on the competition ladder
- current resources – e.g. fit and injured players.

Balance sheets define where an organisation is in a financial sense. The organisation's strategic plan may define the forecast financial position (i.e. the position the organisation wishes to achieve, e.g. being debt free; and those positions the organisation wishes to avoid, e.g. 90 per cent of funds borrowed, or insolvency).

Statement of Cash Flows

Accounting practice now requires a report on financial management from the perspective of cash flows. This report is distinct from the other two reports. The report identifies all money flows whether they relate to performance or position. The report represents the extent of financial activity that has been undertaken during the period. The external version of the report differentiates between three different types of flows:

- operating, e.g. revenue and operation expenditure
- investing, e.g. acquisition of new assets
- financing, e.g. new borrowings or loan repayments.

Cash flow forecasting is an essential component of budgeting and control. For reasons of simplicity and clarity, an internal cash flow statement should follow the categorisation detailed above. In effect, cash is the necessary 'oxygen' for an organisation to achieve performance. Cash is a scarce resource, and its use requires planning, controlling and reporting, i.e. managing.

Budget

(Income and Expenditure, Financial Position Reports and Cash Flows)

The budget document is a projected representation of the three reports above. It is the forecast plan for progress over a given period (income and expenditure budget), for a desired position (balance sheet budget) and for cash flows. It incorporates and expresses primarily in financial terms the activities required to follow the strategies for meeting the organisation's goals and objectives. It should be supported by, and incorporate to the extent that it does not confuse, key non-financial statistics such as:

- number of members
- number of participants

- number of training courses
- average coaching qualification achieved.

Budgets expressed in these terms facilitate ongoing performance measurement, monitoring and control.

Why Financial Budgeting and Control?

Internal Requirements

The preceding paragraphs have put the case for defining target positions and measuring progress, using finance as a common unit of measure, given the lack of alternatives. Earlier chapters will have defined the essential roles of managers to plan, organise, direct and evaluate. Such roles require the support of financial management tools and procedures. Through budgeting and control a sport manager seeks to:

- Achieve equitable and defensible resource allocation, e.g. each portfolio area is uniformly effective and efficient (or is funded to those criteria).
- Identify those lesser priority projects that will miss funding if revenue falls, i.e. supply costed options to provide some choice for the decision makers. Resource allocation is equivalent to any purchasing decision in which the aim is to obtain maximum benefit from a set level of funds.
- Monitor progress against a plan, and to obtain and evaluate the explanations provided for departures from budget, i.e. planning without monitoring is equivalent to monitoring without planning. To gain the benefits both must be undertaken.

Note that a budget variance itself is not a mortal sin. Rather, the issue is whether the expenditure can be substantiated against the various criteria:

- for the benefit of the organisation;
- in pursuit of the prioritised goals;
- with economic, efficient and effective use of resources;
- within the established control regime, i.e. within delegated limits; and
- Achieve a benchmark position for initiating remedial action, e.g. how can a current adverse travel budget variable be reduced and recovered?

However, it has to be acknowledged that finance is just one dimension, and that it is valid to assess organisations from a number of perspectives, e.g. morale, size, a market share, infrastructure. The significance of the financial function will be determined by size and to what extent the organisation is commercial, and accountable to external parties. For example, a very small sport organisation, run totally by volunteers with very limited sponsorship, will have limited requirements for financial reporting and control. Conversely, a large organisation with many people employed, some professional, some volunteers, distributed operations, significant sponsorship, including receipt of public funds, will have stringent requirements for financial reporting and financial control.

The financial dimension is used as the basis for defining the control regime. It includes defining delegations, and responsibilities, and specifying the accountabilities of respective personnel, from organisational governors (elected executives) through sport management to the operational personnel.

Delegations

There is no set formula for establishing delegations, but organisations will define the respective roles (positions) and determine the appropriate delegations (delegated authorities). The general theory is to delegate sufficient authority for a manager or officer to carry out the operational role with relative autonomy with referral to the next higher level for a small proportion of the decisions that fall outside the delegated limit.

The rationale for delegations is to promote effective management and operation whilst maintaining adequate awareness and control. Usually delegations relate to:

- bank signing authorities
- purchasing authorities
- purchase approval authorities
- contracts signing.

External Requirements

Accountability is an essential facet of the governance and management processes. It is the specification of a set of agreed actions or responsibilities for any particular individual or group, and the subsequent measurement of performance against that set of actions. Remedial responses require support through reward and sanction. Organisations have accountabilities to stakeholders (interest groups) through the governors or Board of Trustees to be:

- financially prudent
- efficient and effective in operations
- both statutory and ethically compliant.

Typically sport managers are accountable to the stakeholders (supporters, sponsors, suppliers, participants, and government) through the organisation's governors or trustees.

The governing body will establish objectives, derive specific annual goals from these objectives, and establish the policy and strategic framework within which the organisation is to operate. The sport manager is empowered to translate this direction and framework into more specific action plans and to organise resources to achieve the specified goals. Accordingly, governors and trustees will want to know:

- Whether both the financial and non-financial goals have been achieved. A non-financial goal for some New Zealand sports would be, say, two Olympic medals, or three people in the top 50 rankings.

- Whether the sport manager can account for all resources used being:

- effective
- efficient
- economic
- equitable relative to those goals and the environment.

Note that this criteria applies whether the expenditure is within the budget or not. Budget inclusion is not the sole criterion for expenditure, but part of a more composite criteria.

- Whether progress has been made relative to the financial budget and other plans, but also the state of the organisation's resultant position, e.g. healthy or unhealthy.

Stewardship and Accountability

An organisation has a wide range of accountabilities ranging from performance to compliance. The quasi public nature of many sport and recreation organisations means the interest groups are many and varied. These groups seek, and in time will demand, responsible financial management.

Financial management will allow the identification and reporting of both actuals and budget relating to:

- the level of revenue
- the total level of expenditure, and the levels within expenditure categories, e.g. coaching, travel, training, competition, mass participation, etc
- the net result
- the organisation's current financial position is, i.e. what it owns and what it owes.

Stakeholders will assess performance against:

- the undertakings of the organisation relative to the original plan of service performance
- the comparative performance of other organisations in a similar field
- the intuitive knowledge of what is reasonable behaviour and performance.

The environment is competitive. If an organisation cannot demonstrate appropriate plans, use, or control of resources, then it is likely that the flow of funds will be directed towards better performing organisations.

Communication

In the commercial world virtually all reporting is in financial terms, and financial reports have traditionally been so aggregated that virtually all insight and meaning is lost. In recent years, and predominantly arising from developments in the public sector, there has been a move for a more comprehensive method of annual reporting. Typically it encompasses:

- An Annual Plan of Stated Objectives (being predominantly non-financial).

- An Annual Report (predominantly non-financial) measuring progress against those objectives, and supported by
- A Statement of Resources and a
- A Financial Report, being:
    - an income and expenditure statement
    - statement of financial position
    - statement of cash flows.

In total, the Annual Report forms a comprehensive account from the stewards (governors) on performance against projections, and it enables judgements to be made on the relative value of this performance within an environment of full disclosure.

Statutory Authorities

An entity is required to file statutory tax returns, and annual and statistical returns, to report the status and position of the organisation to various government agencies. The extent of this reporting is dependent upon the legal form. Failure to comply with statutory obligations puts the organisation at risk, both because of the sanctions that will be applied, and through loss of stakeholder confidence that inevitably will follow.

Auditor

The requirement for audit may arise through statute or from the requirements of governors, suppliers, funders or sponsors. The auditor's task is to produce a report stating whether in the opinion of an independent expert (the auditor) the financial reports 'fairly reflect' the actual financial performance and position. The outcome gives the assurance of reliability and serves to demonstrate the accountability of the management. The assurance is, however, quite limited. It is neither an evaluation or review of the body, nor a certification of the organisation's performance. It relates specifically to the report and to the financial systems and procedures (internal control) that underpin them.

Industry Perspective and Responsibility

The sport and leisure sector has the usual diversity of any major sector. There are the large and small players, professional and unprofessional, highly efficient and inefficient. But sport/recreation organisations are different in one key aspect. When a company fails, there is no consequential threat to company structures in general. However, in the sport and leisure sector, because of the huge contributions from volunteers and participants, there is a responsibility to manage the organisation professionally so as to reflect well on the whole sector. Loss of confidence in one organisation often reflects poorly on others in the sector.

Internal Requirements of Financial Management

Perspective and Role

Finance is usually a separate function (responsibility) within an organisation. Other typical functions are marketing, operations, personnel, competition, administration, coaching, and promotion. Functions contribute to an organisation's overall result and final position at any particular point. The non-finance functions require the services of finance to:

- assist with the specification of plans into financial planning documents, i.e. budgets.
- assist in evaluating the effectiveness and efficiency of different ways of resource use, e.g. seeking sponsorship themselves or getting it contracted out.
- measure and report progress against planned resource use and measure and report both progress and position.

Management

A sound and comprehensive financial management system facilitates and supports the tasks of:

- planning
- organising
- leading
- evaluating.

Finance is a critical dimension as it is the denomination in which the organisation's targets are expressed. Financial management outputs are the reports, either internal or external, that are made to the respective stakeholders and interested parties and are distinct from organisational outputs. All parties require reports that are:

- simple to understand
- unambiguous
- sufficiently descriptive
- a blend of both financial and non-financial information
- comparative with either previous years or budget (plan)
- compiled consistently and compliant with prevailing practice and/or statutory requirements.

Referring back to the score board analogy, the reports should ensure that:

- the score is kept according to the latest scoring rules, i.e. to both externally provided and internally formulated policy;
- the score is presented so that people can see it, i.e. large score board or distributed results; and
- the score is communicated both by the plan and the end results to demonstrate accountability.

Operations

From the operational perspective, a financial management system needs to:

- allow organisational plans to be expressed as financial targets and report progress against

goals, facilitating review and response. Many targets may be expressed not in total dollar terms but on a per capita basis, e.g. $3.50 per person per pool visit, or $100 per training day;
- integrate with the other management systems including planning, communicating, reporting and operational systems;
- be efficient to operate, in terms of resource use;
- be easily understood, and user-friendly;
- be flexible, to ensure it will be able to cope with inevitable change;
- be integral, i.e. comprehensive, and structurally and systematically consistent to provide control validity. Stakeholders will require comfort and assurance relating to system integrity, and the auditor will provide a perspective relative to this issue.

Financial Management Processes

Planning

The annual planning process is undertaken within the context of the strategic plan. The strategic plan will have established organisational objectives, goals, milestones and agreed on preferred methods/approaches for achieving these goals. The strategic plan needs to define the various measurement bases used to measure both progress and achievement, e.g. market share, member growth rate, international ranking, etc.

The annual or business plan is a definitive document detailing:

- projects
- activities
- resources to be secured
- operational performance measures, e.g. average coaching clinic sizes, number of 'active' coaching days, or number of school visits per month, per annum.

This planning document requires the support of a document representing the financial dimension, e.g.

- revenue earned
- funds expended
- expenditure type and controls
- financial position at the end of the period.

This document is the Budget. Given there are a number of functions within any organisation, a verification, consultative and prioritising process needs to occur before confirming the budget. The verification process relates to effectiveness of resource use through consultation and prioritisation to reflect the respective interest groups' needs and aims. The objective is to integrate the resource demands to achieve optimal organisational outputs. Key points in the budget building process are:

- to be consistent and congruent with both the strategic and the annual plans as expressed initially in activity and resource use terms, prior to translation into monetary terms;

Budgeting and Financial Control

- to have optional targets and projects to facilitate best matching of limited resources with demands, and provide management with options when needing to respond to a fast changing environment;
- to incorporate specific performance measures (benchmarks) to facilitate evaluation of the budget by the governors (and stakeholders) on the basis of:
  - effectiveness
  - efficiency
  - economy
  - equity;
- to quantify financially the activities, services, and asset use, and reflect such characteristics as lack of linearity with volume changes, e.g. if participants numbers reduce by 30 per cent, do event management activities and costs reduce accordingly?

Organising

The Annual Plan and the Budget are the appropriate reference documents for implementation. Appropriately detailed, they provide management with the delegated powers and with the agreed parameters for initiating/organising any specific action or activity. Management relies on delegated powers. Material departures from these documents will require prior approval from those directing management – trustees/elected executive, etc.

Control

Earlier reference has been made to the requirement for accountability from the various governance and management positions.

The control regime usually matches the organisation hierarchy. If authority has been delegated, the prudent governor/manager must ensure that there are appropriate controls in place to safeguard and to verify that the authority has been exercised in accordance with the plan and organisational policy.

Specifically the control regime will:

- Delegate powers and allocated responsibilities for all officials, e.g. who has cheque signing authority, to what level and with whom?
- Define the policy framework, e.g. what is capital expenditure, how is it approved, and how quickly should it be depreciated?
- Define appropriate procedures, e.g. each portfolio manager (coaching, training, promotions, etc.) to check acceptability of purchases and approve if within their portfolio expenditure limits.
- Ensure a reporting and or a verification discipline to monitor compliance with this regime, i.e. a formal report to detail any internal control departures and to initiate remedial action.

One of the most serious and, unfortunately, frequent breaches of control procedure relates to cheque signing practice. Sport/recreation organisations often have a very limited number of cheque signatories. To counter the inevitable unavailability of one of these signatories, cheques are often signed in advance. This practice is against the rationale for the original control mechanism, and it exposes the organisation to the increased risk of theft, and misapplication of funds. But control can be assessed monthly to verify that expenditure complies with budget in terms of:

- total amount
- expenditure categories
- delegated limits
- material variance with plan, the variances to be substantiated and adequately explained
- targets being achieved
- the financial position being within planning parameters.

Financial Management Structure

The entity concept was referred to earlier. The entity concept is embodied by the Ledger (Chart of Accounts) which lists the individual ledger accounts necessary to describe both:

- progress (income and expenditure section) and
- position (balance sheet section).

In creating an appropriate chart of accounts there is an inevitable trade-off between detail and clarity of information.

The income and expenditure section of the chart is often sectionalised to reflect the organisational structure. These sections are defined as cost or profit centres and used to capture all income and expenditure transactions relative to a particular portfolio, e.g. coaching, promotion, sponsorship, and administration.

The chart of accounts defines the prime financial recording system – the 'General' Ledger system. In addition subsidiary systems, being subsets of the general ledger systems, process substantial volume and detail relating to:

- debtors (accounts receivable sub-system)
- creditors (accounts payable sub-system)
- fixed assets
- payroll.

Further Financial Concepts

As detailed above, financial management systems are based on established concepts and principles. Additional concepts are outlined briefly here to provide a further perspective and to prevent invalid assumptions and responses to reports on progress and position.

Matching Concept

Revenue and expenditure are the two prime financial components constantly being measured and matched. Valid measurement relies on ensuring that when income is recognised or counted (e.g. all race participant fees), then the associated costs of that race (expenses) are recognised at the same time in order to deduce the correct net position (i.e. profit or loss).

Accrual Concept

The accrual concept supports the matching concept and provides substance to reports. It eliminates the shortfalls of cash-based accounting which recognises physical funds received or paid out, because it allows for expenses (and income for that matter) to be incorporated into the report even though neither the cash nor the invoice might be to hand. The matching concept relies on the accrual concept.

Accounting Period (time)

Performance and position is relative to time. Progress (performance) is expressed relative to a specific and notified time period; typically a month or a year. The balance sheet position is that of the last day of that same period, i.e. month or year.

Depreciation

Depreciation is often referred to as a non-cash expense. It occurs when assets are purchased one year and are slowly 'consumed' over a period of years. Depreciation is a charge (non-cash expense) in the accounts that reflects the continual use or consumption of the asset.

If organisations were to purchase only what they needed each month, e.g. phone service, then financial reporting would be straightforward. However, many services are not available, or available economically, in such incremental quantities. Therefore typically an organisation purchases an asset one year for use over many years, e.g. computer, vehicle, sports equipment, etc.

Over the period of the asset's life it contributes to the provision of service and consequently to the receipt of income. To produce valid financial statements, accounts need to reflect the substance of this asset use for each period.

Example:

If a computer cost $10,000 at the beginning of year 1 and has no value or further use at the end of year 5, financial reports must reflect the asset consumption over that period.

Depreciation formula	
e.g. Original cost	$10,000
Asset life	5 years
Per annum depreciation expense	$2,000

Income and Expenditure Account

	A (Without Depreciation) $	B (With Depreciation) $
Revenue	100,000	100,000
Expenses		
Wages/salaries	60,000	60,000
Travel	20,000	20,000
Promotion	10,000	10,000
Interest	3,000	3,000
Depn	-	2,000
Surplus	7,000	5,000

Note: Situation A would have a deficit of $3,000 in the first year, if the total cost of the asset ($10,000) is charged against just that first year's income, and a surplus of $7,000 for the subsequent four years: Situation B has a $5,000 surplus when depreciation is levied annually.

Some Key Issues

Processing of Financial Transactions and Reports

An organisation needs to work to its strengths. If financial management systems is not one person's stock in trade, consideration has to be given to obtaining the requisite reports. The focus should be on utilising the reports as managers and governors, not in processing the transactions.

The hours that have been spent in sport and recreation organisations (all organisations for that matter) on developing accounting systems (primarily computer based) is legend. The opportunity cost of such resource diversion is very high. The benefits of utilising a small but professional processing service are significant.

One aspect is not negotiable. Sport managers cannot stay in an information wilderness for anything longer than a few months whilst systems are developed. They have to be realistic and pragmatic. They must gain the first 80 per cent of their needs quickly and then set priorities for the balance through information system development.

Goods and Services Tax (GST)

New Zealand's tax collection mechanism has a vital relationship with financial reports that sport managers will need to understand because the undertaking of business activity over a particular threshold (currently $30,000 p.a.) requires the organisation to add GST to their accounts. However all financial reports are expressed exclusive of GST.

Method Development

Budgets have traditionally been developed from spreadsheets and compared with the previous year's budget or actual. This is referred to as the incremental approach, and incorporates into the new budget all of the 'ills' (inefficiencies, etc.) of the last year. The alternative, zero-base budgeting, requires a fresh start and the validation and substantiation of all budget sums, not just the increment. Current budget method development, and modern practice, emphasises the requirement to budget in physical terms (i.e. activities undertaken), and to express all budget requests as a relationship between inputs (people, services, assets) and outputs (services or products). Such a process facilitates wider and more informed debate as to the efficiency and effectiveness of the resource allocation.

Performance Measurement

It has to be acknowledged that the emphasis on accountability and the consequential requirement for plan specification and management control, has created a strong demand for non-financial performance measures. In particular the commercial performance measurement of profit or contribution to profit is not applicable for not-for-profit organisations. This has led to the development of comprehensive performance measurement hierarchies, and at present these are still in their formative stages. Their essential purpose is to develop a comprehensive and congruent framework within which the various levels of accountabilities can be reported through the organisation.

Indicatively performance indicators need to report:

output
- volume
- quality
- service level

process
- effectiveness
- efficiency
- productivity

input
- economy
- equity
- cost
- quality

Conclusion

Having made the case for adopting the procedures of financial management in the sport/recreational sector, this chapter has provided potential managers with a guide to statements, budgets, planning, and accountability. It has elaborated certain concepts, and attempted to provide explanations *en route* that would encourage readers to gain expertise in a territory that otherwise might be quite foreign to them. It was designed to give confidence in the use of established commercial procedure, that might profitably be extended to areas in which both financial and non-financial management have sometimes been a matter of concern.

Review Questions

1. What are the main purposes of preparing regular income and expenditure statements?
2. What are the main purposes of preparing a balance sheet?
3. What are the prime purposes of a budget and how would you set about creating one?
4. What are the financial accountabilities of a sports manager and to whom are these owed?
5. What is the significance of separating the actual production of the reports from the use of the reports? How can this be effected in any organisation?
6. Why do we require control mechanisms, and how do these help us manage?
7. How would you refute the proposition that finance is for the bean counters, and let's leave them to it?

Suggested Reading

Bannon, J. and Busser, J. (1985), *Sport Club Management,* Champaign, Ill.: Management Learning Laboratories.

Dougherty, N. and Bonanno, D. (1985), *Management Principles in Sport and Leisure Services,* Minneapolis, Minnesota: Burgess Publishing Company.

Mason, J. and Paul, J. (1988), *Modern Sports Administration,* Englewood Cliffs, N.J.: Prentice Hall.

Parkhouse, B. (1991), *The Management of Sport: Its Foundation and Application*, St Louis: Mosby Year Book.

Human Resource Management – The People Decisions

Katie Sadleir

In this chapter you will become familiar with the following terms:

human resource management *volunteers*

professional development *job descriptions*

Introduction

> People decisions are the ultimate – perhaps the only – control of an organisation. People determine the capacity of an organisation. No organisation can do better than the people it has (Drucker, 1990).

Historically, sport was entirely administered by a volunteer workforce. Today the composition of sport management has dramatically changed. There is now a growing tendency for sport organisations to involve paid staff and, as a recent economic and social impact study shows (see Chapter 5), New Zealand's sport and leisure industry supports 22,745 jobs (Jensen, Sullivan, Wilson, Berkeley and Russell, 1993). For example, the National Sport Organisations have a variety of full- and part-time employees. Depending on the organisation's size, these employees occupy the positions of executive directors, coaching directors, national coaches, administration managers, secretaries, marketing managers, development/technical officers and, in some cases, professional athletes. Similar paid employment currently exists at regional and club levels, with many club managers and bar managers now employed on either a full- or part-time basis.

The impact of the increase in the numbers of paid staff upon the traditional volunteer workforce, was the theme of a national conference run by the Hillary Commission in December 1991 entitled 'Managing Organisations'. The conference looked at the relationships that exist between paid staff and volunteers in national organisations. One reason for holding the conference, was a concern that the whole area of human resource management (HRM) within sport management, was being overlooked in furthering such other organisational objectives as increasing membership or improving athletic performance. It was therefore thought imperative that sound HRM procedures should be in place within sport organisations to ensure the quality of service delivery. Martin Stewart-Weeks, a keynote speaker at the above conference, explained the reason for this by stating that human resource management was about maximising the contributions of individuals to improve the performance of the total organisation.

However, if HRM procedures are of critical importance in the attainment of objectives, they should not be targeted solely at the paid staff members but also at the volunteers. Although there has been a change in the people profile of sport management, New Zealand sport and leisure organisations will always be dependent on their volunteer workforce. For example, the 1991 Census recorded that in the course of one week, 87,460 people aged 15 years and over were involved in voluntary work with sports and youth groups. These volunteers contributed a total of 27.6 million hours, estimated to be worth $196 million per year (Jensen *et al.,* 1993).

In acknowledging the important function and role of the volunteer, it is often said that the term 'volunteer' is no longer relevant when assessing the responsibilities that are attached to their positions; at a national executive level there are simply paid and unpaid staff. This perception of the two types of staff was discussed by Ross Grantham, Executive Director of the National Council of YMCAs, in a 1991 presentation to national sports managers on policy volunteers, as follows:

> The first thing to accept is the basic premise that in any efficient, well-run organisation, policy volunteers should, in broad terms, be treated in exactly the same way as paid staff. Although they have different roles, the staff and volunteers are, hopefully, pursuing the same goals. The two main differences are that the volunteers don't get paid, but the staff do, and the volunteers determine policy which the staff then implement through programmes and activities.

Volunteering has developed into a sophisticated activity that now requires a far more serious commitment from both the volunteers and the organisations dependent upon them. The competition to attract the volunteer workforce has become intense, and to gain a competitive edge, organisations face the challenge of establishing HRM systems for managing volunteers in relation to their recruitment, training, recognition and evaluation.

Who are the Human Resource Managers?

It is often unclear as to where the responsibility lies within organisations for decisions related to HRM, because it may change with the scenario at hand.

Paid Staff Managing Volunteers

The most straightforward scenario is that of paid staff managing volunteers. An example of this could be a regional sports trust that runs a holiday programme and involves volunteer students as unpaid staff. Thus the organisation has a clear responsibility for developing a volunteer policy that enhances volunteer involvement rather than exploits the volunteer labour market. The challenge is for the organisation to develop a policy which is focused on the motivation and needs of the volunteer in addition to those of the organisation.

Volunteers Managing Volunteers

The situation where volunteers report to other volunteers is common at all levels of sport delivery. Here the responsibility of developing a HRM policy could lie with any of the elected officers, i.e. club captain or chairperson. Organisations that want to be really proficient in their dealings with volunteers may opt either to appoint or elect, on an annual basis, a volunteer coordinator to fulfil the role of the human resource manager. This type of position has been evident in some social service and traditional recreation organisations, but is only just starting to develop within sporting groups. The tasks of the volunteer coordinator may include:

- determining where volunteers are needed
- writing job descriptions
- planning recruitment drives
- organising interviews with volunteers
- holding regular meetings with volunteers
- organising training
- supervising where appropriate
- keeping up-to-date records on volunteer involvement
- motivating and encouraging volunteers
- undertaking performance reviews of volunteers
- providing appropriate acknowledgement schemes.

(Hillary Commission for Recreation and Sport, 1991a)

Volunteers Managing Paid Staff

The final scenario is where paid staff members report to volunteer boards. But one of the critical decisions to be made before employing staff is the reporting system they are to follow. Ideally this should be to *one* nominated person, commonly the president or chairperson. This same person or a small working committee would have the responsibility for developing a HRM policy aimed at creating a rewarding and motivating work environment.

Unfortunately problems can arise when a highly qualified staff member, i.e. executive director, reports to a volunteer board with relatively little HRM experience. It is possible that an individual with no business management experience could become, through their years of commitment and dedication to sport, a national executive member faced with the responsibility of managing a paid employee. This sometimes has the potential for an unsatisfactory employment environment. In this situation the executive director must either carry on without HRM policies in place, or must develop a system for managing the manager through the process – and this can lead to difficulties in the area of developing contracts and writing job descriptions, and undertaking performance reviews.

Assessing the Organisation's Needs for Unpaid and Paid Staff

Why are Volunteers Needed?

Before undertaking any type of recruitment campaign, it is important to have a clear understanding of the reasons for recruitment of staff. Reasons most often given by organisations for using volunteers are often selfish and, heavily slanted toward the organisation rather than the volunteer. Such an orientation can unfortunately sometimes result in neglect of the person who is willing to donate time and effort. Organisations may regard volunteers as their second choice rather than their first, and if the finances were available they would rather employ people to do the jobs of volunteers. But saving dollars is not a valid long-term justification for using volunteers (Trederick and Henderson, 1989).

It is therefore important to be clear about the reasons for utilising volunteers and to make sure these are understood by all people within an organisation. It follows that a written, widely circulated document outlining the organisations general policy on volunteers could minimise any misunderstandings. For example, it could be said that volunteers are valuable to organisations because:

- they bring enthusiasm, drive and a wealth of experience into the organisation;
- they offer credibility because they are unsalaried and engage in an activity without thought of financial gain; and
- they form a link between the community and the organisation.

Considerations Before Employing Staff

All too often national volunteer organisations make the decision to employ staff without considering either the impact the position will make on the organisation, or how the role of the position will fit in with the existing roles and responsibilities of paid and unpaid staff. Therefore the decision-making process involved in establishing staffing needs careful consideration. It is also imperative for the skills and strengths of existing staff members and volunteers to be assessed before any job is advertised. Once a thorough skills assessment has taken place, the result may create a series of options:

- Employing part-time rather than full-time staff
- Contracting a person for a short period of time to fulfil the task required
- Restructuring work tasks internally to offer job opportunities for existing staff/volunteers.

(Ministry of Sport and Recreation, Western Australia, 1990)

Establishing a Staffing Need

Review Current Situation

Balance the current roles and responsibilities of current paid and unpaid staff and answer the following:

(a) What are the reasons for having this position?
(b) How else could the duties of the position be carried out?

Creating A New Position

(a) Who currently does tasks required of this position?
(b) How will the objectives of your association be met by the introduction of the position?
(c) How will the position impact on other employees, elected officers and the sport in general?

Refilling An Existing Vacant Position

(a) Can the association do without this position?
(b) How will the objectives of the association be met by refilling the position?
(c) What improvements could be made (e.g. delegation)?
(d) Should the title change?

(Ministry of Sport and Recreation, Western Australia, 1990)

Job Descriptions

Job descriptions are clearly the key to successful HRM systems, because they are the founding documents which form the basis of individual performance agreements. They should at all times be realistic, appropriate, be updated regularly, and contain the following detail:

- A title for the position
- To whom is the position accountable
- General responsibilities (Is the position responsible for supervising staff and money? If so how many and how much?)
- Specific duties listing major work functions
- Key result areas including objectives to be achieved and to be reviewed each year and used as the basis for appraisal of the person in the position (Grossman, 1989).

Job descriptions are not solely for salaried positions, they should also be available for all volunteers. The specifications and detail of the job descriptions should be related closely to the level of responsibility involved. By having job descriptions for all positions the organisation ensures systems are in place regarding accountability.

Volunteers want to be associated with focused, well thought out activities in terms of time commitment and tasks involved (Hillary Commission, 1991b). They are looking for a clear, realistic preview of the job before committing their leisure time. Although producing job descriptions for volunteers could be perceived as a time-consuming task, it is an essential element of planning. For the new volunteer it indicates an organisation that is well prepared and has thought through its need for volunteers. It also gives volunteers a clear idea of what they are getting into.

Job Description

Position:	NZTA National Director of Referees
Responsible To:	NZTA Executive Committee
Location:	Negotiable
Accountable To:	NZTA Technical Panel
Area of Responsibility:	New Zealand
Objectives:	To develop, organise, promote and foster Touch Refereeing in NZ.
Responsibilities:	To plan, coordinate and deliver the NZTA National Refereeing programme including:

    a) Training and Development
    b) Selection
    c) Certification/recognition of achievements and levels of attainment.

To liaise with the NZTA National Director of Tournaments to determine the required number of Referees for NZTA Tournaments.

To formulate the policy and process for the appointment of Referees, Referee Managers, and Referee Appointment and Assessment/Coaching Panel for NZTA Tournaments.

To account for the Refereeing funding, ensuring that all National selection activities are performed within the set budget.

Qualifications:	Proven ability in both written and oral communication skills.
	Self-motivation.
	The ability to coordinate, direct and motivate others.
	NZTA Referee certificates Level 1 and Level 11.
	Level 1 CNZ sport coaching certificate.
	Level 11 CNZ sport coaching certificate or the potential to attain this qualification within 12 months.
	NZTA Coaching certificate Level 1.
	A thorough understanding of the NZTA Levels programmes.
Term:	Two years – expiry 1 July 1995
Hours of work:	As required, 4-10 hours per week.
Honorarium:	1993/94 = Nil

As with salaried staff, the volunteer job description acts as an agreement between the organisation and its volunteers, protecting both if disagreements should occur. Many national organisations now have well thought out job descriptions for their national level volunteers. The Job Description (in abbreviated form on p. 172), was developed by the executive of the New Zealand Touch Association (NZTA) during a recent restructuring of the responsibilities of the National Board for one of five volunteer positions.

Instead of job descriptions, the National Council of YMCAs uses the term Performance Agreement for its national policy volunteers. The performance agreements are prepared in consultation with the volunteer, and roles and responsibilities of each member are clarified before being signed by the National President of the organisation and all newly elected policy volunteers.

National Council of YMCAs of New Zealand
Policy Volunteers Performance Agreement

This performance agreement constitutes a commitment from, National Board Member, to, National President, to further the National Boards philosophy, authority and role as set out below.

I accept the YMCAs' Statement of Purpose as the basic philosophy of the YMCA.

I acknowledge and accept the responsibility inherent in the authority delegated to me by virtue of my election as a National Board member.

My commitment to the National Council of YMCAs of New Zealand is as follows:

- To attend on a regular basis the meetings of the National Board and other sub-groups of that Board as agreed to during the tenure of my appointment.
- To invest time in understanding the issues discussed by the National Board.
- To act as a link between the National Board and associations and individuals within the YMCA, and other community groups.
- To fulfil any special tasks that may be assigned to me by virtue of my election or by the Board.
- To participate in a performance appraisal related to the effectiveness of the National Board and my individual contribution.

Signed: _____ National President
Signed: _____ National Board Member
Date: _____

Recruitment

The principles and steps involved in recruiting volunteers are quite different from those associated with recruiting salaried staff. In this section, discussion will focus on recruitment considerations of volunteers under two separate headings, that of policy volunteers and non-policy volunteers.

Policy Volunteers

Policy volunteers hold executive positions (Grantham, 1991) that are usually outlined within the organisation's constitution, e.g. Chairperson, President, Vice-President, Treasurer, Council Member. Their recruitment process is linked to a democratic election from the wider membership. A common problem is that the variety of criteria by which candidates are selected might not provide an elected board with the range of skills required to function as an effective unit. In some cases members are elected to leadership positions as an acknowledgement for long service involvement, but often the elected representative lacks the competency required for the position. Some national organisations compensate for such deficiencies by writing into the constitution the power for the executive to co-opt people on specific matters.

As a general rule, even if recruitment were solely through the election process, policy volunteers should be selected proactively. For example, before initiating a recruitment campaign it is necessary to know the combination of skills that are required. Once the skills have been listed, membership lists should be perused to identify people who possess them. These people should be actively sought, and their profiles given to membership well in advance of the election so that the voters might be better informed.

Non-policy Volunteers

Non-policy volunteers do not hold executive positions, and organisations require a different approach to attract them. There should be an active recruitment campaign to present ideas about the reasons why volunteers are needed and what their jobs will involve. The key to successful recruitment campaigns would be to think past the organisation's needs to those of the volunteer, and to present them in an exciting and challenging way. Recruitment strategies should be planned well in advance to avoid, if at all possible, last-minute approaches. The method and approach taken will depend upon the target group in mind. When organisational needs have been determined, a well thought out recruitment campaign must be designed. Often the most effective method of recruiting is personal and face to face, because it allows for specific information to be gained by both the organisation and the individual. It might also be necessary to think past traditional target sources and look to new recruitment areas such as students in high school, polytechnic and university sport management courses. Many high schools have established programmes aimed at leadership development, from the traditional Duke of Edinburgh Awards to some of the newer Advanced Kiwi Sport Leadership programmes. Often in such courses students are required to work as volunteers within sport organisations. Another untapped resource for volunteer recruitment is the older adult population. The possible involvement of this group is unlimited. With years of experience in many areas, this group of people has the potential to contribute in a variety of ways and may often be looking for new activities.

Induction

Once people have been successfully recruited the induction period begins. By the end of the induction period new recruits should have a clear understanding of performance expectations and requirements, i.e.:

- a clear understanding of the organisation – what it does, who it caters for, where it fits into the sport and recreation industry;
- an understanding of all administration procedures, particularly those that the individual will directly be involved in;
- knowledge of both their job and that of other salaried or volunteer staff and a clear understanding of relationships between people (Trederick and Henderson, 1989).

Performance Reviews/Appraisals

A performance appraisal is a systematic review of an individual employee's job performance to evaluate the effectiveness or adequacy of his or her work (Grossman, 1989). It provides benefits to both the individual and the organisation. The individual benefits by getting concrete feedback on performance levels achieved and on areas needing further training or concentration. The organisation is provided with a picture of how the individual is performing in relation to present goals. It also provides the opportunity to assess the impact and effectiveness of supervision and support from the organisation on the employee.

Formal performance reviews of paid and unpaid staff are a relatively new phenomena within volunteer organisations. They are still not in place in many organisations and where in place they may not yet cover all positions. Again the level of formality of the review should be commensurate with the level of responsibility involved. The appraisal provides the formal mechanism for reviewing the relationship previously established by contract or otherwise between the individual and the organisation. Normally reviews occur at a minimum of once every year. The types of questions to be answered through the process are:

- Did the individual achieve what was set out for the position? If not why not? What were the obstacles and can they be overcome?
- Are the goals the position was trying to achieve still relevant for the period ahead? Are there some new tasks that should be added or taken away?
- Are there some training needs identified which can help the person to become more effective in the period ahead?

The process used to collect information does not have to be overly complex or formal, but it should be undertaken in a professional manner. The system should be open, fair, and systematic without creating unnecessary pressure, and provide ample opportunity for both parties involved to have their say (Stewart-Weeks, 1991). The most important underlying principle is that the review should involve a two-way process between management and staff.

The following two examples are performance review systems in place for executive directors of national organisations. The first is that of the Executive Director of Netball NZ.

Principal Accountabilities	Level of Achievement	Future Expectation	General Comments
1.			
2.			
3.			

The Executive Director reports to the President. Each member of the national executive and other paid employees are given the opportunity to comment on the Executive Director's achievements. The Executive Director and President then meet and complete the process of filling in the other columns. The review process is used to identify both successes and areas for further development. The results are used by the President to identify training needs and to make recommendations on salary increases.

The second example outlines the procedure used by a committee to review the performance of the New Zealand Touch Association's (NZTA) Executive Director. It consists of six stages as follows:

1. The Executive Director undertakes a written report of his or her performance compared to the agreed performance agreement. This report should include:
   - comment on the performance and whether the objective was achieved or not achieved,
   - comment on whether there were any factors (external and internal) that impacted on the achievement of performance.
2. The NZTA executive members are invited to provide submissions to the performance review committee on the performance of the Executive Director.
3. Four provincial associations are selected to provide comment on the performance of the Executive Director – two to be nominated by the NZTA Performance Review Committee and two by the Executive Director.
4. Following receipt of all reports, the responses are collated and included in a draft to form the basis of discussion between the Executive Director and the Chairperson of the NZTA Performance Review Committee.
5. The Executive Director is then given the opportunity to attach further written comments to the draft report.
6. The NZTA Performance Review Committee makes appropriate recommendations to the NZTA executive for consideration.

Whatever system is decided upon, all those involved in the organisation need to know at the beginning of the process what is being evaluated, by whom, how often, what the results of the evaluation are, and for what purpose they will be used.

The above two systems are currently in place, but only for paid employees because there is still a reluctance to set up systems to review the performance of volunteers. Grantham (1991) comments on this in relation to the YMCAs' volunteers as follows:

> Performance appraisals can make a major contribution to the motivation and morale of people at all levels within an organisation. There is considerable benefit to be gained from improved communication and feedback between individuals within an organisation. The appraisal system provides a vehicle for this to happen. A perception that we cannot expect volunteers to participate in formal appraisal has restricted the development and use of appraisal, resulting in a subsequent lowering of performance standards.
>
> We do appraisals to:
> - measure and judge performance,
> - relate individual performance to organisational goals,
> - clarify both the job to be done and the expectations of accomplishment,

- foster increasing competence and growth of staff and volunteers,
- enhance communication,
- serve as a basis of judgement for reward and recognition,
- motivate people, and
- ensure the goals of the organisation are achieved.

Triathlon New Zealand has instigated a simple but effective performance review procedure for all national portfolios holding volunteers. Before the AGM the secretary writes individually to all policy volunteers explaining the purpose and process for the review, and requires them to provide a short paragraph on the successes and disappointments of their work over the preceding 12-month period. They are also asked to comment on changes they would make to existing goals for the next year. This written information is sought from every volunteer regardless of whether or not they are standing for re-election.

Training

The provision of ongoing training and professional development opportunities adds value to individuals and organisations. The organisation that places great importance on staff development benefits greatly as it increases the skills and competencies of employees. An individual who works in a training-orientated organisation is highly motivated to perform. Part of this motivation comes from the positive feeling of working for an organisation that values its employees sufficiently to invest in their development.

Training is so closely linked to performance that it should not be left to chance. Instead an organisation-wide professional development programme should be set up, with opportunities targeting both paid and unpaid staff. For example, the opportunities available for training in the sports industry have grown substantially in recent years. Coaching New Zealand (CNZ) now provides a nationally recognised system of generic coach education courses that target both volunteer and paid coaches. The courses are run regularly through Regional Sports Trusts, and many national organisations have now integrated their own CNZ courses with the sport-specific coach education programmes.

Administration training for volunteers is provided through the Hillary Commission's Volunteer Involvement Programme, and in 1992/93 approximately 6,500 volunteers took part in them. The VIP club administration courses are two-hour workshops run through local authorities and regional sports trusts. The topics covered in the series are:

- Recruiting and retaining volunteers
- The role of the club secretary
- The role of the chairperson
- Marketing and promotion
- Fund-raising
- Strategic and project planning
- The role of the treasurer
- Event management.

Certain courses are targeted at a higher level of sport management training, and are offered on an occasional workshop basis by the New Zealand Recreation Association and the Hillary

Commission. Many national sport service organisations also run national training conferences, and most New Zealand tertiary institutions offer courses related to sport and recreation management, some through correspondence, to accommodate full-time employees who are unable to engage in full-time study.

Acknowledgement/Rewards

Rewards, whether intrinsic or extrinsic, are absolutely essential to the maintenance of the organisation. People need to feel that their efforts are appreciated or they will seek involvement elsewhere (Grossman, 1989). In the leisure industry the motivation to work is not solely related to dollars, because many people have a passion for their employment, i.e. their vocation targets their vacation and leisure-time interests. An example of this is outdoor recreation instructors who work for outdoor adventure organisations. The challenge therefore for sport managers is to develop a work environment that creates maximum motivation to perform. This is an important consideration when involving volunteers who work because they want to, rather than because they have to. Their commitment has to be acknowledged in the most appropriate way, and in deciding on a personalised approach, it might help to reconsider the reasons why the person has volunteered, e.g. to learn new skills, to help others, to share talents and abilities, to make new friends, to obtain positions of importance or to have fun. Whatever the reasons, the key to giving appropriate recognition is to make awards relevant to motivations. But too often this is ignored. Volunteers work long hours, and their motivation for continuing to work depends on their feeling valued by others, as well as having their own sense of personal accomplishment.

Conclusion

People, paid or unpaid, are the most important resource in the sport and recreation industry. Often they are poorly treated and taken for granted. This chapter has highlighted some of the considerations which must be made to ensure the effective management of people.

> The level of performance an organisation should expect from its people will always be a direct function of the way they are treated, both formally and informally. If you take your organisation seriously enough to take your people seriously, they will respond and perform. If you don't, you shouldn't be surprised at the results (Stewart-Weeks, 1991).

Review Questions

1. Are there any differences between volunteers and paid staff in relation to HRM issues?
2. What information should be included in a job description?
3. Why are performance reviews important?

References

Drucker, P. (1990), *Managing the Non-Profit Organisation*, Great Britain: Butterworth-Heinemann.

Grantham, R. (1991), 'Policy Volunteers – The Management Challenge', in *Managing Organisations – A Conference on the Relationship Between Paid and Voluntary Staff*,

Wellington: Hillary Commission for Sport, Fitness and Leisure.

Grossman, A.H. (1989), 'Personnel Management', in *Recreation and Leisure Services*, New York: American Alliance for Health, Physical Education, Recreation and Dance.

Hillary Commission for Recreation and Sport (1991a), *Club Administration Manual*, Wellington: Hillary Commission for Recreation and Sport.

Hillary Commission for Recreation and Sport (1991b), *Managing Organisations – A Conference on the Relationship Between Paid and Voluntary Staff*, Wellington: Hillary Commission for Recreation and Sport.

Hillary Commission for Sport, Fitness and Leisure (1993), *Management Matters – A Guide to Leisure Facility Management*, Wellington: Hillary Commission for Sport, Fitness and Leisure.

Jensen, B., Sullivan, C., Wilson, N., Berkeley, M. and Russell, D. (1993), *The Business of Sport and Leisure Report*, Wellington: Hillary Commission for Sport, Fitness and Leisure.

Ministry of Sport and Recreation – Western Australia Government (1990), 'Successful Staff Management : A Practical Guide for Sport Associations', Unpublished.

Stewart-Weeks, M. (1991), 'To Appoint Or Not To Appoint', in *Managing Organisations – A Conference on the Relationship Between Paid and Voluntary Staff*, Wellington: Hillary Commission for Sport, Fitness and Leisure.

Trederick, T. and Henderson, K. (1989), *Volunteers in Leisure: A Management Perspective*, Reston, Virginia: American Alliance for Health, Physical Education, Recreation and Dance.

Suggested Reading

Drucker, P. (1990), *Managing the Non-Profit Organisation*, Great Britain: Butterworth-Heinemann.

Grossman, A.H. (1989), 'Personnel Management', in *Recreation and Leisure Services*, New York: American Alliance for Health, Physical Education, Recreation and Dance.

Hillary Commission for Recreation and Sport (1991), *Club Administration Manual*, Wellington: Hillary Commission for Recreation and Sport.

Hillary Commission for Recreation and Sport (1991), *Managing Organisations – A Conference on the Relationship Between Paid and Voluntary Staff*, Wellington: Hillary Commission for Recreation and Sport.

Leadership Issues in Sport

Steve Tew

In this chapter you will become familiar with the following terms:

vision	*honesty*
shared ownership	*control*
passion	*communication*
influence	

When the best leader's work is done, the people say we did it ourselves (Blanchard, 1985).

Introduction

Sport is part of the social fabric of New Zealand society. New Zealanders are active sport participants, avid sport spectators, and self-proclaimed sport critics. They are exposed to sport options at a young age through KiwiSport, a modified sports programme, in which 93 per cent of primary schools are registered. Sport is also big business, with an estimated contribution to the New Zealand economy of $4.5 million a day from the collective contributions of hundreds of thousands of people (Jensen, Sullivan, Wilson, Berkeley and Russell, 1993). It is an industry which supports 14,530 jobs directly, and a further 8,215 indirectly, and it has a volunteer contribution calculated at 27.6 million hours that is worth approximately $196 million per year (see Chapters 5 and 12).

Who leads this vast human resource? What is the role of a leader in New Zealand sport? What attributes must a leader possess? Who should provide leadership in the future?

Before answering these questions, it is important to define the terms. Goode Vick (1989) defined leadership in terms of influence:

> A leader is a person who has influence with people, which causes them to listen and agree on common goals, to follow his or her advice, and to take action toward these goals.

A leadership position can be gained by appointment, by election, or by using some form of power such as wealth or prestige, or it can be earned. Earned leadership is the most effective because those who occupy leadership positions but are unable to influence people's actions without use of authority, will not be successful long term. In other words, the ability to influence people is gained through respect, honesty, credibility and performance.

Leadership is a vital ingredient of any organisation. It is even more crucial in the context of New Zealand sport organisations that rely on the contributions of so many volunteers. Therefore the leaders of New Zealand sport must harness the efforts of both the volunteers and paid staff to ensure that they share a common purpose and vision. This can only be done, within the New Zealand sport environment, through influence. Coercion will not work. Instead, those responsible for the future of New Zealand sport must be able to influence the actions of their members. They will do this not by trying to force a vision, but by convincing people to take some share or ownership of progress. It is a lesson that John Hart (former All Black Selector and Auckland Coach) exemplified when saying that ultimately much of his approach came from what he learned in industry; how important it was to allow people to express themselves, to encourage their input, and to allow them to participate fully, because there is so much talent which would be suppressed by authoritarianism and rigidity (Thomas, 1993).

Leadership is about the future and not just the present. It is very easy for the busy volunteer, or indeed the under-resourced professional manager, to concentrate their own energies and those of their organisation on the hustle and bustle of today. This is a mistake, because an organisation that does not secure its future, will not enjoy one. Drucker (1992) sums this up succinctly in saying that *the Mission for the present is to set the future in motion.* But this is difficult to bring about in the ever-changing social, economic and political environment of New Zealand in the 1990s. Successive governments deregulated many facets of the business community, and placed the onus on individuals to take responsibility for their own wellbeing. But the need to manage change is not unique to New Zealand, it is now accepted as a constant factor worldwide. According to Sir Colin Marshall, Chief Executive of British Airways, not only has change become a constant, but it is going to come about ever faster. As Chaudhry-Lawton and Lawton (1992) said,

> Improvements in technologies and communications are altering our perspectives. What was high tech yesterday is commonplace today and will be obsolete tomorrow. The world is becoming increasingly 'local', with events more frequently having an impact on a global level. The more we experience – and progress means we are experiencing more and more – so too do our expectations grow.
>
> Greater variety is becoming available in virtually every sphere of life.
>
> Increasingly commonly, at work and leisure, people are being confronted by situations they have never before experienced, whether it is simply the latest in fast-changing fashion fads or, more seriously, the implications for your home market of a plummeting collapse in share prices in a country some 8,000 miles away.

For example, the introduction of Saturday shopping in New Zealand changed the nature of that day's activities significantly. In particular it had implications for children's sport that traditionally is played on Saturday morning and is dependent on the input of countless volunteer parents who are now presented with counter attractions. Also, the advent of 'live' sports broadcasts has obliged many sports to ensure that they attract sufficient numbers of supporters at venues rather than have them watch from the comfort of their homes. The combination of television replays, a critical media, and public have also put considerable pressure on New Zealand sport to eliminate acts of violence and foul play. All of these are issues resulting from change that need to be addressed by the leaders if the future of their sport is to be secure.

Thus, those responsible for the future of New Zealand sport have been and will be required to establish organisational cultures, that are not only capable of operating in a changing environment, but will increasingly become catalysts in the change process. They must put systems in place, develop and share attitudes and values to establish such cultures and manage the change process to ensure that it makes a positive contribution. As Chaudhry-Lawton and Lawton (1992) point out, 'from an organisational point of view, it is critical that all the excitement, fear, restlessness, curiosity and panic that surrounds change, be focused into productive and enjoyable activity'.

Managing change in the context of New Zealand sport organisations presents some unique leadership challenges. Traditionally conservative in nature, the councils and boards of New Zealand sport have not always been well prepared or very willing to accept change. However, history will testify that New Zealand sport has benefited from the contribution of many fine, inspirational leaders, not only on the field of competition, but also around the boardroom table. This is further evidenced by the number of sports captains and leaders who are also leaders in industry and business. For example, David Appleby, a partner in a successful Auckland accounting firm, was the Chairman of New Zealand Hockey for four years. He helped to manage the sport through the potentially difficult task of amalgamating the different associations for men and women into one national body. Sir Ronald Scott, the foundation Chairman of the Hillary Commission for Sport, Fitness and Leisure, often challenged his fellow leaders of New Zealand sport with the statement that 'Gold medals are won around the boardroom table'. It was his opinion that a sport not well managed and led, could not succeed with any regularity in any area of activity, including international competition.

Central to the discussion of a definition of leadership is some consideration of leadership style. Blanchard, Blanchard and Zigarmi (1985) outline four basic leadership styles on a continuum from the extremes of directing to delegating. The *directing* involves control, constant supervision, highly defined structure, and no delegating. The second style on the continuum – *coaching* – continues to be reliant on close supervision, but has room for suggestions and explanations for decisions. The third style – *supporting* – introduces the concept of shared decision making, and involves much less direct supervision but more facilitation. The final style on the continuum is *delegating,* which is typified by a consensus approach to decision making and is reliant on the leader playing no more than a support role and the team taking over all but the ultimate responsibility for a decision, task or series of tasks.

Although it is easy to label and identify differing leadership styles, it is not such a simple matter to decide which style will best suit a particular set of circumstances. A key to good leadership is the ability of the leader to determine what style will best suit the current circumstances. This requires an analysis of the group to be led, their experience, maturity, and confidence, as well as a good understanding of what has to be done. Different people will require and respond best to different styles and approaches and the most effective leaders are those who are able to recognise this and adjust their style accordingly.

The following chart illustrates the continuum. A highly delegated style uses influence rather than authority and will concentrate on policy and major issue decisions, while the directing style will rely heavily on authority and be primarily task orientated.

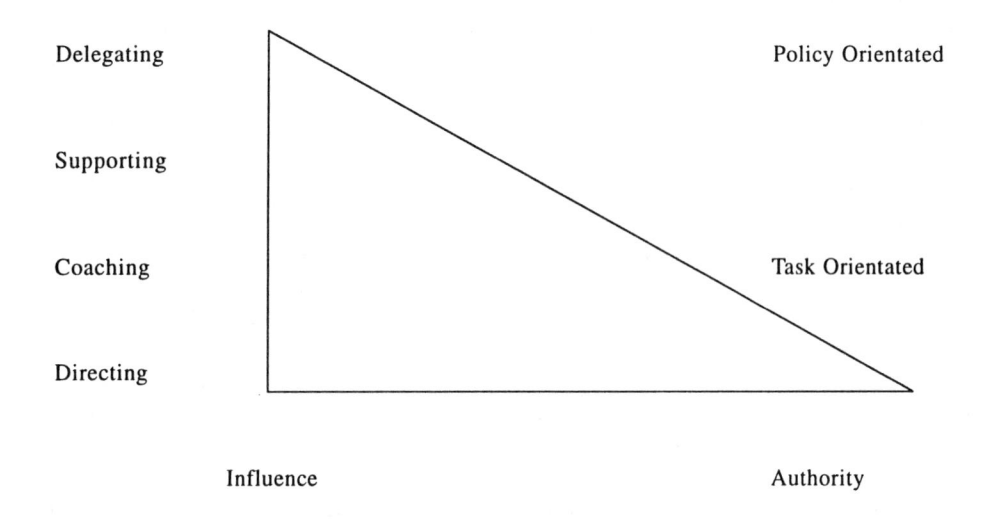

```
Delegating                                          Policy Orientated

Supporting

Coaching                                            Task Orientated

Directing


            Influence                               Authority
```

There are examples of all four styles in New Zealand sport. The sports that are large enough to employ an executive staff are more likely to be plotted on this continuum toward the delegating style, and be focused on policy issues, while those that are totally dependent on volunteer effort are more likely to be task orientated.

Who Leads?

The answer to this question has been complicated because at all levels of New Zealand sport, from the local club to the national governing body, activities have been led by elected or appointed volunteers. The management of New Zealand sport was conducted around the kitchen table and the leadership responsibilities held by the president or chairperson. Yet the standard of leadership provided by these volunteers was generally extremely high. For example, Anne Taylor (OBE) was President of N.Z. Netball from 1978 to 1987, and when she started, netball was the largest women's participation sport, but suffered from low media profile, only modest public interest, and little corporate support. But as a result primarily of her efforts, by the time she stepped down, the game enjoyed the huge advantage of commanding live television coverage, much greater general media interest, and considerable corporate sponsorship. Since then netball has cemented its position as the largest women's sport, and is still enjoying considerable interest from the public. Today when the Silver Ferns, the international team, play, particularly against their arch rivals, the Australians, tickets for the indoor venue are likely to be sold out in advance, and invariably the television ratings for the live telecast are comparable to those of the All Blacks. The recent appointment of the New Zealand coach following the 1993 World Games also attracted widespread media interest.

During Taylor's era, Lois Muir (OBE) built an enviable record as New Zealand coach and became the face of netball to which the public and media could relate. She set high standards for herself and expected nothing less from her players. Even in 1993, five years after retiring as national coach, she still is able to exert considerable influence over the game. Therefore it has to be said that the success of netball's development into one of New Zealand's most popular sports in the widest possible sense, must be credited to the ability of these two women to 'lead' the hundreds of thousands of netball players, coaches and administrators.

Ian Wells, as Chairman of N.Z. Tennis for 20 years, is another example of an outstanding sport leader, one who led that organisation through many stages of development. He adapted it to the changes associated with the professionalisation of the game nationally and internationally, and induced the organisation to change its name from the N.Z. Amateur Lawn Tennis Association to N.Z. Tennis (Inc.). It is no longer an amateur body of provincial associations which selected teams to represent New Zealand at Davis and Federation Cup Matches. It is now a business, attempting to identify and recruit youthful talent, and to provide appropriate coaching to develop the talent to compete against the best professional players, some of whom are amongst the highest paid sports people in the world who enjoy backing and support that New Zealand Tennis is simply not able to provide. In addition, N.Z. Tennis offers a valuable support service to its member associations, manages domestic tournaments and leagues, has established a coaching programme for all level of players, and ensures that appropriate tennis facilities are available for the growing number of players and spectators. The tennis organisation has an annual budget of over $1.1m, a playing membership of 55,257, and a huge team of volunteer administrators. Currently it has significant support in the form of a paid sport manager – one of the estimated number of 45 paid senior managers in New Zealand sport who in 1992 were supported by 70 administrative support staff and 78 coaching or technical directors.

The emergence of the sport management *profession* has complicated the issue of leadership, and many organisations have failed to address the question of whether powers of leadership should rest with the elected volunteers, many of whom are in effect unpaid staff, or the paid sport managers by virtue of their professional training and experience. But New Zealand sport has been ably led by representatives of both groups. In fact some of the greatest successes are the result of a combination of the two. For example, N.Z. Hockey has benefited from the joint leadership of David Appleby as Chairman, and Ramesh Patel, the paid Executive Director. But the key to the success of this duo has been the understanding between them in terms of responsibilities. David Appleby provided leadership to the Board, and was the spokesperson when dealing with the media, the sponsors, and other funding agencies such as the Hillary Commission and N.Z. Sports Foundation. He was an articulate and provocative leader, with business and leadership skills that were valuable in such activities. He paired well with Ramesh Patel whose background as an outstanding international player and respected coach gave him credibility with players, coaches and local level administrators. For his part, Ramesh is an astute thinker in the game, with the ability to communicate ideas and theories to a varied audience.

Similarly, the New Zealand Golf Association has been very well led for the past seven years by a duo of the past President and Chairman, the Rt. Hon. Mr. Justice Tom Gault and Executive Director Grant Clements. Golf has enjoyed outstanding success during this period, culminating with a victory at the 1992 World Amateur Championships. New Zealand golfers have become household names and 200,000 school children have participated in the KiwiGolf programme that has brought golf into school playgrounds. Once again that success must be credited against a large number of factors, but a key ingredient has been leadership.

Volunteer Leadership

There are many examples of sports that flourish and continue to be led by volunteers. The N.Z. Rugby Football Union has traditionally been led by an elected chairman. Ces Blazey, a past Chairman, is a good example. He headed New Zealand Rugby during many of its most controversial years and accepted the responsibility willingly, even during the extremely difficult times associated with the 1981 South African Tour. New Zealand Cricket is another example of an organisation strongly led by volunteers that has produced good results. Since 1990 Peter McDermott has provided very sound leadership, and both the Men's XI and the Women's XI performed extremely well in their most recent World Cups, 33 per cent more primary school girls and boys are playing the game in 1993 than 1992, and the most recent One-Day Series against Australia was a sell-out success. Peter's leadership has created the environment for this success. Obviously the contributions of a dedicated professional staff and hundreds of local association volunteers have been vital, but without a strong and focused leadership, the results would not have been so spectacular.

Another example of a volunteer, in this case a government-appointed volunteer, providing guidance, is that of Sir Ronald Scott who first came to the notice of the New Zealand public when he headed the 1974 Commonwealth Games Organising Committee. He was credited for much of the success of those Games, and maintained his influence over New Zealand sport until, in 1984, the then Minister for Sport, asked him to chair the 'Sport on the Move' Inquiry. At that time Sir Ronald had just returned from leading New Zealand's most successful ever Olympic team. As the first Chairman of the Hillary Commission he not only steered the work of the Commission and the professional staff, but also exerted considerable influence over the Commission's clients who collectively are the sport sector. He established a vision for New Zealand sport during the Review he chaired, and its findings were published in *Sport on the Move* (1985). Once formulated, that vision has guided many of the decisions of the Commission, and it has been the foundation for the Commission's programme development and intervention strategies.

Nine years later, with virtually all the recommendations from *Sport on the Move* in place, Sir Ronald decided to retire. The National Government, not surprisingly, chose to replace him with Wilson Whineray (OBE), an outstanding captain of sport and a successful captain of industry. Whineray was rated by many critics as one of the finest All Black captains with a comparable business career as a former Deputy Managing Director, and currently Chairman of one of New Zealand's biggest companies.

The Leader's Role

Although the dynamics of sport organisations are somewhat unique, the role of the leader is not too different from that in any business of a similar size: i.e. the primary function of a leader is to ensure an organisation's future. A leader must create an organisation that can operate effectively in its current environment and is able to deliver value to its customers and stakeholders, while always looking to its future.

The task might be difficult, but according to Martin Stewart-Weeks, (1993), a Sport and Business Management Consultant from Sydney, the following are the key attributes of successful organisations.

- they acknowledge that they are dependent on their customers;
- they recognise that change and security are not opposites. Stability is not security;
- they accept that it is action not rhetoric that works. 'People ignore what you say and respond to what you do';
- they are committed to constant innovation;
- they focus on long-term solutions which avoid 'quick-fix' solutions;
- they accept that there is no one to blame for the future but themselves.

It is the leader's task to establish a culture that enables these attributes to prevail, by establishing an organisation that incorporates a shared vision and values, a sense of mission, and clearly defined strategies. The leader must develop and implement sound human resource management practices; introduce appropriate structures and systems and strong financial resource management; and market the sport so that it is positioned well and presents a positive profile.

These elements which must interact and are all important, are well summarised by Stewart-Weeks in the diagram below that he calls the organisation effectiveness quadrant. All four quadrants are linked and vital to the success of the organisation. All contribute to the 'culture' and are influenced significantly by leadership.

Organisation Effectiveness Quadrant

Human Resource Management		Financial Resource Management	
	Vision and Values	Mission and Strategy	
STRUCTURE AND SYSTEMS		MARKETING: • Profile • Image • Position	

An organisation must have a vision that will shape its future, and provide a reference for current or day-to-day decisions. A vision must challenge and establish demanding targets, but also be realistic. A good leader will ensure an organisation is focused on this vision, which along with the values of an organisation, will direct its behaviour. The leader must ensure that there is an appropriate fit between the vision and values, the mission and strategies, and the systems, structures and skills within an organisation. These all contribute to the 'culture' of the organisation.

Adapting work from Rosabeth Moss Kanter, Stewart-Weeks identifies the four 'F's' as crucial considerations for a leader when establishing the 'culture' of an organisation, i.e. to make it:

- focused - having a set of objectives that guide the action of everyone at every level
- fast - getting the right things done quickly
- flexible - encouraging decentralised decision making and strategic planning
- friendly - encouraging alliances and partnerships, listens to customers.

An organisation must be all of these and the leaders must be able to harness another crucial ingredient – passion – to be successful. Passion is a particularly important resource in the business of sport. Fortunately, New Zealanders generally are passionate about their sport, as is evidenced by the numbers of volunteers in sport. The leaders of New Zealand sport must ensure that the systems they establish harness this passion as a positive contribution to the ownership of their business.

'Ownership' of the vision is vital if it is to have any chance of being achieved. If the membership of an organisation does not believe in the vision, then it is doomed. This poses a particularly difficult leadership challenge within sport organisations. It is difficult to communicate a vision to all levels of a sport. The club, association and provincial structure of most sports makes it extremely unlikely that the national leader will be able to communicate directly with the average club player or volunteer, but the vision must be accepted and communicated by the *leaders* at each level. Therefore a consistent and workable communication strategy must be followed to achieve this.

Many sports expend considerable energy and resources to develop a vision, and a plan to action that vision, but then fail to explain or sell these to their memberships, or stakeholders. However, during 1993, the Hillary Commission published a Draft 5-Year Strategic Plan for the Sport and Physical Leisure Industry. The Draft Plan, *Moving a Nation,* was itself the product of much consultation with its key client groups (National Sport and Physical Leisure Organisations; Territorial Local Authorities; and Regional Sports Trusts). Then, to enhance ownership of the Plan, the Commission established a comprehensive consultative process. First it invited the key personnel of each major client group to attend a National Forum where the eight visions contained in *Moving a Nation* were explained. Then the Commission Management, led by its Chief Executive, Peter Dale, held numerous Forums throughout the country to communicate these visions and to receive face-to-face feedback. It sought and considered further input by way of formal, written submissions and, over a period of two months, received 106 submissions, prior to the preparation of the final document to provide a set of guiding visions for the sport and physical leisure sector. Now it will be the responsibility of individual sports and their leaders to determine their role in enacting those visions.

What Attributes Must a Leader Possess?

Taking into account the above roles for leaders of New Zealand sport, what are the key attributes a leader must possess? *Vision* and *passion* are vital. A good leader must be a visionary and be able to conceptualise and 'sell' a picture of the future. Sport has in the past had an advantage over some other sectors of business. Its leaders have come from within the ranks of that sport. They have therefore possessed a natural passion for that activity. John Reid, the Chief Executive of Auckland Cricket, is a good example. He transferred his contribution from the test cricket arena to the board-room at Eden Park. Graham Dowling, his counterpart in New Zealand Cricket, was also a very successful test cricketer. It was a natural progression for them and many like them to bring their passion for the game with them into management and leadership roles. Each sport has some unique aspects, and it is important that the leaders of sport are able to capitalise on this uniqueness and build it into their vision.

The new breed of managers will not necessarily have had a background in a particular sport, and must be able to harness the 'passion' within their sport from the membership that they lead. Netball New Zealand in 1992 appointed a male Executive Director with no playing or coaching background in the game. If he is to at least share the leadership responsibilities in netball, then it will be his volunteer board members who provide the necessary passion.

Communication is a key to success. A leader must be a good communicator to articulate visions at many levels. The heads of a New Zealand sport must be able effectively to communicate with the average club member; the provincial or regional association; the elected national board or council; the media; the corporate sponsors; the international federation; and the referees' or umpires' associations. The good leader will also be a very good listener. *Listening* is a crucial skill for the heads of all organisations, but even more so when the goal is to utilise the energy and contribution of the large number of volunteers who underpin New Zealand sport. Someone who is unwilling or unable to hear what the members are saying, will struggle to formulate a vision that will not be owned by the members.

A good leader must also be a *role model*. People follow actions not words, so a leader who preaches one thing and does another, will not command the respect necessary for success. A leader having established systems and procedures must use them, while keeping a constant eye to review, refine and change them as necessary. Closely linked are the attributes of *integrity and honesty*. A leader that is honest and exercises the same values in decision-making will command respect and loyalty. A good leader must be *organised*. People expect a leader to have systems and habits that help bring some order to their efforts. Good time management, punctuality and reliability are all part of being organised, because they allow time for dealing with challenges, responding to opportunities, and constantly shaping the all-important visions, that add meaning to the work of the people whom they lead.

A good leader must also have empathy, i.e. a real understanding of the business and the needs of the people that make up their business. He or she must also be able to apply objectivity to their role. There is obviously a need for balance here. A leader who is unable to leave aside the day-to-day decision making will struggle to create a vision for the future. Good judgement and sound common sense are vital attributes in striking the required balance.

Who Should Provide Leadership in the Future?

Despite the growing number of *professional* managers employed in New Zealand sport in the foreseeable future, the foundation of the business will continue to be built on the efforts of volunteers. The leadership of volunteers is therefore most likely to come from within their ranks. The paid executive will play an increasing role, particularly in the large organisations, but this will be through coordination with the elected leader if good, clear and open working relationships are established between them.

For the smaller organisations in the business of sport, all the leadership will have to come from the volunteers. It will be the passion that they have for their involvement in sport that will provide them with the motivation to make the enormous contribution necessary for the continued development of their sport. For example, Perry Bathgate, Chairman of Trampoline New Zealand, is a dedicated volunteer who provided very sound leadership in his sport and created the vision of hosting the World Trampolining Championship in New Zealand. This was an ambitious undertaking for an organisation with a modest national membership of 191 people, and its success suggests that people like Perry Bathgate will continue to formulate and action a vision for their sport.

In summary, and in an overall industry context, the right leadership will become more important as the Hillary Commission continues to encourage sport organisations to take control and responsibility of their own destinies. One of the Hillary Commission's (1993) visions is to empower sports to take increased control of their own planning and operations.

> Managing a successful sport and leisure organisation requires forward planning and strategic decision making. The key response from the Commission must be a forward commitment of funding for priorities that are set by the organisation itself. The Commission's goal will be to provide funds in bulk form for three years to be expended on the basis of management plans agreed with the Commission. True partnerships will evolve as the Commission contributes to the whole operation and development of a national organisation. Such a partnership implies that the successes and failures of the national organisation will be shared by the Commission.

The Commission's vision is dependent on the ability of its partners to plan for the future, to make strategic decisions with that future in mind, and to have strong and visionary leadership.

Review Questions

1. Does the emergence of a paid sport management profession change the leadership role of the elected, unpaid, volunteer manager?
2. How important as a tool of leadership is communication?
3. What is the leader's role in managing change in an organisation?
4. What is the difference between leadership and management?

References

Blanchard, K., Zigarmi, P. and Zigarmi, D. (1985), *Leadership and the One Minute Manager*, New York: William Morrow and Co.

Chaudhry-Lawton, R. and Lawton, R. (1992), *Ignition! Sparking Organizational Change*, London: Century Business.

Drucker, P. (1992), *Managing the Non-Profit Organization*, Oxford, Great Britain: Butterworth-Heinemann Ltd.

Fox, K. (1993), 'Maintaining Balance in a Pluristic World: Critical Thinking and Ethical Leadership in Recreation', *Recreation Canada,* vol. 51, no. 1, pp. 39-42.

Goode Vick, C. (1989), *You Can Be A Leader*, Champaign, Illinois: Sagamore Publishing.

Hillary Commission for Sport, Fitness and Leisure (1993), *Moving a Nation*, Wellington: Hillary Commission for Sport, Fitness and Leisure.

Jarvi, C.K. (1993), 'Leaders Who Meet Today's Changing Needs', *Parks & Recreation*, vol. 28 no. 3, pp. 60-64, 162.

Jensen, B., Sullivan, C., Wilson, N., Berkeley, M. and Russell, D. (1993), *The Business of Sport and Leisure Report*, Wellington: Hillary Commission for Sport, Fitness and Leisure.

Russell, D. and Wilson, N. (1991), *Life in New Zealand Commission Report Volume 1: Executive Overview,* Dunedin, New Zealand: University of Otago.

Sports Development Inquiry Committee (1985), *Sport On The Move: Report of the Sports Development Inquiry*, Wellington: The Ministry of Recreation and Sport.

Stewart-Weeks, M. (1991), *The Microeconomic Reform of Sport: Case Studies in Restructuring National Sporting Organisations; Australian Sports Commission National Executive Directors' Workshop*, Sydney: The Albany Consulting Group.

Stewart-Weeks, M. (1993), *The People Decisions: Improving Human Resource Management for Better Performance in Sport, Fitness and Leisure Organisations: A One-Day Workshop for Full-time Staff; Wellington, Christchurch, Auckland,* Sydney: The Albany Consulting Group.

Thomas, P. (1993), *Straight from The Hart*, Auckland: Moa Beckett.

Suggested Reading

Covey, S.R. (1989), *The 7 Habits of Highly Effective People*, New York: Simon and Schuster.

Moss Kanter, R. (1992), *When Giants Learn to Dance, Mastering the Challenges of Strategy Management and Careers in the 1990s*, New York: Simon and Schuster.

Senge, P.M. (1990), *The Fifth Discipline, The Art and Practice of the Learning Organisation*, New York: Doubleday/Currency.

Sports Marketing

Peter McDermott and Ron Garland

> **In this chapter you will become familiar with the following terms:**
>
> *consumer benefits*
>
> *franchising*
>
> *lifestyle marketing*
>
> *market research*
>
> *conversion chain*
>
> *performance measures*
>
> *intangibility*
>
> *subjectivity*
>
> *branding*
>
> *barriers to conversion*
>
> *market plan*
>
> *product extension*

There are many definitions of marketing similar to the following: 'the performance of activities that direct the flow of goods and services from producer to user to satisfy the customer and accomplish the organisation's objectives' (McCarthy, 1975).

Marketing of sport, however, differs substantially from traditional marketing. Marketing of sports activities or events is related to a concept known as life-style marketing, which Hanan (1980) describes as a strategy for seizing the concept of a market according to its most meaningful recurrent patterns of attitudes and activities, and then tailoring products and their promotional strategies to fit these patterns. Basically, marketing practice has a unity irrespective of the product or service being sold, but the challenge is choosing those concepts, tools and tactics that are appropriate in each context.

Successful retail marketing ensures that sports are able to provide financial support for increasing participation, and developing the product and its components also ensures that sport is able to maintain its profile as a leisure activity. Marketing and the promotion of sports activities in New Zealand has only achieved business status since the early 1970s. As other chapters in this book show, already it has had a marked effect on the manner in which sport is organised and even the way in which it is played and presented. This chapter will focus upon consumer needs, marketing processes, product branding, objectives, stakeholders, market plan and price. Several examples are taken from New Zealand cricket to demonstrate what could be achieved in the marketing of any sport.

Sport managers committed to increasing participation must ensure they are able to recognise customer needs and how their sport is able to satisfy these needs. Once recognition has been achieved and the benefits identified, the marketing of the sport to the potential participants must be formulated, recognising the features which influence consumer decisions as to which activity or activities they choose to pursue. Selling points of sport include:

- health benefits from active, physical activities
- personal satisfaction through achieving standards of performance either as an individual or as a member of a team
- opportunity to develop unique skills and achieve personal recognition amongst peers
- social interaction opportunities
- physical wellbeing and enjoyment.

To some extent most sports do provide these opportunities, but the use of them is dependent upon and influenced by the following factors:

- social and cultural factors
- family and peer pressures
- identification with role models involved in particular sports
- inspirational success of national or representative teams
- regional and access influences
- promotional and presentation activities of sport organisations
- economic factors
- media influence, particularly television.

Marketing Processes

Marketing of sport can be divided into the two processes of production and promotion. Well organised sport organisations could be departmentalised as follows:

Production	Management	Marketing and Promotion
Increased participation Improved performance support Maintaining memberships Development of representative players/ teams and role models	Financial controls Staff and representative administration Price and costing of activities Budgeting	Selling of attendances Attracting media standard Increasing television exposure and ratings Increasing and/or maintaining sponsorships

Historically, sport marketing in New Zealand has been unplanned and haphazard. In many sports there is virtually no effort to plan and promote activities. In amateur organisations sports have traditionally been production driven, administered by current or previous participants, with little regard for customer requirements. Many such administrators have come from production segments of the sport, having themselves been grass-roots participants and administrators. Successful sport organisations, whilst recognising the contribution of such individuals, are now obliged to become market driven, and to recognise the need to adapt sport and their associated products to both modern participant and spectator requirements. Otherwise these organisations will not attract their share of financial sponsorship and will languish for want of cashflow, benefits, and business acumen.

Attendances at sports events prior to modern communication developments in society were generally influenced by:

- lack of mobility of the population
- social conditions
- financial and economic conditions
- lack of competition and alternative attractions
- poor access to facilities and local venues
- peer and family pressure.

The 1930s era, for example, was characterised by substantial attendances at rugby, rugby league, boxing, wrestling, and horse racing.

Of the sports and pastimes mentioned, horse racing is an example of one which has not changed to meet present-day customer needs. For example, typically the racing clubs are administered by committees drawn from members, trainers, and owners. The product presentation is virtually unchanged with little or no attention having been paid to the requirements of prospective consumers. Spectator attendance and following of horse racing has been falling steadily as a consequence of the sport's inability to market its benefits and attractions in competition with new sports where the needs of the public and members have been recognised. In the time in which horse racing has developed extremely slowly (if at all), other sports have improved both their products (for example, by rule changes) and the the products' presentation (for example, clothing and uniform changes).

In particular limited-over cricket, one-day internationals, day-night cricket, and coloured clothing have helped add excitement for spectators. In both rugby and rugby league certain variations to the rules have improved the flow and speed of the game. These three sports have all introduced marketing and promotion techniques to meet customer requirements and competitive activities. There has also been more competition and rivalry between sports for consumer attention, and this can be seen with the new entrepreneurial sports emanating from the United States – basketball, baseball and gridiron. With these and similar sports, comes the concept of 'franchising' of a sports team or club, where a commercial organisation or entrepreneur 'owns' a club, team or sporting activity. This means that the activity is marketed and promoted, with the production element of players 'purchased' or imported from the proceeds of the successful marketing activities. In these instances the entrepreneurial activity often overtook the development and production function of the sport.

It follows that sports now compete with each other for a share of the public's leisure expenditure and uncommitted time. Available activities have increased substantially. Increased media communications, increasing wealth, substantial mobility and transport improvements have led to vast competition not only from other sports but from a wide range of travel, leisure and recreational opportunities. But sport as a producer has substantial identifiable differences to these other goods and services. These significant differences include the unpredictability of the product, inconsistency of quality, strong emotional attachment and identification (with a team, nation or individual), and the subjectivity of judgement of the consumers with respect to the product. Sports events also rely on the quality of venues, the packaging of the entertainment surrounding the main event, the comfort of the accommodation, and the accessibility of the venue. It has also to be remembered that sport as a product is intangible, and, in the words of Veeck and Linn (1965), 'the customer comes out of the park with nothing except a memory'. Thus, sports marketers need to have full awareness of their product, of the needs of participants, of spectators and of supporters. Importantly, sports administrators must identify those items beyond their control, such as the environmental factors, social conditions, economic conditions, and competition. Like any other business management process, the sports marketing process should be strategically and systematically planned. Research, marketing and feedback are essential in the development of a successful sports marketing plan and the attainment of organisational goals.

Branding

As the first step towards establishing such a plan, sports need to identify the various brands within their sport. Within cricket the identifiable brands are:

1) Domestic Four-Day First Class Cricket (Shell Trophy)
2) Domestic One-Day Cricket (Shell Cup)
3) Test Matches
4) International One-Day Cricket.

Then in each instance the different characteristics of each branded product has to be identified, because each brand has different consumers whose reactions need to be determined before an attempt is made to meet them. Thus branding a product not only covers or influences consumers, but serves to identify clearly definable products with differing sponsor appeal. It enables sports to package all the elements of their product satisfactorily to highlight the strengths of each element, to refine and develop positive features, to eliminate weaknesses, and to identify brand consumers and their characteristics. Research has shown very clearly that the profile of a Test Match supporter is different from that of a One-Day Limited Over International supporter.

Objectives

Sport is a business, and like all businesses only survives when income exceeds expenditure. In the case of sport, expenditure includes the costs of development, promotion and administration of the organisation. The objectives of such administration are:

- to ensure satisfactory funding for the sport to continue and develop at all levels;
- to ensure that the sporting activity is able to satisfactorily compete for public support, media exposure, and sponsorship funds in an extremely competitive market.

In New Zealand successful sport organisations are driven from the grass-roots development of the product, with a professional marketing administration ensuring that consumer requirements are met. As such, the objectives in most New Zealand sports are significantly more community based than their counterparts in the United States. There, the franchise holder or owner of a team or sports event is motivated by return on investment in normal economic terms. Such an entrepreneur may have little commitment to the development of the sport, and accordingly endeavours to generate funds with the object of importing skills to continue to enhance the marketability of the team. The consequence of such actions is that there is a substantially higher level of amateur participation in organised sport in New Zealand than there is in the United States where entrepreneurial activity dominates organised sport.

Market Research

Once product, brands and objectives have been clearly defined, managers can use market research to identify the potential consumers, market segments, strengths and weaknesses of the product, and develop a marketing strategy. For example, in June 1991, New Zealand Cricket engaged the services of Forsyte Research of Auckland to collect, collate and prepare information to assist with the successful marketing and promotion of the sport. As an organising body, New Zealand Cricket Inc. is charged with the responsibility for marketing and developing cricket as a national sport. New Zealand Cricket had a number of strategies open to it to increase revenues:

- to maintain and consolidate the existing customer base by meeting the needs of *regular patrons*
- to build the level of regular attendance by cementing *occasional patrons to regular patrons*
- to expand the pool of *regular* and *occasional patrons* by cementing *occasional followers* into at least *occasional patrons*.

It soon became clear that New Zealand Cricket needed to discover and circumvent likely barriers to the conversion of patrons, and in the process to consider the role of television as a competitor for the existing and potential cricket audience.

At the outset it was important for the researchers to understand cricket's presence in New Zealand and to ascertain the level of interest it attracts. Accordingly, they sought to establish a conversion chain of consumers grouped into the three categories mentioned previously – occasional follower, occasional patron, and regular patron – but added a fourth (new follower) as follows:

| (A) New Follower | → | (B) Occasional Follower | → | (C) Occasional Patron | → | (D) Regular Patron |

Members of each category were differentiated by:

- their degree of general interest in sport
- their degree of interest in cricket

- their level of knowledge of the sport and its personalities
- attendance behaviour
- motivations and barriers
- their level of interest and support in individual brands of New Zealand Cricket.

The objective of New Zealand Cricket was to move consumers through the chain from category A through to category D. To achieve the objective the research included comparative conversion chains for competing sports or activities such as rugby union, rugby league, netball, soccer and tennis. Barriers to movement up the conversion chain were also identified here and suggested improvements to services (and removal of barriers) identified. Similarly, the demographics of the four identified categories in the conversion chain were established.

As part of the initial research, 508 adults were interviewed by telephone in the five main centres (Auckland, Hamilton, Wellington, Christchurch and Dunedin). The occasional patron (category C) was identified as a person who aimed to attend at least one or two matches a season. These occasional patrons made up one quarter (26 per cent) of the sample, and most (73 per cent) of them were males aged between 20 years and 49 years.

Barriers relating to cricket were identified as:

- 'boring sport'
- 'takes too long to finish'
- 'don't understand the rules'
- 'New Zealand team doesn't perform well'
- poor facilities (seating, car parking, access to food and beverage)
- crowd behaviour at cricket
- preference for television coverage.

But the research also made it clear that the barriers could be circumvented by marketing strategies that made use of:

- atmosphere of One-Day Internationals
- more serene atmosphere of Test matches
- success of New Zealand teams
- excitement of watching live sport
- stimulating national pride
- quality of teams and of individual performances.

Market Plan

Once demographics, barriers, and positive aspects of participation in the sport and its potential consumers have been established, sport marketers must define the target market and the manner in which it is to be satisfied. They should develop a marketing plan or strategy which is highly focused and directed at specific categories of consumer or consumer groups. Similarly the sport marketer should also focus on individual brands or products within the sport which best satisfy requirements and direct marketing efforts accordingly. The sport marketer may choose to segment the market and to classify potential consumers on the basis of their needs and the ability of the sport to satisfy these needs. The marketer must not only define the target market but also the manner in which it is to be satisfied. The measure of the ability to satisfy the consumer requirements will be the moving of spectators from category A towards category D on the conversion chain (p. 195). Consumers within these categories are defined as having reasonable interest in the sport through actual attendances, television ratings, media support and membership of clubs and venue facilities.

In the case of cricket the categories A and D were disregarded, because the non-follower category had barriers which were considered virtually insurmountable, and the Regular Patron category comprised individuals whose needs were almost completely satisfied, and required only the confirmation of their position. In cricket the target market was therefore those in categories B and C, with a view to moving them to category D. For instance, the profile of the Occasional Patron satisfactorily matched with those who supported the One-Day International branded product, because as a generalisation, One-Day supporters attend for the entertainment and not for the intricacies of the game of cricket itself. But One-Day Internationals do attract a broad range of supporters, each seeking to observe different aspects of the game. In particular, the Occasional Patron and Occasional Follower look for the interaction with the crowd, and this distinguishes them from the Regular Patrons who are more motivated by the calibre of the teams and the contest.

Therefore in order to develop One-Day International cricket, the researchers advised the New Zealand Cricket Council to devise strategies that would continue to attract Regular Patrons through the promotion of teams and the contest, and to play down the main market attraction for them. But at the same time the Cricket Council was advised to develop strategies to attract Occasional Patrons and Occasional Followers with hype and entertainment. It was argued that the outcome would encourage potential patrons to make the transition from intention to attend into actual attendance, *viz* the flow chart showing the conversion chain for One-Day Internationals.

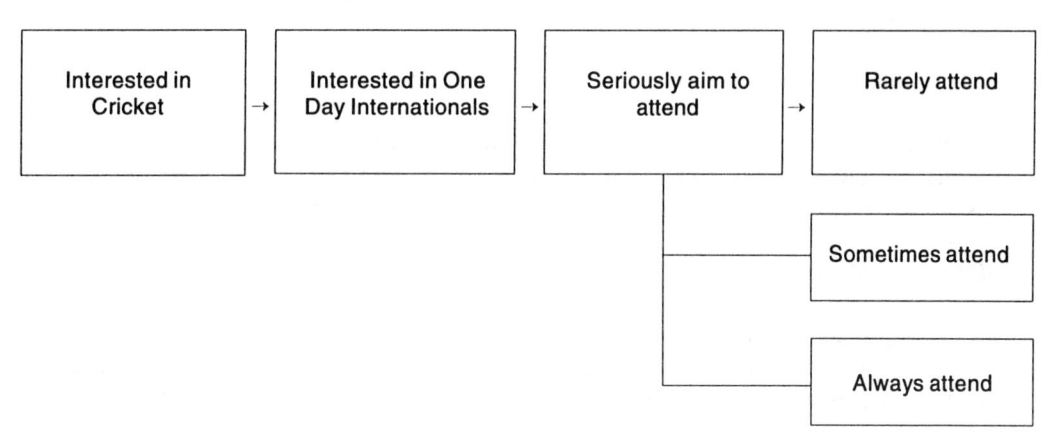

```
┌──────────────┐   ┌──────────────────┐   ┌──────────────┐   ┌──────────────┐
│ Interested in│ → │ Interested in One│ → │Seriously aim │ → │ Rarely attend│
│   Cricket    │   │ Day Internationals│   │  to attend   │   │              │
└──────────────┘   └──────────────────┘   └──────────────┘   └──────────────┘
                                                  │
                                                  │          ┌──────────────┐
                                                  ├───────── │Sometimes attend│
                                                  │          └──────────────┘
                                                  │
                                                  │          ┌──────────────┐
                                                  └───────── │ Always attend│
                                                             └──────────────┘
```

To move consumers along the consumer chain and then down into the 'always attend' category, it is necessary to identify what prevents attendances and what motivates the desire to attend One-Day Internationals. Similar charts can be produced for all brands and read with the overall Consumer Chart, with the researched barriers and motivation to attend identified, with the demographic descriptions of consumers, and with the identification of consumer needs, so that marketing strategies can be planned accordingly. As a result of the marketing research it obtained, the New Zealand Cricket Council improved its venue facilities, restructured its pricing policy, improved its presentation of the product, upgraded entertainment activities involved with each event, and targeted its promotional activities, in the case of One-Day Internationals, at youth (*Young Guns* campaign; *Great Balls of Fire* international branding; and *It's Good to be Back* campaign).

Effective marketing usually means implementing simultaneously many of the strategies and tactics described above. Indeed, the improvement of venue facilities involved:

- more toilets and improvements to existing toilet facilities
- more food and beverage outlets
- the introduction of replay screens.

The review of pricing resulted in:

- uniform pricing across all venues
- the introduction of family group pricing
- free entry to Test matches for children belonging to a cricket club.

Improvements in the way cricket (the product) was *presented* included:

- better coloured uniforms for the players
- playing the national anthem
- better crowd control, allowing players to leave the ground unhindered
- better programmes
- distribution of player profiles to the media
- increased branding in the promotional activity
- increased attention to merchandising at the venues.

And the upgrading of entertainment accompanying each event saw:

- 'pop' bands playing in the intervals (for example, between innings, lunch-times)
- special displays (e.g. sky diving, police dog displays, mini-cricket) in the intervals
- use of the replay screen, and of music over the speaker system.

Performance Measure

Sport marketers, like those in the business world generally, have to be accountable, and, in the case of sport, after an appropriate time various performance measures can be applied to their work. Thus after three years the New Zealand Cricket Council was able to measure:

- increased participation
- increased attendances
- improved television ratings
- increased media coverage
- increased revenues.

These improvements were a result of:

- a controlled and extensive market research programme
- an integrated and focused market strategy
- an improvement in presenting an event
- an improvement in performance of teams as a result of increased investment in production
- the establishment of strong and coordinated relationships with stakeholders and adviser organisations.

Stakeholders, Consultants and Advisory Organisations

There has been an historical tendency for sports organisations to shun the services of consultants and advisory groups. Amateur administrators who had risen from grass-roots activities to national or international positions were often not prepared to accept outside advice or guidance. These self-made administrators were generally product driven (not market driven) and motivated by a lifetime of involvement as players, coaches or administrators. They often were unaware of the concept of consumer needs and requirements and were committed to promoting and driving their own concept of their sport. Such administrators did not recognise the concept of *consumer ownership* of the sport or activity and, accordingly, they were slow to react to public requirements and to outside threats to their sport.

Modern sport managers, on the contrary, recognise the potential help of specialist consultancy or advisory organisations such as sponsorship procuring agents, advertising agents and research organisations. They also recognise the important place held by regional sports groups, participants, administration groups and international teams, all of whom have a part in their sport. It is imperative that ownership of sport remains with the sport and its stakeholders.

Sponsors

Whilst sponsors provide funding assistance for sports organisations, individuals, teams or events, it is important that the roles of both sides *vis-à-vis* the integrity of sport be kept under review. Traditional sponsorship arrangements were prepared by a sporting organisation, identifing the *saleable* elements of the sport or event. These included the naming rights, hospitality opportunities, and other such benefits from association with the sport and its participants. Increasingly, both the sports organisations and the sponsors have come to seek better returns for their sponsorship contracts, particularly with respect to marketing and promotion of their products and services. As the Managing Director of Australia Sports Marketing, which handles Ford's sponsorship of the Australian Open Tennis Tournament, (cited in Phillips, 1993) said, in the recessionary '90s, marketers have become far more accountable for the promotional dollars they spend. He believes this trend has reduced the emotional element in sports sponsorship, and has made marketers scrutinise their options more and ask for a lot more in return. In other words, sports and sponsors need to establish a business relationship rather than a sports/sponsor relationship. Both need to identify their marketing and promotion objectives and endeavour to reconcile them. To do this they have to make a considered approach to the current position of the respective organisations, their marketing and promotional plans, and their total business objectives. The successful reconciliation of objectives will lead to a coordinated marketing approach; and will assist the sport as well as the commercial organisation. Thus, it is important to match a sponsorship with a company's target market, or, in the words of Rodney Northam, General Manager of a sports and event sponsorship agency's sales division, *relevance* is the key. In short:

There is no point in Optus sponsoring the London to Sydney car rally because normally all the cars in that event are old. Optus is modern and needs to be seen as being progressive. A Solar car challenge travelling from Darwin to Adelaide across the desert would be different because the event is environmentally friendly and totally futuristic and would attract the sort of sponsorship Optus should be in (Phillips, 1993).

To take another example, in the light of the anti-smoking campaign and legislation in 1990, New Zealand Cricket Inc. chose to move from Rothmans Tobacco company as a major sponsor, to the Bank of New Zealand. At an early stage a sponsors' council was formed which, with the assistance of mutual advertising agents, defined the strategic goals of not only the Bank of New Zealand and New Zealand Cricket, but also of its associated sub-sponsors. New Zealand Cricket was able to plan its marketing strategies with the knowledge of the objectives of the sponsoring organisations, and so establish a successful business relationship between the sport and its sponsors and maintain a continued exchange of information between all parties. New Zealand Cricket has thus been able to tailor its marketing programme in full confidence that it is compatible with that of its sponsoring organisation.

Advertising Agencies, Marketing Consultants

Fortunately there are similar progressive sport groups in New Zealand that are increasingly utilising the services of professional advertising agencies and marketing consultants to promote their activities and their retail sales. In many instances the introduction to an agency or consultant is through the offices of the sponsorship organisation, thus creating a situation where the agency is able to participate in the reconciliation of respective marketing objectives. The agency appointed in such a manner is also able to package the sport to suit the needs of the sponsor as well as those of the sport organisation. The sponsor is also able to assist the sport with the establishment of a satisfactory advertising budget so as to maximise its use. Notable joint programmes produced in this way include the Steinlager/All Blacks/*Stand by Me* theme; the Bank of New Zealand/New Zealand Cricket/*Pride in New Zealand* theme, and the Dominion Breweries/New Zealand Cricket/*Young Guns* theme.

Media, Television

A major part of any sport organisation's promotion and marketing mix is publicity and public relations. Public relations is a sport's overall effort to create a particular image for itself with its target market or markets and the community in which it operates. Sport organisations need to establish a detailed communication plan identifying appropriate spokespersons and the area in which they are required to respond to media or public enquiries. Senior executives and members of international or representative teams need to be well instructed in the manner in which to respond to media and/or public. Regular news releases and communications must be maintained so that media are fully informed of activities past and present. Role models must be developed and their positive images presented to the public via the media. The opportunity exists in all sections of the media for a sports organisation to promote and project a positive image of its sport, its benefits and its image.

Delivery of the promotional message is becoming increasingly competitive, and restricted access to television coverage for sport in New Zealand places pressure on all but the most popular sports to plan effective marketing campaigns. The helpful influence and effect of television coverage of events enable the sports concerned to:

- develop their product for a popular medium
- seek feedback as to the quality of the product
- promote future events and activities
- create income earning opportunities from signage and sponsorship
- develop easily identifiable role models
- provide opportunities for promotion of the sport generally.

Television ratings, whilst limited in their application by their statistical non-analytical nature, can also provide satisfactory performance measures, particularly in comparison with other activities and entertainment opportunities. For example, in 1993 the ratings for a New Zealand v Australia Rugby League Test Match – staged and televised (delayed) on a Friday night, exceeded that of New Zealand v Australia Bledisloe Cup Test Match – staged and televised (live) on a Saturday afternoon. In the case of the Rugby League the total audience was larger, although it represented a lower percentage of available viewers. The message to the administrations of the respective sports from this comparison is that there is a continuing shift to night-time entertainment, and that the timing of the fixture is an extremely important part of staging the event.

Sales Promotions

Sales promotion is another part of the promotional mix, and includes any other activity that cannot be called advertising or publicity. Sport organisations may devise selling tactics which can be promoted with an event. Included amongst these activities are tactics (gimmicks) such as free tickets, competitions, lucky draws and gifts. Recently cricket organisations have introduced $1.00 per day entry to Test matches, free days for sponsors, and club days, which have served the objective of satisfactorily promoting the fixture and encouraging attendance which would not otherwise have happened. The objective is to involve the public and to encourage their further participation (represented by movement up the conversion chart), and this compensates for the failure in that particular instance to achieve excess of income over expenditure.

Price

Price is another of the elements in marketing, but market research indicates that pricing does not have a major influence upon the decision of the consumer to attend a fixture. What is important is for pricing to be competitive with the pricing of other similar events.

Prices can be determined by a number of factors: recovery of costs; market conditions; value; competition; scarcity; and special features that include social acceptability and status. For example, the prices for the Henley Rowing Regatta, Wimbledon Tennis and Lords Cricket Test bear no relation to value offered as a sports event, but do have added value in terms of social status and scarcity. Prices can also be directed to assist with the image the sport wishes to project. For instance, the creation of a family pass, favourably priced, at Test Cricket, led to a considerable increase in the number of families and young people attending. The key to successful pricing strategies is to react to market demands and the elasticity of that demand. The effect of minor price fluctuations has historically appeared not to affect demand. In most cases it appears price alone does not affect demand – promotional strategies and the quality of the product may alter perceived values and accordingly affect reaction to price.

Consumers equate price with value, and discounted or free products must be equated with little or no value. Bill Veeck, an American sports marketer, declares that he would never give tickets away, no matter how poorly his teams were performing. To Veeck, tickets are the one thing he has to sell and to give them away would be to cheapen the product (Veeck and Linn, 1962).

Value, Product, Promotion and Venue

The sport product is really a mixture of both product and service. Both products and services are offered for sale, and both satisfy the needs of customers. However, it is the benefits derived from the products or services (rather than the products themselves) that actually persuade customers to buy a product or service.

The services aspect of sport is easy to understand. Like any service, a sporting event is staged (created) and consumed simultaneously and cannot be stored (at least the *live* action cannot be stored). Hence the service part of sport is a perishable commodity – empty seats or unsold tickets are opportunity losses, sales lost forever. The intangible nature of services (and sport is no exception) – not being able to see or test the performance before buying your ticket – means the consumer has to rely on the reputation of the contest, the stager of the event and the product extension (venue, facilities, and entertainment). As mentioned already, the sports product by itself is unlikely to satisfy consumer needs beyond the very small percentage of followers who are totally committed or dedicated. In a modern competitive situation the product extension such as venue, facilities, entertainment, and atmosphere, become crucial to the total product.

Sport events in themselves are intangible and subjective; a good performance by a team or individual as judged by one sector of the audience may be considered indifferent by another sector, depending upon the view of the event they get, the expectations they have of the event, the perceptions of the participants they may have, and the differing values they may place on the skills involved. In preparing an event, the sport marketer should undertake market research to modify the event in an effort to satisfy consumer ends and adapt to market requirements. Cricket as a product was in decline until the advent of the amended One-Day Limited Over Game. The next stage was to identify the strengths of modifications and to further adapt the product with rule changes, introduction of coloured clothing, and the innovation of Day/Night fixtures. In making the adjustments to the product, the sports organisations concerned recognised the need to ensure that product extensions further satisfied consumer needs. These extensions incuded:

- venues and venue facilities
- parking facilities and transport requirements
- safety and security of crowd areas
- pre-fixture and half-time entertainment packages
- replay screens
- food and beverage facilities and availability
- picnic and tailgate party areas
- clean and secure bathroom/toilet facilities

- clear explanation of events, participants and rules
- comfort of surroundings including satisfactory seating and shelter
- child-care facilities
- access areas to players for autographs and public relations activities.

These factors all directly affect the retail consumer decision to attend or support an event. Additional product extensions which affect the image of the sport or event include:

- sponsor facilities
- hospitality facilities
- media areas
- communication facilities
- interview room
- players' lounges
- members' lounges and facilities.

Many of the above factors are beyond the control of the sport marketer, and they reflect the need for a continued business relationship between the sport marketer, the venue marketer, the participants, the media, the sponsors and the consumer.

When assessing the value of the product, account must be taken of all these elements, whilst the promotion of the event will also highlight aspects of the product extension which will serve to influence or reinforce a consumer decision to attend an event.

Conclusion

Whilst the marketing of sport is unique and has distinctive differences to the marketing of standard products and services, its various elements are compatible with modern marketing techniques. Despite the uncertainties of quality, expectations and perceptions relating to sport as a lifestyle experience, the models of marketing are essential for sport – if it is to compete in the modern leisure market. Sport groups in New Zealand have been slow to recognise that marketing and promotion of their sport or activity is essential for its survival. There are still too many examples of producer-driven and controlled organisations who believe the very existence of the sport is sufficient for its survival and expansion. Fortunately, the advance of professional and demanding sponsors, sophisticated media outlets, professional playing teams and increased communications has meant sports organisations are recognising and reacting to the need for marketing. The existence of a number of well promoted, professionally organised sporting alternatives for the New Zealand public, either as participants or as spectators, continues to testify to the wellbeing of New Zealand generally.

Sport marketing will continue to develop to satisfy consumer needs, and in the process have an exciting future with increased opportunities and entertainment. In summary, the major factors influencing sport marketing will include:

- increasing competition from all forms of leisure activity
- increasing cultural awareness and price
- continued growth of sports
- expansion and improvement of electronic media and communications

- increasing use of electronic aids
- high standards of performance
- vast sponsorship support and publicity
- increasing importance of role models
- substantial improvement to venues and facilities
- innovative product extensions and promotional gimmicks
- increasing leisure time
- increasing wealth.

Sports organisations must continually be projecting their plans on a minimum three to five-year basis and beyond. Endeavouring to visualise the market, social conditions and sport's place in society in the year 2010 is an exercise which should at some time preoccupy the modern sports administrator. Perhaps if racing clubs had taken this approach in the 1960s they might not be in the grave position they now occupy.

Review Questions

1. Review the role of market research and the conversion chain in identifying New Zealand Cricket's market plan.
2. Show how sport's selling points (or consumer benefits) are affected by economic, social and cultural factors.
3. Demonstrate how sports marketing can help match the varying needs from sport with those that both players and spectators have.
4. A sports event is both a product and a service. List the product and service features of such an event and review the differences between products and services.
5. Outline your argument for convincing a friend to attend your favourite sports event rather than visiting McDonalds to spend her or his leisure dollar.
6. You have been hired as a marketing consultant to market your favourite sporting code at national level from next year. Using the New Zealand Cricket example, what marketing actions would you recommend to help your code's success in the next five years?

References

Hanan, M. (1980), *Life-styled Marketing – How to Position Products for Premium Products*, New York: AAMCON Book Division.
McCarthy, E. (1975), *Basic Marketing* (5th edition), Homewood, Illinois: Richard D. Irwin, Inc.
Phillips, M. (1993), 'Good Sports with Money', *ABM Magazine*.
Veeck, W. and Linn, E. (1962), *Veeck as in Wreck*, New York: Pitman.
Veeck, W. and Linn, E. (1965), *The Hustler Handbook*, New York: Pitman.

Suggested Reading

Bateson, J.E.G. (1992), *Managing Services Marketing: Text and Readings,* Sydney: Dryden Press.
Grönroos, C. (1990), *Service Management and Marketing: Managing the Moment of Truth in Service Competition,* Toronto: Maxwell MacMillan.

Kotler, P. (1986), *Principles of Marketing*, Englewood Cliffs: Prentice-Hall.
Kotler, P. and Andreasen, A. (1991), *Strategic Marketing for Non-profit Organisations*, Englewood Cliffs: Prentice-Hall.
November, P. (1991), *Marketing in the Land of the Long White Cloud*, Wellington: Unibook.

Public Relations and Sport

Geoff Henley

In this chapter you will become familiar with the following terms:

public support	stakeholders of sport
visibility and profile	brand loyalty
positive image	communications plan

This chapter advocates the greater use of public relations concepts and techniques to enhance the profile of sport. It takes the view that without a strong and positive public profile, sport generally will start to lose out against other forms of recreation, and specific sports will find it difficult to support their domestic and international programmes. It makes clear that public relations is a highly cost-effective method of promoting sport.

How is Sport Seen?

The first step in applying public relations techniques is to see sport from the viewpoint of the participant and the public, and to recognise the diversity of their interests and motivations. The task is not easy, because in sport there are as many different opinions as there are people to voice them. To some, male physical contact sports are simply legalised violence, to others they are a test of strength, to others still they are a clash of *wits, will and weight.*

While sports are seen by different people in different ways there are often some common themes. Some are seen as *now, today,* others as *yesterday, conservative and staid.* Some sports are identified with particular ethnic groups, with certain income or educational and sometimes occupational groups.

Sport is often as controversial off the field as it is on the field, and it incurs endless media speculation about team selection, who is going to sign with whom, or whose eyes were gouged by whom. The sheer emphasis on sport in our culture, and its alleged contribution to violent or overly competitive behaviour, have in recent years become issues in themselves. Claims about over-exposure of sport in the media have at times been put forward by groups, particularly arts and welfare groups, that are not in the limelight and need to attract attention. Also, the word *sport* has in the past had moral connotations. 'Giving a sporting chance' has connotations of fairness and equity. To what extent sport is still seen as conveying such moral values is difficult to assess, but the association with commercial values is seen by some to have reduced its moral influence.

Whatever regard sport is held in, the key to the long-term viability of any sport is its ability to attract the interest of a wider public and to understand what it is those people are looking for from any particular game.

Why is Public Support So Important?

Public interest leads to public support which leads to vital financial and moral support for the sport. It provides *capital* for the long-term growth of that sport and it provides a huge incentive for performance and excellence.

Generally, the higher players rise in a game, the less able they are to support themselves. With an increasing gap between serious and social players, and financial pressures generally, the less willing are social players to finance the *adventures* of the serious. Therefore it is necessary for sports which are ambitious nationally and internationally to gain a share of public support for their sport.

Public support is a scarce resource. It comes in many forms, such as gate-takings, sponsorship, and support for fundraising. However, these are not sufficient for everyone, and sports inevitably compete with one another to win a larger share of that resource. To do this, traditionally sports have used the achievements of their international performers. In sports with limited international popularity, such as rugby union, rugby league, netball and cricket, New Zealand has been among the top performers, and their profile in this country has been high. But in the truly international sports, such as tennis, soccer, hockey, golf, athletics and skiing, success has been hard won and public support much more difficult to gain.

Increasingly, sports are recognising that the attractiveness of their domestic competition, the quality of their junior coaching, and the support they give their players, are as important to international success as the international competition itself. They find it increasingly more important to be seen as progressive and contributing to the community through coaching and development.

Brand Loyalty

Sports are becoming more and more strongly associated with products and brands (see Chapter 14). A sport with strong positive brand values will do well. To market a brand it is essential to understand the needs and attitudes of the consumer of that brand. The first point is to be aware that the interests of the sport consumer are changing. In the same way that marketers of commercial products are bemoaning a growing fickleness in the customer, sport managers are becoming more aware of the same characteristics in the consumer of sport.

Talented young people are now more commonly making a conscious choice about which sport they will use as the *vehicle* for their talents. In their turn, sponsors are very particular about the profile of the game they are being asked to sponsor, and they are increasingly making choices based on commercial criteria rather than sentiment.

Successful sports will increasingly become successful brands, and these brands will come to be viewed in a similar manner to a commercial brand. Management of such brands will require the development of a different mindset for many administrators.

It is interesting to examine the 1993 launch of the All Black Supporters Club in this regard. This club, intended as a fundraiser for the All Blacks, arguably the most powerful sporting brand in the country, has to date met with limited success despite significant investment in television advertising. It may be that the public no longer sees rugby and the All Blacks, which after all receives massive sponsorships, as legitimate recipients of the charitable dollar (effectively what they are being asked to provide). Perhaps they see the proposed supporters club as a commercial brand which should be able to make its way in the world as does any other brand.

Undoubtedly, pressure for funding has forced sports to become more commercial. They have to recognise that while this approach opens up new avenues in the entertainment market, it closes others in the community service sector.

Who are the Audiences of Sport?

The primary audiences or supporters of sport are those people closest to the game – players, former players, and officials. Their attitudes to a sport are influenced by others involved within the sport. They in turn influence others.

Amongst players there are varying ages, skill levels and interests. But there is often a huge gulf between the so-called *serious* and *social* players, especially at the club level. Take a large participation and competitive sport such as tennis. Why do people play the game? Because it is an enjoyable pastime, because it is challenging, international, located close to home, has an active social dimension, caters for all ages, has good facilities, mixed sexes and good for matchmaking, and can be played by two people? Why do people tramp – to get away from the city, to enjoy the environment, to be with friends, to test themselves physically, to get off on masochism? Why do watchers support a game? They may have friends involved or an historical association. They may enjoy the athleticism, skill or excitement of the game. They may have little interest in the game at all – as often seems to be the case of the crowd on the bank at cricket. Instead, they are into entertaining each other and what goes on out in the field sometimes seems irrelevant.

The one common thread is that the sport must give its supporters a tangible reward. It must meet their needs in one or a number of ways. It must *do something for them on the court or field,* but most people also need to feel a deeper involvement in the direction of the game and a sense of identification with it.

Stakeholders of Sport

For this reason it is helpful to see the supporters of sport as being potential stakeholders. All have a stake in that sport no matter how small, and as long as the sport continues to give them a *return,* they will continue to *invest.*

Watchers want to see skill, speed, power, grace, energy and style. They want to experience drama, pathos, intensity, elation. Players of virtually all sports are becoming aware of the need to deliver on these expectations if they are to retain the support of watching stakeholders. It is not enough for the players to win a test match, the performance must be pleasing to the watcher's eye.

Players are stakeholders too. The return they seek from sport is recognition or fame, personal satisfaction, exercise, friendship and so on. They invest their effort in the hope of a return from the investment of other stakeholders and the total performance of the sport.

A sport is rather like a financial investment that requires the right balance of inputs and outputs to operate effectively. Those who do not have the right formula demonstrably suffer in a competitive world. Stakeholding involves give and take. Gaining the right balance of give and take between all stakeholders is the key to modern sports management.

What is public relations and what can it do for sport?

Contrary to popular belief, public relations is not about selling more hospitality boxes, although good PR could result in buoyant sales. Nor is it about getting more mentions in the local media to satisfy the sponsor, although that may be a helpful by-product of PR activity.

Public relations is about building the commitment of stakeholders to a sport. It seeks to reward stakeholders for their support in the most cost-effective manner possible. It has an important role to play in attracting watchers (the public), because it is watcher support (on TV or on site) that drives sponsorship, and it is sponsorship that allows a sport to reward its player stakeholders with quality games, first-class facilities and challenging competitions.

Public relations seeks to target communication accurately at stakeholders and potential stakeholders to build their confidence and interest in the particular sport.

Who are the stakeholders of your sport and what are they looking for?

Very few sports seem to have taken a systematic approach to determining this information. Many administrators take the view that they have played the game, they know what it is about and that is sufficient. It is rather like a person saying 'I drink lots of beer, frequent hotels and have done so for years, therefore I could market the product without the help of anyone else'.

Sport is dynamic, changing and evolving. The environment around it is changing. The structure and pattern of participation is also changing rapidly. Reasons for participation today are often quite different from 20 years ago.

In the same way that the male supermarket shopper is becoming a commercial force to be reckoned with, so also is the child's mother when it comes to choosing a sport. People's needs and interests change as they move with the times through the life cycle.

Commitment to a brand for life is being replaced with *sampling* and *grazing.* Young men are moving from a square meal of rugby in the winter and cricket in the summer, to snacking on a wide range of involvements. The growth of women's soccer, and mixed games such as touch, are breaking the traditional mould of netball as the sole game for women in the winter.

People are often prepared to pay more to buy involvement in sport on a casual basis, such as hiring a tennis court for an hour, than to join a club and to undertake their share of maintaining facilities through working bees, or being available every Saturday, without fail, for games.

Stakeholders now have to be identified, understood and provided with an attractive package, or they have a tendency to walk. The idea of researching the membership of a sport and those in the stand is still regarded as expensive and unnecessary, but managers who are doing it are beginning to reap the rewards. They are using the following techniques:

- **Focus groups,** i.e. homogeneous or composite groups of stakeholders sharing what they are seeking, and finding. This technique can highlight the emotive as well as the rational reasons for participation.

- **Exit Polling,** i.e. identifying people who have left or are about to leave the sport (as players, administrators or watchers) to understand the issues and why and what, if anything, the sport can do to continue to attract and retain either others like them or alternatives.

- **Auditing,** i.e. interviewing a wide range of stakeholders individually to identify what they are looking for from the sport and whether they are getting the rewards. This is also a useful technique for understanding how a particular sport is seen, i.e. conservative/progressive, contemporary/old fashioned, well organised/muddled, focused/confused, and so on. It also identifies key issues for the future of a sport.

Is the Product Right?

Who is the game designed for? The answer needs to take account of the interests of all stakeholders, not just the players. A great deal of effort has been expended analysing games and making rule changes to ensure the game is challenging and entertaining.

The format of local, national and international competitions is also important. To add drama and intensity, a number of sports have recently moved to semi-final and final structures rather than a round-robin competition. Such moves have often been frustrated in the past by players who see a league final as a sudden-death situation, reflecting performance on the day rather than consistency of performance. The fact is that another group of stakeholders, the viewing public, who support the sponsors, want more excitement and drama, and their needs must be met for the sport to survive.

Safety in sport is a similar issue, excitement and risk must be balanced. While on the one hand risk produces excitement, it also can produce serious injury.

Creating a Vision (see Figure 15.1)

A sport needs a vision that is sufficiently broad for all stakeholders to subscribe to, yet sufficiently specific to be motivational. A vision is the rational/emotive glue that holds the stakeholders together. It is the 'holy grail' that is out there in front of everybody. Around the vision is built the management plan, which is the rational plan of action for the sport.

A vision is particularly important for minority sports. They do not have the financial capital at the disposal of larger sports. Their capital is almost solely the commitment, enthusiasm and interest of stakeholders. A vision is a method of harnessing that human capital for the development of the sport. Yet too often the stakeholders are not sufficiently informed or motivated. They are not provided with a focus around which they can make their contribution and are criticised by sports administrators as being apathetic.

Figure 15.1

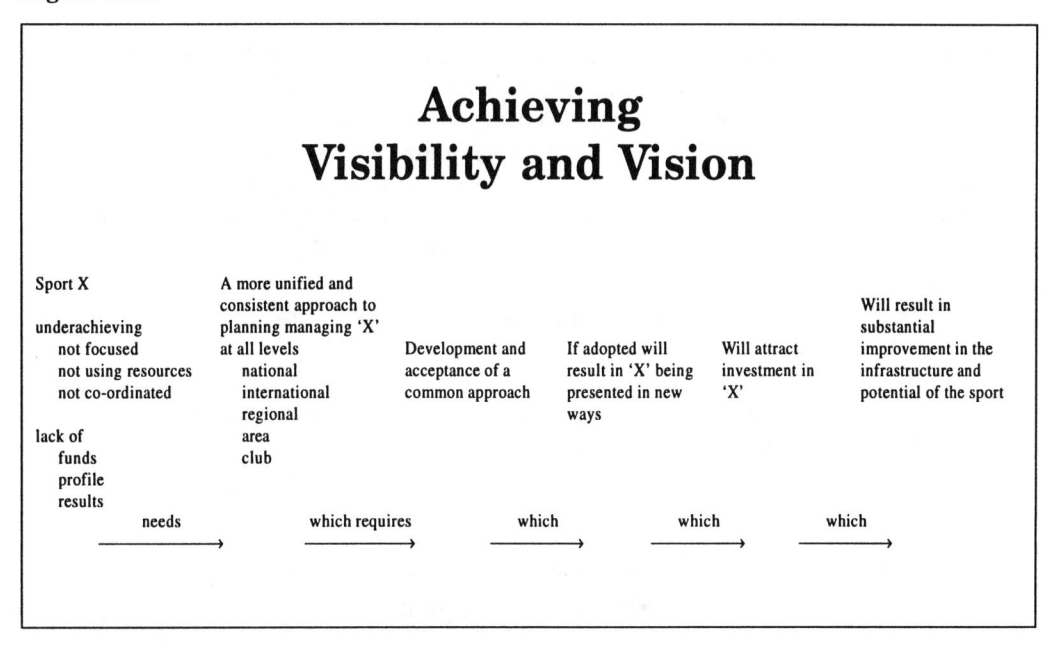

Achieving Visibility and Vision

Sport X	A more unified and consistent approach to planning managing 'X' at all levels				Will result in substantial improvement in the infrastructure and potential of the sport
underachieving					
not focused		Development and acceptance of a common approach	If adopted will result in 'X' being presented in new ways	Will attract investment in 'X'	
not using resources	national				
not co-ordinated	international				
	regional				
lack of	area				
funds	club				
profile					
results					
needs →	which requires →	which →	which →	which →	

▶ Building a Positive Image for a Sport

Doing the right thing and being seen to do the right thing is vitally important, as rugby has found in the last few years with the disciplining of players. A positive image not only comes from how a sport deals with 'ugly' play, but how well it is organised, supervised and presented. An administrator of a junior club recently made the observation that the drop of 50 player participants from one year to the next was directly attributable 'to the poor image of the game nationally'.

Sports need to have positive appeal, not only to players but to 'influencers', such as the mothers who seek experiences either to educate and improve themselves or their children, or provide a positive recreational outlet.

▶ Building a Communications Plan

The key to a good image and positive brand values is an effective communications plan.

A communications plan is an extension of a marketing plan, and it should be designed to activate and motivate stakeholders to support the direction of the sport. The practical elements of a communications plan are deceptively simple. They include:

- *Situation analysis*
  An analysis of the strengths, weaknesses, threats and opportunities facing a sport. An accurate picture of the issues facing a sport can be gained by the use of focus groups,

polls and audits as outlined above.

Many sports officials simply 'stick their finger in the air' to see which way the wind is blowing. It is those sports which are becoming more businesslike about these matters that will succeed.

- *Stakeholder analysis*

A thoroughgoing examination of the needs of each group of stakeholders is essential – Who are they? What do we want from them? What have we got to offer them?

Figure 15.2 demonstrates that stakeholders have varying levels of commitment or *exposure* to a game. A programme of communication recognises the priority of stakeholders and can work its way out from the centre of the most intense interest through the concentric 'circles'. A successful sport will be communicating to all stakeholders and seeking to maintain or increase their contribution.

- *Objectives*

A clear set of objectives is required to ensure that communication activities are measurable.

- *Programme of activities*

The range of potential activities is enormous and can include newsletters, videos, road shows, briefings, media activity and so on.

Figure 15.2

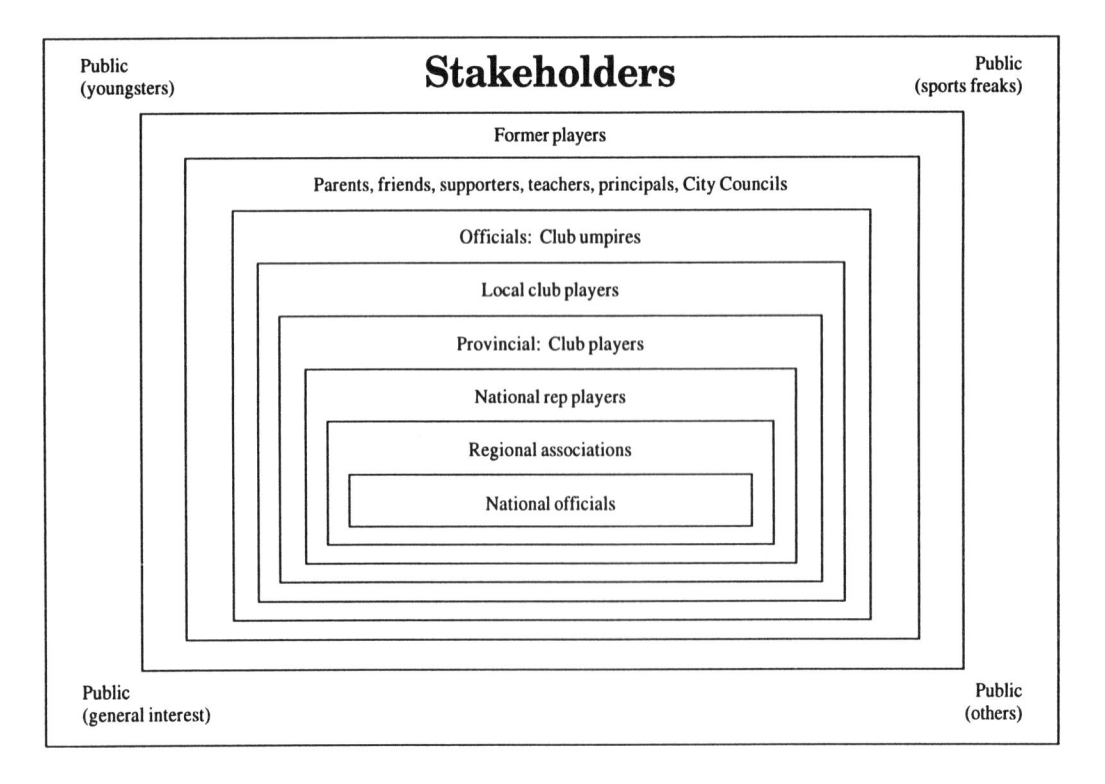

Public (youngsters) — **Stakeholders** — Public (sports freaks)

- Former players
- Parents, friends, supporters, teachers, principals, City Councils
- Officials: Club umpires
- Local club players
- Provincial: Club players
- National rep players
- Regional associations
- National officials

Public (general interest) — Public (others)

- *Evaluation*
  Evaluation is one of those tasks that often falls through the cracks. Proper evaluation can save considerable effort and help to prevent the same mistake occurring twice.

▶ **Techniques for Building Visibility and Profile** (see Figure 15.3)

- *Media*
  With all the changes that have taken place in the organisation and development of the media in the last five years, it is difficult to assess whether coverage of sport has increased or decreased (see Chapter 18). Also, the pressure of the recession on newspaper revenues has seen a decline in the overall size of newspapers and therefore of sports coverage. On the other hand there has been a huge surge of activity in the radio market, although little of it has been directed at the sports listener.

  The introduction of sports magazine programmes on television has probably increased coverage of minor sports, but live coverage has been confined to a few frontline sports, such as World Cup Cricket, and in some cases overseas competition, such as League's Winfield Cup.

  Visibility, especially through the media, has become a key ingredient in the fortunes of sports. Up until now second-tier sports, such as softball, hockey, soccer, and basketball, have had a very low profile. But to effect an improvement there is no substitute for continual relationship building with the media. This involves:
    - regular contact with media reporters and editors – seeking ways of presenting sport that are fresh, different and interesting;

Figure 15.3

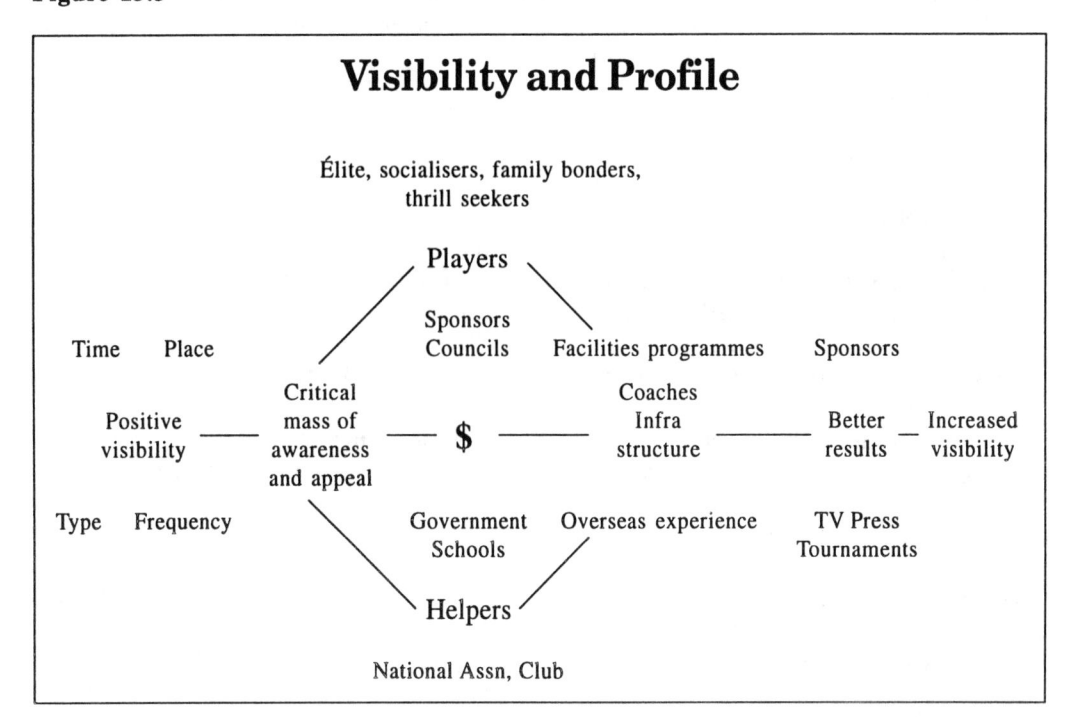

Visibility and Profile

Élite, socialisers, family bonders, thrill seekers

Players
Sponsors
Councils — Facilities programmes — Sponsors

Time   Place

Positive visibility — Critical mass of awareness and appeal — $ — Coaches Infra structure — Better results — Increased visibility

Type   Frequency

Government Schools — Overseas experience — TV Press Tournaments

Helpers

National Assn, Club

- making a special effort to inform media representatives and invite them to key events, and meetings;
- regularly supplying information in a digestible form;
- providing opportunities for the media suited to their medium, e.g. visual material for TV;
- allowing the media to get closer to the game, to the inner sanctum of management of the sport and the playing of the game.

- *Encouraging personalities*
  Within sports there are ambivalent feelings about promoting personalities, often out of fear of the tail wagging the dog. However, it is vital that the strong personalities in sport are allowed to come through. They add colour and drama. People are interested in people, and role models are essential to young people.

- *Coordinating public relations locally and nationally*
  Communication of the game is necessary at both the national and local level. With media becoming more localised and targeted to specific groups in the community, there is huge scope for local promotion of sport or use of targeted media, e.g. certain age groups. Therefore regional television community newspapers and local radio are an important vehicle of local exposure. Public relations should operate to a plan with national and local implementers.

- *Keeping the members involved*
  Internal communication is vital but is often neglected. Many sports see internal communication as little more than a newsletter. To keep members really involved and committed, particularly those in the inner rings of the concentric 'circles' diagram (p. 212), there is a need for purposeful activity such as:
    - meetings
    - road shows
    - presentations
    - social events
    - celebrations

  Although many sports concentrate on recruiting new players and supporters, their real problems lie in the continuous loss of players at critical stages in the life cycle, e.g. such as leaving school, or in the early to mid-20s. Maintaining a strong tie with existing participants and recognising their changing needs is vital. A clear and regularly communicated vision is vital. Stakeholders need to be carried along as elements of the vision are achieved and the sport progresses.

  Some of these things sound simple and basic, but it is often the basics that are not done properly – after all getting the basics right is the essence of any successful sporting performance.

What are the Easy Answers?

The fact is that there are no easy answers to building a successful sport. With the help of public relations techniques the profile and visibility of a sport can be enhanced. Visibility leads to critical mass which leads to more resources for the infrastructure. This in turn leads to better results and therefore increased visibility. It can be a positive circle for some sports and a vicious circle for others.

The situation of minority sports is especially difficult because they lack the critical mass for the incredibly competitive environment they exist in. The key to success is to harness the talents and capabilities of members on and off the field and build a strong, positive sentiment about the direction of the sport with all stakeholders.

Review Questions

1. What is the value of the 'stakeholder' concept when planning a public relations programme for a sport?
2. What are the implications of moving sport more towards a commercial model.
3. How does a sport create a vision that is inclusive rather than exclusive, that does not for example, focus on the interests of the élite to the exclusion of other members?
4. How can public relations enhance the positive attributes of membership of a sport as against some of the negative associations?

Suggested Reading

Francis, B. (1992), *Promote your Sport*, Auckland: Bateman.
Helitzer, M. (1992), *The Dream Job: Sports Publicity, Promotion and Public Relations,* USP: Ohio.

Sponsorship and Sport

Paul Carrad

In this chapter you will become familiar with the following terms:

sponsorship

sponsorship proposal

corporate marketing objectives

point of difference

product sector exclusivity

event marketing

leveraging

post-analysis

Introduction

The history of sponsorship of sport in New Zealand is not well documented but, as one might expect for a country with a passion for sport, sponsorship seems to have developed at a pace at least equal to, if not ahead of, world trends. Whatever the original traces, 1983 saw a quantum leap in the scale and professionalism of sports sponsorship with the launch of the Los Angeles Olympic Appeal. It was then that the traditional 'philanthropic' approach to sponsorship was superseded by a strongly commercial approach. The Los Angeles Olympic Appeal also saw the emergence of television leveraging, product sector exclusivity and a smaller group of exclusive sponsors contributing larger amounts. These factors are still very much part of obtaining sponsorship for todays' major sporting events and they feature strongly in New Zealand's challenge for the next America's Cup in 1995/96, with only four major sponsors, all participating on a heavily leveraged basis.

Whilst the sports sponsorship market has grown an estimated ten-fold since 1983, increased competition from many other sectors has created a very demanding marketplace. Events and sports in the sports arena that have clung to traditional methods are struggling now to secure sponsors. They have to realise that sponsorship in the 1990s is driven by the ability to deliver messages to defined audiences. Sport sponsorship has become inextricably linked with media value and measurements. Sponsorship should be viewed as simply another form of advertising and must be accounted for in similar terms.

Also, it must be accepted that all sport organisations face an ongoing requirement for funding, and sponsorship provides an increasingly important mechanism for securing that funding. It is no longer a simple matter to secure and retain sponsorship income. Whilst the sponsorship market has grown to an estimated $93 million per annum (Jensen, Sullivan, Wilson, Berkeley and Russell, 1993), the competition for sponsorship dollars and the professionalism now required by sponsoring entities is dictating the need for higher than ever standards of presentation, evaluation and performance. For this reason the present chapter describes the parameters and framework within which organisations seeking sponsorship must now operate. The sponsorship process is laid out as a step-by-step guide, preceded by a definition section.

Definitions

Sponsorship

- a contribution of cash, goods and/or services provided by the 'sponsoring' organisation in return for quantifiable and qualified recognition or returns provided by the 'sponsored' party.

Event marketing

- sponsorship is generally related to an event or activity and as such needs marketing in its own right – a process referred to as *event marketing*. Sponsorship correctly event marketed is a powerful marketing tool and accordingly should be presented to the prospective sponsor in a format that demonstrates a dynamic contribution to the achievement of that sponsor's business goals.

Leveraging

- the process whereby the purchaser of a product (sponsor) receives added value. Media leveraging is increasingly common. Example: a newspaper special supplement can add increased value in editorial terms from the number of extra sales generated.

Product sector exclusivity

- where each sponsor has a clearly defined product category and has exclusive sponsorship rights within that category. Example: banking might extend to include retail, investment or merchant banking and a range of other financial products such as superannuation or life insurance, or each one of these could be a product sector in itself.

Guide to Obtaining Sponsorship

The following factors must be considered when seeking and managing sponsorship:

- Integrating sponsorship and corporate/brand marketing
- Understanding an event or activity
- Corporate marketing objectives
- Research the prospective sponsor
- Evaluating needs and requirements
- The event – point of difference
- Event – assessment
- Developing the sponsorship proposal plan
- Judging an event or sport as a product
- Corporate criteria
- A competitive marketplace.

Each of these guiding factors is considered in more detail:

1. *Integrating sponsorship and corporate/brand marketing*

In developing sponsorship programmes one must first identify the personality, image, theme, positioning and other relevant attributes of the event. Invariably those who seek support know their organisations well, but it is important to evaluate how the event might be considered from an outsider's point of view. Looking at an individual sport, it is important to consider:

- How popular is it?
- How popular could it be? (growth)
- What sort of people are most interested in it?
- How old are the participants?
- What are the lifestyles and personalities of these people?

Example: Looking at Golf

- Very popular and is well out in front in terms of time spent playing.
- Growing steadily, reinforced by international successes.
- All people, but especially the age 45 plus group (both males and females).
- Reaching all people including hard-to-reach upper socio-economic levels.
- Includes many retired or semi-retired people who have high disposable income or investments.
- Attractive television sport, especially at professional level.

2. Understanding an event or activity

The process of understanding an event and describing its personal and/or quality connotations is an important first step in seeking out and finding a compatible sponsoring partner. This process draws on innovative lateral thinking and energy – important prerequisites in event marketing. It is essential to think about the sponsorship opportunities from a prospective sponsor's point of view, and how they fit with the marketing objectives and strategies of those sponsors.

3. Corporate marketing objectives

Sponsorship is used by companies as both a strategic and tactical marketing tool and is usually part of a broader marketing mix. Therefore a sponsorship proposal must be presented to a prospective sponsor in the context of a complete marketing plan and integrated with those other components. Questions that should be addressed are:

- How will this sponsorship opportunity relate to a prospective sponsor's brand advertising?
- Will this sponsorship facilitate a reduction in direct media spend or will it complement or reinforce existing media spend?
- Will the sponsorship deliver improved communications with key accounts, staff or suppliers – for example, through hospitality?
- Will staff motivation and commitment be enhanced?
- Are there enough branding opportunities tied in with the event to demonstrate sponsorship value?

Remember that sponsors are not donors – they are generally commercially active and looking for a return on investment, and applicants must be able to demonstrate how an event can help them achieve their objectives or a return on their investment.

4. Research the prospective sponsor

A fundamental principle of successfully seeking sponsorship is to know your prospect. Carefully research prime prospects. Find out everything you can about their:

- marketing objectives
- advertising style and content
- brand or corporate image
- distribution networks
- product attributes
- positioning statements.

This process will help to identify sponsors who are not especially well known and again the use of lateral thinking is important and can often help to identify enthusiastic and valuable sponsors other than the traditional highly visible companies. For example, if a company has an anchor or a ship in its logo this is not necessarily a reason for it to sponsor an event in the nautical arena! Does the National Bank sponsor an equestrian event, for example?

Figure 16.1

Sponsorship Fits the Strategic & Tactical Options
for Achievement of Marketing Objectives

```
         ┌─────────────────────────┐
         │ Company Business Plan   │
         │ Corporate Philosophy    │
         └───────────┬─────────────┘
                     │
         ┌───────────┴─────────────┐
         │ Marketing Plan          │
         │ (or Brand Plan)         │
         └───────────┬─────────────┘
     ┌───────────────┼───────────────┐
┌────┴─────┐  ┌──────┴──────┐  ┌─────┴─────┐
│Quantified│  │Communication│  │Distribution│
│Sales     │  │Objectives   │  │Objectives  │
│Objectives│  │             │  │            │
└────┬─────┘  └──────┬──────┘  └─────┬─────┘
     └───────────────┼───────────────┘
              Strategic and Tactical Objectives
     ┌───────────────┼───────────────┐
  ┌──┴──┐     ┌──────┴──────┐    ┌───┴────────┐
  │Sales│     │Communication│    │Distribution│
  └──┬──┘     └──────┬──────┘    └───┬────────┘
```

Sales	Communication	Distribution
Sales Force Recruitment	Advertising	Dealer Relations
Sales Force Training	Public Relations	New Dealers
Sales Force Incentivisation	Sales Promotions	Dealer Incentives
Sales Force Motivation	Direct Response	Dealer Education
Trade Incentivisation	Sponsorship	
Trade Education		

```
                    ┌──────────┐
                    │ Consumer │
                    └──────────┘
```

5. *Evaluating the sport organisation's needs and requirements*

Whilst being commercially driven, sponsors will of necessity be interested in the sports manager, the organisation and its activities. They will be interested in more than just how much it will cost. They will want to know:

- what the funds will be used for
- whether the event will proceed regardless of their decision
- whether the event will benefit the wider community
- whether the event will assist the organisation to achieve its objectives.

Analysis of this kind identifies the areas of organisational activities that will be attractive to a sponsor, and allows the sports managers to immediately present those areas in a favourable light. Sponsors will generally want to see their funds being used to add value to a project rather than being used to reduce an overdraft! For example, sponsorship may be associated with:

- a new clubhouse
- team travel
- a professional coach
- training equipment
- a special event.

6. *The event – point of difference*

Before identifying sponsors and making presentations, it is necessary to look at the event itself, because the marketplace is inundated with individuals, groups, organisations and charities seeking sponsorship support. The question sponsorship seekers must ask is – *'Why our event?'* What is the specific point of difference? The task for the sponsorship seeker is to break through the clutter.

So competitive is the sponsorship market, that the sponsorship seeker must have something different, must present well and most importantly, the event must be well researched and thought out to have any chance of success. The opportunity presented must be a near perfect match with the marketing and communications objectives and strategies of the prospective sponsors. The nature and structure of the event and the range of benefits for the sponsor must be clearly identified.

7. *Event assessment*

Each prospective sponsor (particularly sophisticated brand marketeers) will have developed their own checklist or procedures for evaluating sponsorship opportunities or proposals. In essence these criteria will all revolve around the central theme of 'What's in it for me?', or 'What return will I get on my investment?' A basic critique might include the following questions:

- what are the image qualities of the event I am being asked to sponsor?
- what type and size of audience will it reach?
- what added value will it deliver to my product or brand image?
- what extra resources will the opportunity require in order to realise its potential?
- what level and quality of brand exposure will be delivered?
- what guarantee of delivery exists?
- will it be an ongoing commitment?

8. *Developing the sponsorship proposal plan*

There are four key steps which can be used as a focus for developing the sponsorship proposal, implementing and managing the event and analysing the results:

- the offer
- the proposal
- the event marketing plan
- post-analysis.

The assembly of all the necessary information and construction of the proposal must be carefully undertaken. The quality and style of presentation will have a large impact on the likely success. The final document must be in a form suitable for easy distribution and must clearly communicate the salient points. Supplementary information and supporting detail is best supplied in Annexe form.

9. *Judging an event or sport as a product*

Potential sponsors will look to make a commercial decision based on whether the return on investment is justified. Therefore sponsorship proposals should provide the answers to some or all of the following sub-questions as appropriate:

- What are the image and quality connotations that the sponsorship will deliver by association?
- What type of people will it reach? How many and how often?
- What is the level of direct market support available through the sponsorship?
- What level of sponsorship support would the sport or event provide?
- What level of additional marketing support will be required by the sponsor?
- How will the sponsor receive brand or product exposure?
- What are the ongoing opportunities?

Remember each sponsorship opportunity needs to be treated as a product and marketed as such in its own right.

10. *Corporate criteria*

Sponsorship opportunities are evaluated in many ways by potential sponsors, most of whom will have a checklist of criteria not too dissimilar to the following list, i.e.

- Is the event compatible with their company or brand?
  Example: ENZA's sponsorship of the skier Annelise Coberger fits their product positioning of high energy and technology.

- Are there any political or commercial risk factors?
  Example: Boycotts or drug scandals.

- What is the event or sports target audience?
  Example: Gymnastics has a primary target audience of females aged 5-15, with their parents as a secondary audience.

- Is the event relevant to the company's target audience?
  Example: The AMP New Zealand Open Golf Championship provides a near perfect

match for AMP Insurance, its policy-holders and investors.

- Will the event reach all or part of the company's target audiences?
  Example: Golf reaches a mass market audience as well as several hard-to-reach niche markets such as the higher socio-economic levels and professional people.

- How often will it reach the audience? What is the type of communication and frequency?
  Example: The Nissan Mobil 500 Wellington Street Race is televised and reaches thousands of viewers in countries such as Japan, SE Asia and Australia, which are important to New Zealand companies, and it also gains further valuable exposure through international motoring magazines.

- What is the time-frame of the event or sport? Is it a 'one off' or are there ongoing opportunities? Will it mushroom to an unmanageable level?
  Example: Sponsors of the International Rugby Hall of Fame are offered a defined eight-year term.

- Is corporate hospitality offered? Communication is the key to good business, and hospitality delivers quality communication.
  Example: The Nissan Mobil 500 delivers premium viewing and a memorable occasion for key clients.

- Will the event happen regardless of sponsorship? Events should not generally be dependent entirely on sponsorship for them to occur. Rather, sponsorship should add value to the event.
  Example: The AMP New Zealand Open Golf Championship is substantially enhanced by AMP's provision of the prize-money and television coverage.

- Is the event newsworthy?
  Example: Sponsors will often want details of commitments from the media, particularly from the various television channels. Peter Blake's catamaran, ENZA, delivered television coverage to over 100 countries.

- Is the media well catered for?
  Example: Attending journalists provide the window to the world, and consequently the provision of media facilities for the 1990 Commonwealth Games was one of the biggest budget items for that event.

- Are there any associated, leveraged media opportunities? The full range of newspaper features to fully fledged television leveraged packages are increasingly important.
  Example: The television production costs of 'Exhibition Artikos' were offset by bonus television advertising placements. A win situation for sponsor and the channel.

- Is product sector exclusivity offered?
  Example: For Coca Cola, product sector exclusivity could mean the exclusion of all

other drinks including iso-tonic drinks, milk, water, tea, coffee, fruit juice, etc., etc. – not just Pepsi or Schweppes!

- What direct sales opportunities exist? Many sponsorships can deliver immediate sales in reciprocal business.
Example: Moro's ski sponsorship helped secure product sales on New Zealand ski fields.

11. *A competitive marketplace*

Market demands, and competition for sponsorship dollars from a variety of sources, dictate the need for sport to be increasingly professional when seeking sponsorship. As the previous section details, the criteria used for evaluating sponsorships and assessing their value, are quite complex. The following document covers the essential sponsorship objectives and evaluation criteria used by one of New Zealand's largest corporate entities (anonymous).

Company Sponsorship Objectives and Evaluation Criteria

Sponsorship Objectives

(Company name) sponsorships are to be evaluated against five objectives:

Corporate image
- trustworthy, progressive and successful
- increases name and/or product awareness
- projects a sense of corporate responsibility
- builds goodwill among opinion formers and decision makers
- achieves positive media coverage
- is not political, controversial, nor contains elements of danger.

Sales
- fits in with sales/marketing strategy
- increases sales revenue.

Customer care
- provides customer-care beyond product and customer service.

Staff
- motivates staff and encourages pride in the Company
- increases productivity value.

Budget
- fits into existing budgets
- must be cost-effective
- the Company must get a return on the investment
- the budget must include not only the amount requested but also the total costs involved in promoting the sponsorship. The Company's sponsorship involvement must be promoted, otherwise

it may be seen solely as a donation. Sponsorships actually cost more than the amount of money requested, and a typical rule of thumb is that promotional costs should be budgeted at two to three times the amount of the sponsorship request.

Sponsorship Issues

Issues to be considered in evaluating a proposal against these objectives include:

Status of applicant
- is the organisation reputable?
- any adverse ramifications of association with the applicant?
- relevance to (company name)
- political affiliations?
- track record of applicant to date?

Level of control
- who will control (company's name) sponsorship involvement?
- what controls will be put in place to monitor the sponsorship, media and how the company's logo will be used?
- sole sponsorship in preference to joint or multi-sponsorships. This enables (company name) to get naming rights, a higher profile and greater degree of control?

Demand on resources
- what company staff will need to be involved and what resources are available?
- can the company provide the resources needed and still get the benefit?
- is the sponsorship a one-off or long term. If long term, how will the ongoing requirements be met?

Audience potential
- what is the target audience?
- how extensive will media coverage be?
- are there any media coverage guarantees?
- does the publicity angle fit in with (company name) profile?

Measurement

Sponsorship results must be measured. Criteria for measuring what outcomes are hoped to be achieved must be quantified, and techniques for measurement put in place before starting the sponsorship. Evaluation must be ongoing – before, during and after the event. Methods of evaluation include:

- Image criteria established and measured/surveyed.
- Business contacts made are recorded and assessed.
- Media monitoring; record how many times the company's name is mentioned in all media that is not specifically paid for. This can be translated into comparative advertising costs.

Product as Sponsorship

Requests are often made to provide sponsorship support in the form of 'free' product. This should be treated no differently to a request for sponsorship funds, and it should begin with an assertion that (company name) is in the business of (business activity). If an organisation believes its aims are best served by using (company product) then it should be prepared to pay for the product. If (company name) gives the product without the analysis required in this policy, it is signing away business.

Sponsorship Effectiveness

With sponsorship now being regarded as a legitimate marketing tool, the provision of quality information at all stages of sponsorship becomes imperative. The hunch philosophy of yesteryear is rapidly being replaced with scientific-based judgement, yet there is still uncertainty. Remember David Ogilvy's great claim that only 50 per cent of advertising works – the problem being which 50 per cent. The same is probably true of sponsorship.

The three key ways in which sponsorship effectiveness can be tracked are:

- Direct media comparison
- Attitudinal change
- Brand switching.

1. *Direct media comparison*

Media value is just one benefit of sponsorship with other benefits being loosely categorised under terms such as direct association, image reinforcement, client entertainment, customer loyalty, staff motivation and others. Valuing the media component is achieved by adding up the total number of seconds obtained in television coverage, news reports, and radio mentions, together with amount of exposure in newspaper columns, editorials, photo essays and magazine coverage, and on posters, letterheads, tickets, and invitations.

> *Example:* To assess the value of television signage exposure.
> Number of seconds the brand/logo is in clear camera shot = 600 seconds.
> Divide number of seconds by 30 = number of equivalent 30 second television commercials, i.e. 600 divided by 30 = 20 x 30 second television commercials.
> Rate card value of 20 x 30 second television commercials = 20 x $2,500 = $50,000.
> Application of an arbitrary compensatory multiplier 0.3 = $15,000.
> The value of television exposure so generated could be assessed at $15,000.

It is important to remember that the application of a compensatory multiplier is an arbitrary factor.

Signage exposure is generally written down by comparison to the cost of spot placement, because there is not the same opportunity to demonstrate the product or to create an image about the product or brand, although, in support of sponsorship, what is being bought into as brand or product exposure is *association with the values of the sponsored event*. In other words, the image and quality connotations of the event rub off on the sponsor's brand or product.

> *Example*: The AMP Society turned to sponsorship of the New Zealand Open Golf Championship to help reposition the company. In a very cost-effective manner and in a short space of time, AMP threw off its outdated image, and it positioned itself as a modern

dynamic and successful company. With the positioning *We'll be There* exposed through event signage, AMP also reinforced their key consumer proposition of intending to be around for the future or when clients would need them.

2. *Attitudinal shift*

Leading research houses are now developing models for tracking corporate image in relationship to sponsorship programmes as well as traditional advertising. The basic premise for such tracking studies is:

> The more consumer respondents are interested in or involved with a certain sponsored object, the more they will be aware of all aspects concerning that particular object, and therefore, the greater the effect the sponsor's communications may have on them. But awareness levels are not the ultimate aim. Sponsoring companies are more likely to be seeking to improve their communications effectiveness and change the perception of their company (Eilander and Koenders, 1991).

> *Example:* Successful companies care about the environment within which they operate. They generally take a responsible attitude within the community and are concerned about their corporate image. An unfavourable corporate image can be an impediment to sales.

3. *Brand Switching*

Tracking studies are useful in identifying changes and trends in preferred brand status. Consumers are influenced in their choice of brand by the brand values they perceive. Sponsorship adds different values to a brand and as a result is likely to generate brand switching amongst those influenced by the sponsorship communication. Perhaps a more straightforward way of tracking brand switching is to look at the sales graph!

Conclusion

From the principles as well as the different examples provided from commercial practice, it should be clear that there is no simple and static relationship between the parties. Rather, to succeed, attention has to be paid by both parties to the current needs and objectives of the other, and they need to be prepared to make some adjustment without compromise on essentials for a viable existence. The task for sports managers is not to take sponsors for granted, but to recognise that they do not have unlimited funds at their disposal for the promotion of the product through any one promotional area. The objective of this chapter is to prepare managers for some of the obstacles that they must negotiate if they are to achieve successful relationships with sponsoring companies.

Review Questions

1. What is meant by the term product sector exclusivity?
2. How and why should sponsorship proposals be linked to prospective sponsor's marketing objectives?
3. Outline the key factors that must be considered when seeking sponsorship?

References

Eilander, G. and Koenders, H. (1991), 'Communication Research into the Effects of Short and Long-Term Sponsorship', paper presented to the Sponsorship Europe Conference '91.

Jensen, B., Sullivan, C., Wilson, N., Berkeley, M. and Russell, D. (1993), *The Business of Sport and Leisure Report*, Wellington: Hillary Commission for Sport, Fitness and Leisure.

Suggested Reading

Gill, B. (1992), *The Ultimate Guide for Planning Developing and Managing Sponsorship and Event Marketing*, Wellington: Strategic Media.

Event Management

Arthur Klap

In this chapter you will become familiar with the following terms:

event management	*critical path*
organisational structure	*debriefing*
communications	*media plan*

It is not a sudden revelation that has lead to the current focus on event management as a discipline, because events have always had to be well managed if they were to be successful. What has changed is that the participants and spectators now seem to demand a more consistently high standard of organisation for events in which they are involved. This applies as much to the local club tennis tournament as it does to the Olympic Games. Seemingly gone are the days when an asphalt tennis court with no club facilities was regarded as a perfectly satisfactory venue for a tournament. There is also a demand for value for money. A $3 fun run can be poor value, while a $400 bike ride can be considered cheap because of the quality of the services provided. Increasingly, this demand for better organisation and value for money has meant that more and more time is demanded from organisers, who are still, in the main, volunteers. Therefore organisations could save themselves a considerable amount of time were they to follow simple event management principles.

The two key skills required by successful event managers are first, an ability to break complex organisational problems down to manageable tasks, and second, the ability to relate to people. That is, a systematic and methodical approach combined with people skills greatly increases the probability of an event being successful. Both will be considered in some detail in this chapter in relation to major events that have succeeded as well as to some that failed.

Event Management in New Zealand

There have always been organised events, but two key factors in the milieu of sports have had a profound impact upon event management. The first is the increasing importance of sponsorship (see Chapter 16). Until the mid-seventies sponsorship was largely viewed as a donation that helped make an event better. However, as businesses started to look more closely at how and where their promotional dollar was being spent, they became more sophisticated and hence more demanding in the assessment of their sponsorship. This led to an increased demand for a 'professionally run event', not necessarily for the employment of professional event managers but for an improvement in the quality of event organisation and planning.

The second factor was that events and sports became very expensive enterprises to run and they developed a dependence upon sponsorship in order to survive. If there was no sponsorship, there was no event. As a result, the organisers of events had to not only become more skilled in their event management but they also had to take into account the needs of the sponsor.

For the record, it should be said that the 1974 Commonwealth Games in Christchurch was the first sports event in New Zealand where television played a prominent part. The role of the media suddenly shifted from merely reporting on the proceedings, to one of providing a prominent link between the sport, the sponsor and the public. Yet through the seventies, events remained largely organised by volunteers and few sports employed full-time administrators. Even major sports, such as rugby and especially netball, treated sponsors as donors, and all of them encountered financial problems. But it was perhaps first in the arts where administrators recognised the importance of sponsorship and professional quality event management. Without sponsorship it had become increasingly difficult for them to produce plays, have full-time orchestras, and quality arts festivals. This led to the establishment of the QEII Arts Council, a major factor in improving the professional management of arts activities and organisations.

Organisational Structures

No matter how big or small an event, the first requirement is to put in place an organisational structure that meets the needs of that event. Unfortunately too many events are still one-man bands. This all-inclusive, dictatorial style of management can result in successful events, but once that key person burns out or leaves, there is usually total disarray. One person carrying all the cards can also make an event vulnerable, with a strong likelihood that some aspect of the organisation will not be up to the mark.

Much more efficient, satisfying and long-lasting is a structure that spreads the responsibilities and involves more people in the decision making. Depending upon the size of the event, the number of people in the structure can vary from just a few, through to hundreds, as is the case for major international events.

Types of Structures

The overall responsibility of many events rests with a designated community or sports committee that usually begins with elected volunteers but comes to employ paid staff. Those given the task of organising the event are therefore often not free to make decisions in isolation and need to be responsible to an Events Committee. The structure of the organisation is then usually based around the key decision-making areas. From within the Events Committee there may well be separate people given responsibility to oversee each key area. In the NZ Masters Games example, shown below, the Committee had different people responsible for merchandise, marketing the social programme, and special events.

The Masters Games are held annually with Dunedin and Wanganui alternating as the venues. Each city has its own organising committee elected by the sports involved, and a link between the two is provided by an advisory Games Co-ordinator. The Games are a major exercise held over nine days and involving vast numbers of volunteers, around 50 sports and attracting 4,800 competitors in 1993. The initial Games in 1989 attracted 1,600 competitors in 30 sports over seven days. Since then, as the Games have grown so has the structure and the number of paid personnel, as the structure used for the 1994 Games in Dunedin indicates (see Figure 17.1). The Games Committee consists of volunteers, while everyone else in the structure is a paid employee, although some are employed for little more than the period of the Games. Hence for much of the planning period it is the volunteer within the Games Committee who is responsible for the planning, but not for the implementation.

Figure 17.1

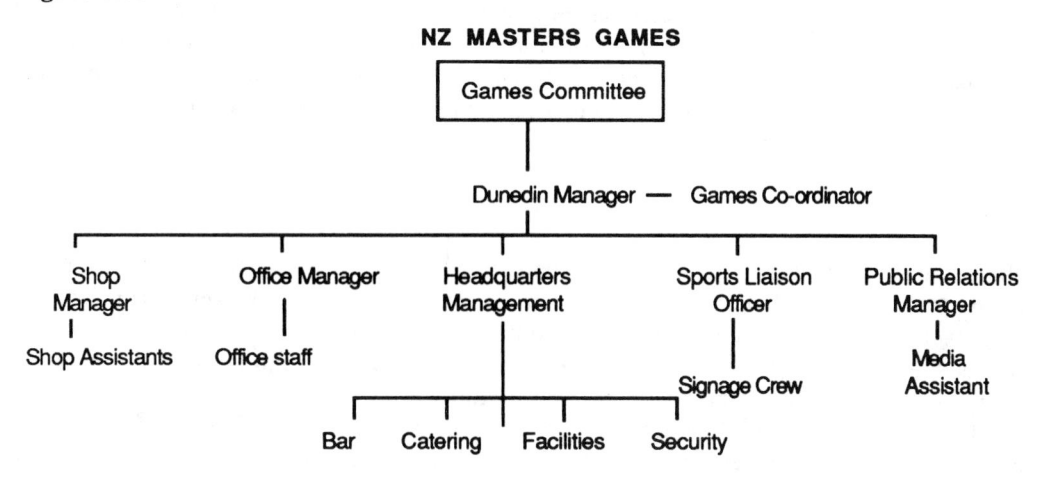

NZ MASTERS GAMES

```
                        Games Committee
                              │
                              │
               Dunedin Manager ─── Games Co-ordinator
    ┌──────────┬──────────────┼──────────────┬──────────────┐
   Shop      Office        Headquarters    Sports         Public Relations
  Manager    Manager       Management      Liaison        Manager
    │          │               │           Officer            │
  Shop       Office            │              │             Media
Assistants   staff              │         Signage Crew     Assistant
                    ┌──────┬───┴───┬────────┐
                   Bar  Catering Facilities Security
```

A more complex structure is that which will be used for the one-off 1994 Triathlon World Championships in Wellington. For this event the organisation has to meet not only the needs of the event, but also to link in with the national governing body (Triathlon NZ) and the international body (International Triathlon Union) (Figure 17.2). This obligation to link is a very important consideration for many sports because it means that some (if not all) of the final decision making can be taken away from the event manager, and it may lead to considerable tensions between the local organisers and the international body. Often this is because the local organisers have not made themselves aware of their international requirements.

The international structure for triathlon world championships is:

Figure 17.2

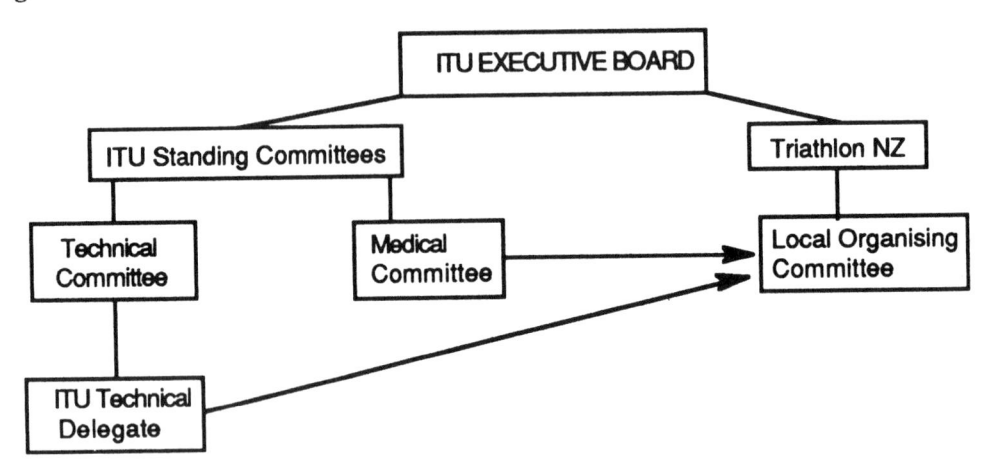

```
                    ITU EXECUTIVE BOARD
                   /                    \
        ITU Standing Committees      Triathlon NZ
        /          |                       \
  Technical    Medical              Local Organising
  Committee    Committee            Committee
       |
  ITU Technical
  Delegate
```

A triathlon is one of sport's most complex events to organise because it combines three sports that are held in the sea as well as on public roads. For the event organisation to be effective it is necessary to have a strong system of delegation so that no one person has to cover too many areas. The structure in Figure 17.3 (p.233) is based on the key areas of responsibility for course control, race support, competitor and volunteer liaison, finance, marketing, and linkage with Triathlon NZ and Wellington City Council. An interesting feature is that the financial control is kept separate through the involvement of Coopers and Lybrand as independent financial managers.

Job Descriptions

No matter how small the task allotted in the structure, it helps immeasurably if a clear and simple task sheet or job description is written. At the completion of the event, the debriefing must include a review of all such job descriptions. Copies should be kept so that each year it is a simple task for someone new to carry on. Whether a volunteer or paid employee, everyone likes to know from the outset what is expected of them. A written job description, ideally accompanied with time deadlines greatly increases the job satisfaction. It also helps avoid those situations where resentment builds up when a person discovers too late that the job that they have to carry out is far greater than expected. They should know what is expected of them before they start.

Equally as important as a written task description is for those in minor positions to know the overall picture. Too often the 'person on the gate' knows little about the overall organisation, and so cannot answer questions from the public or respond effectively if something goes wrong.

Figure 17.3

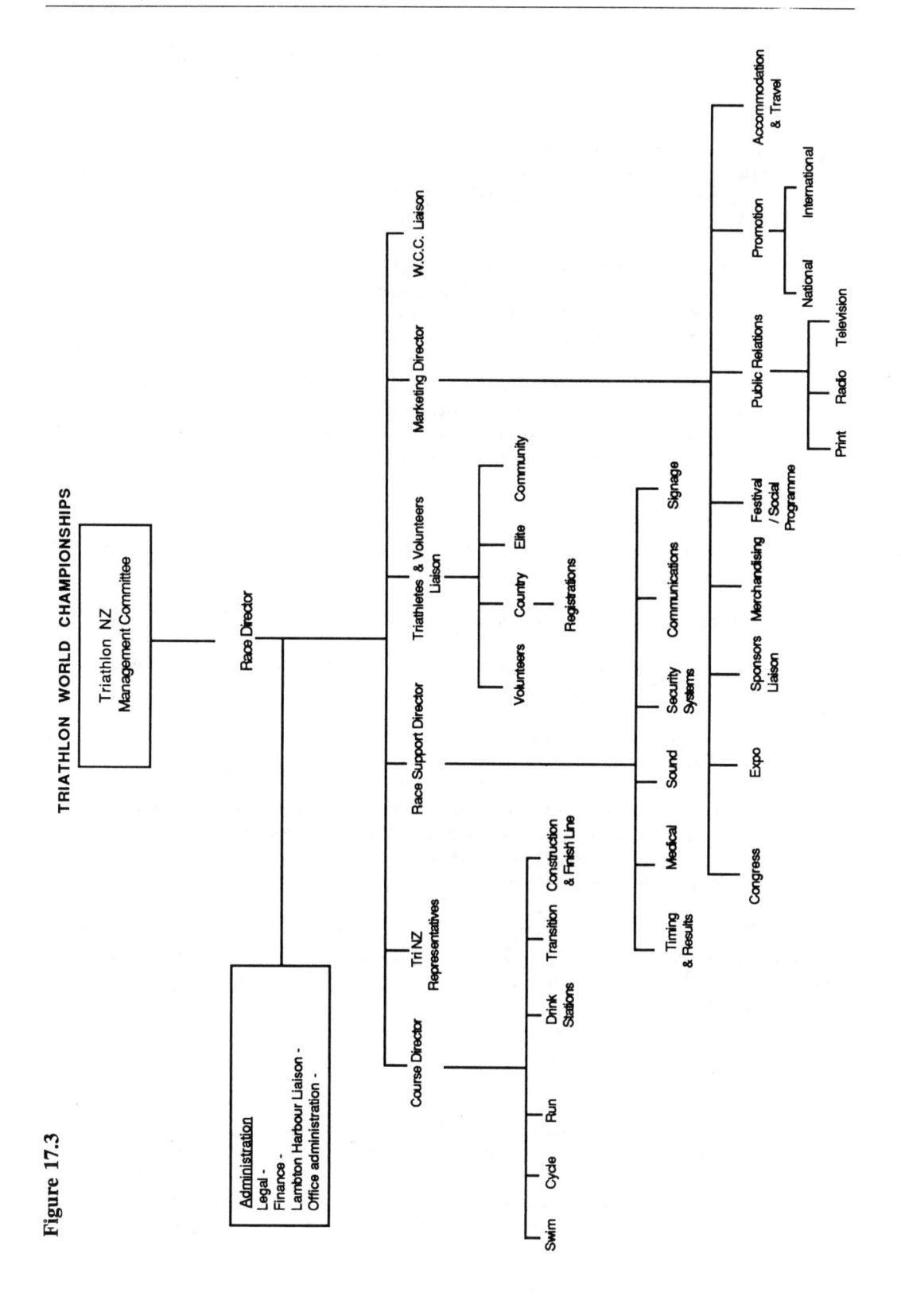

TRIATHLON WORLD CHAMPIONSHIPS

- Triathlon NZ Management Committee
  - Race Director
    - Administration
      - Legal -
      - Finance -
      - Lambton Harbour Liaison -
      - Office administration -
    - Course Director
      - Tri NZ Representatives
      - Swim
      - Cycle
      - Run
      - Drink Stations
      - Transition
      - Construction & Finish Line
    - Race Support Director
      - Timing & Results
      - Medical
      - Sound
      - Security Systems
      - Communications
      - Signage
    - Triathletes & Volunteers Liaison
      - Volunteers
      - Country
      - Elite
      - Community
      - Registrations
    - Marketing Director
      - Congress
      - Expo
      - Sponsors Liaison
      - Merchandising
      - Festival / Social Programme
      - Public Relations
        - Print
        - Radio
        - Television
      - Promotion
        - National
        - International
      - Accommodation & Travel
      - W.C.C. Liaison

The following job description is from the New Zealand Masters Games in Dunedin.

Shop Manager

The Shop Manager shall be responsible to the NZ Masters Games Executive Committee through the Dunedin Manager.
The Shop Manager shall ensure that the Games shop is efficiently run throughout the Games period by ensuring that the following responsibilities are carried out :

1. The shop will be open as follows (all dates 1994):
   Wednesday 2 February – Thursday 3 February, 8am – 6pm
   Friday 4 February – Saturday 12 February, 8am – 8pm
   Sunday 13 February, 8am – 5pm.

2. The shop shall be set up with facilities that will include counters, cash register, clothes racks and hangers, storage, wrapping material, display facilities, till float, credit card facilities, calculator, changing room. Where a charge is necessary for any of the above, prior agreement must be obtained from the Dunedin Manager.

3. The return of all shop equipment.

4. Have a management system put in place prior to the Games that will ensure a reliable reconciliation can be made on a daily basis of stock and sales.

5. Daily bankings in conjunction with the Office Manager.

6. Re-order merchandise in consultation with the Dunedin Manager. All orders to be made on an official Games Order form.

Any variation to set prices must be made with the approval of the Dunedin Manager and one member of the Executive Committee.

The shop assistants will be responsible to the Shop Manager and volunteers will also be used.
The period of the contract shall be from 1 September 1993 until acceptance of a final report by the Executive Committee. This report shall be submitted within 10 days of the conclusion of the Games and shall include a full cash and stock reconciliation.

Similarly, the following job description is for the voluntary position of Run Director for the Triathlon World Championships. Pre-event planning is critical, so it is important to know dates by when certain tasks have to be completed. The triathlon is planned for November 27, 1994.

Run Director

Task	Time Frame
* Draw a plan of the run, identifying all areas requiring marshalls, fencing, marking, cones and signposting	July 1993
* List and cost all items required for the run.	July 1993
* Produce a budget for the run section.	July 1993
* List where all items to be obtained from and when.	August 1993

      * Produce a timechart for race day.   September 1993
      * Ensure that the run is accurately measured.   October 1993
      * Obtain the marshalls for the run.   November 1993
      * Obtain all items required for the run.   November 1993
      * Full dress rehearsal event.   February 1994
      * Organise all aspects of the run section on race day according to ITU rules.   November 1994

Communications

A difficulty for many events is that many of the people involved have little regular contact with each other. Unlike a business situation in which employees spend most of the working day together at a venue, in event management the only occasion when everyone is together is on event day. This means that it is particularly important that within the event organisation there is planned regular communication through all levels. Most events are driven by the key organisers, so communication will tend to be downwards from the decision makers. However, there still needs to be the opportunity for communication to occur back up to the decision makers.

At the decision-making levels it will be necessary to have regular meetings involving all those directly concerned. For example, the executive committee will meet on a regular basis to make key decisions and to monitor progress. At a lower level, those involved within a particular area should meet when required to update each other on progress in each other's area.

Outside these meetings it is important that the event manager has a planned programme of written communication with sectors of the organisation as well as with the organisation as a whole.

Whatever the system or form of communication both within and outside the organisation, it is important that decisions and instructions are confirmed in writing. At a later stage in the planning it may become very important to have some written record of the decisions made and to whom they were communicated.

Financial Considerations

Too often events have proceeded, even though a careful analysis would have shown that the event was heading for financial disaster. The rule is to quit before it is too late! Too many events have been organised with unrealistic expectations of income, poor budgeting, and an absence of financial control. For many people the financial side of event management is at best an unimportant aspect of the event management, or at worst something to be ignored.

The unfortunate Sesqui Celebrations in Wellington in 1990 will forever be remembered for their spectacular and very public financial collapse just days into its planned operational period. That a large number of people had visited the Sesqui site in the opening days went largely unnoticed. Although there were planning mistakes made in the overall organisation of the Festival, it was the poor financial planning that lead to its early demise. The occasion was intended to celebrate Wellington's 150th anniversary. Unfortunately a number of organisations and local bodies were involved in the establishment of the organising body without having a clear organisational structure. At no time was it clearly established who had the overall responsibility for closely monitoring progress and independently assessing projections and budgets. Obvious later, in the cold light of day, the organisers grossly overestimated income. After the event there were any number of lay people pointing out the ridiculously unrealistic figures for expected daily visitor numbers. Easy to be wise after the event perhaps, but event organisers must be realistic in their income projections. At the very least they must know the break-even points and have assessed the likelihood of obtaining the required number of participants, i.e. *What is the risk?*

Budgeting

Someone taking over the management of an established event for the first time should ignore the previous year's budget and financial statement, if in fact there happens to be either of these. The first task is to brainstorm all potential areas of expenditure and income under the obvious catch-all categories such as administration, marketing, event control, social events, and merchandising. Within each category all cost areas should be listed and only then should previous financial records be viewed for any item that might have been missed.

Step two is to obtain initial costings for all expenditure areas. Step three is to identify and write down guaranteed income areas. Step four is to total both expenditure and income and see if there is either a surplus or a shortfall. If there is a shortfall, questions arise as to how the difference can be met? What number of spectators/competitors are required to break even? What total level of sponsorship will be required? At this point it will be important to assess whether it is realistic to run the event or whether sponsorship will be required to meet the shortfall or reduce the risk. If that is the case, how long can a decision be delayed before you are committed to the event?

If the above analysis is still negative, then the budget may need to be revisited. Are there any areas of the budget that can be trimmed and yet still meet the demands of the event participants?

Cash Flow

It is particularly useful to know in advance when expenditure will be incurred. For many events the bulk of income and expenditure is concentrated over a very short time span. However, there is probably some expenditure that is incurred very early in the planning, followed by a lull until just prior to the event. Knowing this can be an asset when negotiating with sponsors for the money to be available when required. Perhaps 25 per cent of the sponsorship can be paid immediately to cover initial expenditure, but further sponsorship may not be required until the successful completion of the event. The result is that the sponsor might be able to spread payments over more than one financial year, thus increasing the attractiveness of the sponsorship.

Another option might be to offer a reduction in the level of sponsorship if the full amount is paid well in advance of the event. This could open up the opportunity either to make purchases immediately, and so avoid possible future increases in costs, or to obtain some further income from investing the early income.

To work out cash flow is a simple task of going through the budget allocating expenditure and income on a month-by-month basis, and calculating the monthly balance. The cash flow can then often be manipulated to flatten out the highs and lift the lows by shifting the timing of purchases or their payments.

Keeping Records

Whatever recording system is chosen, it must enable the manager at any time to quickly assess the financial status of the event. This requires a clearly set out budget and then the production of regular (monthly) income and expenditure statements that also show the budgeted figures.

One simple strategy is to separate the ordering of goods from their payment, and this can be done by ensuring that no invoice is paid unless accompanied by an order form. Upon receiving the invoice, the event accountant checks that it is accompanied by an order form and, if so, whether it is a budgeted item and within budget. If the invoice passes all these checks the accountant then prepares the cheque, but is not a signatory.

Event Planning

The end result of any event planning should be that everything is in place before the event starts. The hard work should usually be prior to the event so that the good event manager can almost relax once the gun goes. Ideally there should be nothing left to do but enjoy the spectacle of an event, knowing that the organisation is functioning as efficiently as planned.

To achieve this nirvana, the key elements in the pre-planning are :

- Organisational structure in place
- Budget completed
- Job/task descriptions in place for all positions
- People allocated to responsibilities (positions)
- A time-frame placed alongside all tasks
- A critical path developed.

Critical Path

The intention should be to have tasks completed as early in the planning as possible, so that the pressure on the organisation is reduced to a minimum in the final days. For each area of the planning there will be dates by which an action will have to be finalised. Often it is a case of working backwards and identifying those critical points. It is then necessary to further identify what actions need to have taken place before then. For example, the date for printing of posters and entry forms for a netball tournament is governed by how long before the tournament players need to receive the information. To get the material printed requires decisions on costings, design and tournament information. These in turn require venues to be booked, the tournament format to be finalised, entry fees to be set, and sponsorships to be obtained. A simple critical path for this task would be:

	- 1 year	-9 months	-6 months	-4 months	0 months
Tournament	Format finalised	Venues booked			Tournament held
Print material			Costings & design complete	Printed	
Finance	Budget set	Sponsorships obtained			

Marketing

In event management the concept of marketing is still poorly understood (see Chapter 14). Most sports still produce the same old product and then wait for the participation to occur, but they are starting to change under pressure from other and newer sports as well as other forms of entertainment. Sport is competing with a much wider variety of choices for the leisure time of people than ever before and two marketing approaches have occurred to help them. The first is to adapt an existing sport or event to meet the needs of the potential competitor or spectator. A spectacularly successful example of this approach was the introduction of the one-day game in cricket under the influence of media magnate Kerry Packer who recognised the importance of entertainment and the role that television in particular could play to promote the sport. On the field he introduced coloured team clothing, fielding restrictions, the white ball and the day/night game. In his television coverage he brought in more cameras to provide closer footage with every bit of the action shown through the use of multiple angles and close-ups.

The result was a huge increase in support for cricket from the general public. A new audience was attracted to the new sport. It was a marketing exercise aimed at the spectator rather than the participant. For a similar reason the New Zealand Rugby Union has made a number of radical rule changes in recent years, that were aimed at increasing the pace of the game and its appeal to the players and the public.

The second approach is to develop an event or sport based upon the immediate appeal to the sporting public. Such events can have a very short life-span as the focus of the public shifts to new areas. The development of these new events has been aided by technology which has introduced some revolutionary changes. Some examples of such events in New Zealand are the Coast to Coast multisport event that crosses the South Island, the mass recreational cycle rides such as the round Taupo ride and the Hillary Commission's Big Coast mountain bike rides, and the snow-boarding events in the ski resorts.

The Product

A clear understanding of key elements of an event is critical to effective promotion. Who is the event targeted at, why will they want to compete, how can they best be reached and what other forms of entertainment are competing for the same target market? The Coast to Coast is an example of an event that has changed over the years from an event for tough, outdoor adventure types to one with much wider mass appeal. Organiser Robin Judkins has a knack for understanding who his competitors are and why they want to participate. Clearly there is a challenge factor, but for many the social component and the sense of occasion are equally important. The majority of the competitors are not tough, macho, outdoors types. In fact many have never touched a canoe prior to deciding to participate, although they might perhaps previously have done some cross-country running and cycling.

Judkins' event competitors are not from other multisport events but from other 'adventure/ social' options such as Club Med holidays, or going to Hong Kong to watch an international seven-a-side Rugby tournament.

A common mistake of event organisers trying to emulate Judkin's success, is to try for bigger and tougher events under the mistaken impression that people are attracted to the Coast to Coast only because of its toughness. Only when an organiser understands the target market can an effective promotional campaign be undertaken.

Promotion

The most effective form of promotion is person to person but this is clearly not possible for most events. What then are the options open to event organisers, most of whom will have very limited budgets for promotional activities? These involve:

- print, radio and television advertising
- direct marketing
- print material, e.g. posters, brochures
- expos, displays and special promotions.

Advertising

Advertising can only be effective if seen or heard by the target audience. For many events there are specialist magazines or newsletters that are read by the enthusiasts. However, general readership magazines can be very effective if their readership includes those who would be interested in the event, and if their advertising rates are not too high.

Newspapers are useful more for the attraction of spectators than participants, because they reach a wider audience and so increase the chances of reaching potential spectators.

National television advertising is seldom used except for major sports events. However, regional television advertising can have a high impact and be cost effective at off-peak times of the year. For example, in New Zealand the January summer holiday period is a quiet advertising time, yet many events happen then, and their exposure on television can be very cost effective at that time of the year.

Radio advertising tends to play a bigger role than television for many events, but the proliferation of radio stations in the cities has resulted in each of them usually having only between 10 and 20 per cent market share. The result is that the selection of a particular radio station for sports coverage is difficult because their target reach is often not very high.

Direct Marketing

Direct marketing is increasingly more important than indirect in the promotion of (participatory) events, and several organisers have developed extensive databases from entry forms that can be divided into interest groupings to suit direct mailings for subsequent events. Such direct targetings are very cost effective and these databases have become valuable assets.

However, the Privacy Act 1992 has restricted the use of entry form information since July 1, 1993, without the express permission of participants about the use of material they are providing. In particular it will no longer be possible for event organisers to pass on entrant information to sponsors for follow-up marketing.

Another aspect of direct marketing that has proved effective is the targeting of promotional material by travel-related businesses. Organisations such as Air New Zealand's Koru Club obtain information from members on their interests, and they mail information and related travel packages to people who could be interested in that event. For example, all those who indicated an interest in rugby would be sent information on the Hong Kong International Sevens tournament, in the hope that they might book flights and accommodation with the airline.

Print Material

The use of posters, promotional brochures, flyers and entry forms remains the most common form of promotion. Often these will be mailed direct to potential participants or mailed to venues frequented by similar people, i.e. specific sports clubs, sports centres and sports shops. The quality of the print material is the first indicator of the likely quality of the event. Yet many events organisers put very little planning into the promotional design and quality of their printed material.

Expos, Displays and Special Promotions

When held at other events or venues where the target audience is present, displays and a combination of personal selling can be very effective. But because the period of availability can be limited, this form of promotion is often best employed when promoting an event internationally.

Public Relations

Critical for most events is the level of media coverage that can be obtained, but surprisingly few events actually allocate responsibility for publicity to one person. Instead the job is usually an additional responsibility for one of the main organisers, and often results in less than satisfactory support from the media.

To try to ensure that an event receives good media coverage it is important that there be a planned approach to the media, and that the publicity manager has a clear understanding of what journalists are likely to perceive to be 'newsworthy'. Otherwise, although publicity through the news media might be 'free', the event manager will have no control over it at all.

Radio

The difficulty with radio news is that it comprises only a handful of very short news items. This means that the radio news editors can be very selective and make it difficult for an event to feature. However, it is also important for the radio news to be current, with a continual changing of the news content. This opens up the opportunities to obtain news coverage, with numerous opportunities for interviews on a variety of interest programmes. Although often outside peak times, these interviews can be an easy way for event managers to reach a wider public.

Print Media

The print media consists of both the daily newspapers and magazines. Generally it is easier to obtain good newspaper support in smaller centres, because they do not have the same pressure for major national and international news items as in the larger metropolitan areas. Newspapers have a short lead time into publication and will take written briefs, but magazines are the opposite and are often working on stories many months in advance, with journalists writing their own articles.

Television

The most difficult of all the media is television, because there has to be a strong news content before an item will be considered, and there has to be television footage of an event to provide background to the material. But with limited television news crew resources even in the main centres, television news presence at events in New Zealand is very difficult to obtain. The other avenue for television publicity is through a sports or news documentary, the cost of which – excepting the big four of rugby, rugby league, netball and cricket – is often met by the event organiser. This has often meant that the sponsorship dollar has gone towards not only the cost of producing a television item but also to the cost of the television credits the sponsor thereby obtains. If the event is to be introduced by its full name, including that of the sponsor, it can usually be made a requirement that the sponsor also purchases the 'credits'. Because many sponsors want to see their sponsorship support shown on television, event managers are increasingly having to divert the sponsorship dollar away from the event and towards television instead.

Media Plan

The most common mistake is for managers to contact the media too late or even not at all. They focus so much upon the event management, that they leave a planned publicity campaign until last. It is important early in the planning to map out the who, what, how and when of the media campaign, in order to increase the likelihood of receiving the maximum publicity possible. A media plan requires :

- A full list of all the media that need to be reached, with the names of individual contacts wherever possible.
- A draft programme of lead-in news releases together with the dates, and the actual time slots to catch deadlines for when they are to be released. Some examples of possible 'announcements' are:

    * 12 months prior - announcement of the event to happen in a year
    * 9 months prior   - principal sponsor
    * 6 months prior   - prize money
    * 3 months prior   - stars, celebrities confirm they are coming
    * 2 months prior   - event will produce $$$$$ for the local economy
    * 1 month prior   - more stars confirmed
    * 3 weeks prior   - event 'declared a winner' by a star participant
    * week prior   - previews/ interviews, etc.

- A structure and system for ensuring that the media plan is actioned prior to the event.
- A structure and system to ensure that the media are hosted during the event.

Administration

There must be a system to record all aspects of the event management. The same principle applies as for the finances, with records kept of all decisions, and a filing system to facilitate easy reference. However, many events have poor recording systems, resulting in the 'wheel needing to be re-invented' next time, or when something goes wrong there is no record of what actually occurred earlier in the planning that might have caused it. Therefore it is important that event managers confirm in writing all communications for reference purposes should there be any misunderstanding later on.

Event Implementation

The successful event manager should be able to concentrate on the unexpected during the event and leave the running of it to the delegated people. Last minute planning creates too much stress. If all the early planning has been successfully implemented there should be someone in charge of each area of responsibility with sufficient knowledge to be able to handle most problems likely to arise.

Debriefing

Once the event is over for the participants it is, unfortunately, not over for the organisers. An event debriefing involving key personnel must be held as soon after the event as possible to ensure that important points are not forgotten. The first step in any debriefing should be to consider the overall success or failure of the event. It is too easy to go straight for those areas that need to be improved with the result that a highly successful event could appear to have been a failure. Once the overall outcome has been assessed, it is the responsibility of the key directors to review performance of their section and recommend changes for next time. A group meeting of all directors can then consider the overview and make recommendations for future consideration.

Summary

Event management in New Zealand is becoming increasingly more professional in quality. Over the last decade numerous events have been a credit to their organisers, even though there will have been room for improvement in at least one aspect of their work. However, there have also been some spectacular examples of very poorly managed events, with many more falling short of expected standards. It is hoped that the advent of a more professional approach to event management education, and the development of an event managers' network, will result in an increase in the quality of event management.

Review Questions

1. What effects has sponsorship had on the management of events?
2. Explain the importance of critical paths in the planning process.
3. Select a sports event and demonstrate how you would use marketing to attract participants to it.
4. What is a media plan and can it assist in the obtaining of event publicity?

Suggested Reading

Wilkinson, D.G. (1988), *The Event Management and Marketing Institute*, Canada: The Event Management and Marketing Institute.

Media Sport

Judy McGregor

In this chapter you will become familiar with the following terms:

media sport	*social construction of news*
commodification of sport	*entertainment genres*
hero and heroine construction	*empowerment by television*
gender equity	*symbolic annihilation*
sexist language	*media management*
newsworthiness	*news sources*
media strategy	

Introduction

A powerful nexus exists between sport and the mass media that is profoundly influencing the public face of sport. Sport for many has become media sport. The term media sport refers to the sporting representations which are screened on television, broadcast by radio and published by the print media, and their audience effects. Media sport does not mirror reality, but it is a manufactured, socially constructed product that according to Davis (1990: 159) is:

... grounded on the premise that we live in a fundamentally ambiguous social world – a world in which persons, objects and actions have no inherent or essential meaning. If meaning is not inherent, then it must be created – imposed on action, events or things through human action.

Media sport is selected and highlighted from a vast array of sporting activities, and there is nothing natural or inevitable about the selection. In New Zealand, for example, sport programming on television bears little relation to participation rates in sport as gathered by the Hillary Commission's *Life in New Zealand* (LINZ) survey in 1991. Instead, media sport is based on certain criteria and assumptions about what will make good viewing, listening or reading. Therefore sport managers need to acknowledge the impact of sport media and develop their own strategies to influence the social construction of sport news and programming. This chapter reviews the contemporary sport mediascape in New Zealand, and asks whether the sport media are serving the public interest. It concludes by providing some observations on the relationship between sport managers and the sport media.

The Sport Mediascape in New Zealand

The Impact of Television

Numerous commentators have looked at the pervasive influence of television on sport. For example Altheide and Snow (1991: 217) in their analysis of the contemporary media condition express the opinion that over the last three decades, organised sport and television have become inseparable. Sage (1990: 115) quotes an American sports journalist, Leonard Shecter, who declared: 'Television *buys* sports... . Television tells sports what to do. It *is* sports and it runs them the way it does most other things, more flamboyantly than honestly'.

Much of the research into television sport is concerned with the impact of television on sport. Commentators such as Sage (1990) and Barnett (1990) state that television dictates the way sport is played to fit in with the entertainment and financial requirements of television. They also note that organised sport allows itself to be manipulated by television and accedes to changes in the structures and processes of sport to guarantee television coverage. Altheide and Snow (1991: 217), quoting Duncan and Brummett (1987), state that 'sport, operating through an entertainment perspective and other media formats, has undergone major changes in fundamental characteristics, such as rules of play, style of play, stadium theatrics, economic structure, media markets and hero construction'.

The commodification of sport into an entertainment format has occurred in partnership with television. One example of a sport modifying its game to suit television's needs in the New Zealand context, was the 1992 change to the format of Friday night Auckland rugby, so that games were played in quarters instead of two periods of play broken by the traditional half-time break. This format change better suited the entertainment genre of the television rugby spectacle, and it allowed for scheduling of more commercials during the four breaks made in the game. However, despite the intense publicity in advance, the new rugby on Friday night did not 'rate' in terms of television audience appeal, and it was quickly shelved.

An example of stadium theatrics comes from the world athletics scene, where the costumes of athletes have become more shiny and more streamlined for television cameras. Such an emphasis on 'outfits' and personal appearance pays homage to the notion of sport as a performance, which is central to media sport. Altheide and Snow (1991: 225) trace the origins to baseball players wearing tailored uniforms to emphasise a svelte look for the television cameras, followed by permanent hair waving, gold chains, stylish footwear, gloves, glasses, Florence Joyner's designer costumes for the 1988 Olympic Games, and the latest wrinkle, the shaved hair design on the scalp. Since then have come the male athletes' bodysuits worn by Afro-American athletes at the 1992 Barcelona Olympics, and the modern, luminous and 'day-glo' colours of the boards, sails and wetsuits worn by board and wind surfers, such as New Zealand Olympic gold medallist Barbara Kendall.

Media sport creates heroes and heroines of gigantic proportions, but it can also make or break the 'profile' and 'image' of sports people. The emphasis on winning, on status, on élite players, and on personalisation by the media, has meant a media growth industry in player profiles and human interest stories. No longer is it enough for media sport to simply provide run of play commentary or the results of the day's play. Instead, audience attention is retained by television during much of the mundane play by the insertion of player profiles that allow for the hero or heroine characterisation of sport stars. The most recent example of hero construction is the *Moro Sports Extra* programme of 7 June 1993 that featured New Zealand rugby league star Jason Donnelly. Here Donnelly (the hero) was presented as a straight-living sport star in contrast with a relative (the villain) who had been involved in, but acquitted of, a serious crime in New Zealand and who had been branded a rough player. In contrast to such media glorification of sport people is the media denigration accorded fallen heroes, such as former All Black Richard Loe, banned from rugby in the 1993 season for an eye-gouging incident.

Barnett (1990: 56) describes the all-encompassing influence of television on sport by saying:

> Throughout the developed world, at almost every level beyond recreational parks and back gardens, television considerations have influenced, often dictated, the progress of sports. Prize money has escalated beyond the wildest dreams of early participants. Rules have been changed. Events have been tailored, rescheduled or abandoned. Amateurism has almost vanished in all but name.

He also makes a second point, often overlooked in sociological analyses of the sport/media nexus, which is that television has 'empowered' some viewers by allowing them access to sport they would otherwise not see. Other observers of the television/sport relationship point to the important financial considerations of media sport, and Sage (1990: 123) in particular states that sport and television have become mutual beneficiaries in one of capitalism's most lucrative associations. Some of the largest sponsorship money available to sport in New Zealand, such as that from brewery and oil companies and food conglomerates, attaches itself not to the sport *per se* but to television sport. It seems that it is the television exposure rather than sport participation by players and spectators which provides the pay-off to sponsors.

In New Zealand now, there is evidence that the outrageous bidding wars for television rights to exclusively broadcast large sport events are becoming part of the competitive culture between the two 'free-to-air' channels, Television New Zealand and its rival Television Three, and the pay channel Sky which provides 24-hour sport, courtesy of satellite linkages. In addition, sport is used to sell advertising, and because sport as a television spectacle has more pace and can be more exciting than other forms of programming, it is a logical vehicle for advertising. Altheide and Snow (1991) claim that television programmes are commercials for commercials, and 'viewers are packaged for advertisers'.

Another linkage between 'professional sport and capital' is the employment by the media of former professional athletes. Television New Zealand's head of sport, John Knowles, has confirmed that it is TVNZ's policy to try to convert past and present sport stars into television personalities. He was quoted in the *Listener* (May 1, 1993) as saying that one of the things about television is that it relies on stars. A star is a mixture of someone who is well-known and who is an excellent performer. The *Listener* felt this phenomenon of sport star conversion was worthy of a cover story. As this chapter was being written, TVNZ's Monday night sports programme *Moro Sports Extra* was using sport stars April Ieremia (netball), Brent Todd (rugby league), Jeff Crowe (cricket) and Stu Wilson (rugby) as reporters, even though they might have a limited journalistic input into the items they present. According to the *Listener*, over 75 sport people have been used in this way by television and radio as broadcasters in association with about fifteen sports.

In addition, former New Zealand cricket captain, Jeremy Coney, has become a regular presenter of sport news on TV One's premier nightly news programme at 6 p.m. As the pressure to entertain through media sport has risen, so too has the role of the sportscaster. Another example here is the popular former rugby league Kiwi coach Graham Lowe, whose coaching days are over, but whose rise as a media celebrity selected for his appearance, his expert knowledge of the game, and his ability to participate on screen in the contest, makes him one of what Altheide and Snow (1991) have described as the 'new players'. Lowe even has a programme segment 'Lowedown' in the TV One's Monday night sports programme named after him.

How Much Sport is in the Media?

Television researchers (Lealand, 1991; Atkinson, 1992) examining the nature of television content since the deregulation of broadcasting in New Zealand, have noted an increase in the amount of sport broadcast. Lealand, in research for New Zealand On Air (the Broadcasting Commission), indicated that sports coverage increased by a remarkable 141 per cent in 1990, from 686 hours in 1989 to 1653 hours in 1990. While he states that much of this increase could be attributed to the prolonged coverage of the January Commonwealth Games in Auckland in that year, the increased coverage of netball, rugby, cricket and tennis in primetime also contributed to this total. Atkinson (1992) examined Television New Zealand's One Network News between 1985 and 1992, and noted an increase in sport as a percentage of the total week's programme time from just over 20 per cent to 57 per cent. And John Knowles of TVNZ (Television New Zealand), indicated personally to members of the sport media lobby group FIRST (Female Images and Representation in Sport TaskForce) at a meeting in 1992, that there was some internal concern that too much sport was screened by his organisation, and that those setting policy and principles had to be guided by the notion of balanced programming.

But the increase in sport on television is similar to the pattern overseas. Barnett (1990) analysed British television and found that 'the opportunities for watching sport had nearly doubled over the last ten years'. He commented that one reason for the increase in sports coverage was that compared to the cost of producing plays, current affairs programmes or even quiz shows, sports coverage apparently was cheaper, and therefore gave better value for money.

The same increase in sport coverage pervades other media as well as television. According to Sage (1990), American radio stations broadcast more than 400,000 hours of sport annually. In New Zealand the growth and popularity of sport talkback, and the regular rows over whether cricket commentary or the broadcasting of Parliament should be a programming priority, testify to the greater audience appeal of radio sport over political debate.

The print media have traditionally allocated around 20 per cent of newsroom resources and pagination to sports coverage. It is within the New Zealand experience too, that experienced sports reporters often graduate into newsroom management, and often become newspaper editors, and this career path reinforces the priority attached to sports coverage in the print media. Looking to the future, revolutions in satellite and cable technology, and the deregulated broadcasting environment, will provide increased opportunity for media sport. It is safe to say there will be more airtime available to fill, and it could mean that media sport will simply become an incidental marketing tool – a commodity packaged as a sponsor's product sandwiched between other sponsor's products or the commercials. Barnett (1990), in his British analysis of the future of television sport, expresses the bleak conclusion that in many respects 'the second fifty years of television sport may prove to be significantly less beneficial, both to the audience and to sport itself, than the half century which has just ended'.

Which Sport is Media Sport?

Overwhelmingly media sport is male sport. The subordination of women's sport internationally as a media image has been systematically recorded since the mid-1970s. With regard to the press, Brown (1991: 21) is among those who confirm that the percentage of total space devoted to women's sport is marginal when compared to men's sport, and he cited authorities who found the same gender imbalance in United States, Germany, Finland and Australia. To that list can be added New Zealand. McGregor and Melville (1992) in a print media study of seven New Zealand newspapers, found the coverage of womens' sport news amounted to only 12.4 per cent of the total space devoted to sports news compared to 75.5 per cent for that of males, and 12.1 per cent for mixed sport stories that featured male and female competitors in the same story (Table 18.1). Taken separately, the results showed that no newspaper analysed managed to devote more than 20 per cent of its total sport news coverage to female sports. Three newspapers analysed devoted less than 10 per cent of their total sports coverage to women's sport. The provincial newspaper which was included in the survey devoted 6.18 per cent of space to women's sport and allocated twelve times more space to male sport than to female sport in its sport over the week-long period studied. The results were consistent with those of a previous study of the New Zealand press by the government appointed *Committee on Women* confirming, the near invisibility of New Zealand women in media sport (Cooper, 1981).

Table 18.1: Showing the cm^2 total space devoted to sport news editorial and photographs by gender in seven New Zealand newspapers.

	Male		Female		Mixed		Total
	cm^2	% of Total	cm^2	% of Total	cm^2	% of Total	cm^2
Dailies	66182		11722		11928		89831
Sundays	21812		2689		2246		26748
TOTAL	87994	75.5	14411	12.4	14174	12.1	116579

Gender equity in media sport is influenced by the overwhelming male domination of media sport. While there has been an increasing feminisation of New Zealand journalism that has closed up the gender gap in newsrooms, evidently this feminisation has not spread to print media sport journalism, where only a handful of female journalists are attracted to, and sustained in the work. One of the few women ever to become a newspaper sports editor at a metropolitan or provincial level in this country is now working outside journalism. Her departure further reduced the number of positive role models for women as print sport journalists. Television has fared only marginally better in this regard, although it has to be acknowledged that the producer of the *Moro Sports Extra* programme is a woman.

New Zealand is not alone in having few women sports journalists. McKay (1991: 97) made the point that despite international accomplishments of Australian sportswomen and their participation in virtually all sport, 'the electronic and print media coverage of sport in Australia is overwhelmingly devoted to and contributed to by men'. By default, males set the media sport agenda, decide which sport should be covered and the prominence and emphasis of its presentation. Males are the only gender to take part in newsroom socialisation, the process by which journalists absorb newsroom rituals and news values. Therefore it is no surprise that the male perspective dominates media sport.

Two recent pieces of New Zealand research have looked at women's coverage in television sport. Ferkins (1992) found that women received 20 per cent of television sport coverage compared with 67.8 per cent by men, 11.7 per cent mixed coverage, and 0.5 per cent unidentified, and they fare even worse in television news coverage. Massey University researchers, including the author, are continuing to monitor aspects of television's sport coverage throughout 1993, with funding help from the university's research fund and the 1993 Suffrage Centennial Year Trust Whakatu Wahine. Their sample of 37 days of the main daily news programmes of Television One and Television Three in 1992, has shown that of the 505 sports news items broadcast during the period studied, 401 (79.4 per cent) featured male sport, while 45 (8.9 per cent) featured women's sport, and 59 (11.7 per cent) featured mixed sport (Table 18.2).

Table 18:2: Male, female and mixed sport items taken from 37 days randomly chosen from May, June and July 1992.

	Number of Items	% of Total
Female	45	8.9
Male	401	79.4
Mixed	59	11.7
Total	505	100

Again these results were similar to a previous study conducted by O'Leary and Roberts (1985), and they show that the New Zealand media has made no progress in redressing the gender imbalance in coverage of sport.

The survey went further to indicate which sport by gender was covered in the news items, and it found male rugby with the greatest number, followed by male rugby league, male soccer, men's racing, men's cricket, male golf, and tennis (Table 18:3 over page). Female netball was the most prominent for female media attention, but it ranked with male yachting in an equal 10th place.

Table 18.3: News items showing the frequency of female, male, and mixed television sports.

All Items on the Sports News					
Female	**No.**	**Male**	**No.**	**Mixed**	**No.**
Netball	8	Rugby	117	Olympics	17
Golf	6	Rugby League	94	Tennis	7
Tennis	6	Soccer	37	Athletics	4
Athletics	6	Motor racing	27	Equestrian	4
Cycling	3	Cricket	19	Underwater Hockey	2
Hockey	3	Golf	15	Squash	2
Tabletennis	2	Tennis	14	Rugby	2
Volleyball	1	Athletics	14	Yachting	2
Skiing	1	Cycling	10	Cycling	1
Tae Kwon Do	1	Yachting	8	Speed Skating	1
Squash	1	Boxing	7	Swimming	1
		Basketball	5	Sports/Drugs	1
		Hockey	4	Rowing	1
		Snooker	4		
		Weightlifting	2		
		Ice Hockey	1		
		Gridiron	1		
		Underwater Hockey	1		
		Canoeing	1		
		Equestrian	1		
Total	**38**	**Total**	**382**	**Total**	**45**

To the quantitative research can be added the scholarship that focused on the qualitative analysis of media sport writing in Australia. McKay (1991) comments that even the meagre coverage of women in sport over there, overwhelmingly portrays women in peripheral roles, trivialises their accomplishments, and treats them as sex objects.

Massey University researchers have begun to look at qualitative dimensions of media sport in New Zealand to complement the quantitative studies. They find that the lack of coverage of women's sport is compounded by the trivialisation of women in sport. An example is Television One's repeated portrayal of New Zealand swimmer Toni Jeffs as 'unpatriotic' and a 'rebel' who wore a tattoo, drank red wine, enjoyed steak and received sponsorship from a Wellington Strip Club to get to the 1992 Barcelona Olympics. Both the invisibility of women in media sport and stereotypical representations of them impacts negatively on sponsorship opportunities. Top New Zealand sportswomen such as windsurfer Barbara Kendall, skier Annelise Coberger and marathoner Lorraine Moller, have all had difficulties attracting sponsorship because of their negligible media profile, despite their world-class sport status. When the feminist media lobby group, FIRST, complained to the Broadcasting Standards Authority about the near invisibility of sports women in the 6 p.m. news on TV One and TV Three, the authority in its decision (1993) said:

The arguments about the imbalance of the coverage of women's sport which are well documented overseas include the lack of sufficient highly visible role models, the lack of awareness of opportunities, the lack of encouragement to participate, and the lack of sponsorship and other financial support.

It can also be said that when females are mentioned in the media, sexist language is still being used to portray them, and the references are male-oriented; in other words the image of female athletes is largely constructed by males (Sage, 1990).

Tuchman (1978) used the term 'symbolic annihilation' to describe both the invisibility of women as a media image, and the trivialisation of women when they *were* represented in the media. Media sport is a major arena of this symbolic annihilation. The claim can be made that the neglect in both the quantity and quality of coverage of women's sport undermines female participation and achievement in sport.

A particular feature of New Zealand's contemporary sport panorama is the current high level of achievement by New Zealand sportswomen at a rate of at least four 'world beaters' a year and, as Ferkins (1992) comments, this is no less than the achievements of male athletes. Coney (1992) reported that at the Barcelona Olympics in 1992, for example, New Zealand women athletes made up 30 per cent of the team (43 women and 99 men) but won 43 per cent of the medals on a points system of three for gold, two for silver and one for bronze, and the only gold medal was won by a sportswoman. But still media sport is male. As this chapter was being written, a national Sunday newspaper the *Sunday Star,* distinguished itself in its issue of 6 June 1993 by carrying not *one* single story about women's sport in its entire sports section, and it featured only netball, in six-point type, in the results section. One might wonder whether women's sport was cancelled on that particular Queen's Birthday weekend, and the answer is not that there was no women's sport but rather that it did not become media sport.

The male-dominant media images of sport confirm Connell's (1990) notion of 'hegemonic masculinity', i.e. the culturally idealised form of masculine character which underlines the connecting of masculinity to toughness and competitiveness, as well as the subordination of women. Thus media sport both helps to create and to reinforce stereotypical images that men are newsworthy as 'natural' sportsmen, and tries to perpetuate the myth that sport leadership, competitiveness, team membership, physical and mental strength and endurance, are exclusively to be regarded as attributes of the male.

Is Sport Participation Reflected in Media Sport?

Four major sports dominate media sport, as has been mentioned previously – i.e. male rugby, male rugby league, male cricket and female netball – and even these sports are unequally treated. While data on overall sports participation rates in New Zealand is difficult to obtain, the LINZ (1991) study showed that of the most popular male and female sports by participation, about 10 per cent of all New Zealand men over 15 years played rugby union, and 7 per cent of all women over 15 years play netball. Yet, in the television news survey conducted by Massey University researchers, 117 items on the sports news featured rugby union, and only eight featured netball. The period studied coincided with the appropriate season for these two major codes.

And even widespread grassroots participation in particular sports is no guarantee of a media profile, regardless of gender. Several sports have become cinderellas in terms of television coverage, and these include lawn bowls, gymnastics, softball, soccer, hockey, masters sport, school sport and sport involving disabled athletes, simply because those selecting media sport do not believe they will 'rate' in terms of audience size. The most spectacular example of the unbalanced treatment accorded sport, by comparison with the participation rates in the sport, is the media's treatment of touch rugby. Touch rugby has become one of the fastest growing mixed sports in New Zealand. Yet it is not a media sport. It receives minimal news media attention despite its popularity. Traditional rugby bags attention, whereas 'new' rugby is ignored.

Does Media Sport Serve the Public Interest?

Media sport caters for a number of clients whom Rowe (1991) describes as employers, advertisers, sponsors, governments, the aesthetic and professional demands of each medium, peers and finally sport associations, sport people and audiences. He states the obvious in saying that it is naive to believe that all these interests can be reconciled. Media sport is big business, and according to Sage (1990: 135) the media are effective and powerful organisations for promoting hegemonic ideology, for the advancement and reproduction of dominant interests.

But does this mean that the public should acquiesce in the face of the agenda set for them by media sport? New Zealanders are entitled to question broadcasting priorities when Television New Zealand uses public monies via the broadcasting licence fee, and New Zealand on Air provides funding to screen such sport as Australian rugby league rather than to commit their resources to the coverage of indigenous sports. The Broadcasting Commission is required by law, s.36 and s.37 of the *Broadcasting Act* 1989, to reflect and develop New Zealand identity and culture by promoting programmes about New Zealand and New Zealand interests; and by promoting, in its funding of the production of programmes, a sustained commitment by television and radio broadcasters to programming reflecting New Zealand identity and culture. Apart from the tenuous links through the numbers of New Zealanders playing Australian rugby league, the question can be asked as to whether the screening of Australian rugby league reflects New Zealand's identity.

TVNZ's coverage of Aussie Rugby League is evidence of the chicken and egg argument facing sport seeking a media profile. It states that 'minority' sport and women's sport do not rate highly with viewers and therefore it should not be covered. But there was no initial imperative to make Australian rugby league games compelling viewing. Instead, television *built* the following of league. The Broadcasting Standards Authority commented in a March 1993 decision that TVNZ implicitly acknowledged that television coverage of Australian rugby league had probably fostered the participation in and media coverage of that particular (male) sport (p.5). One might well ask why the same philosophy of TV nurturing a media sport cannot be applied to other New Zealand sports that have a wide following but need help.

How to Manage the Sport Media

There are a number of persuasive reasons why sport coaches, officials, administrators, managers and sports people themselves need to be 'street wise' about the sport media. The most obvious is the business/sport symbiosis which sees the sport media providing profile as a pay-off for sponsorship or delivering audiences for commercials. But knowledge about news media and mass media processes is important for those interested in the management of sport, because of the power of the media, as has already been mentioned, to construct heroes and heroines in sport and equally to destroy the reputations of sports people who fall from grace.

Developing expertise in managing media sport, particularly sport news management, requires tenacity and experience. This is because there is no universal agreement amongst journalists themselves as to what constitutes the 'news'. Nowhere is there a set of rules or codes as to what 'makes' the news. Instead, a socially constructed product such as sport news is selected and presented against subjective criteria which could change from day to day, from journalist to journalist, and from sub-editor to sub-editor, and so on to the proprietors. Bennett (1992), who discusses the perils of mass-mediated democracy, considers it impossible to define just what constitutes news, beyond the technologies, organisational routines and market forces that drive its production. This ambiguity makes it difficult to provide a recipe of media sport management for sports managers to follow. In the absence of a definitive code, however, the following pointers should be of help to sport managers.

Knowledge of News Processes

Sport managers need to know how the news media works so they can best use it to serve their sport. They need to know such factors as:

- which media should be targeted?
- what the prevailing editorial philosophy is of the particular medium?
- what is 'newsworthiness' (for example, why is 'bad news' highlighted ahead of 'good news')?
- what makes a good 'human interest' story, or photographic or film opportunity?
- the deadlines of the appropriate news media, particularly when many news organisations are suffering from constraints in journalistic resources
- how to do basic newswork themselves to ensure coverage of, say, weekend competition in the Sunday press.

Professionalism as a Source

Journalists *need* sport managers and sport people as sources for their stories. The more professional the potential source is in dealing with the news media, the more likely they will become a primary source in a story. Good sources cultivate their relationships with journalists, feed them 'tips' when appropriate, are available at nights and the weekends to suit the parameters of the journalist's job, and have a good understanding of the competitive nature of journalism so they do not antagonise reporters they know well by giving a newcomer the story first. Source/journalist relationships need to be nurtured, and sport managers need to allocate time for both the professional relationship and the socialisation necessary to cultivate them.

Preparation of Players

Good sport managers need to prepare their charges for the news media 'assault'. Pre-game comment, post-game disappointments and triumphs recorded live by television and radio, deliver good and bad losers into the nation's living rooms. Sporting thuggery is action-replayed. Bad behaviour on the sport field is instantaneously recorded and revealed. Top players need to be coached in television skills, and good sport managers should provide video training in which players can see themselves as they answer hard questions and then can practice televised, 'dignity-in-defeat' remarks. The contemporary media condition is that *all* will be revealed. Sport people need to know, too, that media sport makes them role models for generations of aspiring young players.

Limiting Damage and Countering Negative Publicity

Not all sport publicity can be good, and sport managers need to be prepared for negative coverage. Limiting the damage of bad publicity needs a media strategy. Sport managers caught by surprise on the end of the phone with bad news by a reporter should not, for example, simply react and prattle loosely. It is a journalistic aphorism that loose lips make good copy. Instead, media-wise sport managers arrange to ring the reporter back, then carefully consider the response they wish to make before communicating again. Equally, in this circumstance, trying to avoid the news media, or resorting to the proverbial 'no comment', may simply serve to heighten and prolong media interest. The Bruce Taylor affair is an example of such media hype in the absence of the sportsman making himself available at the initial stages of the story's development in 1993. In this case the media's coverage of the former New Zealand cricket great whose gambling addiction led to his downfall, warranted judicial admonition at the time of his sentencing. But by then the news media damage was done.

Building Community Linkages with the Media

The media has the backing of powerful business interests with a strong tradition of sport sponsorship and endorsement. They realise the financial potential of such involvement, and the media appreciates that sport provides them with valuable community linkages. Therefore sport managers need to draw in the media as participants in their planning of events. Many fun-runs organised by harrier clubs, for example, are endorsed and supported by the news media as community building exercises. Auckland's annual Round the Bays run would not have been the success it was in its heyday without the former *Auckland Star.* The growth and strength of community newspapers in New Zealand provides a largely untapped reservoir of support for sport. Talkback radio callers, too, have the opportunity to slip in unsolicited 'free plugs' for sports events, and sport managers need to exploit these opportunities.

Consumer Muscle

The media, unless challenged, have both the means to resist criticism by ignoring it, and the means to massage their own image by its promotion, self congratulation and commentary. Ferkins (1992) urges the aggrieved consumer to use mechanisms such as those of the Broadcasting Standards Authority in relation to radio and television, and of the New Zealand Press Council in relation to the print media. While this may be a useful strategy in relation to news media excesses or abuses, it is largely unhelpful in relation to media omissions, because both bodies are reluctant to consider the wider issue of what is *not* covered as media sport. A better strategy for sport managers who are concerned about non-coverage, might be for them to tackle the media's commercial rationale. Their suggestions to an editor that the media product will not be read, listened to, or watched, *unless* there is coverage of a particular sport could be a strong tactic, particularly if this feedback is organised amongst those involved in sport. Letting the news media know that sports people will support those of them who *do* cover their sport well, is a powerful commercial incentive in a fiercely competitive environment.

Conclusion

Sport is inextricably entwined with the media, and media sport, which is a socially constructed reality, is for many, the only sport they experience. Media sport is an arena for big business to accumulate capital and make profits. It also facilitates promotion and reinforcement of dominant ideologies and interests in society. In New Zealand this is strongly reflected in the dismal coverage of women's sport and so-called 'minority' sport. Because media sport is so pervasive, sport managers need to develop a knowledge and understanding of news media processes so they can exploit publicity opportunities.

Review Questions

1. Define media sport as a socially constructed product.
2. Explain why the nexus between sport and the media is so powerful.
3. Analyse which public groups are served by media sport.
4. Construct a media plan for a particular sport organisation, team or personality, utilising the suggestions provided in the chapter.

References

Altheide, D.L. and Snow, R.P. (1991), *Media Worlds in the Post-journalism Era*, New York: Aldine De Gruyter.
Atkinson, J. (1992), 'The State, the Media and the Democracy', University of Auckland Winter Lecture Series (unpublished).
Barnett, S. (1990), *Games and Sets: The Changing Face of Sport on Television*, London: BFI Publishing.
Bennett, W.L. (1992), 'White Noise: The Perils of Mass Mediated Democracy', *Communication Monographs*, Vol 59, pp.401-406.
Broadcasting Standards Authority, Decision No.30/93 (1993), Wellington: Government Printer.
Brown, P. (1990), 'Women, the Media and Equity in Sport: An Australian Perspective', Paper presented to the World Congress Leisure and Tourism, Sydney 16-19 July 1991.
Coney, S. (1992), 'Boys Can Only Talk About It', *Dominion Sunday Times*, 9 August 1992, p.11.
Connell, R.W. (1990), 'An Iron Man: The Body and Some Contradictions of Hegemonic Masculinity', in Messner, M.A. and Sabo, D.F. (eds), *Sport, Men, and the Gender Order: Critical Feminist Perspectives*, Champaign, Il.: Human Kinetics Books, pp.83-95.
Cooper, R. (1981), *Investigation of Discrimination in Sporting and Other Leisure Activities*, Wellington: The Treasury.
Davis, D.K. (1990), 'News and Politics', in Swanson, D.L. and Nimmo, D. (eds), *New Directions in Political Communication*, California: Sage, pp.147-186.
Ferkins, L. (1992), *New Zealand Women in Sport: An Untapped Media Resource*, Hillary Commission: New Zealand.
Lealand, G. (1991), 'Selling the Airwaves: The Impact of Broadcasting Deregulation on Local Context and Audience in New Zealand', Paper delivered to the New Zealand Broadcasting Industry Summit (unpublished).

Life in New Zealand (LINZ) Survey, (1991), Wellington: Hillary Commission.

Listener, 1 May 1993, p.21.

McGregor, J. and Melville, P. (1992), 'The Invisible Face of Women's Sport in the New Zealand Press', *Leisure Options: Australian Journal of Leisure and Recreation,* 2 (4), 18-28.

McKay, J. (1991), 'Bimbos and Rambos in Sport: The Mass Media as a Barrier to Women's Participation in Sport', in Proceedings of the joint seminar on *Equity for Women in Sport,* held by the House of Representatives Standing Committee on Legal and Constitutional Affairs and the Australian Sports Commission, February, Parliament House, Canberra, 14-21.

O'Leary, E. and Roberts, N.S. (1985), 'Bad Track Record', *New Zealand Listener,* 15-21 June, pp.15-21.

Rowe, D. (1991, Winter), Sport and the Media, *Metro,* pp.42-49.

Sage, G.H. (1990), *Power and Ideology in American Sport,* Champaign, Il: Human Kinetics Books.

Tuchman, G. (1978), 'The Symbolic Annihilation of Women by the Mass Media', in Tuchman, G. Daniels, A.K. and Benet, J. (eds), *Health and Home/Images of Women in the Mass Media,* New York: Oxford University Press, pp.3-38.

Sport and the Law

David Howman

In this chapter you will become familiar with the following terms:

legal entity	*incorporation*
constitution	*contract*
Employment Contracts Act 1991	*restraint of trade*
disciplinary procedures	*natural justice*
Health and Safety in Employment Act 1992	*character merchandising*
Fair Trading Act 1986	*defamation*
Resources Management Act 1991	*Sports Drug Agency*
taxation of income	
Accident Rehabilitation and Compensation Insurance Act 1991	

The law is one of the major methods which civilised society uses to determine the rights of individuals. As it affects human rights in every aspect of day-to-day existence, so too it touches upon those who participate or are otherwise involved in sport. The increase in professional sport, the growth and expansion of sport generally, the importance of sport in New Zealand, the heightened awareness and focus upon individual rights all tend to lead to a reliance upon the law and the courts to protect sport people and their interests. The 1992 case involving Richard Loe and the New Zealand Rugby Union is but one example of this, where the 'prosecution' and penalty imposed on a player for an act of violence became a matter of wider public interest and debate.

It is suggested that in the future more and more individuals will exercise their legal rights by going to court when they consider that sport organisations fail to fulfil their legal obligations, or fail to provide fair, internal remedies for handling disputes or discipline.

This chapter will give a cover in brief of the way in which the law impacts on sport in New Zealand. It is intended to provide a general overview of the major legal issues but not an exhaustive account. It touches on sporting bodies as legal entities, matters concerning contracts, discipline, accident injuries and safety, sponsorship, facilities, drugs, and finance. Its aim is both to inform and to warn sport people of the traps that might befall them.

The Sporting Body and its Legal Entity

There is no simple law governing sport organisations. Each organisation typically will have a legal entity or personality, which through providing rules and a mechanism to operate efficiently and effectively, will protect its members and run its sporting activities. In New Zealand an organisation will typically be legally formed by incorporation under the Incorporated Societies Act 1908, the Charitable Trusts Act 1957 or the Companies Act 1993. Incorporation enables the sport group to record its objectives and purpose, and establish the authority or powers it gives to those responsible for running it. These matters will be contained in a constitution or set of rules.

A typical constitution will set out the organisation's powers, objectives, membership criteria, executive or management committee powers, meeting procedure and voting, financial requirements and procedures for disciplinary measures. To prevent legal challenges it is very important that a sport runs according to its constitution, and does only what it is empowered to do. The constitution provides the organisation with legal authority to establish the rights and obligations of its members. At the same time it provides members with an avenue of recourse should their rights not be respected. This means that all sport organisations should carefully review their constitutions or rules to ensure they still properly and adequately govern their present-day circumstances. In New Zealand this is now a vital concern because a number of constitutions were crafted in the early part of this century and they do not cover current issues such as drugs in sport, disciplinary processes and the employment of paid staff.

Incorporation has other benefits. For example, registration pursuant to the Incorporated Societies Act protects members from being sued personally, but the sport body can sue and be sued in its own right, i.e., it has its own legal personality. The constitution should be a living document as it is the heart of the organisation. It follows that officers of sport organisations should have a good working knowledge of their constitution or set of rules. One matter which should not be ignored is the requirement to return annual accounts to the Registrar of Incorporated Societies. Failure to do so may result in the striking off of the organisation, and subsequent loss of identity and the protection given by the Act.

It is important to note here that office bearers may have legal responsibilities, and indeed liabilities, as a result of holding office. This varies according to the sport body and its form of incorporation, and the documentation entered into by office bearers. A recent case in Australia is a salutary example of such responsibility, when office bearers in a tennis club who had signed personal guarantees with a bank, found some years later that the bank wished to call up those guarantees and pursued the individuals personally.

Contractual Matters

The contract is one of the basic factors of our legal system. A contract is an agreement between two parties containing promises by each which they intend to be enforceable at law. Although it is commonly thought that a contract must be in writing and signed in some peculiar legal form, that is not correct. An oral contract may be just as binding, and, indeed, a contract can be construed from an exchange of letters, or the acceptance of an offer with a letter.

In sport there are many examples of contracts, ranging from player contracts and sponsorship contracts to employment contracts for administrators or groundspeople. In each case there needs to be careful identification of a number of factors to ensure that the contract is enforceable and not void. For example, minors and those who are mentally ill do not usually have the capacity to enter into contracts. Also each party to the agreement must be fully and properly identified, and the substance of the deal be fully set out so that each party clearly understands the obligations and requirements imposed on it. As a general rule contracts should provide for termination, and a mechanism for relieving responsibility or demanding compliance should one party be in breach. In other words care needs to be taken in sport contracts for the worst case situation to be covered and the not-so-serious breach anticipated.

Player contracts in New Zealand are now common. Several major sports, including cricket, netball, tennis, athletics and swimming, have detailed contracts for their national members. Those who are selected in Olympic and Commonwealth Games teams are also required to complete a contract where individual and management responsibilities are clearly set out for the period of the Games. Fortunately, to date there has been little need for either the sports body or the individual to have recourse to the courts in relation to such agreements, but it is important for the individual that personal rights are jealously guarded and protected.

It is in fact becoming more common in New Zealand for player contracts to have an arbitration clause to cover disputes. Under such clauses the parties will agree to resolve any argument by referring to an umpire or arbitrator for a decision, rather than go to court. Overseas there is a trend, particularly in Europe, for all sports disputes to be so referred. In addition to what was said earlier about the form of contracts, for employment contracts it is necessary to comply with the Employment Contracts Act 1991. This law requires all employment contracts between an employer and an employee to be in writing, and among other requirements to have a personal grievance and dispute clause. Other statutes regulate minimum terms for employees, such as statutory holidays, annual leave, sick leave, holiday pay (Holidays Act 1981) and wage rates (Minimum Wage Act 1983).

In sport, difficulties may arise in determining whether an individual is an employee of the sports organisation or has some other status. An individual who is *under the control* of the organisation, who receives some form of consideration (e.g. payment, expenses, clothing or gear) and who is an integral part of the organisation may be an employee. This of course has implications for tax and accident compensation levies as well as compliance with the laws mentioned. If the individual is not an employee then responsibility for tax does not lie with the organisation but rather the individual, and failure to comply does not result in further obligations or liabilities for the organisation. As this is a fast-developing area, carrying with it considerable potential financial responsibility, it is crucial that the definition of employee status is carefully checked. Some players will in fact be independent contractors, and not employees, but each case requires separate consideration.

An element of player contracts which has received attention in the New Zealand courts is that of restraint of trade. The courts have traditionally recognised an individual's right to work, and the doctrine protects that right and promotes free and competitive trade conditions. The New Zealand Rugby League discovered this doctrine when one of its players Tony Kemp (David, 1992) challenged a restraint clause precluding him from playing further in the Winfield Cup for Newcastle. The High Court ruled that the clause breached his right to work and upheld his challenge. The irony of this case, however, was the cost to Kemp financially. His legal fees were far greater than his player fees, and he lost a subsequent case against the Taxation Board in Australia when he sought to have his legal fees classified as a deductible expense.

Disciplinary Matters

The New Zealand Rugby Union has come under close public and media scrutiny in recent years with its handling of disciplinary matters for its players. Cases involving prominent All Blacks Alan Whetton, Jamie Joseph, Andy Earl and the previously mentioned Richard Loe have all been in the spotlight. Rugby has in its rules a carefully drafted set of procedures in its *Black Book* to ensure disciplinary matters are dealt with properly. The High Court in Richard Loe's case endorsed those procedures as being appropriate for the sporting code to follow in accordance with principles of natural justice. At law an individual charged with breaching a sports rule must be dealt with in accordance with the principles of *natural justice*. This often quoted phrase simply means the organisation must ensure that the individual should be given adequate notice of a hearing, be told of the substance or nature of the accusation, be given the opportunity to hear the evidence and to respond to it. Finally, the organisation needs to ensure the decision-making tribunal is impartial and acts in good faith. All hearings must be conducted within the powers or rules of the organisation.

Any failure to adhere to the principles of natural justice could result in the decision being challenged in court. Such challenges can of course bring large expense and bad publicity to the sport and should be avoided. It can be anticipated that individuals wrongly disciplined, suspended or banned in any way, will seek appropriate financial redress from the body responsible, and large law suits will follow accordingly. That in itself should be sufficient spur for sport organisations to conduct their disciplinary hearings properly and fairly.

Another matter that should be mentioned here is the coexistence of the laws of the country and the laws of the game. An individual can be punished under both for an incident in a sporting fixture without there being double jeopardy. For example, a player could be charged and convicted of an assault under the Crimes Act 1961, and also disciplined and suspended by the sport body. It may seem unfair that an individual be dealt two punishments for one offence, but it simply recognises the duties of citizens as separate from their duties as members of an organisation. Keith Hancox, the former Chief Executive of the New Zealand Sports Foundation, learned that when following criminal convictions in 1991, he was removed from the membership of the Sports Hall of Fame. Hancox challenged that process in the High court but failed to convince the court to grant him an injunction.

Accidents, Injury and Safety

Given the risks of injury in most sports, it is important to consider the legal remedies open to the injured player. In New Zealand the Accident Rehabilitation and Compensation Insurance Act 1992 gives an injured player some financial relief. Unlike its predecessor, however, there is now some doubt that it will provide exhaustive cover, and certainly it does not fully compensate the individual.

The Act covers those who are injured by an *accident,* which is described as 'a specific event or series of events that involves the application of force or resistance external to the body'. Thus a slowly degenerating injury may not be covered but most instant injuries will come within the Act. However, it is one thing to be covered by the Act, yet another to be compensated or compensated adequately.

Even if covered by the Act, the compensation payable is restricted to loss of earnings compensation (payable at a rate of 80 per cent of earnings), an allowance assessed on the extent of disability (maximum payment of $40 per week for 100 per cent disability), and assistance towards medical and allied costs. In many cases there will be insufficient compensation to meet all the medical costs. Private medical insurance therefore becomes an option that all sport players must consider. There is still the possibility of suing the individual, or the individual's sport organisation, for punitive or exemplary damages if the injury was caused maliciously or intentionally. But the Act specifically bars individuals from suing for compensatory damages, and as yet there is little if any litigation action for exemplary damages. It might safely be predicted that it will only be a matter of time before such a claim is made. Sport organisations need therefore to be ready and properly protected by insurance or other schemes.

They also need to pay close attention to the recently enacted Health and Safety in Employment Act 1992, which highlights the need to have in place prevention mechanisms in the workplace. Where a sport is played or participated in in a workplace, for example a gym or a swimming pool, then the responsibilities and duties under the Act must be maintained. The Act requires every employer and employee in the workplace to maintain a healthy and safe place of employment. The duties extend to persons in control of a place of work, to persons in charge and to principals who have engaged sub-contractors to complete a task. This means the owner, manager or operator of the gym or pool.

This Act also requires a hazard management system, a register of accidents, emergency procedures, safety equipment, training of employees and protection requirements to be in place. Failure to comply with the Act could result in being charged with a quasi-criminal offence and penalties of up to $100,000 or imprisonment for up to twelve months for those in breach.

The Health and Safety in Employment Act 1992 and its obligations have not yet been tested in court, but already sports organisations are discussing and setting standards to ensure compliance. It is another example of recent legislation putting accountability back on those providing facilities, and it is somewhat inconsistent with the no-fault compensation principles behind Accident Compensation. The trend towards accountability may be expected to continue, and therefore with it the responsibilities, obligations and liabilities of sport organisations will continue to increase.

▶ **Sponsorship** (See also Chapter 16)

The commercialisation of sports is typified by the dominance of sponsors. The All Blacks are rarely seen without the *Steinlager* label somewhere on their clothing, the New Zealand cricket team is covered with *DB Draught,* and of course *Smokefree* frequently appears in sporting contexts. Such sponsorship provides the financial support that is vital for the promotion of sport in New Zealand. It comes either from the private or corporate sector, or the public sector (the Hillary Commission in particular), and sometimes from a combination of both (the New Zealand Sports Foundation) or the specifically legislated body – The Health Sponsorship Council. There may also be a corporate link with the Hillary Commission, as has occurred with the Firestone Tyre Company sponsoring *Fair Play* in sport.

In New Zealand now it is not unusual for an individual to have to wear different gear or clothing when playing for club, province and country. When those responsibilities are balanced against the individual's obligations under a personal sponsorship, it is easy to anticipate dispute. This occurred in Australia this year when the Cronulla Rugby League Club entered a sponsorship agreement with the Reebok sports shoe company. One of its key players Andrew Ettingshausen had an existing contract with a competing company, Asics, and a dispute arose. Fortunately it was settled without the delay and expense of going to court.

Sport organisations and individuals entering these contracts should ensure that crucial elements of control are not lost to the sponsor. The player or club should not be deflected from the sporting pursuit by such sponsorship demands as media contact before and after the games. Therefore matters such as photo approval, naming rights and sponsor's rights must all be carefully considered.

Character merchandising is another area which requires legal intervention and assistance. The obvious example in the United States is Michael Jordan, the basketball player, but in New Zealand, sports personalities such as Susan Devoy, Martin Crowe, Sean Fitzpatrick and Gary Freeman feature prominently. Their agreements involve the use of the name, signature or likeness of the personality to sell the product or service. They involve intellectual property rights, and the use or transfer of such rights, all of which require careful limits and explanations. If overlooked, the potential damage to sporting reputations is difficult to recover.

The Fair Trading Act 1986 is an important vehicle for protecting a sport person's reputation. The Act prevents persons or businesses in the trade of providing goods and services from engaging in conduct which is misleading or deceptive or likely to be so. It also prohibits advertising or misrepresenting goods and services. As providers of leisure services, organisations need to be aware of these requirements when they operate their businesses. It also becomes important for them when advertising events to ensure accurate advertising occurs in accordance with the requirements of their particular sponsors. If the public is likely to be misled by such advertising, the court may grant an injunction to prevent that advertisement from being published.

Finally, the law of defamation protects the reputation of individuals. This has not often been used in New Zealand for sporting individuals but has recently been used successfully by Kangaroo Rugby League star Andrew Ettingshausen in Australia (David, 1992) to win an action against a Sydney newspaper for publishing a nude photograph of him, claiming such publication was defamatory. Although his initial award of $A350,000 had just been set aside by an appeal court, by the time this book went to press the finding of liability remains a subject for further argument.

Facilities

While the debate in Wellington over a multi-sport stadium continues, it is pertinent to consider the laws which relate to sports facilities and their role. There are legal requirements for buildings, leases, provision of food and beverages, lighting, drainage, and parking, all of which require approval, permits, licences or agreements from different legally constituted local and central authorities.

For example, consents may be required under the Resource Management Act 1991, the Reserves Act 1957, or various local government by-laws. The Food Act 1981 and the Sale of Liquor Act 1989 also have provisions for compliance. Even if Wellington through its Basin Reserve Trust should wish to develop a multi-purpose sports ground at the Basin Reserve, it will have many legal matters to comply with or to seek consent for before the development becomes reality. Some of these processes will involve the right for the public to object or oppose, and the legal procedures, particularly under the Resource Management Act, could be both lengthy and expensive.

Drugs in Sport

New Zealand introduced a policy against the use of performance enhancing drugs in sport in 1989, and this is presently implemented by the Sports Drug Agency. Although not yet established by statute, as is the Australian Agency, the Sports Drug Agency is responsible for the collection of samples for analysis. The Agency presently operates as a committee of the Hillary Commission and relies upon Commission funding to operate. At a cost of more than $300 per test, it is an expensive operation.

The policy in New Zealand means that each sport reliant upon Hillary Commission funding must endorse the policy, and ensure its own constitution properly covers testing and any subsequent disciplinary action. In an age where already huge sums have been spent on the international scene by athletes such as Butch Reynolds, Katrina Krabbe and Martin Vinnicombe in challenging drug tests, sport needs to be extremely careful to properly implement its rules. For example, Martin Vinnicombe, an Australian Olympic cyclist, tested positive for steroids while in Canada. But although he admitted taking drugs and was banned, he challenged the results on technical grounds. His complaint, which was that the wrong forms and thereby the wrong procedures were followed, was eventually upheld by the courts. Vinnicombe succeeded in recovering damages and caused sport to expend vast sums on legal fees. New Zealand hopes that similar problems do not surface here.

Privacy Issues

The promotion and protection of an individual's privacy is also a responsibility for sport with the passing of the Privacy Act 1993. This Act establishes principles on the collection, use and disclosure of personal information, such as names and addresses, by public and private organisations. It also provides principles for the right of individuals to access and correct information those organisations hold. The Act therefore impacts on sport in a number of ways, particularly in publication of lists of members and other information, and must be complied with carefully, notably by the appointment of a privacy officer.

Financial Issues (see also Chapter 11)

Financial accountability is now high on the list of responsibilities for sport. Whether that accountability be to a sponsor, a public body, or the Inland Revenue Department, it is important and often mandatory that the law is adhered to. For example, annual accounts for Incorporated Societies must be lodged with the Registrar, the goods and services taxes must be paid and returns provided for GST registered bodies or persons, and income tax or PAYE paid. Individuals also must be aware of their taxation responsibilities and understand whether payments are income or could be regarded as capital and not liable for taxation. Generally inducement payments or benefit payments can be viewed as capital payments, not income.

Those involved in sport should realise that, just as in other legal areas, the fact that the money has been earned from sport or leisure does not remove it from laws relating to taxation of income. It of course follows that expenses incurred in earning the income may be classified as deductions from that income.

Conclusion

This chapter has touched on several areas of the law which commonly invade the world of sport. Each topic in itself warrants a chapter, indeed some are already the separate subjects of whole books. It is suggested that there will be other issues which inevitably grow from these, and that the law in sport will continue to expand in New Zealand as it has already in other countries. This means that all those involved in sport, whether playing, coaching, administering or managing, will need to look to lawyers for advice and to the law to ensure compliance. However, once again they are warned to seek this advice early, to comply with it carefully, and to seek mediation or arbitration through reputable third parties as a more speedy and less expensive alternative to using the civil court system.

Review Questions

1) What benefits are conferred by an organisation establishing itself as a legal entity?
2) What is the essence of a contract?
3) What is implied by the phrase 'natural justice'?
4) Discuss some of the legal obligations to be considered with regard to providing facilities and staging particular sporting events.

References

David, P.W. (1992), 'Sport and the Law – A New Field for Lawyers', *New Zealand Recent Law Review*, pp. 80-92.

Suggested Reading

Grayson, E. (1988), *Sport and the Law*, London: Butterworths.
Greenberg, M. (1993), *Sports Law Practice*, Virginia, USA: Michie.
Healey, D. (1989), *Sport and the Law*, NSW, Sydney: New South Wales University Press.
Kelly, G.M. (1987), *Sport and the Law – an Australian Perspective*, Sydney: Law Book Company.

Ethics and Sport Management

Jon Doig

In this chapter you will become familiar with the following terms:

ethics	*implementation of codes of ethics*
code of ethics	*compliance*
professions	*enforcement*

Introduction

The increasing inter-relationship between sport and business has raised a number of ethical dilemmas for the developing sport management sector. This chapter discusses some of those issues and possible ways of addressing them.

The extent that sport itself is underpinned by, and operates to strong ethical considerations has long been an area of debate both in New Zealand and overseas. Many, the International Olympic Committee (1986) for example, point to the positive traits of the sporting spirit which binds competitors, whilst others, such as Hodge (1989), question the extent of the supposed character building process in modern sport, and Simson and Jennings (1992) are critical of the dealings of some prominent international sport leaders. Further, some commentators have been critical of the ethical link to violence (Stothart, 1993), or have even renounced sport because of events such as the Olympic Games, described as 'a festival for television, big business, cheating, maleness, white European sports codes and patriotism' (Ross, 1993).

While some have argued that these influences have been part and parcel of sport since its inception, and claim that 'you can't change history' (South, 1993), it is clear that sport administrators are faced with the quandary of managing a product that is idealised by some, but has several obvious negative factors for other sections of the community. It is also clear that sport is increasingly subject to and identified with the same influences as those affecting the wider community, and is full of the same ethical and moral dilemmas (Cordes, 1990; Branvold, 1991).

Sporting organisations and sport people constantly measure and reassess their actions against their own predetermined rules and regulations. These are often based on unwritten ethical standards which may or may not change as the ethics of the communities in which they live alter. For example, the rules of soccer and rugby were written in the nineteenth century but those of soccer have changed little since then, while those of rugby have changed frequently. This has meant either stability with little flexibility to adapt to changing demands, or flexibility with little stability.

The emergence of new sports such as Triathlon have strongly highlighted this situation. Its direct approach to issues such as athlete payments has contrasted with those of its component activities, athletics, swimming and cycling, each of which, with their long established rules and regulations, have struggled to come to grips with the distinction between professional and amateur status. Their protestations of adherence to amateur ideals while becoming more of a business than recreation are not always well received. Seeing some athletes in 'amateur' sports being paid, or their organisations appearing to make large amounts of money from gate fees, sponsorships or television rights, has contributed to the confusion and disillusionment as to the aims of some sports, especially when it is not made clear how the performers or overall participants will benefit.

This confusion is evident for example in the reaction to New Zealand rugby player Richard Loe's High Court case regarding a suspension for foul play on the field, and to the suspension and subsequent banning of Canadian sprinter Ben Johnson for drug taking. Both instances involved strong ethical decisions being taken by sport organisations. It is interesting to note that the second of these would likely have carried no criminal penalty if the drugs had been taken outside the sporting arena, because only drug dealing and being found in possession of drugs, rather than the taking of certain prescribed classes of drugs, is specified as a crime. However, the former act of eye gouging would constitute an assault were if off the playing field, and as such it would be subject to criminal law.

The now infamous (in New Zealand) incident involving underarm bowling in an international cricket match between Australia and New Zealand also provides stark evidence of this public reaction. In this particular case no written rules of the sport were even broken, but an underlying ethical line was deemed to have been crossed when the Australian captain ordered the last ball to be delivered in such a way that the batsman could not score sufficient runs to win the match. In all three cases the rules governing the incidents were reassessed immediately following public debate about the underlying ethics and values applying in each case. It is clear that the behaviour of sport people whose actions in and out of the sporting arena were deemed unacceptable in the wider community, is now being more closely scrutinised (Cordes, 1990). The community's expectations of untainted success however, are as high as ever, and this has placed many sports and sport people under considerable stress in trying to meet unrealistic standards of performance.

Definitions

To prevent statements about ethics being misinterpreted or becoming little more than empty words or clichés, it is important to clarify what is generally meant by these terms before their importance to sport, business and sport management can be fully understood.

Ethics

Ethics have been variously described as:

- What should I do? (Shea, cited in Sands and Smith, 1988).
- A way of life (Zeigler, 1988).
- What is good and right for human beings (Strange and Hopkins, 1992).

Values

Values have been described as something that is good, including governance of law, freedom, equality of opportunity, and the right to privacy (Zeigler, 1988).

Morals

Although the meaning of morals is generally accepted as being the same as for ethics, Strange and Hopkins (1992) noted that use of the term in sport and business is now less used due to its religious connotations. Instead, terms such as 'fair play' are increasingly being used as an alternative.

Codes of Ethics

Codes of Ethics have been described as systematic collections of rules and regulations relating to the values of a given society. When formalised, they often become laws and provide clear statements of expected behaviour of members of an organisation. According to Zeigler (1988) they are more detailed than the short idealistic statements of belief that he termed creeds. The British Institute of Sport Coaches (1989) went further in making a distinction between Codes of Ethics and Codes of Conduct. Codes of Ethics were seen to provide guidelines for expected standards of personal responsibility and competency. Codes of Conduct were more concerned with the implementation of principles embodied in the Codes of Ethics such as public criticism, misconduct, criminal conviction and misrepresentation. But the position is not entirely clear because Pitchforth, Brien and Battye (1993) go so far as to say that in business, mission statements and codes of practices are forms of codes of ethics.

Fair Play Charters

In some sports, Fair Play Charters are also tantamount to a Code of Ethics, because they set out the spirit in which games should be played.

Fair Play or Sportsmanship

Fair Play or Sportsmanship generally means abiding not only by the written rules of an activity, but by the spirit, or the unwritten ethics, understood by the participants. The International Olympic Committee (1986) considers the Olympic Oath to apply both to observing the rules and behaving in a sporting spirit.

Sport's Ethical Base

A focus on the need to promote *fair play* was strongly emphasised when the international rules for the first organised sports such as cricket and soccer were drawn up over one hundred years ago. Prominent among them was 'ungentlemanly conduct', and conventions required batsmen to declare themselves out by 'walking' before an umpire gave the decision. Such principles have continued to be reflected in the rules of newer organisations which have evolved since, such as volleyball and touch. They rely on the individual player's own ethical standards as well as on those enforced by referees and umpires.

The emphasis on ethics at an international level is reflected in the functions of national or government organisations such as the Hillary Commission for Sport, Fitness and Leisure. It was established in 1987 by the New Zealand Government following an inquiry into sport. The report of that Inquiry, *Sport on the Move* (1985), included in its recommendations strong opinions on the state of New Zealand sport and on the increasing prevalence of violent or antisocial behaviour. The result when the Commission was formed was that its statutory responsibilities included:

- promoting the full use of leisure;
- facilitating equal opportunities for participation by all New Zealanders;
- encouraging persons to make the most effective use of their abilities and aptitudes;
- facilitating the physical, mental and social wellbeing of New Zealanders, and enhancing their quality of life;
- promoting attitudes and behaviour that are conducive to good conduct and fair play among all persons involved in or associated with sport and recreation;
- promoting community-based and group recreation, and appropriate indigenous and ethical forms of sport and recreation.

Recreation and Sport Act (1987)

These functions were emphasised in the Act's initial Statement of Intent, and reiterated in the programmes such as *KiwiSport, Drugs in Sport* and *Fair Play* it established soon after its formation, and in its later Corporate Plans. These international and national statements of responsibility, along with the laws of the country, support the constitutions and activities of clubs and individuals, and set the framework of expected behaviour for those administering and playing sport. Increasingly these are also being backed up by published codes and charters, such as the Hillary Commission's *Fair Play Charters* that are produced not only for players but for schools, administrators, coaches, officials, parents, educators, media and sponsors. They are now being adopted and promoted by sports at all levels as an effective way to promote sports benefits while publicly dealing with negative issues.

Business Ethics

With the increasing business and commercial emphasis in the management of sport, a question arises about their respective ethical codes. The primary objective of business – of making a profit for shareholders – is essentially different from that of sport, but the wider business community is rediscovering the importance of having a strong, clearly communicated ethical base. This has become more relevant when analysing the excesses of the late 1980s, subsequent company failure rates, and loss of public confidence following the 1987 stock market crash. As a result, success in management is now increasingly being measured by performance in addressing ethical issues as well as customer service, leadership and profits. Management commentators are promoting, and people are understanding, that an ethical base not only means good business for companies, but it can also mean higher productivity and profits, and a stability of workforce and customers (Strange and Hopkins, 1992, Peterson, 1992). Studies of companies such as Cadbury, Johnson and Johnson, and the Body Shop show that their clearly communicated ethics were a major reason for their successful operation prior to the crash of 1987, during the crash, and afterwards as well (Pitchforth et al., 1993). Others, such as Maloy (1993), have claimed that innovation also stems from having clear values.

While the 'greed is good' mentality, characterised by the character Gordon Gekko in the film *Wall Street*, is no longer universally in vogue, recognition of, and unease with, the growing links between sport and business within the sporting community, has fanned the embers of the ethical debate as far as sports managers are concerned. In particular, issues such as sponsor and television demands on sports and individual athletes are now being raised. The recent practice where a small number of sports are either being paid to allow television coverage or are receiving it at no cost, whilst most others receive little coverage or are having to pay for it, is being openly queried.

Ethics and Sport Management

The adoption of codes of ethics helps to define the standards of practice and the expectations of those who work as, and are served by, professionals (Peterson, 1992). Their ethical base is also important in helping to identify sport management as a distinct and important profession. Already the growth of employment opportunities in the sport sector and the desire for professional respect has manifested itself in codes of ethics for groups such as coaches, physical trainers, and sport scientists. The need for a written code of ethics to confirm the emergence of sports management as a profession was recognised by Zeigler (1989) in his discussion on the establishment of the North American Society for Sport Management. A significant step in the development of sport management as a profession in New Zealand came in 1993, when the New Zealand Recreation Association adopted the following ethical code agreed to by members as a condition of acceptance of membership.

Code of Ethics

It is the duty of all members of the Association to familiarise themselves with the code of ethics and to observe the code not only in the letter but also in spirit.

1. Members shall exercise their professional and technical skill and judgement to the best of their ability

and shall discharge their professional skill and responsibility with integrity.
2. Members shall be loyal to the Association and active in its work.
3. Members shall not conduct themselves in such a manner as to prejudice the professional status or reputation of the Association.
4. Members shall at all times recognise their responsibilities to their employer or client, the public, fellow employees, the Association and its members.
5. Members shall not make comparisons with, or statements about, other members that are not based on verifiable facts.
6. Members shall not disclose any confidential information or matter related to their work or the business of their client, without the express authority of their employer or client.
7. Members shall not entertain or accept any covert reward, or profit, or use (for personal gain) any information obtained in their professional capacity.
8. Members shall in any dealing with their employer or client disclose any financial or other interest they may have which may impair their professional judgement.
9. Members shall not misrepresent their competence nor, without disclosing its limits, undertake work beyond it.
10. Members shall involve themselves in continuing education and training and encourage staff to do likewise.

(NZ Recreation Association 1993)

Writing and Implementing Codes of Ethics

Any code that is to be effective and have other than lip service paid to it, should be drawn up according to the following guidelines.

Successful codes of ethics have been shown to be:

- public
- understandable
- not contradictory
- stable but reviewable
- useable
- specify what regulatory mechanisms are used if there is a breach
- impartial.

(From Pitchforth *et al.*, 1993)

When writing a code of ethics for a sport, club, business or profession, the writer must consider:

- What is it required for?
- What specific issues are to be addressed?
- What ideals is the organisation based on?
- Does it focus on individual responsibility?
- Does it have identified time-frames for implementation?
- Does it have a review mechanism?
- What does it cost to implement?

- What are the legal implications?
- Is it appropriate to the organisation's culture?
- How will it be communicated?
- How much does it commit the organisation to?
- Are there likely to be any conflicts of loyalty between ethics of individuals and the organisation?
- Is everyone, especially the leaders of the organisation, committed to it?
- Is a case study library available so individuals can refer to actual rather than theoretical instances of adherence or breach?
- Is it fair?
- Is it enforceable?

(Adapted from, Peterson, 1992 and Pitchforth *et al.*, 1993)

When implementing a code of ethics its distribution should be followed by a structured training programme to introduce and involve all those affected by it. There must be total commitment from the top of the organisation and it must be understood that although it is being put in place permanently, it must be constantly reviewed to ensure it stays relevant.

Limitations of Codes of Ethics

Commentators such as South (1992) have criticised Fair Play Charters (Codes of Ethics) as being *just words,* which while universally approved, are not universally adhered to. Sands and Smith in their study of ethics of teachers and coaches in 1982 noted that while some individuals believe they are acting ethically, they are in fact acting unethically. Codes also fail either when they are too general or too specific for individuals to relate to, or are not supported by the organisation, or when an individual's ethics conflict with those of the organisation, or if they are seen to apply to ideals only reached by saints!

Compliance with Ethical Codes

Problems may occur with regard to interpretation of codes of ethics within large sports clubs that contain different ethnic and/or age groups (i.e. a generation or cultural gap*).* Problems in sport also arise when officials have differing interpretations of rules when officiating with teams outside of their own club, region or country. Adherence to codes also drops when the benefits from not complying are judged by the individual to outweigh the consequences of being caught. Hodge (1989) noted that morality was often seen as an expensive luxury when the primary goal was winning or when an organisation's ethics force the abdication of an individual's own ethics. McIntosh (1979) found that some professional soccer players would behave unethically to give their team an advantage, as also would senior New Zealand business managers (Strange and Hopkins, 1992).

The importance of role models, peers or leaders of organisations addressing this issue is made by writers including McIntosh (1979), Hodge (1989), South (1992), Simson and Jennings (1992), Maloy (1993), and Ross (1993). Lack of, or inconsistent, action by these people was seen as tacit endorsement or encouragement of unethical behaviour.

Enforcement of Codes of Ethics

To enforce codes of ethics some organisations have established structures which adjudicate cases of alleged ethical breaches. Committees are preferred to remove the possibility of any personal bias from single adjudicators. One of the biggest criticisms of codes is that they are either not enforced (Pitchforth *et al.*, 1993) or ignored in pressure or convenient circumstances (Smith and Sands, 1982, Strange and Hopkins, 1992, and Hodge, 1989). To take one example, the National Strength and Conditioning Association's Code of Ethics (1989) has an enforcement policy which clearly defines its committee's powers in terms of:

- jurisdiction
- grounds for discipline
- types of discipline
- powers and duties
- disciplinary procedures.

It regularly publishes guidelines along with the Codes themselves in a magazine which is sent to all members.

In assessing any alleged unethical practice the following steps should be taken:

- It should first be determined if a breach occurred and its cause.
- The offender should be dealt with appropriately according to the organisation's predefined rules including the right to be heard.
- The Code should then be re-evaluated and if necessary be altered to reflect changing conditions.

Should Ethics be Taught?

The teaching of ethics is not only recognised as being achievable (Kanaby, 1990), but overdue and a necessity. Although an old subject, it has recently been described as a 'new challenge' that needs to be brought out into the open (Pitchforth *et al.*, 1993). However, it has been noted that until recently there have been few courses available in New Zealand or overseas in ethics training for either business or sport managers (Zeigler, 1988; Strange and Hopkins, 1992). Whilst there is a renewed awareness of the need for clear individual and organisational ethics to be reasserted, a recent New Zealand survey of business people found that although 94 per cent thought ethics could be taught, only 27 per cent had attended any courses on the subject, and 85 per cent cited lack of information as a main hindrance (Strange and Hopkins, 1992).

The need for ethics courses to help managers develop sound ethical choices is clear. In all cases, effective teaching of organisational or situational ethics can only be successful if it is building on a solid individual and organisational ethical base which may be formally or informally instilled.

In sport, management issues discussed in these courses should be current and assessed from a variety of roles such as those of the athlete, coach, sponsor, administrator or spectator. These would help in the development of a balanced analysis from a range of ethical positions, including those of the organisation and they could be based on case studies of actual sport issues.

Cavanaugh (cited in Parkhouse, 1991) outlines a clear structure and a flow chart by which ethical decisions in practice can be made (Figure 20:1),

Figure 20:1: Flow chart of key questions relating to ethical issues.

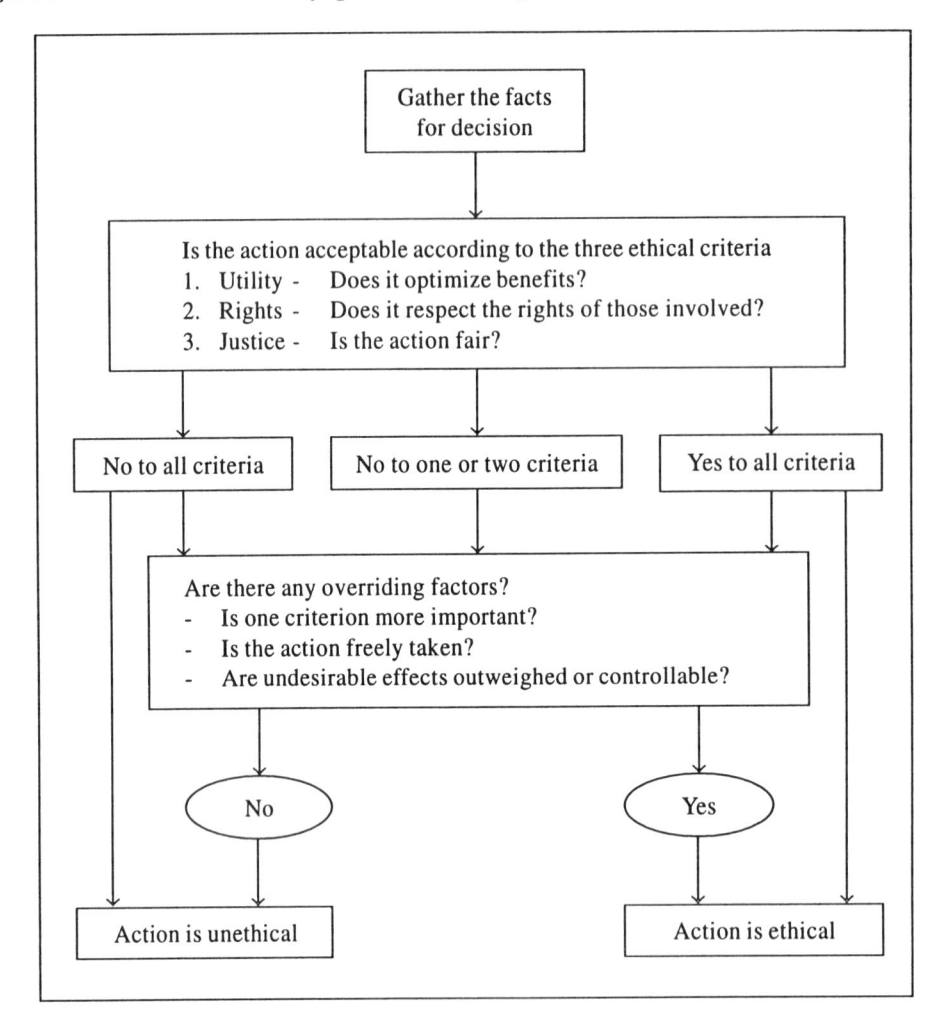

```
                    ┌─────────────────────┐
                    │  Gather the facts   │
                    │    for decision     │
                    └──────────┬──────────┘
                               ▼
        ┌──────────────────────────────────────────────┐
        │ Is the action acceptable according to the    │
        │ three ethical criteria                       │
        │   1. Utility  - Does it optimize benefits?   │
        │   2. Rights   - Does it respect the rights   │
        │                 of those involved?           │
        │   3. Justice  - Is the action fair?          │
        └──────┬──────────────┬───────────────┬────────┘
               ▼              ▼               ▼
      ┌───────────────┐ ┌──────────────┐ ┌────────────────┐
      │ No to all     │ │ No to one or │ │ Yes to all     │
      │ criteria      │ │ two criteria │ │ criteria       │
      └───────┬───────┘ └──────┬───────┘ └────────┬───────┘
              │                ▼                  │
              │   ┌──────────────────────────────────┐
              │   │ Are there any overriding factors?│
              │   │  - Is one criterion more         │
              │   │    important?                    │
              │   │  - Is the action freely taken?   │
              │   │  - Are undesirable effects       │
              │   │    outweighed or controllable?   │
              │   └────────┬─────────────┬───────────┘
              │            ▼             ▼
              │          ( No )        ( Yes )
              ▼            │             │
      ┌───────────────────┐│             │┌──────────────────┐
      │ Action is         ││             ││ Action is        │
      │ unethical         │◀             ▶│ ethical          │
      └───────────────────┘               └──────────────────┘
```

▶ **Common Ethical Issues Raised in Sport**

In day-to-day sport management many of the following issues have been and are being continually addressed:

- use of performance-enhancing drugs
- banning of sports or activities due to likelihood of physical danger to individuals
- banning or amending sports or activities involving animals
- gender equity
- racism

- use of sports as a political or nationalistic tool
- responsibility for field violence
- demands of sponsors on the timing and structure of sports events
- gambling by participants on outcomes of their events
- funding of high-performance versus participatory activities
- equivalent funding of performance by people with disabilities
- amateur and professional status
- the age at which children should be introduced to intensive training or competition
- encouraging athletes to train and compete in their home, country, or province where they can act as role models for their sport or club, versus encouragement to train wherever the best conditions for training and competition are
- altering pitch size or conditions to suit the home team
- treating 'star' players differently financially
- accrediting coaches before appointment to prominent positions.

There is no single right or wrong answer in each case, but the answers may be affected by factors such as health, finance and other resources or constraints. The extent of these influences will also be determined by the strength of the ethical base of each individual affected, and its matching with that of their organisations.

Conclusion

Although all decisions relating to the participation and administration of sport are underpinned by ethical considerations, lack of its expression in a changing sporting and external environment can cause many problems. This chapter examines the ethical base of sport and its links to business, and touches on some key issues facing sport. It also provides guidelines to establishing and implementing a Code of Ethics as a basis for making decisions in sport.

Review Questions

1. What information should a Code of Ethics contain?
2. What are the major considerations to take into account when writing a Code of Ethics?
3. What are the key factors leading to successful implementation of a Code of Ethics?

References

Branvold, S. (1991), 'Ethics', in B. Parkhouse, (ed.), *The Management of Sport: The Foundation and Application*, St Louis, MO: Mosby Year Book, pp.365-381.
British Institute of Sport Coaches (1989), *Code of Ethics and Code of Conduct*, Leeds: British Institute of Sports Coaches.
Cordes, K.A. (1990), 'Ethics in Sport: Writing Seminar', in *Commonwealth and International Conference on Physical Education, Sport, Health and Dance. Recreation and Leisure Conference Proceedings*, Auckland: Recreation Association New Zealand, pp.163-167.
Hillary Commission (1990), *Fair Play Codes*, Wellington, Hillary Commission for Sport, Fitness and Leisure.
Hodge, K.P. (1989), 'Character Building in Sport: Fact or Fiction', *New Zealand Journal of Sports Medicine*, Winter, 17, (2), pp. 23-25.

International Olympic Committee (1986), *Sport Leadership Course*, Lausanne: Olympic Solidarity, pp.43-47.
Journal of Sports Management (1988), January, 2(1), pp.70.
Kanaby, R.F. (1990), 'Ethics – Integrity – Values: What Place do they have in our Programs?', *Scholastic Coach*, November 86, pp.11-12.
Maloy, B.P. (1993), 'Beyond the Balance Sheet', *Athlete Business*, January, pp.29-31.
McIntosh, P. (1979), *'Fair Play: Ethics in Sport and Education'*, London: Heinemann Books.
National Strength and Conditioning Association (1989), 'Code of Ethics', *National Strength and Conditioning Association Journal*, December/January.
New Zealand Recreation Association (1993), *Code of Ethics.*
Parkhouse, B. (1991), 'The Management of Sport: Its Foundation and Applications', St Louis, MO: Mosby Year Book.
Peterson, J.A. (1992), 'Developing a Business Code of Ethics', *Fitness Management*, February, pp.22-23.
Pitchforth, R., Brien, A. and Battye, J. (1993), 'Designing and Implementing a Code of Ethics', Palmerston North, Massey University, unpublished.
Recreation and Sport Act (1987), Wellington: Government Print, pp.7.
Ross, B. (1993), 'Point of View Agenda 21: Cleaning up our Educational Environment', *Journal of Physical Education in New Zealand*, 26 (2) p.2.
Sands, R. and Smith, T. (1988), 'Physical Education. Teachers and Coaches: A Comparison of Ethics', *NZ Journal of Health, Physical Education and Recreation,* 15(2), pp.40-43.
Simson, V. and Jennings, A. (1992), *The Lords of the Rings – Money, Power and Drugs in the Modern Olympics*, London: Simon and Schuster.
South, B.(1993), 'Fair Play Code Just So Much Malarky', *Sunday Star*, 11 April.
Sports Council,(1991), *Coaching Matters: A Review of Coaching and Coach Education in the United Kingdom*, London, Sports Council, pp.26-27.
Sport Development Inquiry Committee (1985), *Sport on the Move: Report of the Sport Development Inquiry*, Wellington: Government Print, pp.136-142.
Stothart, R. (1993), 'The Phillip Smithells Memorial Lecture', *Journal of Physical Education, New Zealand*, 26(2), pp.12-14.
Strange, T. and Hopkins G. (1992), 'Ethics: Can they be Taught?', *Management*, December, pp. 9-54.
Zeigler E.F. (1980), 'Applications of a Scientific Ethics Approach to Sports Decisions', *Quest* 32(1), pp.8-21.
Zeigler, E.F. (1988), 'The Dimensionality of an Ethical Code', in Galasso P.J. (ed.), *Philosophy of Sport and Physical Activity*, Toronto, Canadian Scholars Press, pp.358-369.
Zeigler E.F. (1989), 'Proposed Creed and Code of Professional Ethics for the North American Society for Sport Management', *Journal of Sport Management*, 3, pp.2-4.

Suggested Reading

Hillary Commission (1990), *Fair Play Codes*, Wellington: Hillary Commission.
Hodge, K.P. (1989), *Character Building in Sport: Fact or Fiction, New Zealand Journal of Sports Medicine*: Winter, 17 (2).

McIntosh, P. (1979), *Fair Play: Ethics in Sport and Education*, London: Heineman Books.
Pitchforth, R., Brien, A. and Battye, J. (1993), 'Designing and Implementing a Code of Ethics', Palmerston North, Massey University, unpublished.
Sands, R. and Smith, T. (1988), 'Physical Education. Teachers and Coaches: A Comparison of Ethics', *NZ Journal of Health Physical Education and Recreation*, 15 (2).
Simson, V. and Jennings, A. (1992), *The Lords of the Rings – Money, Power and Drugs in the Modern Olympics*, London: Simon and Schuster.
Sport Development Inquiry Committee (1985), *Sport on the Move: Report of the Sport Development Inquiry*, Wellington: Government Print.

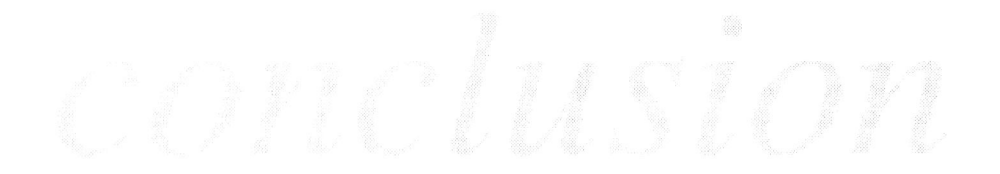

Looking Ahead:

Sport Management Towards 2000

Chris Collins
Linda Trenberth

In this chapter you will become familiar with the following terms:

continuity and change

application of technology and science

commodification of sport

the 'greying' of New Zealand

immigrant receiving

urbanised and northern drift

primacy of the consumer

declining volunteer structures

economic recession and the economically disadvantaged

demographic diversity between ethnic sub-populations

professionalisation of the sport

commercialisation of sport

future trends

regional variations

changing family structures

culture of convenience

targeted assistance programmes

> I am a businessman managing blue chip athletes and blue chip company sponsors. It is not a difficult formula. I ask 'What are you coming to us for? What is your ultimate objective? What are your plans to achieve that?' We have got to see a financial plan, management plans, international preparation, programmes, better use of coaching, sports science and technology and talent identification. We must think smarter.[1]
>
> B. Ineson, New Zealand Sports Foundation, 1993

Introduction

The chapters in this book have shown that sport has become a serious business in New Zealand. As discussed in Chapters 2 and 3, sport has played an important role in various aspects of our culture, including the development of our national identity. New Zealanders, of course, have always taken their sport seriously, but if sport is to survive and exist in a form which is of benefit to the community, sports leaders must become ever more serious about the way in which they manage its development.

There have always been good models of sport management available, but with the changing nature of social and economic conditions, they are now not merely an optional extra; they are a prerequisite for sport organisations who wish to be viable as they move into the 21st century. Sport organisations which are not positioned appropriately to anticipate both the new challenges and the opportunities will be swamped by the onrushing waves of change within society. They can ill afford an attitude of 'business as usual'.

There has been an explosion of interest in the future in recent years, fuelled by a vast array of literature on the topic, with careers and consultancies established on the so-called expertise of predicting the future. Predicting change is exciting, and has considerably more appeal than describing the present, but if the emphasis is merely on change, the analysis can be quite misleading. This is because change usually emerges out of a 'combination of existing social conditions and the efforts of people to shape those conditions to fit their visions of what life should be' (Coakley, 1990: 370). As Coakley goes on to note, some people and groups are more able to influence the future. Others, because of vested interests, commit their efforts to keeping things the same, and resist any change.

Continuity and Change

Kelly (1987) advocates an analysis of the future based on two contrasting principles: first the continuity principle, where the best predictor of the future is past behaviour; and second, the change principle, which is simply that nothing stays the same. An examination of sport in New Zealand over the last century clearly reveals both principles of continuity and change at work. Chapter 2 outlines the way in which sport developed out of the cultural heritages of the early colonialists. The overall pattern, however, was quickly shaped by the frontier nature of the society in which settlers indulged in many forms of spontaneous and rugged physical recreation, with few uniform rules and standards. As New Zealand moved from a frontier to a more settled society, an increasing communal organisation and formalisation of sport became evident. Later when the twentieth century unfolded and New Zealand developed into what might be referred to as a 'modern society', there was a move away from mass activities and structured team and club sports towards the growth of individual sporting pursuits. The new sports involved increasingly sophisticated technology, and created new opportunities for the commercial sector to explore.

Stewart (1990) noted a similar change in Australia in the late 1970s and early 1980s with the development of exercise-to-music and general conditioning movements, of individual high-cost activities such as skiing and sailboarding, of sport and exercise as a vehicle for personal growth, and the encroachment of North American sports and exercise models. He went further to suggest that the changes mirrored both a shift in the cultural mood from the more romantic, naturalistic, and socio-medical influences of the late 1960s and early 1970s, toward the influence of technology and the societal fascination with narcissism. The late 1980s onwards, he suggested, were characterised by a growing professionalisation of the sport and exercise industry, and a growing application of technology and science. Thus although triathlons and multi-sport challenges might seem to hint at the pioneering spirit and a return to romanticism and more naturalistic influences, on closer investigation Stewart (ibid.: 186) suggested otherwise:

> ... triathlons are also highly regulated, and thus are codified, competitive and supported by a combination of sophisticated technology (lightweight, high-performance bicycles) and medical science (a weighty literature covering nutrition and sporting performance, the biomechanical principles of swimming, running and cycle technique, footwear design, injury prevention and treatment, and training regimens).

A prime example of such an event is the Great Lake Challenge held in the central North Island of New Zealand, which requires competitors to ski, run, road cycle, mountain bike, canoe, and water ski. To be competitive, participants undoubtedly need a variety of skills and physical conditioning, but they also need advanced-level skis, boots and poles, good running shoes, a road-racing bike, a racing mountain bike, a racing down-river canoe, and access to a high-powered ski boat with appropriate accessories for long-distance water ski racing. For both competitors and organisers, the costs of equipment and logistics, the organisation required, the time commitment for both the race itself and pre-race training, are all significant. Yet such events are growing in number, and they are attracting a widening spectrum of participants and growing interest from media and commerce.

Growing Commercialisation

The growing commercialisation of sport in New Zealand has been highlighted in several chapters of this text. Sport, it was argued, is now a commodity which has become increasingly absorbed into the capitalist industrial system. This 'commodification' of sport means that it is being 'reconstructed within a framework of production, marketing, consumption and prices' (Stewart, 1990: 186). The major ramifications were discussed in Chapter 2, and are summarised again on the following page. As outlined in Chapter 3, government policy and philosophies have supported this trend towards increased commercialism. In New Zealand the changing nature of the role of the state as provider in sport and recreation has shifted from the egalitarian goals of the 'welfare reformist' phase of the 1970s. Previously the emphasis was on the proactive role of the public sector in meeting the needs of groups who were disadvantaged, so that recreation and sport provision were supported as a 'need' and a 'right', as well as a vehicle for other social welfare and political benefits. But subsequently, and for various reasons, the role of the state changed to one perhaps more accurately described as a 'managerialist critique' that presented a corporatised approach. This, together with the influence of the political New Right with its goal to reduce state spending, led to a more commercial orientation and policy directed towards commercial styles of sports management. As stated in Chapter 3, whereas facilitation might have been the new word of the late 1970s and early 1980s, business values and processes such as strategic planning, profitability and accountability have come to dominate in the 1990s, and they seem now to be setting the course for the opening of the next century.

Ramifications of the Commodification of Sport

- Sport and general fitness have become arenas for commercial sponsorship and investment and for major property development, gambling (both legal and illegal) and highly competitive selling of specialised clothing, equipment, facilities, books and magazines.
- Older cultural or sporting forms have either been replaced or simply swept aside by the cult of the new, the novel, and the fashionable, in the pursuit of 'market share'.
- Values which today sustain team sports such as rugby and cricket, are no longer those which nurtured and sustained their predecessors during the colonial period.
- Leisure has ceased to be a separate sphere of life, free of the pressures which mark other spheres. More areas of our lives have become monetised, so that the freedoms gained from work are increasingly the object of attention of the markets.
- Performance criteria have become as stringent in sport as in 'work', and the division between them has grown increasingly blurred.
- Institutionalised dislocation has arisen between suppliers and consumers of sport. The provision of sport, even of amateur sport, has become increasingly dominated by market considerations.
- Distinction has emerged in sports funding, and increasingly, élite sportsmen and sportswomen are able to attract financial support.
- Commercial considerations have also begun to exert strong influences over the actual structure of sports events.

[Adapted from Chapter 2]

Future Trends

It is important not to speculate too much about the trends and patterns for the future, and to be aware that commentators like to point towards catchy and exciting changes. Naisbitt and Aburdene's (1990) *Megatrends 2000,* for example, could be described as buoyantly optimistic, placing considerable confidence in science and technology, the marketplace, and on the aspirations of the human spirit, with scarcely a look at possible dislocations. It is easy to be wrong. Sine (1991: 6) notes the way in which Khan and Weiner's (1967) optimistic *The Year 2000* missed the dislocations of the seventies and eighties, and how Reich's classic, *The Greening of America*, predicted the continuation of the sixties' counterculture into the 21st century, but missed out the yuppies. Similarly, it is tempting to overstate the role of technology in the development of sport in the coming decades. Commentators such as Johnson (1974) point to the possible future *technosport* scenario for example, and there is no question that technology will continue to have an impact, and will be a key factor in the ongoing commodification of sport. But Kelly (1987: 10) cautions against technological determinism arguing that most technologies are never implemented to their fullest potential, because they must be 'cost-effective, consistent with established skills and values, complementary to other dimensions of life, available, and satisfying in some way'.

The Changing Human Face of New Zealand

One of the significant factors for the future in New Zealand, as in most Western societies, will be the changing composition and location of the population. The 'greying' of New Zealand will be particularly rapid in the first quarter of the century as the baby boomers (those born between the end of the Second World War and the early 1960s) move on from late middle age into retirement (see insert box on *An Aging Society*).

Family make-up is also changing, consistent with decades of increased divorces and later age of marriage. There are increasing numbers of single-parent families, and a declining fertility rate, combined with the trend for women to delay childbirth. The declining family sizes, combined with the aging population factor, presents a future scenario in which a shift is likely to occur in societal resources, away from children and towards the elderly.

An Aging Society

The 'greying of New Zealand' will be a significant factor in the future, although this trend in New Zealand will lag behind that of other developed countries. During the 1990s the 45-59 year age group will increase by 30 per cent. The number of those 60 years and over is projected to grow every decade, especially between 2001 and 2031 (an increase of about 20 per cent each decade – more than double the percentage increases in the 1970s and 1980s). The population aged 80 years plus, is expected to grow even more rapidly, especially in the 1990s, the 2020s and the 2030s. The number in the 80 years plus aged group will treble from 1991 to 2031, and women will outnumber men in this group by three to two.

The changes in the age structure will have major implications for economic and social planning. Significantly the dependency ratio (taken as those aged under 16 and over 64 years) to working age population (16 – 64 years) is expected to increase from 1991 to 2031, reflecting the sharp upturn in the aged dependency ratio, which will almost double during this period. In 1991 there were 5.7 workers for every 65-year old and over adult; by 2031 it is projected that this ratio will have altered to 3.1 workers for every 65-year old and over adult.

Demographic diversity between ethnic sub-populations

There will be differences between ethnic groups in terms of age structures, as rates of natural increase and patterns of international migration will ensure that there are different demographic prospects for particular sub-groups of New Zealand's population. There are three different demographic transitions occurring simultaneously:
- The non-Maori populations are following the European pattern – low fertility and a shift towards an older population structure.
- The Maori population is in a transitional state between developed and developing countries and is characterised by low fertility and a young age structure.
- The Pacific Island Polynesian population is in an earlier stage of transition, characterised by high fertility and a young age structure.

The projections are, therefore, for considerable demographic diversity between ethnic sub-populations within New Zealand.

[Adapted from Department of Statistics' publications, *The Human Face of New Zealand* (1990) and *Demographic Trends, 1992* (1993).]

Some Major Characteristics and Outlook for New Zealand's Population

Growth:

Currently New Zealand's population is growing more rapidly than that of most developed countries, although the rate of growth will drop over the next 60 years. The population is projected to increase from 3.37m in 1991 to 4.02m by 2016.

The Greying of New Zealand

(See Insert Box on An Aging Society)

Immigrant receiving

In an international context, New Zealand is characterised as an immigrant-receiving country. In 1992 Asia (6,835), Hong Kong (2,865) Taiwan (1050) and Japan (993) were the most important sources of permanent long-term gains.

Changing family structures

There has been a drop in the marriage rate, which is indicative of the strong trend towards delayed marriage and increasing numbers of New Zealanders remaining single, as well as the emergence of cohabitation before marriage as an important new lifestyle. For example, in 1971 only 11 per cent of women aged 25-29 had never married; by 1991 it had increased to 39 per cent. For the 30-34 year age group the increase was from 6 per cent to 20 per cent. Similarly a rise in divorce rates since 1985 has increased in most age groups, and the number of marriages dissolving within 5 years, has risen by over two fifths. Also New Zealand women are having fewer children, and having them later in their lives.

Urbanised and northern drift

New Zealand's population is highly urbanised (85 per cent of population in urban centres in 1991), and is unlikely to shift over the next 60 years. This distributional inertia is in contrast to considerable redistribution occurring in other countries, particularly in Europe. But the northern drift will continue: at least 92 per cent of total growth will occur in the North Island, with 80 per cent of total growth occurring in the northern part of North Island (Northland, Auckland, Waikato and Bay of Plenty). By the year 2016, 53 per cent of New Zealanders are expected to be living in these regions, with Auckland becoming more crowded with one in three New Zealanders living there. By contrast, regions such as Gisborne, Taranaki, the West Coast and Southland are likely to have fewer people there than at present.

[Adapted from Department of Statistics publications, *The Human Face of New Zealand* (1990) and *Demographic Trends, 1992* (1993).]

Similarly the ethnic and racial make-up of New Zealand has been undergoing steady change. The past predominance of British and European immigrants has been replaced by that of immigrants from the Pacific Islands and Asia, with the demographic structure of the ethnic sub-group populations being quite different from that of the European (Pakeha) population. Sports policy planners and managers need to recognise these differences and realise the opportunity that these patterns present. In the United States, for example, the tendency 'toward greater opportunity for minority groups in sports is one of the most salient trends at the present, and it will, if futurist predictions are correct, continue in the coming years' (Eitzen and Sage, 1993).

The outlook suggests that New Zealand will remain a predominantly urbanised society. The population will continue to increase slowly, with most of the growth occurring in the north of the North Island (see insert box on population changes). There will be significant regional variability in the sizes of the young population, the labour force, and the elderly population, which is likely to increase. These differences will require effective regionally-focused skills for formulating, implementing and evaluating the management of sport in ways which are sensitive to distinctive population structures and needs. Already National Sports Organisations are having to come to grips with the dominance of the North Island and the major centres because of population pressures, and this dominance will only strengthen.

The demographic characteristics of New Zealand's population will be a critical factor in determining the future direction of sport, but because patterns are even more evident in other developed countries, sport policy-makers and managers can learn from overseas experience. Clearly such demographic trends will result in a reallocation of resources, and 'with a maturing adult population, the stereotypical age-appropriate activities must be dismissed and programs and services focus on the nature of the experience individuals receive' (van der Smissen, 1991). For example, the raised profile of Masters sports tournaments is already evident and is likely to continue, and retirement communities are becoming established with the leisure/sport interests of their members in mind. Major growth is also predicted in participant sports wherever large groups of middle-aged people settle. In the United States, for example, Eitzen and Sage (1993: 381) suggest that by 2036 both participant and spectator sports programs will be more prominent among the 40 plus age group than among younger people.

The power of sport to increase ratings or sell newspapers/magazines is likely to strengthen as the population ages, particularly as technology develops to provide even better and more dramatic coverage. Following sport via the media is a popular activity for many senior citizens. This may in turn have some impact on spectator attendances of other age groups at sporting events, and therefore sport managers will have to manage their assets carefully for the best return, both financially and in terms of profile. As outlined in Chapter 18, obtaining media coverage, most particularly television, is already a problem for many minor sports. In New Zealand only the big four – rugby, league, cricket and netball – are paid rights fees by television to be screened. Other 'minor' sports, such as squash, hockey, golf, basketball and even tennis, are having to find large sums of money to obtain television exposure (South, 1993). The vicious circle of requiring television coverage to attract sponsorship, yet having to use sponsorship funds to pay the high cost of television coverage, is likely to become worse for minor sports. Unless there are policy changes within the media, financially and profile-wise, many sports face an increasingly difficult future.

The Economy: Stuck in the Doldrums?

On the wider political scene, New Zealand has been going through difficult times economically. The economic recession of 1987-1992 has been longer and the most severe since the Great

Depression of the 1930s. As Dalziel (1992: 216) states, our 'welfare system was not built to withstand the pressures of a quarter of a million people unable to find work and five consecutive years of low or negative economic growth'. According to Dalziel, governments since 1984 have adopted a primary focus of attempting to create a stable environment of low inflation, fiscal balance and external balance (i.e. in the balance of payments) within which the private sector can effectively operate, leading to economic recovery in deregulated markets. He argues that other macroeconomic objectives, such as economic growth, full employment, and income distribution, have been placed on the back burner or left to the private sector. Needless to say, the merits or otherwise of such a focus have generated much debate. Certainly government policies during this time have wrought sweeping changes on New Zealand society. There is growing evidence, however, that the impact of government policy in areas such as housing, health-care, education, and Accident Compensation, has fallen disproportionately on low- to middle-income families, women, Maori, Pacific Islanders and the elderly, with couples without children, single people and the wealthy being much less affected (Boston, 1992). Waldegrave and Frater (1991) have demonstrated that while a reduction in disposable income occurs across all households regardless of income ranges and work-force participation status, those who lose the least in dollar terms, are those without children, and those in the middle- to high-income groups (see also Stephens, 1992). Overall, Boston (1992: 15) argues, the evidence suggests that New Zealand is becoming a less egalitarian society with growing disparities between rich and poor, and that such developments are likely to prove socially and politically divisive and exacerbate racial tensions. At one end there are those struggling to find money for rent, food, doctors visits and so forth, while at the other the primary concern is maximising return on investments and minimising investment taxation rates.

Sport management entrepreneurs should do well with the middle- to high-income earners, and the growth of high-profile, high-cost sporting activities such as multi-sport events, windsurfing, skiing, and yachting are testimony to such potential. As van der Smissen (1991: 389) states, generally they service the affluent who expect to have the amenities provided. There is evidence of growth and good prospects for aspects of the commercial sport industry, as discussed in Chapter 5. For the affluent in particular, the 1990s will be a decade of a 'culture of convenience' and an era of the 'primacy of the consumer'(van der Smissen, 1991). People will want time-saving and convenient services, ease of parking, aesthetically pleasing decor and design, hassle-free administrative procedures, well-designed and comfortable changing facilities and so forth. Sport and fitness participation, argues van der Smissen, will become as much an issue of lifestyle, fashion and social status as a matter of time. Individuals will be seeking experiences, rather than just products, and multi-faceted programming and multi-service emphases will be critical for success in what will be an intensely competitive and highly marketed environment. Facility versatility in terms of attracting new markets, and facility flexibility to accommodate special events will be the focus for facility management. While the small size of New Zealand's population will limit the amount of growth that can occur in these areas, there is little doubt that some sport services will prosper during the next decade.

However, given the pressure on the low- to middle-income earners, sport management entrepreneurs will find it difficult to do well financially with activities targeted at these groups. Many clubs at the local level already struggle to obtain players' subscriptions, and there is evidence that unemployment is a factor in non-payment. In 1993 the Wellington Rugby Club, for example, reported a 20 per cent drop in subscription payment due to unemployment, despite the fact that 'subs' have not increased for five years (*Evening Post*, Friday 1 October, 1993). The Club is reportedly now considering 'subs' for the unemployed. In an effort to counter this problem, Avalon Rugby Club, which is located in a high unemployment area, cut its 1993 membership fees to a New Zealand-wide low of $30, with the unemployed permitted to pay a minimum of $5 per week. The result was an increase in subscriptions and a 98 per cent payment rate (*Evening Post*, ibid.). Clearly sport managers, particularly of clubs at local levels, will have to be innovative and enterprising in order to survive, and must take into account the financial profile of the area they draw upon.

In most cases sports clubs at the local level are fighting a tough, and often losing battle. North's Rugby Club in Porirua, for example, bemoans the fact that often 80-90 per cent of its committee's time is spent on finance, leaving it unable to concentrate on other aspects of managing and promoting the game (*Evening Post*, ibid.). Improving technology also makes some sports more expensive to play, and exacerbates the financial difficulties. Hockey is a prime example of a game that used to be relatively inexpensive, when played on grass. Now that it is played more and more on artificial surfaces, as for example in Palmerston North, players are having to pay substantial fees to cover the cost of providing the artificial turf.

While there is plenty of rhetoric about the signs of an economic recovery, there are few signs of the benefits of the promised growth trickling down to the unemployed or the low- to middle-income earners, and this does not augur well for many sport clubs and organisations. These issues pose real problems for sports leaders and our society in general, particularly as user-pays philosophies are intruding into more and more areas of the lives of New Zealanders, with the impact falling on those who can least afford it. Targeted assistance programmes for the economically disadvantaged, such as single women with children, the elderly, the unemployed and low-income earners, will need to be more rigorously explored if sport and recreation opportunity is to be accessible to all New Zealanders. The 'leisure passport' schemes being considered by some local authorities, such as Palmerston North, provide such an example, because they promise to ensure that recreation and sport participation remain affordable to the economically disadvantaged.

Where Have all the People Gone?

In terms of human resources, sport will also continue to be under considerable pressure. Women have traditionally been important contributors as a volunteer 'work-force' underpinning sport structures and supporting the participants themselves, serving on committees, and providing transport and food. But increasing numbers of women are now entering the paid work-force (usually at the lower paid end, and in the service sector) perhaps reflecting the increased divorce rates and the resultant need for women to be self-supporting, the increased numbers of single-parent families, the increased requirements for women's income to support households and the impact of the 'women's movement' (Kelly, 1987). Working women with children have the least discretionary time of any sector of the population, and far less time to contribute as volunteers, or indeed as participants. Further exacerbating this is the increasing tendency for service sector employment to require irregular and 'off-time' work schedules, so that the opportunity for recreation and sport involvement is less confined to weekends, evenings and vacations (Kelly, *ibid*).

Furthermore, the entire baby-boom generation is under considerable pressure, particularly those in the middle-class sector, as they have been enculturated to expect everything that their parents had, and a little bit more besides. As Sine (1991) notes, the problem with this expectation is that economically their parents caught the 'big wave', but in spite of the fact that the quarter-acre section, home ownership and affluent lifestyles are increasingly difficult to attain, there is no evidence that the baby boomers will give up trying to attain it. In a considerably tighter economic environment, they are pursuing the material success that a previous generation enjoyed. Consequently the baby boomers work two jobs, extra hours, and become dual income families in order to meet income requirements in their pursuit of the 'Western dream'. The result is a scarcity of time and for some, as Kelly (1987) states, time eventually becomes more scarce than income. The growing time pressures are not only debilitating in terms of both physical and mental health, and corrosive to relationships, as is hinted at by the increasing incidence of marriage break-ups, but they also seriously erode the volunteer input of an entire generation. Volunteer-based organisations are being stretched to the limit by a diminishing pool of human resources, and this is significantly impacting on sport at the local level. The relatively well off Paraparaumu Athletics club, for example, recently reported that its main problem was not finance, but the sharply dropping numbers of volunteers; getting people to help is now a struggle compared to the past when 'there were always people on the bank only too happy to help' (*Evening Post*, Friday 1 October, 1993).

Similar examples abound, although for most they reflect a combination of financial and human resource difficulties. It is clear that unless there are some fundamental changes in values underpinning this current generation, it will become increasingly difficult for sports clubs and organisations to operate primarily on volunteer management. As Kelly (1987: 28) states, the combination of 'smaller families, increased family dissolution, the separation of work and residential locales, geographical mobility increased by employment shifts, and increased at-home entertainment have all affected the development of skills for activities that require regular interaction with other people'. It will, he argues, become increasingly difficult to gather a group for activities such as team sports, political action or organisational building. Therefore volunteer management programmes such as that of the Hillary Commission, will be critical in strengthening this volunteer resource.

Managing for a Responsible Future

Assuming there are no unforeseen crises, the economy in the 1990s will probably continue to go through its cycles of growth, recession and growth. As discussed in Chapter 4, since expenditure on sport comes from disposable income, sport management is most likely to thrive when the economy is growing at a healthy rate. But New Zealand sport cannot wait for an economic recovery which might or might not be just around the corner. Sport managers must be rigorous and business-like now in the management of their scarce resources. There are often complaints that little benefit is seen at the local level from the subs paid to national offices, or of the funding provided at the national level. Sport managers at the national level must avoid the temptation to establish expensive bureaucracies – with salaries and perks to match – and must administer and plan for the future of sport in a realistic way which is appropriate to membership, financial, and competitiveness profiles. Business management methods must be adopted, but the business executive mind-sets, to do with lifestyles and aspirations, should be kept firmly in check. Furthermore, past glories must be exactly that – past. The future must be planned, with the learned experiences of the past informing the process, but with the current realities directing the future hopes.

Complaints at the local level, however, are not always legitimate. They do not always have the broader picture in mind, and their own management practices are often ad hoc and, occasionally, poorly directed. J.J. Stewart, a former NZRFU Councillor, All Black Coach, and New Zealand Council for Recreation and Sport Councillor, frequently cites the example of local clubs using funds to build Members' Lounges, when they could more effectively employ coaching coordinators or fund their own junior sport development in some other way.

Good and well directed business management practices are required at every level, if a sport is to survive into the 21st century. If New Zealanders wish to be participants, rather than just spectators, they must direct their energies and programmes to strengthen the local level management of sport, and to target assistance towards certain sports or clubs which are drawing on economically disadvantaged groups.

The Golden Dream

The 2000 Sydney Olympic Games pose a great opportunity for New Zealand on a number of fronts, one of which is of course sport. They also, however, pose a threat of misdirected energies. Already a golden glitter is appearing in the eyes of many sport leaders. Yet the debate as to the validity of the trickle-down effect in economics could equally be applied to sport. Certainly most teachers will testify to the impact in the playground when New Zealand performs well in the international arena, and many sports report a surge in interest following international successes, but the actual long-term effect must be carefully evaluated. Even if one were to accept the 'trickle-down effect' theory, questions must still be posed about a sport's ability to capitalise on international success. Can the sport cope with increased demand? Is its grass-roots coaching structure sufficiently strong? Does it have appropriate competition and management structures at the local and national level? Such issues are critical and must be considered alongside resource allocation demands for élite level sport. The grass-roots level must not be neglected. National sport managers and leaders must avoid the temptation to be seduced by the more glamorous élite level competitive hopes.

No high-profile international event will be the panacea for a sport's current difficulties or tough times. It presents opportunities, but its merits as a goal for a sport must be considered in the wider context of the sport's overall objectives and of the most cost-effective and viable way to achieve those objectives. If the goal is merely to win medals, then many sports will be disappointed and their resources will be squandered.

Likewise national sport leaders and politicians need to be clear as to the merit of medals and international success. If the goal is to raise the profile of New Zealand, or to increase tourism, resourcing should come via the appropriate sources. If, however, the overall goals for sport and leisure policy are to encourage New Zealanders to become more active, as well as for some to achieve sporting excellence, then the allocation of resources should appropriately reflect those goals.

Sensitive New Age Sport?

As stated in Chapter 3, the institution of sport tends towards conservatism and its politicisation usually lags behind that of other areas of culture. But sport is not separate from society, and is in fact frequently a showcase, particularly given the increasing degree of media involvement and the creation of 'media sport'. In the 1980s the NZRFU learnt some harsh lessons about the damage to a sport which can be caused by alienating large sections of the community. Sport leaders and managers in the 1990s will not be able to afford to ignore societal concerns about human rights, equality, cultural and various other social issues. Ensuring appropriate opportunities for disadvantaged sections of the population will be important aspects to address in the future, and sport leaders should not be seen to be 'dragging the chain'.

Societal concerns about issues such as safety, violence, and drug, alcohol and sexual abuse are also reaching new heights, and given its high level of visibility, sport will increasingly come under the spotlight on these matters. The initiatives of sports such as the NZRFU in adapting rules to improve player safety and the establishment of procedures to curb violence on the field are commendable, and it has led the rugby world in its efforts to address such issues. The old attitudes of 'what happens on the field should be left on the field' are inappropriate. As van der Smissen (1991: 393) states, the sport manager of the 1990s must know not only how to handle disruptive and undesirable behaviour in sport, 'but also how to foster desirable behaviour through sport and physical activity'.

Finally, as outlined in Chapter 20, sport leaders and managers must adopt appropriate business ethics alongside the business management approaches to administering sport. Mismanagement of sport finances has attracted significant media coverage with incidents such as the Hancock affair. Not only should management of the sport resources, both people and finance, be based on appropriate ethical standards, it should also be seen to be so. Backroom deals, the underhand tactics, and the plays for power were once sadly endemic in sport, and frequently they did little more than service egos rather than act for the good of sport, the participants, or the wider community. Sport managers and leaders must adopt appropriate procedures and practices which treat people with dignity, as they efficiently and effectively utilise the limited resource base to contribute to the enhancement of the experiences and the achievement of excellence by participants.

Conclusion

This book offers a theoretical and an applied approach to strengthen the administrative structures of sport. The outcomes, combined with the thrust of government, business and funding agencies could help New Zealand achieve success at events such as the 2000 Sydney Olympics, as well as foster participation at the lower levels through the diversity of 'recreational' sport clubs. The trend towards a professional sport scene must not be allowed to become a barrier to wider participation, as local clubs – divorced from the national scene – follow their own limited agendas for survival. Sport leaders must acquire and apply managerial skills as tools to enable sport for all to survive and thrive.

To achieve an outcome of success towards 2000, government and business must increase their investment in sport. The funding agencies must also continue to recognise the importance of volunteers whose commitment sustains viable sport structures. They must also provide and secure long-term professional executive assistance, particularly for smaller sports, to ensure that management meets the needs of professional athletes, (i.e. those who sacrifice jobs/careers to achieve national and personal recognition). Fortunately, the strategic plans of the Hillary Commission for Fitness Leisure and Sport are firmly intent upon strengthening the place of sport in schools, and the pay-off should come in the next generation with a more active and participating population at all levels, and in the achievement of sporting excellence by élite level athletes.

Such a major thrust requires sport managers with business skills. In the past people have worked as promoters, organisers and coaching directors, but none without an appropriate managerial approach will be able to enter the competitive commercial market. They must be sensitive to changing trends and be able to make the appropriate moves to benefit their sport. They will have many roles to perform and competencies to acquire.

Certainly the indications are that sport and physical activity will continue to be important features of New Zealand society. Those sport managers who take the trouble to acquire the requisite skills will reap the fruits of their labour, as will the participants, supporters, organisers, sponsors, community and nation.

Review and Discussion Questions

1. When describing the future, why are the principles of continuity and change important? How are these principles evidenced in New Zealand's past?
2. What are some of the consequences of the commodification of sport?
3. What are the implications of an aging society for New Zealand sport managers?
4. Describe examples of demographic diversity between ethnic sub-populations.
5. How has the economic recession impacted on sport?
6. What does van der Smissen mean by the 'culture of convenience' and the 'privacy of the consumer', when describing the future?
7. What are possible reasons for the declining volunteer input into sport organisations?
8. What hopes and dangers do the Sydney 2000 Games present for New Zealand sport?

Note

1 Sunday Times, October 24, p.42, 1993.

References

Boston, J. (1992), 'Redesigning New Zealand's Welfare State', in Boston, J. and Dalziel, P. (eds), *The Decent Society* (pp.1-18), Auckland: Oxford University Press.
Coakley, J. (1990), *Sport in Society: Issues and Controversies*, St Louis: Times Mirror/ Mosby.
Dalziel, P. (1992), 'Policies for a Just Society', in Boston, J. and Dalziel, P. (eds), *The Decent Society* (pp. 208-223), Auckland: Oxford University Press.
Department of Statistics (1990), *The Human Face of New Zealand*, Wellington: Department of Statistics.
Department of Statistics (1993), *Demographic Trends 1992*, Wellington: Department of Statistics.
Eitzen D. and Sage, G. (1993), *Sociology of North American Sport*, U.S.A.: Wm. C. Brown Communications Inc.
Johnson, W.O. (1974), 'From here to 2000', *Sports Illustrated*, 41(26), 73-83. Cited by Coakley (1990).
Kelly, J. (1987), *Recreation Trends, Toward the Year 2000*, Champaign, Ill.: Management

Learning Laboratories, LTD.

Naisbitt, J. and Aburdene, P. (1990), *Megatrends 2000: Ten New Directions for the 1990s*, New York: William Morrow.

Sine, T. (1991), *Wild Hope*, Dallas, USA: Word Publishing.

South, B. (1993), 'Squeezing Out Minor Sports', *Sport Monthly*, 12, March, pp.62-64.

Stephens, B. (1992), 'Budgeting with Benefit Cuts', in Boston, J. and Dalziel, P. (eds), *The Decent Society* (pp. 100-125), Auckland: Oxford University Press.

Stewart, B. (1990), 'Leisure and the Changing Patterns of Sport and Exercise', in Rowe, D. and Lawrence, G. (eds), *Sport and Leisure: Trends in Australian Popular Culture*, Sydney: Harcourt Brace Jovanovich.

van der Smissen, B. (1991), 'Future Directions in Sport Management', in Parkhouse, B. (ed.), *The Management of Sport, Its Foundation and Application* (pp. 381-404), St. Louis, MO: Mosby Year Book Inc.

Waldegrave, C. and Frater, P. (eds) (1991), *The National Government Budgets of the First Year in Office: A Social Assessment*, Wellington: Business and Economic Research Limited.

Suggested Reading

Kelly, J. (1987), *Recreation Trends, Toward the Year 2000*, Champaign, Ill.: Management Learning Laboratories, LTD.

van der Smissen, B. (1991), 'Future Directions in Sport Management', in Parkhouse, B. (ed.), *The Management of Sport, Its Foundation and Application* (pp. 381-404), St. Louis, MO: Mosby Year Book Inc.

about the contributors

▶ **Editors**

Linda Trenberth is a lecturer in the Department of Management Systems in the Business Studies Faculty at Massey University. She has a B.Ed. from Massey University, a Dip. Teaching and an M.A. (Applied) in Recreation and Leisure Studies from Victoria University. Linda lectures in the University's sport management programme. Her research has been in the area of leisure and mental health and she is currently undertaking doctoral research into the relationship between leisure, stress and health. Linda is Director of Publications for the Australian and New Zealand Association for Leisure Studies (ANZALS). She has been a New Zealand representative in gymnastics and her recreational interests now include jogging, dance and spending time with her family.

Chris Collins is the Director of Recreation and Sport at Massey University and is responsible for the recreation and sporting services and facilities at the University. He also lectures in the University's sports programme. Chris has a Dip. Phys. Ed. from the University of Otago, a Dip.Teaching, and an M.A. (Applied) from Victoria University in Recreation Administration and Leisure Studies. His research has been in the area of leisure and religion and he has also published in the area of economics of recreation provision. His recreational interests include rugby coaching (currently coaching the University senior A team), scuba diving, skiing and windsurfing.

▶ **Contributing Authors**

Deborah Battell is a Senior Consultant with KPMG, Wellington. She has a B.A. in English and Education, and an M.B.A. from Victoria University. Deborah has reviewed or managed reviews of twelve sporting or recreational organisations for the Hillary Commission and the Lottery Grants Board. She has also assisted some of these organisations to implement her recommendations, an experience which has given her an excellent understanding of the challenges facing sporting organisations. Deborah specialises in strategic planning, organisational review and evaluation. Her recreational interests include walking, tramping, films and music.

Paul Carrad is a Director of Strategic Media Limited, specialising in media placement, sponsorship and event marketing. Paul attended Otago University (maths, physics, marketing and management) and then moved into event management and marketing through hotel management. Major events include: The Nissan Mobil 500; Executive Producer - Last Great Capping Show; Talent Coordinator - Telethon; AMP New Zealand Open Golf Championship; Los Angeles Olympic Appeal, XIVth Commonwealth Games; Firestone Fairplay Programme; redevelopment of the Royal Port Nicolson Yacht Club; Expo 92 - New Zealand Pavilion; New Zealand International Festival of the Arts; FIS Ski Championships, World Amateur Golf Championships; International Rugby Hall of Fame. Experience in Government Relations, Public Policy and Public Relations came through several years as a Director of Link Consultants Limited, which led to specialising in sponsorship and event marketing through his own company Sport Link Limited. Paul is an active yachtsman, skier, swimmer and glider pilot (instructor's rating). He is also a councillor of the New Zealand Yachting Federation and Chairman of the Wellington Yachting Association.

David Cullwick is a partner in Ernst and Young, Wellington and is responsible nationally for strategic management consulting. He has a Ph.D. in Management and Marketing from North Western University, Illinois, USA. He was Foundation Professor of Marketing at Victoria University of Wellington from 1973 until 1987. Currently he is Chairman, Maranui Water Polo Club, and previously was on the National Council of the New Zealand Association for Disabled Skiers. In December 1992 he presented seminars on Strategic Planning in Sport for the Hillary Commission. He has an active interest with tennis, skiing, sailing and learning golf.

Grant Cushman is Professor and Head of the Department of Parks, Recreation and Tourism at Lincoln University. He has a Dip. Phys. Ed. from the University of Otago and an M.Sc. and Ph.D. in leisure studies from the University of Illinois. Grant teaches leisure theory and recreation policy. His research interests include leisure and public/social policy, leisure participation, urban studies and urban leisure management. He is a member of the Board of Directors of the World Leisure and Recreation Association, a vice-president of that organisation's Research Commission, and is a member of the Research Committee on Leisure, of the International Sociological Association. His recreational interests include jogging, stamp collecting, fishing and reading.

Jon Doig is currently employed as a manager with the Hillary Commission for Sport, Fitness and Leisure. His areas of responsibility include coordinating the Commission's Coaching, Sport Science and Drugs in Sport programmes. Previous initiatives he has worked on include launching and operating the Commission's Fair Play programme from 1990 until 1991. His educational qualifications include a Bachelor's degree in Physical Education and Science from the University of Otago. A former competitive swimmer and swimming instructor, he now fills his leisure time with casual soccer, squash and outdoor activities. Jon attended the World University Games in 1991 and 1993 in a managerial capacity.

Ron Garland is a senior lecturer in marketing in the Business Studies Faculty at Massey University. He has a B.A. (Hons) and M.A. from the University of Otago and spent ten years in the New Zealand market research industry before joining Massey University. Ron is just beginning his doctoral research in the area of customer loyalty and customer satisfaction. His recreational interests include cricket, golf, jogging and trout fishing.

About the Contributors

Bob Gidlow is a Senior Lecturer in the Department of Parks, Recreation and Tourism at Lincoln University. He has an M.A. in sociology from the University of Canterbury at Kent. Bob teaches social and leisure theory. His present research interests are focused on a sociological and social geographical study of dual-career families and leisure (with Harvey Perkins). His recreational interests include listening to classical music, drinking wine, reading, sailing, fly fishing and gardening.

Bevan Grant is the Director of Leisure Studies at the University of Waikato and the current President of the Physical Education Association of New Zealand. He has a B.Ed. and an M.A. from Victoria, Canada and a Ph.D. from the University of Otago. He is an advocate of play being part of lifestyle, and in recent years has been committed to researching, developing and promoting alternative forms of physical activity programmes for school students and 'older' adults. He has traded participating in sport for the opportunity to spend more time in the outdoors and in particular enjoys walking, fly fishing and 'gentle' cycling.

Graeme Hall is a Director of the Performance Improvement Group in Coopers and Lybrand's Management Consulting Division. He has a background in corporate finance management and marketing and has a B.Com. from Canterbury University. Over the last four years Graeme has been involved, primarily in the State sector, in advising on and reviewing management and financial management systems. He has worked closely in an advisory capacity with the Hillary Commission and a number of its clients, and has evaluated grant recipient performance. Graeme brings a specialised and comprehensive yet pragmatic approach to sport management. His recreational interests include running, swimming and tennis, and he is an avid spectator of sport.

Geoff Henley is a public relations consultant of eight years and a director of Network Communications (NZ) Limited. As a consultant he works with clients in the health, welfare and sport sectors. As a member of the Board of the New Zealand Hockey Federation and coach of a Wellington premier men's hockey team, Geoff is active in the sport sector. He has advised a number of sport organisations on public relations strategies and programmes. In 1986 he was the director of the Government's Sports Development Inquiry which produced the report *Sport on the Move* which formed a blueprint for the development of sport through into the 1990s.

Anne Hindson is a lecturer in the Department of Parks, Recreation and Tourism at Lincoln University. She has a B.A. and is currently completing a Masters of Commerce and Management in human resource development from Lincoln University. Anne teaches sport management and recreation management papers. Her research interests focus on sport management, policy issues, and human resource development and management. Her sporting interests include squash, touch rugby, tennis and water-skiing, with involvement at competitive and representative levels.

David Howman is a senior litigation partner with Simpson Grierson Butler White, Barristers and Solicitors, Wellington and Auckland. He is counsel for many national sports bodies and prominent sports people, and is presently the New Zealand Executive member on the Australian and New Zealand Sports Law Association. In addition to being a Board member for New Zealand Tennis, David is the Complaints Review Commissioner for the New Zealand Rugby Union and presently legal advisor to the Hillary Commission. His recreational interests include running, tennis and golf.

Benedikte Jensen is currently a policy analyst with the Department of Social Welfare. Until 1993 she worked as an economist at Business and Economic Research Limited (BERL). While with BERL she led the inter-disciplinary project team which produced *The Business of Sport and Leisure: The Economic and Social Impact of Sport and Leisure in New Zealand.* Benedikte has a B.A. (Hons) in Economic History from Victoria University. Her recreational interests include jogging, skiing and tennis.

Arthur Klapp is Managing Director of Sports Impact Limited, a sports event management company based in Wellington. Arthur has a B.Sc. and a B.Com. from Otago University, a Diploma in Teaching and a Diploma in Recreation and Sport. He is a former professional freestyle skier who first became involved in sports event management by organising the New Zealand Freestyle Skiing Championships in 1976. He has since organised several hundred events and the New Zealand Masters Games. Arthur is an ex primary school teacher, community sports advisor in Blenheim and promotions advisor for the former New Zealand Council for Recreation and Sport. His recreational interests include triathlon, mountain biking and skiing.

Peter McDermott is a Director of James Dale Associates Limited, specialising in sports marketing and leisure consultancy to national sporting organisations, commercial sponsors and sports/leisure bodies generally. He is also a Director of several other commercial organisations. Peter has been Chairman of New Zealand Cricket since 1990, is a past Deputy Chairman of the Waitakere Regional Sports Trust, member of the Auckland Cricket Association Board of Control, member of the International Cricket Council and Chairman of the New Zealand and International Golden Oldies Cricket committees.

Judy McGregor is a senior lecturer in communications in the Department of Human Resource Management, Business Studies Faculty at Massey University. She has a B.A. from Waikato University, an L.L.B. from Victoria University and a post-graduate diploma in legal studies from Auckland University. Judy has twenty years experience as a journalist and is a former editor of the *Sunday News* and of the now defunct *Auckland Star*. She is undertaking doctoral research at Massey University examining the reporting of the 1993 General Election. Judy is one of the founders of the feminist media group F.I.R.S.T. (Female Images and Representation in Sport Taskforce) which is working for better coverage of women's sport by the media. Judy's recreational interests include running, walking, sailing and New Zealand art.

Katie Sadleir is manager of Volunteers and Professional Development at the Hillary Commission for Sport, Fitness and Leisure. She has a Diploma in Parks and Recreation Management from Lincoln University, Canterbury and an M.A. (Applied) in Recreation and Leisure Studies from Victoria University, Wellington. In Katie's first year with the Hillary Commission she was responsible for the development of the Volunteer Involvement Programme, an initiative developed specifically for the training of volunteer administrators. From 1989-1991 Katie was also Chairperson of the New Zealand Synchronised Swimming Authority, a sport in which she has achieved much success, the highlight being the winning of a bronze medal at the 1986 Commonwealth Games in Edinburgh. Katie will attend the 1994 Commonwealth Games, this time as a volunteer manager. Her recreational interests include jogging, cycling and picture framing.

About the Contributors

Bob Stephens is a Senior Lecturer in Economics and Public Policy at Victoria University of Wellington. He has an Honours degree in Economics from the University of Melbourne, Australia, and a Masters degree in Economics from the London School of Economics. Bob has worked in industry in Australia, for the National Board for Prices and Incomes in the United Kingdom and as a research officer for a large British trade union, before coming to New Zealand. He was a member of the 1985 review of Recreation and Government in New Zealand, and has analysed the economic impact of the Paparoa National Park, the role of user charges in recreation, and the use of economic instruments for the greenhouse effect. His other research interests include tax, social, and industrial policies. Bob is involved in cross-country running and tramping.

Bob Stothart is the Associate Principal at Wellington College of Education, former Director for New Zealand Council of Recreation and Sport, Senior Lecturer (Recreation) at Victoria University, and Physical Education Adviser and Senior Education Officer in the Department of Education. He has an M.A. and a Dip. Tchg, and is a Fellow of PENZ. His career interests are in sport, recreation and physical education. He is passionate about New Zealand art, wine, literature and the outdoors and is an active skier, golfer and leisure pursuer.

Mary Stuart is Executive Director of the New Zealand Sports Assembly and former Executive Director of Coaching New Zealand. She has a B.A. in Political Science and an M.A. (Applied) from Victoria University in Recreation Administration. Mary's main sporting interest is Badminton, in which she has served as player, umpire, coach, administrator, and team manager at all levels. She was the Badminton Section Manager at the 1986 Commonwealth Games and is an executive member of the New Zealand Olympic and Commonwealth Games Committee. Mary has also served on the physical educational curriculum review. Her recreational interests include gardening, sport and reading.

Steve Tew is General Manager of the Hillary Commission, and is responsible for the management of all the Hillary Commission programme and funding initiatives. He leads a team of 20 professional management and support staff. Prior to his appointment at the Hillary Commission he was the first Executive Director of the New Zealand Universities Sports Union. As an appointed volunteer, he has led New Zealand teams to the World University Games in Zagreb in 1987 and Buffalo in 1993. He holds a B.A. and an M.A. (Applied) in Recreation Administration from Victoria University. Steve's recreational interests include skiing, gardening, reading and good wine.

Lorraine Vincent is Executive Director of the Manawatu Sports Foundation in Palmerston North. She was New Zealand's youngest and only woman Sports Editor when appointed to that position with Manawatu's *Evening Standard* newspaper in 1985 aged 25. These days she still has an active interest in journalism and she has a passion for tramping. She represented New Zealand as an age-group cricket representative and has competed in cricket, soccer and athletes at provincial level.

index

A
Accident Compensation 38, 49, 65, 78, 108, 258, 260, 283
accidents, injury and safety 260
accountability 15, 21, 53, 55, 90, 103, 104, 116, 121, 130, 131, 145, 151, 156, 157, 158, 159, 161, 165, 171, 260, 263, 279
accounting period 151, 163
accrual concept 151, 163
amalgamation of Local Authorities 102
arbitration 258, 263
auditing 210

B
brand loyalty 206, 207
branding 191, 192, 194, 198
British Empire 35, 49
budget 49, 61, 65, 77, 78, 118, 119, 131, 132, 141, 151, 152, 153, 154, 155, 157, 159, 160, 161, 162, 165, 166, 172, 184, 200, 223, 224, 234, 236, 237
Bursary Physical Education 91, 94
business ethics 268, 287

C
canopy structures 100
CANZ 103, 105, 107
central government 33, 38, 65, 68, 71, 77, 78, 79, 81
central government expenditure 77, 78
character merchandising 256, 261
chart of accounts 151, 162
church 30, 31
class structure 28, 30
Coaching New Zealand 103, 177
codes of conduct 266
codes of ethics 264, 266, 268, 269, 270, 271
colonial development 28

commercial sector 20, 33, 34, 38, 64, 66, 68, 71, 74, 75, 76, 83, 116, 122, 277
commercialisation 15, 27, 35, 37, 39, 113, 120, 121, 261, 278
commodification of sport 36, 243, 244, 276, 279, 288
common unit of measure 151, 152, 153, 155
communications plan 206, 211, 212
community development 35, 37, 50
competency 113, 114, 115, 117, 118, 119, 121, 122, 174, 266
conflict theory 17, 22
constitution 174, 256, 257, 262
consumer preferences 63
contractual matters 258
conversion chain 191, 195, 196, 197, 204
Crimes Act 1961 259
critical theory 17, 22
cultural continuity 27, 28, 277
culture 27, 34, 35, 46, 65, 85, 86, 87, 90, 92, 124, 134, 186, 207, 245, 251, 270, 276, 277, 283, 287, 288, 289

D
defamation 256, 261
definition of sport 17, 19, 59, 60, 72
definition of sport industry 20
depreciation 151, 163, 164
derived demand 62
disciplinary matters 259
discretionary income 34, 61, 63
drugs 34, 36, 249, 257, 262, 265, 267, 272

E
economic description of sport 60
economic significance of sport 72
elastic demand 62

elasticity of demand 59, 62, 63
employment contracts 256, 258
entity concept 151, 153, 162
event marketing 216, 217, 219, 222
event planning 234, 237
exit polling 210
externalities 59

F

Fair Play Charters 266, 267, 270
Fair Trading Act 1986 256, 261
financial accountability 263
financial management 19, 115, 116, 117, 128, 131, 132, 135, 152, 153, 154, 155, 157, 158, 159, 160, 162, 164, 165, 166
focus groups 210, 212
franchising 191
frontier society 27, 29
functionalism 22
funding strategies 108
future trends 276, 279

G

gender differences 32
gender equity 243, 248, 272
girls and physical education 87-88
goods and services tax (GST) 73, 151, 164, 263
government involvement 33, 35, 44, 47, 49-53, 56, 65
grass-roots structures 100
gross domestic product (GDP) 18, 71, 73, 74, 76, 77, 79, 80, 81, 82, 83, 84
gross output 71, 73, 74, 75, 80

H

Health and Safety in Employment Act 1992 256, 260
hedonic pricing 67
hegemony 43, 44
hegemonic masculinity 250
hierarchy of authority 43, 54, 55, 56
Hillary Commission for Recreation and Sport 38, 43, 51, 53, 101, 169, 179
Hillary Commission for Sport, Fitness and Leisure 13, 16, 51, 102, 122, 182, 267, 273
Holidays Act 1981 258

I

income effect 61
incorporation 153, 256, 257
inelastic demand 62
institutional nature of sport 46, 287

J

job descriptions 129, 133, 167, 169, 170, 171, 172, 173, 232

K

key capabilities 136, 139, 140, 143, 145, 150
KiwiSport 51, 91, 95, 104, 267
KiwiSport Leadership Award 91, 95

L

Labour Government 33, 38, 48, 49, 50, 51, 52, 53
leadership styles 182
ledger 151, 162
legal entity 256, 257, 263
legal responsibilities 257
leveraging 216, 217
life-style marketing 191
local authorities 35, 60, 64, 65, 79, 102, 103, 104, 105, 177, 187, 284
local government 32, 33, 35, 38, 68, 71, 73, 77, 79, 81, 102, 103, 105, 262
Local Government and Technical Services Unit 102
local government expenditure 79

M

management versus administration 17, 20
managerialist critique 43, 52
managing change 182, 189
Maori 28, 29, 30, 32, 33, 35, 46, 48, 51, 96, 280, 281, 283
marginal price 63
market demand 62
market failure 53, 59, 62, 65
market plan 191, 192, 196, 204
market prices 62, 67
market research 103, 191, 195, 199, 201, 202, 204
mass media 37, 243, 251
matching concept 151, 162, 163
media plan 229, 241, 242, 254
Minimum Wage Act 1983 258
Ministry of Recreation and Sport 35, 38, 43, 44, 50

modern society 17, 27, 34, 35, 56
morals 266

N

National Government 50, 51, 53, 185, 289
National Party 34, 44, 49, 50, 51

nationalistic values 43, 45
nationhood 32, 35
New Right 43, 52, 53, 278
New Zealand Council for Recreation and Sport 43, 50, 89, 286
New Zealand Qualifications Authority (NZQA) 85, 96
New Zealand Secondary Schools Sports Council 91, 95
New Zealand Sports Assembly 50, 52, 105, 108
non-profit sector 20, 64, 66, 71, 72, 80, 83

O

objectives 20, 21, 54, 64, 65, 66, 86, 128, 216, 218, 219, 220, 221, 224, 225, 227, 257, 283, 286
opportunity cost 68, 164
organisation effectiveness 186
organisational structures 21, 230
outputs-based accounting 124, 132

P

performance measures 128, 129, 130, 133, 139, 151, 160, 161, 165, 191, 198, 201
physical education 19, 85, 86, 88, 89, 90, 91, 92, 93, 94, 95, 96, 97, 115
physical education syllabus 86, 89
Physical Welfare and Recreation Act 27, 33, 39, 43, 50
Picot reforms 90
principles of natural justice 259
Privacy Act 1993 239, 262
privacy issues 262
product sector exclusivity 216, 217, 223, 227
Profit and Loss Account 153
public sector 20, 27, 33, 34, 35, 38, 50, 53, 64, 68, 71, 72, 77, 79, 83, 128, 157, 261, 278

R

Recreation and Sport Act 1987 27, 35, 38, 39, 43, 50, 51, 267
recruiting volunteers 173
Regional Network Sports Trust 105
Regional Sports Trusts (RSTs) 99, 101, 103, 104, 105, 109, 177, 187
relative prices 62
replacement ratio 61
resource allocation 151, 155, 165, 286
Resource Management Act 1991 262
restraint of trade 256, 259
Rothmans Foundation 88
rugby union 32, 38, 60, 196, 207, 238, 250, 257, 259

S

settled society 27, 30, 277
sport education 77, 79, 85, 91, 92, 93, 94, 105
Sport Fitness and Leisure Act 1992 43, 51
Sport, Fitness, Recreation Industry Training Organisation (SFRITO) 85, 96
Sport on the Move 19, 51, 89, 102, 185, 267
sport service organisations 105, 178
sport-related tourism 18, 71, 72, 82, 83, 84
Sportfit 85, 91, 94, 95
Sportfit/Regional Partnership 91, 95
Sportfit/School Partnership 91, 95
sports-media complex 27, 37, 38
sport management defined 22
sportsmanship 29, 87, 105, 267
statement of cash flows 151, 153, 154, 158
statement of financial position 151, 153, 154, 158
statement of income and expenditure 151, 153
stewardship 151, 157
strategic plan 99, 104, 108, 109, 110, 121, 126, 129, 130, 133, 134, 136, 137, 139, 140, 141, 148, 149, 150, 151, 154, 160, 187
strategy development 140, 141
strategy implementation 140
structured competition in school sport 93
substitution effect 61
supply and demand 60, 62
symbolic annihilation 243, 250

T

tertiary education 96
Thomas Report 86
Tomorrow's Schools 90
traditional pluralism 43, 52
triathlon world championships 231, 232, 234

V

value added 71, 73, 74, 75, 79, 80, 82, 83
valuing benefits from sport 67
violence 143, 182, 206, 257, 264, 273, 287
visibility and profile 206, 213
voluntary sector 18, 33, 34
volunteer imvolvement programme (VIP) 99, 103, 177

W

welfare reformism 43, 52
work-leisure choices 59, 60

W.C.S LIBRARY

INDUSTRIAL RAILWAYS in COLOUR
THE NORTH EAST
A Railway Bylines Special

Copyright IRWELL PRESS Ltd.,
ISBN 1-903266-72-6
ISBN 978-1-903266-72-4
First published
in 2006 by Irwell Press Ltd.,
59A, High Street, Clophill,
Bedfordshire MK45 4BE
Printed by Alden Group Ltd., Oxford

This portrait of industrial railways in North East England is very much a personal view of the scene during the first half of 1968 and is certainly not comprehensive. For example, one of the places I did not visit was the well known and extensive National Coal Board system at Ashington, probably because the engines were relatively modern and the photographic possibilities not particularly outstanding. At the beginning of the year over sixty NCB and private industrial sites in Northumberland and Durham had steam engines, although in some cases they were stored out of use. Almost a third of these locations are featured here. Overall, the North East's industrial railways presented a wonderful array of machines in very varied settings. Engines ranged in age from the 1863 Lewin 0-4-0ST at Seaham Harbour to a 1957 Robert Stephenson & Hawthorn 0-6-0ST at Burradon. They also came in various sizes, from a diminutive vertical-boiler Head Wrightson 0-4-0 at Stockton to the magnificent 0-6-2T locos at Philadelphia. There were also unusual specimens, such as the 'long-boiler' at Derwenthaugh, the well-tank at Wallsend Slipway and crane tanks at Doxford's shipyard in Sunderland. In marked contrast to BR's then corporate blue and grey livery, the engines were variously adorned in green, red, blue, black and yellow.

My interest in this long-vanished aspect of the life and character of so many parts of Northumberland and Durham started towards the end of a geography degree course at Durham University from 1965 to 1968. Between lectures, tutorials, essays and the like, together with plenty of socialising with fellow students from Van Mildert and other colleges, it was very enjoyable to explore the North East. Trips by train and bus included investigating the residue of BR steam in the area. Fond memories of K1s and Q6s at Tyne Dock, Ivatt moguls at Blyth and WDs and J27s at Sunderland will last forever. With this scene about to vanish for good, I came across a booklet entitled 'Tyneside Steam 1967' and purchased the subsequent edition which appeared early in 1968. Together, they opened up a whole new world of industrial locos. Some illustrations of my ensuing adventures are reproduced here. One of my intentions at the time was to portray the engines in their natural environment wherever possible. Hopefully, the varied settings including colliery yards, back lanes, shipyard machinery, riverside vistas and rural valleys will add to the enjoyment. I am indebted to Mick Hubbard for scanning my slides and the hospitality of Phil, Steve and Daphne was essential while I was writing this book. Matt deserves special thanks for rescuing my work when the computer blew up!
Paul Anderson, Leicester.

Right. In one of the many obscure corners of Doxford's shipyard at Sunderland on Wednesday 1 May 1968, 0-4-0CT ROKER, built by Robert Stephenson & Hawthorn in 1940, works number 7006, moves off with a plate wagon as another crane tank waits for a clear road to take up its next duty.

INDUSTRIAL RAILWAYS in COLOUR - NORTH EAST

1 Philadelphia

The NCB system based at Philadelphia, between Houghton-le-Spring and Washington in County Durham, was the gem of the North East in terms of industrial steam during 1968. There were two sheds, one active, the other decidedly derelict and housing withdrawn locos. Nearby was the area Central Workshops, usually overhauling up to four steam engines. This was the hub of the erstwhile Lambton, Hetton & Joicey network, which once covered a large part of mid-Durham. Philadelphia had an impressive pedigree, the line through the village having originated as the Newbottle Waggonway of 1815 which carried coal down to staithes on the River Wear. This operation continued for a century and a half, NCB locos working to Sunderland over BR metals until the mid-1960s. In 1968, the big engines at Philadelphia were a legacy of such duties.

Above. Robert Stephenson 0-6-2T No.42 awaits a new crew at Philadelphia coaling stage on Thursday 13 June 1968. Its bunker has just been replenished from one of the elderly timber-bodied wagons bearing the legend 'NCB LAMBTON'.

A Railway Bylines Special

INDUSTRIAL RAILWAYS in COLOUR - NORTH EAST

During 1968, with BR steam-hauled mineral traffic just a memory in County Durham, it was still possible to see big engines working hard as they pulled long trains through Philadelphia. Furthermore, this NCB operation featured double track and signalling characteristic of main lines. On the overcast morning of Monday 27 May 1968, Robert Stephenson 0-6-2T No.42 climbs the last few yards of the ascent to Philadelphia summit with a loaded coal train from Herrington Colliery to the BR exchange sidings at Penshaw. It was built in 1920, works number 3801. Note the limited dimensions of the cab, a characteristic feature of Lambton engines which worked over the NER/LNER/BR line to the staithes at Sunderland where there was a tunnel with very restricted clearances. Philadelphia loco sheds and workshops are beyond the crossing in the background.

A Railway Bylines Special

INDUSTRIAL RAILWAYS in COLOUR - NORTH EAST

Robert Stephenson No.42 resting at Philadelphia around 1pm on Thursday 13 June 1968, prior to its afternoon duties. Typically, there was still plenty of activity while it snoozed. On this occasion, Vulcan Austerity 0-6-0ST No.58, built in 1945 to works number 5299, blasts past with sixteen loaded wagons from Herrington Colliery to Penshaw. This engine featured a rounded cab roof, a legacy of its erstwhile duties at Sunderland. Of the dozen or so 0-4-0ST and 0-6-0ST locos based here at the time, most had this trimmed profile. No.42 was one of three Robert Stephenson 0-6-2Ts at Philadelphia in 1968. No.5, of 1909 vintage, was being overhauled while No.10, built the same year, languished in the derelict shed.

A Railway Bylines Special

INDUSTRIAL RAILWAYS in COLOUR - NORTH EAST

The Lambton Engine Works at Philadelphia had four locos under repair on Thursday 13 June 1968. Prominent in the foreground is Robert Stephenson 0-6-2T No.5, built at Darlington in 1909, works number 3377. It awaits springs and a repaint. An Austerity is receiving attention at the far end of the building and 1904 Kitson 0-6-2T No.29 was also present, having been in the shops for some time.

A Railway Bylines Special

INDUSTRIAL RAILWAYS in COLOUR - NORTH EAST

Two of Philadelphia's smaller engines, generally used for shunting work, rest outside the loco shed during the lunch break on Thursday 13 June 1968. On the left is No. 63, a Robert Stephenson & Hawthorn outside-cylinder 0-6-0ST dating from 1949, works number 7600. It has a conventional cab. To the right is No. 45, an inside-cylinder 0-6-0ST built by Hawthorn Leslie in 1912 to works number 2932. This one has a cab roof with the distinctive round profile necessary for working through the tunnel to Sunderland staithes.

Green-liveried 1907 Kitson 0-6-2T No.31, the Leeds manufacturer's number 4533, had been working earlier in the year, but languished in store on Thursday 20 June 1968. Note the attractive angled cab, reminiscent of far more modern diesels. There were another two big Kitson side tanks at Philadelphia at the time, sister loco No.30 also dating from 1907 and No.29 of 1904 vintage. The former was stored while the latter had spent some time in Lambton Engine Works. Other historic locos reposing beneath the ancient timbers of the former running shed were No.52, an 1899 Nielson Reid 0-6-2T from the Taff Vale Railway and No.27, the much-rebuilt Robert Stephenson 0-6-0T which was ex-North Eastern Railway and originally entered service in 1846.

INDUSTRIAL RAILWAYS in COLOUR - NORTH EAST

A final view of Robert Stephenson 0-6-2T No.42 amid smoke, shafts of sunshine and seemingly an apparition on Thursday 13 June 1968. Light catches water from the hose as it is lowered after washing down coal in the bunker during preparations to get this hard working engine ready for its afternoon shift.

Yet another gem at Philadelphia was the carcass of an 1837 Hackworth 0-6-0 standing proudly on a plinth near the workshops. For many years it had been used as a snowplough, but had to be coated with thick black paint to prevent further decay of its rusty ironwork prior to preservation. The plaque tells its story.

2 Ravensworth

In complete contrast to Philadelphia, the NCB operation at Ravensworth Park on the eastern flank of the Team Valley three miles south of Gateshead was a very modest affair involving just one engine. There was definitely a personal touch here. The crew of the Peckett saddle tank kept their charge in lovely condition, its green paint and brasswork gleaming in bright sunshine. There was plenty of time for this 'tender loving care' between trips to a small pit on the western side of the valley. Furthermore, the crew were very friendly and revelled in entertaining enthusiasts. To be fair, Philadelphia men were accommodating as well, but they had less time for personal attention, let alone cleaning engines! East of Ravensworth Park, a rope-worked incline led to Ravensworth Ann Colliery.

Left. Driver Jim McIvor oils No.66 CHARLES NELSON at Ravensworth Park on Friday 2 February 1968, having given the already sparkling paintwork yet another polish.

Following the cleaning session at Ravensworth Park shed on Friday 2 February 1968, CHARLES NELSON had taken on coal and water before moving up to the office building where the motion was oiled. The Peckett outside-cylinder 0-4-0ST was built at Bristol in 1928, works number 1748. In this view, the engine is shunting empties prior to dropping them off at the small Ravensworth Park pit, three quarters of a mile north west of Lamesley. Note the assorted wagons, two of them lettered NCB BOWES. The Team Valley and Low Fell on the outskirts of Gateshead form the backdrop.

INDUSTRIAL RAILWAYS in COLOUR - NORTH EAST

During the cold afternoon of Friday 2 February 1968, No.66 had deposited its empty wagons at the little Ravensworth Park mine and duly returned with a full load of coal. The Peckett saddle tank looks splendid as it prepares to push its train to the bottom of the incline up to Ravensworth Ann. With the setting sun casting long shadows, the far side of the Team Valley is getting darker and County Durham is in for a bitter night.

12 A Railway Bylines Special

INDUSTRIAL RAILWAYS in COLOUR - NORTH EAST

The dying rays of sunshine on Friday 2 February 1968 pay tribute to the gleaming paintwork of CHARLES NELSON as it propels another rake of empty wagons bound for Ravensworth Park across the indifferent concrete viaduct at the southern end of the Team Valley Trading Estate. A venerable steam engine crossing a dull modern bridge was incongruous enough, but there were other poignant contrasts in the immediate vicinity. The Trading Estate was created to counter the decline of traditional industries on Tyneside. It was built across the course of the Team Wagonway, which ran from Lamesley to staithes at Dunston and was one of the enterprises which helped develop commerce in the area a couple of centuries ago.

A Railway Bylines Special   13

Once one of many in the North East, the rope-worked incline between Ravensworth Park and Ravensworth Ann was a rare feature on Tyneside by the time this view was taken on the cold afternoon of Wednesday 31 January 1968. A cloud-laden sky seeping a hint of weak sunshine provides the atmosphere as a load of coal is dragged out of the Team Valley. This location is not far from Ravensworth Ann colliery and less than quarter mile from the busy A1 Great North Road.

Ravensworth Ann mine was adjacent to the A1, about a mile south of Low Fell and near the delightfully named settlement of Galloping Green. The steam engine here was No.67 PELAW, a 1947 outside-cylinder Peckett 0-4-0ST, works number 2093. It operated between the top of the incline from Ravensworth Park and the bottom of an incline to Wrenkenton colliery, which was 350ft above the Team Valley. Seen here on Wednesday 31 January 1968, PELAW is shunting Ravensworth Ann a couple of weeks before the pit closed. Fortunately, the engine found other employment and was at Ravensworth Park the following May.

A Railway Bylines Special

3 Doxford

Shipbuilding was still a significant industry in Sunderland during 1968 and Doxford's yard was rather special as far as industrial engines were concerned. Situated on the south bank of the Wear at Pallion, just upstream from the massive Queen Alexandra bridge, this site was regularly shunted by four neat little crane tanks dating from World War 2. The setting was spectacular for photography and the company welcomed enthusiasts, providing written permission was obtained. ROKER, HENDON, SOUTHWICK and MILLFIELD scurried about, picking up, transporting and depositing steel plates, girders and other bits and pieces, with a backdrop of huge framework where ships were taking shape. There was also a charming sight each afternoon when the engines were 'put to bed' in their shed, almost a scene out of 'Thomas the Tank Engine' books!

Above. SOUTHWICK, one of Doxford's four crane tanks, works in its natural setting on Monday 17 June 1968 with a hull taking shape in the background and venerable machinery flanking it.

INDUSTRIAL RAILWAYS in COLOUR - NORTH EAST

On Monday 17 June 1968, HENDON unloads steel sections from a BR bogie bolster wagon which had been brought down to the yard via exchange sidings on a stub of the erstwhile Durham - Sunderland line. This Robert Stephenson & Hawthorn crane tank, works number 7007, was delivered in 1940. Dominating the scene is the North Eastern Railway/Sunderland Corporation Queen Alexandra Bridge, a huge structure with little aesthetic merit, yet seemingly revelling in its own bulk. The centre span weighed a massive 2,600 tons, the heaviest in Britain at the time. It was a very costly white elephant for the railway, the mineral line on the top deck being in use for merely twelve years, from 1909 to 1921.

A Railway Bylines Special 17

INDUSTRIAL RAILWAYS in COLOUR - NORTH EAST

SOUTHWICK, built by Robert Stephenson & Hawthorn in 1942, works number 7069, is silhouetted against the gantry of an empty slipway as it builds up steam ready to take plates from the pressing shed to a prefabrication shop on Wednesday 1 May 1968. The colossal centre span of Queen Alexandra Bridge closes the view.

The crane tanks at Doxford's yard may have been diminutive, but they were totally suited to the job and the crane itself was an impressive piece of equipment, having its own cylinders which performed the turning and lifting functions. SOUTHWICK loads pressed steel sheets on to a bogie wagon during the morning of Wednesday 1 May 1968.

INDUSTRIAL RAILWAYS in COLOUR - NORTH EAST

Its crane at rest on the specially designed chimney cap, and little steam in evidence, SOUTHWICK trundles off towards the plating shop on Wednesday 1 May 1968. Note the huge buffers, surely some of the largest on any engine anywhere in the country. In the background, one of Doxford's order for freighters from a Liverpool firm takes shape.

INDUSTRIAL RAILWAYS in COLOUR - NORTH EAST

SOUTHWICK, having deposited the bucket it is seen transporting in an earlier view, returns down the yard and treats the large shed to a generous helping of smoke. The date is Monday 17 June 1968. More ancient machinery adds to the scene and Queen Alexandra bridge forms an almost inevitable backdrop. The only Doxford crane tank not illustrated so far iS MILLFIELD, built by Robert Stephenson & Hawthorn in 1942, works number 7070.

A Railway Bylines Special

INDUSTRIAL RAILWAYS in COLOUR - NORTH EAST

The Doxford yard also had a Peckett 0-4-0ST GENERAL, built in Bristol during 1944 to works number 2049. The engine had been purchased from Tilbury Docks a few years earlier and transferred wagons up and down the steep incline affording access to exchange sidings with BR. It was kept in sparkling condition, not really a luxury afforded to the hard-working crane tanks. Once again, Queen Alexandra Bridge forms a dramatic backdrop on Monday 17 June 1968. Note the driver's headgear, a trilby hat of all things! The bits of wood in front of the smokebox are probably kindling sticks for starting the fire on Tuesday morning.

A Railway Bylines Special

INDUSTRIAL RAILWAYS in COLOUR - NORTH EAST

Bedtime for HENDON, MILLFIELD, SOUTHWICK, ROKER and GENERAL on Monday 17 June 1968. Little more to be said. This was a superb location to see industrial steam engines at work in a spectacular setting. Doxford's yard closed early in 1971 but fortunately four crane tanks went for preservation at Bressingham, Dinting and the North Yorkshire Moors Railway.

A Railway Bylines Special   23

4 Wallsend

Continuing the maritime theme, but in this instance a yard where ships were repaired rather than built, Wallsend Slipway & Engineering Co Ltd was located on the north bank of the Tyne four miles east of Newcastle. The firm had two vintage engines, both oil-fired. One of them was a conventional Peckett 0-4-0ST which was in daily use. The other was an unusual Borrows 0-4-0 well tank which had been demoted to a standby engine. These locos worked against a splendid backdrop of the Tyne and its myriad industries. One of their duties was to tow ships into the dry dock by means of a steel hawser. On thankfully rare occasions an errant vessel would drift sideways, thereby encouraging the engine to join it! Needless to say, the crew rapidly left the footplate, although no loco ever fell into the water.

Left. Wallsend's 1914 outside-cylinder Peckett 0-4-0ST No.2 LION, works number 1351, is seen here on Wednesday 6 March 1968 with Jarrow forming the skyline on the far bank of the Tyne.

INDUSTRIAL RAILWAYS in COLOUR - NORTH EAST

The gigantic crane at Wallsend Slipway dominates this view of the firm's distinctive 0-4-0WT on Wednesday 6 March 1968. No.3 was built by E Borrows & Sons of St Helens in 1898, works number 37, the first of its type produced by the firm. It was kept in reserve and stored in the open, a situation which had sullied the coat of light green paint recently applied by local enthusiasts. A somewhat ugly oil tank on the roof gave the otherwise well-proportioned loco a somewhat top heavy appearance. Unlike LION, which had a substantial panel to provide comfort for the driver when a cutting easterly wind whipped down the river, No.3 had to make do with loose sheeting for the cab door. On retirement, the loco went to the North Yorkshire Moors Railway.

A Railway Bylines Special

5 Seaham Harbour

Completing this trio of industrial loco sites associated with shipping is Seaham Harbour, on the Durham coast six miles south of Sunderland. The town was long associated with the transfer of coal from inland mines to coastal vessels. Two lengthy waggonways tapping the coalfield east of Durham City originally served the harbour, namely the Rainton & Seaham of 1828 and the South Hetton Railway of 1835. As mineral lines, both still performed their original function over a century and a quarter later. Seaham Harbour Dock Company employed half a dozen saddle tanks during the mid-1960s, but by 1968 they had all been replaced by diesels. However, there was a miraculous steam survivor in the form of a diminutive 0-4-0ST built over a hundred years earlier. Other wonders at Seaham included steam paddle tugs and ancient chaldron wagons.

Above. The South Hetton Railway approach to Seaham Harbour at Parkside, about three quarters of a mile from the docks, on Friday 14 June 1968. Note the shared centre rail in the foreground of this self-acting incline.

One of the gems of the North East industrial steam scene four decades ago was Seaham Harbour's No.18, the outside-cylinder 0-4-0ST built by Stephen Lewin's Dorset Foundry at Poole way back in 1863. There was no known works number. Seen here on Thursday 20 June 1968, it had only worked for one day so far that year. This loco was still around by virtue of its lack of stature, an essential asset to negotiate the low level lines when repair work was required on the harbour walls in summer. The author's companion on the footstep, about 6ft tall, provides a useful scale. In 1975 the engine went to Beamish Museum.

INDUSTRIAL RAILWAYS in COLOUR - NORTH EAST

This view shows Seaham's tiny tank loco in its natural habitat on Thursday 20 June 1968. Two varieties of relatively modern metal-bodied mineral wagons are visible in the distance, while on the left is a decidedly modern diesel. A couple of years earlier, the harbour and its associated marshalling yard had been shunted by a stud of ex-Dorman Long saddle tanks, but these were ousted by a batch of five new 0-6-0 diesel hydraulics purchased from English Electric's Vulcan works at Newton-le-Willows in 1967. The 0-4-0 diesel in this scene is a Rolls Royce machine from the former Sentinel factory at Shrewsbury.

As old as the Lewin saddle tank, and just as interesting, were the few surviving chaldron wagons at Seaham Harbour. Incredibly, these primitive 2½ ton wooden-bodied veterans were still used on colliery work a few years before this photograph was taken on Thursday 20 June 1968. At the time, they were employed on occasional internal duties. Chaldron wagons featured in several prints depicting horse-haulage and early steam engines on Tyneside, but their genuine deployment during the latter part of the 20th century was truly remarkable. These particular examples dated from the 1860s when there were still wagonways which had not been converted to modern mineral lines.

6 Derwenthaugh

The River Derwent drains the Durham fells above Consett and joins the Tyne near Blaydon, three miles west of Gateshead. Flat land bordering the confluence, known as Derwent Haugh, was the shipping point for three waggonways from local pits in Blaydon and the Derwent valley by the 1780s. Almost two centuries later, Derwenthaugh was a splendid place to see industrial locos at work. The NCB shed once served an extensive network stretching to mines up in the hills, but by 1968 this system had been cut back to Winlanton Mill, two miles upstream from Derwenthaugh. It was a very scenic line with wooded valley slopes as a backdrop. Derwenthaugh operated 24 hours a day, 7 days a week, most of the work being undertaken by two 0-6-0ST Austerities. Two venerable engines were in store. However, the main attraction was an ex-Consett Iron Co. 'long-boiler' 0-6-0 pannier tank, the oldest working NCB loco in the whole country.

Left. Star of the show at Derwenthaugh was 0-6-0PT No.41, seen here on Wednesday 24 April 1968 with the dislodged safety valve cover causing a somewhat erratic emission of steam.

INDUSTRIAL RAILWAYS in COLOUR - NORTH EAST

Three venerable engines languished at the back of Derwenthaugh shed on Monday 17 June 1968, two of them intact and one partially dismantled. The loco in the process of being cut up was No.42, seen to the right of this view. Identical to still-active No.41, this ex-Consett Iron Co. 0-6-0PT was built by Kitson to works number 2510 in 1883. Beyond it is No.65 HENRY C EMBLETON, a rather fine Hawthorn Leslie outside-cylinder 0-6-0T dating from 1930, works number 3766. The other gem dumped here was No.5 MAJOR, an elegant Kitson inside-cylinder 0-6-0T built back in 1905 to works number 4295.

A Railway Bylines Special

INDUSTRIAL RAILWAYS in COLOUR - NORTH EAST

Derwenthaugh No.90 shunts at Winlanton Mill on Wednesday 24 April 1968, its usual duty at the time. This Austerity-style 0-6-0ST was built in 1955 by Hunslet of Leeds, works number 3833, making it a comparative youngster on NCB metals. A couple of Austerities, assisted by Nos.41 and 78, kept the system going. The latter was a Robert Stephenson & Hawthorn outside-cylinder 0-4-0ST built at Darlington in 1949 to works number 7538.

On Wednesday 24 April 1968, No.41 was derailed while shunting at Winlanton, its leading driving wheels having ridden over a point blade. Derwenthaugh's breakdown train, comprising two ancient vans propelled by 0-4-0ST No.78, soon arrived. Work then began on jacking up the loco, moving it over to the correct alignment and lowering the wheels on to the track again. The operation is nearing completion in this view, with timbers supporting the buffer beam about to be removed.

INDUSTRIAL RAILWAYS in COLOUR - NORTH EAST

Job done, and the Derwenthaugh workers gather round to survey their achievement as No.41 gets up steam ready to resume its duties on Wednesday 24 April 1968. This ancient 0-6-0 pannier tank, the last of the Consett Iron Co class A engines, was built by Kitson of Leeds in 1883, works number 2509. Half-dismantled sister loco No.42, languishing near the shed, was works number 2510. These 'long-boilers' were very reminiscent of contemporary Edward Fletcher designs for the North Eastern Railway.

INDUSTRIAL RAILWAYS in COLOUR - NORTH EAST

Having completely recovered from its derailment ordeal, No.41 shunts the breakdown wagons at Winlanton on Wednesday 24 April 1968. The engine later returned to Derwenthaugh with these two vans and the rake of loaded wagons it was sent to collect before the mishap. No.78 had gone back light an hour or so earlier. The attractive Derwent valley wooded backdrop was typical of the line around Winlanton.

A Railway Bylines Special 35

7 Durham Collieries

When the NCB was formed in 1947, every nationalised mine in the country was allocated to a Division, the Northumberland & Durham Division embracing pits throughout the North East. This was sub-divided into Areas, six of them in County Durham. By 1968, amalgamations had reduced those south of the Tyne to just two, North Durham Area and South Durham Area. Incidentally, locomotives retained their original Area numbers, causing duplication and general confusion! Fifteen North Durham sites in the territory between Gateshead, Consett, Durham City and Sunderland had steam engines. In some cases they were out of use and two of the most significant places, Philadelphia and Derwenthaugh, have already been illustrated. Marley Hill, Morrison Busty and Springwell feature here. There was industrial steam at sixteen South Durham collieries to the east and south of Durham City. Shotton, Wheatley Hill, Thornley and Thrislington provide a flavour of the scene during the late 1960s.

Above. Marley Hill No.28 climbs the upper reaches of the Bowes Railway on Friday 21 June 1968 against a beautiful background formed by the fells above Rowlands Gill and the Derwent valley.

One of the most interesting NCB lines in the North Durham Area was that which passed through Marley Hill, four miles south west of Gateshead and around 550ft above sea level. In 1968, Marley Hill had the last surviving steam shed on the famous Bowes Railway, which abounded in steep gradients. Some of these were still very apparent four decades ago. The steam-worked western section served Byermoor Colliery and Hobson Colliery at its extremity, the latter almost 750ft above sea level. A punishing climb between Byermoor and Hobson required two hard-working locos to lift a modest load of just six or seven loaded wagons up to the washer, as clearly illustrated by this view on Friday 21 June 1968. At the front is Barclay outside-cylinder 0-4-0ST No.85, built at Kilmarnock in 1949, works number 2274. Doing its bit at the rear is No.28, an inside-cylinder Austerity 0-6-0ST produced by Vulcan Foundry at Newton-le-Willows in 1945, works number 5298. This particular run at the bank stalled, but the second attempt was successful.

INDUSTRIAL RAILWAYS in COLOUR - NORTH EAST

The gradient to Hobson Colliery is obvious in this scene on Monday 17 June 1968, as Barclay No.85 and Vulcan No.28 battle uphill with their short train of metal hoppers and wooden-bodied wagons. At the time, the Bowes Railway featured three forms of traction on its route from Hobson to Jarrow. Steam engines worked the top section from Hobson to Kibblesworth. From Kibblesworth to Galloping Green, Springwell and Wardley, the transect of the Team Valley, rope-worked balanced self-acting inclines were employed. Diesel locos operated the line from Wardley to Jarrow staithes. Other engines at Marley Hill in 1968 included No.22, a Hawthorn Leslie 0-6-0ST of 1915 vintage, and No.83, a Hunslet Austerity 0-6-0ST dating from 1949. Hobson and Byermoor mines closed in summer 1968, leaving Nos.28 and 83 to handle traffic from Marley Hill colliery on alternate weeks.

A Railway Bylines Special

Morrison Busty colliery, on the southern edge of Annfield Plain roughly five miles south west of Marley Hill and four miles east of Consett, employed two steam engines to move coal from the pithead to BR exchange sidings at New Kyo. By summer 1968, these were both elderly machines. No.4, a 1923 Hudswell Clarke outside-cylinder 0-4-0ST, usually worked 24 hours a day, Monday to Friday. Veteran No.3 TWIZELL, a Robert Stephenson inside-cylinder 0-6-0T dating from 1891, operated from 6.00am to 11.30am on Saturday. Both were tucked up in the locked shed on this Friday 21 June visit. Ironically, much newer locos at the mine had been cast aside. Robert Stephenson & Hawthorn outside-cylinder 0-6-0ST No.79, built in 1949 to works number 7545, had been made redundant by the arrival of TWIZELL. Beyond it is partially cut-up RSH No.34, an almost identical engine dating from 1938, works number 6943.

Sadly, this was the fate of so many industrial steam engines in the North East and elsewhere, especially those with little historic value as far as preservation was concerned. At Morrison Busty on Friday 21 June 1968, two previously hard-working engines less than twenty years old were being turned into scrap metal. On the left is No.80, a Robert Stephenson & Hawthorn outside-cylinder 0-6-0ST which was built at Darlington in 1949, works number 7546. To the right is No.84, from the same manufacturer later in the year and carrying works number 7641.

INDUSTRIAL RAILWAYS in COLOUR - NORTH EAST

Springwell Colliery was on the Bowes Railway, 3 miles south east of Gateshead and a mile or so from Washington. By the time this view was taken on the dull rainy afternoon of Wednesday 8 May 1968, diesels had taken over shunting duties. However, three inside-cylinder steam locos of considerable interest were in the yard awaiting scrapping. All of them wore a dignified dark blue livery with red lining and had obviously been looked after prior to their demise. In the foreground is No.26, a 1930 Hunslet 0-6-0T, works number 1506. Behind it is No.25, A massive Hawthorn Leslie 0-6-0ST dating from 1923, works number 3569. In the distance is No.24, a smaller Hawthorn Leslie 0-6-0ST of 1902 vintage, works number 2545.

A Railway Bylines Special 41

Shotton Colliery, in the South Durham Area, was seven miles east of Durham City and still employed two vintage steam locos when this view was taken during the overcast afternoon of Wednesday 15 May 1968. On the left is the un-numbered Peckett outside-cylinder 0-6-0ST, built in 1914 to works number 1310. Out of steam to the right is a similarly anonymous Barclay outside-cylinder 0-6-0ST, constructed in 1904 and bearing works number 1015. The former carried a green livery and the latter was painted blue, although both of them were somewhat work-stained. This is an interesting snapshot of these two engines, as the Peckett was basically a spare and had not worked for years prior to March 1968. With the Barclay out of commission awaiting re-tubing, its younger shedmate was required to shunt the mine for a few months.

INDUSTRIAL RAILWAYS in COLOUR - NORTH EAST

Billowing clouds against a bright blue sky formed the background to a pure mining environment at Shotton on the afternoon of Thursday 20 June 1968. The elderly Peckett 0-6-0ST is dutifully moving BR hopper wagons around the yard. Note the piercing emission from its steam brake. Incidentally, Shotton Colliery still had steam-powered winding gear for its shafts. Around this time, the splendid Hawthorn Leslie 0-6-0ST STAGSHAW arrived from Wheatley Hill as a standby.

A Railway Bylines Special   43

INDUSTRIAL RAILWAYS in COLOUR - NORTH EAST

Another aspect of Shotton's Peckett 0-6-0ST in its natural setting is portrayed in this scene around 3pm on Thursday 20 June 1968. A back lane, so typical of Durham pit villages, provides a glimpse of the engine as it shunts wagons in the colliery yard. There are mine buildings on the left and back yards of terraced houses to the right. Shotton itself is a tiny medieval village on the flanks of Castle Eden Burn and boasted a hall in its own grounds. The much larger and newer settlement of Shotton Colliery is about a mile to the north west and had a passenger station called Shotton Bridge on the Sunderland - Stockton line until June 1952. Note the total lack of grafitti and rubbish!

44   A Railway Bylines Special

INDUSTRIAL RAILWAYS in COLOUR - NORTH EAST

Wheatley Hill Colliery, which stood 1½ miles south west of Shotton Colliery, closed on 2 May 1968. Prior to its demise, the mine was shunted by 1958 Barclay 0-6-0 diesel No.2, but something special provided back-up motive power. This was STAGSHAW, a very impressive 1927 Hawthorn Leslie outside-cylinder 0-6-0ST, works number 3513. The loco is seen here in the shed on Wednesday 15 May 1968, before it moved to Shotton. An unusual and quite appealing bright yellow livery was applied, the diesel sharing this distinctive hue.

A Railway Bylines Special

INDUSTRIAL RAILWAYS in COLOUR - NORTH EAST

Thornley Colliery was just over a mile west of Wheatley Hill and is seen here on Wednesday 15 May 1968. Earlier in the year, the yard had been shunted by outside-cylinder 0-4-0ST No.148 TAURUS which was built by Hawthorn Leslie in 1919, works number 3384. By this time the engine was stored and languished on the left of this view. Barclay 0-6-0 diesel No.2, ex-Wheatley Hill, was the main performer with 1949 Barclay 0-4-0ST No.52 as standby. The latter had been transferred from closed Bowburn Colliery. No.17, out of use on the right, was a particularly interesting machine. Built in 1918 by Kerr, Stuart of Stoke on Trent, works number 3098, this outside-cylinder 0-6-0T was part of an order for South America which was subsequently cancelled. Sister loco No.27, works number 3100, was in pieces in the workshop.

Thrislington colliery was at the top of a rope-worked incline, which could be seen from the East Coast main line where it passed through Ferryhill gap, eight miles south of Durham City. The pit was actually near the village of Cornforth, on a plateau almost 200ft above the valley used by the Darlington- Newcastle railway. Two neat little outside-cylinder Barclay 0-4-0ST locos in attractive dark red livery were allocated to Thrislington. One of them, No.57, built in 1957 to works number 2341, was out of use when this photograph was taken on Wednesday 15 May 1968. There are rails down there somewhere!

INDUSTRIAL RAILWAYS in COLOUR - NORTH EAST

A spectacular duty for Thrislington's engines was the steep ascent to the coal drops. 1950 Barclay 0-4-0ST No.50, works number 2277, storms the bank with a solitary BR hopper on Wednesday 15 May 1968. Note the short wheelbase and diminutive stature of the loco compared with its wagon. But appearances can be deceptive, for these small machines were very capable performers. Furthermore, Thrislington kept both of them clean.

48   A Railway Bylines Special

INDUSTRIAL RAILWAYS in COLOUR - NORTH EAST

By the time this view was taken on Thursday 20 June 1968, a much larger engine had been transferred to Thrislington for regular duties. It was No.140, an angular and rather grubby 1948 Hudswell Clarke outside-cylinder 0-6-0T, works number 1821, which came from nearby Mainsforth colliery. As a result, Barclay No.50 became the standby loco and No.57 was sent for scrap. The newcomer is seen here after a hard day's work against a bizarre man-made backdrop of pyramids of coal.

A Railway Bylines Special 49

INDUSTRIAL RAILWAYS in COLOUR - NORTH EAST

8 Wearmouth

This NCB North Durham Area site has been singled out for particular attention because of its unusual location near the centre of a major town, which has since become a city, and the rather endearing scruffy nature of the place! There were actually two mines on the north bank of the River Wear at Sunderland. Wearmouth Colliery was in Monkwearmouth, close to the historic station of the same name and the distinctive North Eastern Railway bridge over the river. A two-mile branch of surprisingly photogenic character ran west to Hylton Colliery. In 1967, eleven steam engines were based at Wearmouth and Hylton, although many of them were spare or awaiting cutting-up. By mid-1968, the only serviceable loco dated from 1909, much newer machines having already been scrapped. Wearmouth had *two* engines bearing No.2, illustrating the Division numbering confusion.

Above. Lazy black smoke and a good dose of steam emanated from JEAN in Wearmouth Colliery yard on Monday 17 June 1968, reminding residents of the nearby terraced houses that their back yards overlooked a particularly grimy industrial site.

Its relatively short career over, Wearmouth No.39 awaits scrapping on Monday 17 June 1968. This Robert Stephenson & Hawthorn outside-cylinder 0-4-0ST, built in 1953 to works number 7757, had recently been a spare engine at Hylton. The distinctive cab betrays the fact that it was originally intended for the staithes at Sunderland on the Philadelphia network.

By Monday 17 June 1968 two engines were awaiting scrapping at Wearmouth. On the right is un-numbered DIANA, a Robert Stephenson & Hawthorn inside-cylinder 0-6-0T built in 1946, works number 7304, which looked as if it had not had a lick of paint since new. The other was one of the two Wearmouth locos bearing No.2, in this instance a neat 1922 Hawthorn Leslie outside-cylinder 0-4-0ST, works number 3493. Its bright, fully-lined blue paintwork suggests a fairly recent overhaul. The other No.2 was a Hunslet Austerity 0-6-0ST, built during 1944 to works number 3191, which was still busy a few months earlier. Debris in the foreground is indicative of a decaying industrial site, a marked contrast to the brave new tower block on the far right. Within a matter of years, many such buildings were regarded as even more of an urban blight than dirty sites such as Wearmouth Colliery.

On Monday 17 June 1968, the only serviceable steam engine at Wearmouth was JEAN, an elegant Hawthorn Leslie 0-6-0T built in 1909, works number 2769. The loco had been under repair a few months earlier and emerged with a new coat of paint on the side tanks and frames. With a full head of steam and virtually no smoke emanating from the chimney, JEAN prepared to shunt a rake of BR metal hoppers. The veteran had seen off much newer compatriots at Wearmouth in 1967-68, including a pair of Robert Stephenson & Hawthorn 0-6-0ST locos dating from 1952 and an 0-4-0ST from the same manufacturer, built as recently as 1954. Other machines employed by Wearmouth and Hylton at the time were a 1957 Hibberd 'Planet' 4-wheel diesel numbered 2505/78, a 1955 North British 0-6-0 diesel, No.1, from Philadelphia and a 1965 Hunslet 0-6-0 diesel electric, No.501.

9 Northumberland Collieries

In 1968 twelve Northumberland Area sites employed steam locomotives. They were located over a very wide area, from Shilbottle south of Alnwick to Bardon Mill east of Haltwhistle and Backworth near Whitley Bay. However, the largest concentration was on the coastal plain north of Tyneside. This group included the large Ashington system, basically a 6 mile loop linking the mines at Linton, Ellington and Lynemouth with the marshalling yards at Ashington. Of seventeen engines allocated here, up to twelve were in use on weekdays. Closure of Ellington, the very last colliery in the North East, was announced during January 2005. By 1968, NCB operations in Northumberland were largely in the hands of 0-6-0ST locos dating from 1943 to 1957, although there were one or two veterans. Attention here is focused on Backworth, Burradon and Bardon Mill, respectively featuring very clean engines, a daily slog and a delightfully scenic setting.

Above. Backworth Colliery's No.47 shunts BR mineral wagons past a neat little signal cabin protecting the Shiremoor-Seghill road on Tuesday 18 June 1968, delaying a United Bristol Lodekka providing one of many local services in the Northumberland coalfield.

INDUSTRIAL RAILWAYS in COLOUR - NORTH EAST

During the late 1960s, most coal mined in south east Northumberland was carried by BR either to Cambois power station at Blyth or staithes on the Tyne. The days of the independent railways were almost over, but one system carried shipping coal in its own wagons hauled by it own locomotives over its own track. This was Backworth colliery railway, which ran from Fenwick and Backworth pits west of Whitley Bay to staithes at Whitehill Point near North Shields. Backworth shed and colliery were close to the BR station of the same name on the North Tyneside loop. Shunting there on Tuesday 23 January 1968 was No.48, an Austerity 0-6-0ST built by Hunslet in 1943 to works number 2864. They did not come much cleaner than this.

A Railway Bylines Special 55

INDUSTRIAL RAILWAYS in COLOUR - NORTH EAST

Backworth No.47, an outside-cylinder 0-6-0ST built by Robert Stephenson & Hawthorn in 1955 to works number 7849, takes water at the shed on Tuesday 18 June 1968. Its deep blue paintwork and even the bright red buffer beams and rods are very clean. This was normal at Backworth and the NCB coat-of-arms on the bunker sides added a touch of class. Note the customary modes of transport for workers at the time: cycling and walking. A couple of the system's bright red wagons are seen here, usually and remarkably, in the same clean state as the engines. They were probably destined for the Tyne staithes at Whitehill Point. A banking engine would assist the climb to Allotment, just south of Shiremoor.

A Railway Bylines Special

INDUSTRIAL RAILWAYS in COLOUR - NORTH EAST

A touch of primitive coaling at Backworth shed on Tuesday 23 January 1968. Locos present in the view are ex-Ministry of Supply Austerities Nos.6 and 33, the former having it bunker replenished. No.6 was built by Bagnall in 1944, works number 2749. No.33 was a Robert Stephenson & Hawthorn product, also dating from 1944, works number 7177. Of the ten engines allocated to Backworth in 1968, no less than eight were required in traffic every weekday. During this visit, the author enjoyed a meal in the colliery canteen. It consisted of pie, potatoes and veg., plus pudding, costing 2s 4d - just over 10p in today's money!

A Railway Bylines Special　　57

INDUSTRIAL RAILWAYS in COLOUR - NORTH EAST

Burradon, 2½ miles west of Backworth and five miles north of Newcastle, had two NCB loco sheds which provided motive power for Burradon, Dudley, Havannah and Seaton Burn collieries, together with Weetslade Washer. A very good time and place to see plenty of action on the system was between 2.45pm and 3.30pm at the A189 Bedlington-Newcastle road crossing, when locos were returning to the sidings at Burradon with loads of coal at the end of a day's shift. On one such occasion, the bitterly cold early afternoon of Tuesday 23 January 1968, Robert Stephenson & Hawthorn outside - cylinder 0-6-0ST No.42 approaches the crossing with a heavy train, holding up the Triumph Herald estate. The engine was built in 1953, works number 7759.

INDUSTRIAL RAILWAYS in COLOUR - NORTH EAST

The star working at Burradon was the 'Dudley Pilot' which left Dudley Colliery, a mile or so north west of its home base, about 9.30am and 4.30pm every weekday. To reach Burradon it had a six-mile trek via Seghill, the BR Blyth & Tyne line and a connection from Holywell cabin. During the latter stage of its journey, the train usually had the help of a banking engine. Assistance was a familiar feature at Burradon. On Tuesday 23 January 1968, a couple of 0-6-0ST locos heave a train across fields on the final approach to Burradon Colliery.

A Railway Bylines Special 59

INDUSTRIAL RAILWAYS in COLOUR - NORTH EAST

Burradon was typical of colliery villages throughout the Northumberland and Durham coalfield. With miners dwellings and a lovely gas lamp framing it, an 0-6-0ST adds to the atmospheric nature of the place on Tuesday 23 January 1968. Despite its modern motive power at the time, Burradon was not a haven for conventional inside-cylinder 'Austerities', so typical elsewhere. Of the twelve steam locos allocated to the two sheds, eight were outside–cylinder Robert Stephenson & Hawthorn 0-6-0ST machines dating from 1946 to 1957.

Bardon Mill Colliery was a somewhat eccentric outpost of the Northumberland coalfield, ten miles west of Hexham and over thirty miles from Newcastle and the other collieries north of the Tyne. It was shunted by elderly Hawthorn Leslie 0-4-0ST C19, built in 1906 to works number 2660. This delightful engine is seen shunting empty BR hopper wagons on Wednesday 19 June 1968 against a lovely backdrop of Thorngrafton Common on the northern slope of the Tyne Valley.

10 Miscellany

This personal view of North East industrial locos during 1968 concludes with a look at three subjects which differ somewhat from the steam engines featured up to now. Incidentally, diesels have been almost completely ignored for two reasons. Firstly, there was too much interesting steam about; secondly, I took no photographs of them! Narrow gauge systems are also absent as they were not a significant feature of Northumberland and Durham. Illustrated here are three rather specialised machines built for industrial service. The Head Wrightson vertical-boiler loco was very useful on lightweight track. Steeple-cab electrics employed below coke retorts had a very short length of track to work on. The Harton overhead electrics were not only unusual, but led an almost secretive and elusive life. The North East industrial scene was nothing if not varied!

Above. Before the diminutive Lewin 0-4-0ST took up harbour repair work at Seaham Harbour in 1960, such duties were undertaken by vertical boiler 0-4-0s built by the Stockton firm of Head Wrightson. Fortunately, the company had the foresight to rescue one of its products from maritime redundancy and put it on display back at headquarters. Seen here on the somewhat overcast morning of Friday 7 June 1968, the primitive engine dated from 1877. A couple of chaldron wagons, also from Seaham Harbour, showed that quite a bit of thought had been put into this particular preservation effort.

INDUSTRIAL RAILWAYS in COLOUR - NORTH EAST

Very specialised little 0-4-0 electric locos once worked at coke works in the North East, as elsewhere, but by 1968 they were becoming a rarity. The hostile environment meant that neither overhead nor third rail current supply was practicable, so a side wire supplied the necessary energy. At Lambton Coke works on the Philadelphia system during the afternoon of Wednesday 28 February 1968, burning fuel is being pushed out of one of the retorts into the coke car. This will shortly be propelled to the tall tower on the right where a drenching will cool the coke and send a plume of steam high into the air.

INDUSTRIAL RAILWAYS in COLOUR - NORTH EAST

Observant passengers alighting from the North Shields – South Shields ferry in 1968 may well have noticed the terminus of an overhead electric railway as they climbed the pier ramp on the south bank of the Tyne.   This was one point on an interesting, complex and rather shy system which formerly belonged to the Harton Coal Company. Much coal from Westoe and Whitburn collieries at the far end of the network was transferred to coastal colliers at South Shields low staithes for transport to London. No less than thirteen overhead electric locos were based at Westoe at the time. They dated from 1907 to 1959 and were variously built by Siemens, Kerr Stuart, Allgemeine Elektricitaats Gesellschaft of Berlin and English Electric. One of the newer machines creeps through South Shields towards the staithes on Tuesday 18 June 1968.